D0422035

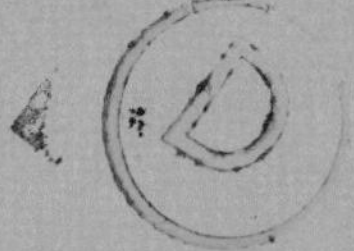

ANOINTED TO SERVE

The Story of
The Assemblies of God

By

WILLIAM W. MENZIES, Ph. D.

GOSPEL PUBLISHING HOUSE

SPRINGFIELD, MISSOURI

02-0465

LIBRARY OF CONGRESS CATALOG CARD NUMBER: 79-146707

4th Printing 1984
ISBN 0-88243-465-9

Printed in the United States of America

DEDICATED TO THE MEMORY

OF

JOSEPH ROSWELL FLOWER

A FATHER IN THE FAITH

JUNE 17, 1888–JULY 23, 1970

"MARANATHA"

CONTENTS

APPENDIXES

Foreword

Periodically, throughout the long centuries since the Apostolic Age, the Holy Spirit has breathed fresh life into Christ's Church. At the end of the 19th century new stirrings of life began to appear in obscure places where earnest prayer for revival was ascending to heaven, particularly among the Holiness people hungering for a new outpouring of the Holy Spirit. Simultaneously, in unrelated places, manifestations of the Holy Spirit began to appear in profusion uncommon in modern times, attended by great conviction for sin and a sense of the imminence of the return of the Lord. Remarkable healings occurred, both of body and soul. This was the beginning of the latter-day outpouring promised by Joel the Seer!

To be sure, this was not the only time since the first century that God's Spirit had moved in similar display of the divine presence. However, it has indeed been remarkable that this charismatic revival has *survived!* Other great spiritual awakenings, accompanied by speaking in tongues and other evidences of the manifest presence, were driven into the limbo of heresy and fanaticism in previous days. Not until the Great Revival of the 20th century has a charismatic stirring survived sufficiently long to gain acceptance and toleration by mainstream orthodox Christianity. Today, the anointing and gifts of the Holy Spirit, once despised and rejected by the larger church world, are more and more in evidence across a broad spectrum of Christian communions! The Pentecostal revival is here to stay!

Crucial in the preservation of the fruits of the Pentecostal revival has been the organization known as the ASSEMBLIES OF GOD. In 1914, following a period of baffling rejection by all segments of the American church world, with great reluctance, but recognizing the urgency of the task, farsighted men gathered in Hot Springs, Arkansas, to establish a "cooperative fellowship" for the conservation of the work of God. There have been other organizations, as well, that carried a similar burden, and that God has wonderfully blessed, but the Assemblies of God has enjoyed a role of leadership in the American Pentecostal Movement that places it in a strategic position historically.

As a new decade dawns, it is highly appropriate that the story of the dramatic developments within the Assemblies of God be brought up to date. Recent years have brought important decisions and changes. In 1967 the Assemblies of God launched upon an in-depth self-study, the fruits of which have embarked the fellowship on a renewed commitment to the ideals articulated by the early pioneers nearly 60 years ago. Fresh winds of revival and new vitality in growth are already being reported as the Five-Year-Plan of Advance moves ahead into the decade of the 1970's. To tell this story, the Publications Board of the General Council commissioned William Menzies in the fall of 1968 to undertake the task of telling the story of the Assemblies of God. The result is the distilled essence of more than a year of diligent work by the author.

The burden of the book is very adequately expressed in the title, *Anointed to Serve*. Here is the tale of early pioneers who stood firm and straight when adversaries assailed their distinctive testimony, of courageous men and women who caught a vision of a world perishing for want of compassionate witnesses. Here is the story of those "whose hearts God touched," who exercised faith to believe that God would surely move mountains to bring deliverance to captives held in brokenness by the Devil and his hosts. Here is the story of creative enterprise, of ministers and laymen, working together in a great fellowship to do the bidding of the Master. This is the story of the Assemblies of God.

Yet, it is more than the story of a movement. It is intended to provoke faith in the God of heaven. As you, dear reader, pore over the fascinating pages that follow, may the Holy Spirit kindle a flame in your heart! Let the Lord be glorified! Let us attempt great things in His name, for we have learned to expect great things from His hand!

August, 1970 THOMAS F. ZIMMERMAN

Introduction

It is now apparent that the modern Pentecostal revival which began in obscurity just after the beginning of the 20th century has assumed a magnitude that compels the attention of religious observers the world around.

> It is estimated that there are ten million Pentecostals in the world, of which four million are to be found in the United States. In Chile 14 percent of the population belongs to the Pentecostal movement, constituting 700,000 members out of 835,000 Protestants. In Italy and Russia the Pentecostals are the group with the highest growth rate. The Russian Pentecostal community is reported to be the largest in Europe. In France and Norway and some other European countries the Pentecostals represent the largest of the free churches. In Latin America they outnumber the traditional Protestants by at least four to one, and in some areas the rate of Pentecostal growth is from three to five times the population increase. One out of two Puerto Rican Protestants is a Pentecostal, and in New York City Spanish-speaking immigrants have founded 250 Pentecostal churches. . . . Any group which can boast of being the fastest growing movement within the Christian tradition must be reckoned with.[1]

In addition to the amazing growth of the recognized Pentecostal bodies, Pentecostal phenomena have been appearing in the historic churches with increasing regularity since the mid 1950's. Because of this new "penetration" it is virtually impossible to assess the true dimensions of this remarkable 20th-century revival.

What is the Pentecostal Movement? The Pentecostal Movement is that group of sects within the Christian Church which is characterized by the belief that the occurrence mentioned in Acts 2 on the Day of Pentecost not only signaled the birth of the Church, but described an experience available to believers in all ages. The experience of an enduement with power, called the "baptism in the Holy Spirit," is believed to be evidenced by the accompanying sign of "speaking with other tongues as the Spirit gives utterance." This experience is to be distinguished from the traditional

---

[1]Kilian McDonnell, "The Ecumenical Significance of the Pentecostal Movement," *Worship*, XL (December, 1966), pp. 608-9.

Holiness teaching of a "second blessing." Although both groups believe that there is a definite crisis experience subsequent to regeneration taught in the Bible, the Holiness understanding is that this experience is for the sanctification of the believer, whereas the Pentecostal understanding is that this experience is primarily an enduement for service.[2] In addition, the Pentecostal Movement has made a large place in its worship for the manifestations of the Spirit described in 1 Corinthians 12-14.

Although the Pentecostal Movement is a worldwide phenomenon, our study will be limited to the United States. It is not the intention of this volume to survey the Pentecostal Movement broadly, but rather to scrutinize a key representative body in depth. It is the author's contention, after extensive interviews with Pentecostal leaders, evangelical churchmen, and representatives from the larger church world, that the Assemblies of God, largest of the American Pentecostal bodies, is indeed the most representative of the Pentecostal organizations, and can serve usefully as a microcosm of the Pentecostal Movement as a whole.[3]

How did this book come about? First of all, the story of the modern Pentecostal revival is a story worth telling. It is significant news. Secondly, so much has been occurring very recently that in spite of the appearance of several valuable histories in the last 15 years, few books have been designed to give much attention to events since World War II, preferring to concentrate on the fascinating story of the origins of the modern revival. Aware of the need for an updating of the story of the Assemblies of God, the Board of Publications requested the author to undertake such an assignment, late in 1968.[4] He had recently been awarded a Ph.D. degree

---

[2]Gordon Atter, *The Third Force* (Peterborough, Ontario: The College Press, 1962), pp. 6, 7.

[3]Ten interviews with non-Assemblies of God leaders in the Pentecostal and evangelical segments of the Church all support this contention. This also seems to be the consensus of leading scholars who have written on Pentecostalism. See, for example, Nils Bloch-Hoell, *The Pentecostal Movement* (Oslo: Universitatsforlaget, 1964), p. 62. Also, Morton T. Kelsey, *Tongue Speaking* (Garden City, N.Y.: Doubleday and Company, 1964), pp. 84-85. John T. Nichol sees in the Assemblies of God all the major elements of tension and development present in the Pentecostal Movement (interview, July 21, 1967).

[4]"The Assemblies of God; 1941-1967: the Consolidation of a Revival Movement" (unpublished Ph.D. dissertation, The University of Iowa, 1968).

at the University of Iowa in the field of American church history.

The writer traveled about 14,000 miles in the course of his research. More than 20 libraries were visited from coast to coast. In addition, nearly two months were spent in the archives of the Assemblies of God headquarters in Springfield, Missouri. Because of the limited amount of written materials, and because of the concern for very recent information, considerable emphasis was given to personal interviews and correspondence. Nearly 100 Assemblies of God leaders were personally interviewed, including all the resident Executive Presbytery, all the department heads at the headquarters offices, all the major editors, several district officials, pastors, evangelists, missionaries, and lay people. Six of the nine college presidents were interviewed. Particularly valuable was extensive conversation with such well-known elder statesmen as J. Roswell Flower, Ernest S. Williams, Noel Perkin, Gayle F. Lewis, Frank M. Boyd, and Ralph M. Riggs, men whose vantage point scans the Pentecostal Movement from its beginnings.

More than two dozen interviews were conducted with key individuals in three circles; five chief executives of Pentecostal bodies; several leaders in the evangelical world, such as Clyde Taylor and Carl Henry; and in the larger church world, important church historians and scholars.

Of special significance in the research was the happy conjunction of the writer's sabbatical year from Central Bible College with the inauguration of the denomination's momentous critical self-study, the "Committee on Advance." The writer was extended the unique privilege of sitting in sessions of that committee as a special observer. The climate of diagnosis that has pervaded the denomination since the institution of that Committee has provided a most favorable one for inquiry and discussion. The candor and earnestness of the leadership of the fellowship have contributed enormously to the usefulness of this research project.

The book is divided into two major parts. Part One deals with the formative years, culminating with the onset of American participation in World War II, which seems to have been an important watershed in the history of the Assemblies of God. The historical background surrounding the birth of the modern Pentecostal revival, the recounting of the initial phases of the revival, and events leading to the organization of the Assemblies of God in 1914 are included in the first part of the book. The formative phase includes as well the development of the infant fellowship from 1914 to 1927, when a formal constitution was adopted. The first part of the story concludes with the relatively tranquil years prior to World War II in which the Assemblies of God grew very rapidly, with a very simple organizational structure, and in virtual isolation from the rest of the church world.

Part Two carries the story forward from the entry of the United States into World War II up to 1970. Initially, there was a period of tremendous proliferation of new service agencies, roughly spanning the period from 1941 to 1953. From 1953 onward there was an attempt to coordinate the sprawling enterprises that had been brought into being by the vigorous, growing Assemblies of God. A plateau of growth was reached by the late 1950's, which lasted about a decade. More recently there is evidence of fresh vitality and a renewed sense of direction appearing which give bright promise of continued spiritual revival and evangelistic outreach in the years that lie ahead. Of special interest in this period has been the acceptance of Pentecostals by evangelical Christians. This dramatic change has occurred since World War II.

While domestic growth tended to level off, for a time at least, during these years, Assemblies of God missionary activity continued at a remarkable pace, with no signs of slackening on the horizon. This amazing development has occurred in spite of the necessary adaptation of fresh strategies to meet a rapidly changing international situation. The story of Assemblies of God missions is a fascinating tale all its own, far beyond the scope of this book, a story that is to be told in a companion volume that will appear in the near future.

The writer trusts that this attempt at an in-depth study of the Assemblies of God will provide the reader sufficient information in a single volume so that he will not only come away with a clear picture of the historical dimensions of the Pentecostal revival, but will also capture something of the inner moods, aspirations, and dynamics of the men and women who comprise this vibrant fellowship. It is hoped, further, that in an age in which the kaleidoscope of disturbing world events creates a sense of deep pessimism among discerning people, the recounting of this story of a profound and significant revival will stimulate the reader to greater faith in our Saviour and King, Jesus Christ, the triumphant Lord of history!

The writer is indebted to numerous people for the production of this manuscript. Grateful acknowledgment is due the executive brethren at Assemblies of God headquarters in Springfield, Missouri, for their kindliness and encouragement, and for their generosity in making available to the writer indispensable records and documents. General Superintendent Zimmerman, in particular, has provided aid and counsel. Miss Grace Carroll, Research Secretary at headquarters, has furnished invaluable assistance, not only in the accumulation of data, but in the critical reading of the manuscript. Numerous department personnel and editorial people contributed hours of effort to make the task of the writer possible. Much of the research was undertaken during a sabbatical year provided by the administration of Central Bible College. Much of the latter part of the book is the product of a dissertation submitted to the University of Iowa. The author is indebted to Dr. Sidney E. Mead, chairman of the thesis committee at the university, who was of great help in the completion of that manuscript.

This paper could not have been written without the patience and encouragement of a loving wife and two very understanding boys who have made mine a happy home. A similar debt is owed to my godly parents, Pentecostal pioneers, who faithfully showed the way.

The writer is, above all, indebted to the Lord. He has found the Lord to be faithful and true, the giver of every good gift. And, it was the Lord who, after all, poured out His Holy Spirit on a band of praying people at the outset of this century, giving the United States the refreshing known as the Pentecostal revival, which is what this story is all about.

Part I

THE EARLY YEARS [1900-1941]

1

The Background [Before 1900]

Years of Social Revolution—The Churches in a Period of Crisis—Fundamentalism—The Holiness Revival—Nineteenth-century Contributions to the Pentecostal Movement—Stepping-stones to the Great Revival

The Pentecostal revival did not occur in a vacuum. Before the great outpouring of the Latter Rain there were conditions, both positive and negative, that furnished the context of the Great Revival. In the years prior to the Pentecostal revival our land was in great ferment in a variety of ways, the churches in the main declining in vitality through the process. An important crosscurrent was that fragment of the Church which cried to God for supernatural intervention. The Pentecostal revival came to people who were deeply concerned over the spiritual and moral deterioration abroad in the land, people who prevailed with God in earnest prayer. And it has always been thus, for "If my people, which are called by my name, shall humble themselves, and pray, and seek my face, and turn from their wicked ways; then will I hear from heaven, and will forgive their sin, and will heal their land" (2 Chronicles 7:14). The Pentecostal revival did not add new doctrines; it called the Church back to historic truth. The Pentecostal Movement has stood within the framework of orthodox Christianity, serving the valuable purpose of challenging Christians everywhere to take very seriously the person and work of the Holy Spirit, as described in the Scriptures, and outlined in the great creeds. In a real sense, then, the Pentecostals stand on the shoulders of earnest believers of yesteryear. Before continuing our

journey into the story of that wonderful outpouring itself, let us pause sufficiently to look at the scene against which the story is to be portrayed.

YEARS OF SOCIAL REVOLUTION

The United States in the generation between the Civil War and the advent of the new century underwent a virtual social revolution. Arthur M. Schlesinger points our vividly that this was the era in which the great American cities came to full life.[1] Industrialization and immigration contributed heavily to the rapid urbanization of the nation. Rural migration to industrial centers, once a trickle, now swelled to a flood. By 1900, once rural America had 40 percent of its population in cities of 4,000 or more.[2] Between 1861 and 1900, 14 million Europeans had found new homes in this great land, many of them collecting in ghettos developing in the burgeoning cities. Industrial production rose 600 percent in the same period, and the number of factory workers multiplied from 1.3 million to 5.3 million.[3]

They were turbulent years. Great financial panics brought distress to many in both 1873 and 1893. A gulf seemed to be widening between the great captains of industry and the toilers in the mills who huddled in crowded cities. The railroad strikes of 1877, the bloody Haymarket riot of 1886, and the armed confrontation in the disastrous steel strikes of 1892-94 punctuate the period.[4] It was an era of unprecedented government scandals and a general decline in public morality.[5] Yet, church membership increased from 16 percent in 1850 to 36 percent in 1900, creating the illusion of a nation thriving spiritually.[6]

---

[1]Arthur M. Schlesinger, *The Rise of the City*, 1878-1898 (New York: Macmillan Company, 1933), pp. 64-77.

[2]William W. Sweet, *The Story of Religion in America* (New York: Harper and Brothers, 1950), p. 373.

[3]Nils Bloch-Hoell; *op. cit.*, pp. 9-10.

[4]Henry F. May, *Protestant Churches and Industrial America* (New York: Harper and Brothers, 1949), pp. 91-111.

[5]Klaude Kendrick, *The Promise Fulfilled* (Springfield, Missouri: Gospel Publishing House, 1961), pp. 26-28.

[6]Earle E. Cairns, *Christianity in the United States* (Chicago: Moody Press, 1964), p. 135.

The Churches in a Period of Crisis

THEOLOGICAL BANKRUPTCY

"It is scarcely an exaggeration to say that during the 19th century and well into the 20th century, religion prospered while theology slowly went bankrupt."[7] The great American denominations, successful in having Christianized America, faced a set of challenges for which their post-Civil War complacency seemed to have left them largely unprepared.

Before the closing of the frontier, a series of revivals had refreshed the land. The 19th century had opened with a powerful revival that changed the course of national history. The "Second Awakening" of 1800-01 crushed French deism which had flourished during the American Revolution and the years immediately following. During the decades of the twenties and the thirties and beyond, great revivals profoundly affected life in the eastern cities. The chief instrument in these mighty movings of the Holy Spirit was Charles G. Finney. And, until the Civil War, it was the expectation in most of the church-related colleges that dotted the westward-advancing frontier that there would be an annual spiritual visitation in which young people would be swept into the Kingdom. The last great nationwide revival occurred on the eve of the Civil War in 1858-59, a revival sometimes called the great "Prayer Meeting Revival," for it was characterized by laymen who prayed fervently for a deluge from heaven.[8] So it was that as the nation gravitated toward the Pacific shore, genuine, vital Christianity deeply affected the national fiber. However, sometime after the Civil War, the freshness of vital experience with Christ was exchanged for a moribund "culture-religion" by much of American Protestantism, in which prevailing social values became identified with Christianity. A mood of self-satisfaction, of optimism and complacency, displaced the earnestness and prayerfulness of earlier years in many churches across the land.

---

[7]Henry S. Commager, *The American Mind* (New Haven: Yale University Press, 1959), p. 165.

[8]J. Edwin Orr, *The Light of the Nations* (Grand Rapids: Eerdmans, 1965), pp. 101-9.

ALIEN IDEAS

As social unrest challenged the tranquility of American domestic life, a series of devastating, alien ideas weakened the American churches. Imported from German universities in the post-Civil War years were views that severely threatened the now anemic, flaccid culture-religion of American Protestantism. The popularization of Kantian idealism produced a wave of disturbing Biblical criticism. The authority of inspired Scripture, a basic anchor in orthodox Christianity through the years, was undermined by such subtle philosophizing, presented in such plausible terms to young seminarians. It would be but a few brief years until such views filled the American pulpits and American chairs of theology.

At least as serious was the great force of Hegelian philosophy. The Hegelians had an optimistic view of man, a mood that caught the fancy of success-laden Americans in the late 19th century. Such views nourished various strands of liberal theology, and spawned an army of evolutionists who carried their brand of doctrine into every conceivable branch of human enterprise, from biology and the other sciences into the humanities, and, finally, into Biblical studies and theology as well. "Onward and upward" was the enthusiastic watchword of the day!

THE NEW THEOLOGY

Friedrich Schleiermacher, sometimes called the "father of Modernism," developed a system of theology based on human experience, thus undercutting traditional Biblical authority. Following in his train were a number of prominent German theologians whose views made a deep impact on American churchmen. One such German theologian who was particularly influential was Albrecht Ritschl. His emphasis on the community aspect of religion encouraged belief in sin as primarily corporate, and not therefore essentially personal and individual. Salvation, too, for Ritschl was corporate, in rather sharp contrast to the orthodox view that human ills are primarily individual and require personal salvation for remedy.[9] Finally, Adolph Harnack, eminent church historian and theological scholar, formalized much of the

[9] Cairns, *op. cit.*, p. 148.

mood of critical scholarship, fashioning a system that came to be known as the essence of Modernism.[10] The ideas flourishing in mid-century Germany were transplanted quite successfully to the United States in the latter part of the century, virtually dominating most of the major theological schools by the 1890's. This was the New Theology.

THE NEW SCIENCE

In addition to the currents flowing from theological Germany, the American churches were staggered as well by the implications of the New Science. Darwin's *The Origin of Species,* published in 1859, created considerable tension within the churches, tension that persisted well into the 20th century, a tension that has never been resolved. Various degrees of accommodation were made by American churchmen to the doctrine of evolutionism, much to the dismay of literalists who continued a vigorous resistance, notably at Princeton. Some of the greatest pulpiteers of the day, including Henry Ward Beecher, capitulated to the prevailing wave of popular thought. Evolution, it was argued, was God's way of operating.

THE RISE OF THE SOCIAL GOSPEL

Revivalism, which had been the methodology of most of the great denominations throughout much of the 19th century, notably the Methodists and the Baptists, came under sharp attack. In 1861 Horace Bushnell published *Christian Nurture,* since heralded as a classic in religious education literature. Bushnell, a liberal preacher who had earlier testified to genuine religious experience, held that it was the duty of the church to cultivate a more hospitable environment by social and political means. He held that the individual is born morally neutral, and is susceptible to the educational forces that impinge on his consciousness. The ideal situation is that in which the youngster never knows when he has become a Christian. Education should displace evangelism, for, surely the individual who is taught properly will do right. Christian education and social activism were, in effect, to displace the old-fashioned mourner's bench.

---

[10]Adolf Harnack, *What Is Christianity?* (New York: G.P. Putnam's Sons, 1904).

Faced with grave social evils the churches, now cut loose from traditional moorings and attached firmly to the New Theology, adopted as their technique the Social Gospel. Through the leadership of such men as Josiah Strong, Washington Gladden, and Walter Rauschenbusch, the ills of urban society were attacked with optimistic vigor on the premise of environmentalism. Christianity was largely reduced to social ethics. To be sure many of these men were high-minded, well-intending individuals, deeply concerned about the trauma of the great cities. The tragedy of these years, however, is that it was a broken reed they caught up in their hand to do battle against the cunning of Satan. To illustrate the theological poverty of the Social Gospelers one need but cite the title of Rauschenbusch's famous book, published in 1917, *A Theology for the Social Gospel.* Quite tardily it was felt necessary to fabricate a rationale for the Social Gospel enterprise. The crises of 20th-century dictatorships and the hell of modern war quickly evaporated the shallow, ephemeral thinking that undergirded the naive Social Gospelers who prevailed at the dawn of the century.

Fundamentalism

The religious forces sweeping into the American church in the late 19th century produced consternation among many orthodox believers. Two parallel, sometimes overlapping, movements, Fundamentalism and the Holiness revival, developed in opposition to what was felt to be an alarming trend in the larger church world. Each of these conservative reactions was to have a significant influence on the shaping of the coming Pentecostal revival.

Fundamentalism was the result of a coalition of the "Princeton theology" with dispensationalism, which though not wholly compatible, maintained a united front against Modernism until well into the 20th century. Masserano says, "It is my contention that this 'Coalition theological movement' helped set the stage upon which the Assemblies of God emerged."[11]

---

[11]Frank C. Masserano, "A Study of Worship Forms in the Assemblies of God Denomination" (unpublished Th.M. thesis, Princeton Seminary, 1966), p. 31.

FUNDAMENTALIST DISPENSATIONALISM

Dispensationalism had its origins, as a modern movement, in the British sect, the Plymouth Brethren. J. N. Darby was its chief advocate, having considerable influence even in the United States, which he visited three or four times between 1866 and 1877. He preached in influential pulpits across the country. "More important than his preaching, however, were his Bible studies which he held with the ministers of the different communities in which he visited."[12] By 1876, concerned orthodox leaders had established the "Believers' Meeting for Bible Study." It was so successful that it gained considerable public attention and became a more or less permanent institution. W. J. Erdman, H. M. Parsons, and A. J. Gordon were among its earliest leaders, and they, more than any others, probably deserve the title, "Fathers of Fundamentalism." The Believers' Meeting for Bible Study became known as the Niagara Bible Conference with its move to Niagara-on-the-Lake, Ontario, where it met for 15 years until 1898.

Juxtaposition to this movement was established the International Prophecy Conference, the first conference being held in 1878. While the Bible conferences and the prophecy conference were two separate organizations with separate objectives, the leadership in both was much the same. Darby's influence on these men is easily recognized in their emphasis on Bible Study and Prophecy. Dispensationalism in the Bible Conference movement was a dominant force although in the last years (1897-1901) it was to be challenged by postmillennialism within the group. A. J. Gordon had acted as a mediating force between the different camps, both of whom claimed him as a supporter. After his death in 1895 and the death of J. H. Brookes in 1897, a crisis arose over the premillennial tenets of the pretribulation secret rapture of the church and the "any-moment theory." While it is not our purpose to discuss the conflict, it is important to note that younger leaders (i.e., C. I. Scofield and A. C. Gaebelein) emerged as champions of the "dispensational truth" and so completely took the day, that for the next fifty years friend and foe alike largely identified dispensationalism with premillennialism. The *Scofield Bible,* undoubtedly, has had the greatest influence in the spreading of dispensationalism throughout the country.[13]

---

[12] *Ibid.*, p. 32.
[13] *Ibid.*, pp. 33-34.

THE PRINCETON THEOLOGY

The Princeton theology was the second ingredient in the emerging Fundamentalist Movement. Begun in 1814, at the inception of Princeton Seminary, by A. A. Hodge, this stream of thought was perpetuated throughout the 19th century by such men as Charles Hodge and Benjamin B. Warfield. Its tenets were the core of the Fundamentalist platform: the rational defense of the faith, verbal inspiration of the Bible, the inerrancy of the autographs. "These articles of belief became the shibboleth of the Fundamentalist movement and its doctrine of scripture."[14]

As evidence of the strong Assemblies of God sympathy with the Fundamentalist Movement during the height of the great Fundamentalist-Modernist controversy, more than 200 titles by Fundamentalist-Dispensationalist authors appear in the catalogs of the Gospel Publishing House during the period 1924-1928[15] During the formative years of the denomination, the Fundamentalist influence was conspicuous.[16]

The Holiness Revival

THE EARLY YEARS

An even more important influence in the shaping of Pentecostalism was the Holiness Movement. Although Wesley had taught a doctrine of perfectionism in the 18th century, Methodism in the United States was already losing this distinctive emphasis by mid-19th century. It would be on a much broader plane that the quest for holiness would develop, even becoming a motif of Calvinist-oriented evangelists in the post-Civil War world.

In retrospect, the quest for Christian holiness seems to have been a popular expression of strivings which on a more sophisticated level produced the transcendentalist revolt of Emerson and Thoreau. That such diverse individuals as Horace Bushnell, Phoebe Palmer, Catherine and Edward Beecher, William E. Boardman, Asa Mahan, Frederick Dan Huntington, and John Humphrey Noyes sought a higher life in the years between 1835 and 1845 indicates a wide

---

[14] *Ibid.*, p. 36.

[15] *Ibid.*, p. 53.

[16] Carl Brumback, *Suddenly From Heaven* (Springfield, Missouri: Gospel Publishing House, 1961), p. 131.

surge of thought and feeling of which the events at Oberlin were but a dramatic example.[17]

Oberlin was, of course, the headquarters of Charles Finney, who had been preaching a perfectionistic doctrine since 1836.

LATE 19TH CENTURY

By the time of the Great Revival of 1858, Holiness preaching had reached a veritable flood tide in the United States. Charles G. Finney conducted great union services in Boston, Buffalo, and New York, preaching a Holiness message wherever he went. At the height of the revival, William E. Boardman's book, *The Higher Christian Life,* sold 200,000 copies.[18] The effort to restore the Holiness emphasis to the Methodist Church was not entirely without success, although there were some breaches in local areas. The Wesleyan Methodist Church was organized in 1843 and the Free Methodist Church in 1860, both partially a reaction to the declension in the parent body.

The main thrust of the post-Civil War Holiness Movement was in extradenominational activity, however. In 1867, at Vineland, New Jersey, the National Camp Meeting Association for the Promotion of Holiness came into being, with John Inskip as its president and chief theologian. By 1871, 24 "national" camp meetings had been held, one in 1869 at Round Lake, New York, with 20,000 in attendance.[19]

Eventually, as reaction to the Holiness message hardened in the great denominations late in the century, it was out of such associations that new denominations were born. "Gradually they found themselves more and more unwelcome, and finally between 1893 and 1907 twenty-five separate Holiness denominations came into existence."[20] The leading one to be born in this period was the Church of the Nazarene.

The typical Holiness teaching was that a second experi-

---

[17]Timothy L. Smith, *Revivalism and Social Reform* (New York: Abingdon Press, 1957), p. 113.

[18]Timothy L. Smith, *Called Unto Holiness* (Kansas City: Nazarene Publishing House, 1962), p. 11.

[19]*Ibid.*, pp. 16-21.

[20]Atter, *op. cit.*, p. 19.

ence subsequent to regeneration was to be expected. It was defined in terms of "cleansing," or "eradication." By the 1870's a new emphasis was emerging. Typical of the new emphasis was the Keswick teaching, named after the conference grounds in the northwest of England where it was first popularized. The Keswick view maintained that the second experience was more properly defined as "enduement of power," rather than a cleansing from sin. Other ideas also became associated with the Keswick doctrine, further distinguishing it from the traditional Holiness pattern.

> These teachings—the denial of the eradication of inward sin and the emphasis on premillennialism, faith healing, and the "gifts of the Spirit"—opened a wide breach in the holiness ranks. The conflict spread to America when Dwight L. Moody, R. A. Torrey, first president of Moody Bible Institute, Chicago, Adoniram J. Gordon, father of Gordon College, Boston, A. B. Simpson, founder of the Christian and Missionary Alliance, and the evangelist J. Wilbur Chapman began to propagate in this country the Keswick version of the second blessing.[21]

Not only did reaction begin to solidify in the denominations, and not only did dissension tend to splinter the movement from within, but there was a further cause of decline in the Holiness Movement by the turn of the century.

> For more than a century one of the disturbing factors of the second blessing movement was how to develop distinguishing criteria by which the individual and his associates could have undeniable evidence that he had the spiritual experience of sanctification.[22]

So it appears that the crest of the great Holiness revival was already passing by the time the great Pentecostal effusion burst into history.

---

[21]Timothy L. Smith, *Called Unto Holiness*, pp. 16-21.

[22]Raymond O. Corvin, "Religious and Educational Backgrounds in the Founding of Oral Roberts University" (unpublished Ph.D. dissertation, University of Oklahoma, 1967), p. 114. See also Irvine J. Harrison, "A History of the Assemblies of God" (unpublished Th.D. dissertation, Berkeley Baptist Divinity School, 1954). Harrison observed: "But perfectionism was lacking somewhere. Often those who professed the experience soon found to their dismay that there was much of the 'old man' still alive. Apparently they were mistaken; there must have been something more to their experience which they failed to receive. And so the question arose naturally: 'Is there an evidence, certain and definite, of this experience by which man may know if he has received it or not?' This question filled the pulpits, the schools and the minds of sincere individuals among this great group of holiness folk as the twentieth century dawned upon the world" (p. 59).

Ninteenth-Century Contributions to the Pentecostal Movement

The urban masses, largely unreached by the more sophisticated churches in spite of the heroic efforts of the Social Gospelers, presented a fertile soil in which new movements could flourish. The free church tradition in America, with its toleration for new organizations, contributed, without doubt, to the proliferation of Pentecostal sects at the outset of the revival. It was relatively commonplace for new groups to spring up. The voluntary tradition, in which people *choose* their church connection, an important feature of American society, stimulated aggressive competition among the various denominations and sects, those groups with the greatest vitality and evangelistic zeal gaining a ready foothold in a culture used to the easy movement of members from one loyalty to another. The doctrines of divine healing and speaking in tongues made spiritual experience vivid and real. The Pentecostals came with a clear message, presenting not only the *mystical* presence of God, but the *manifest* presence as well. Heart-hunger for "reality" was realized! The living God was made available to the common man!

The Fundamentalist Movement contributed much to the shaping of Assemblies of God theology, particularly its views on Scripture, on the person and work of Christ, on the shading of its doctrine of sanctification in distinction from the traditional Holiness view, and in its emphasis on the second coming of Christ. Dispensational eschatology was given a kind of "Pentecostal baptism," and the very hermeneutic employed by the Fundamentalists to rule out the possibility of charismatic manifestations in the Church Age was thus neatly inverted to serve Pentecostal purposes![23]

The Holiness Movement contributed immensely to the Pentecostal revival. Its emphasis on spiritual experiences and its tradition of earnestly seeking God created a receptive mood for the Pentecostal revival. The methodology of the camp meeting and the revival were eagerly adapted. From the Keswick wing of the Holiness Movement, chiefly through

---

[23]See, for example, Frank M. Boyd, *Ages and Dispensations* (Springfield, Missouri: Gospel Publishing House, 1949).

the agency of the Christian and Missionary Alliance with its Missionary Training Institute at Nyack, New York, came the Bible institute program, the ecclesiology of the Assemblies of God, the missionary vision, the emphasis on divine healing, much of its early hymnology, and even a significant portion of its early leadership. The Holiness Movement also passed on its Arminian emphasis on human responsibility, a qualification that appears prominently in Assemblies of God theological literature.

Surely, then, the Assemblies of God owes a sizable debt to stalwarts of the faith of bygone days. Let us acknowledge with gratefulness the contributions that many have made to the fellowship. We shall now direct our attention to some who were stepping-stones to the Great Revival.

Stepping-stones to the Great Revival

EARLY CHARISMATIC MOVEMENTS

Bernard Bresson has catalogued 24 charismatic movements and sects appearing between the late second century and the middle 19th century, from Montanism to Edward Irving's Catholic Apostolic Church.[24] Although there were wide variations from group to group, some common characteristics appeared among them. They tended to employ a literalistic interpretation of Scripture, viewing the Apostolic Church as normative for the church of all ages. They reacted against what they felt were corruptions of genuine Christianity, standing out against the prevailing patterns of the contemporary church. They believed themselves to be the repristination of the apostolic community, replete with fresh, direct inspiration from the Holy Spirit. The antagonisms that such groups produced alienated them from the main streams of the church, causing them to be driven off to the periphery where they frequently succumbed amid extravagances of doctrine and practice, leaving behind a history of heresy and fanaticism.[25] They were abortive revivals. It would not be until the modern, 20th-century Pentecostal revival that such a charismatic movement would enjoy the uniqueness of *sur-*

[24]Bernard Bresson, *Studies in Ecstasy* (New York: Vantage Press, 1966), pp. 20-112.

[25]An extensive treatment of such groups and their aberrations is supplied in Ronald Knox, *Enthusiasm* (Oxford: Clarendon Press, 1951).

vival. The outstanding characteristic of the modern revival is that it has endured sufficiently long to be more or less accepted within the broader confines of orthodox evangelical Christianity. This has not happened since the first century!

LATE 19TH-CENTURY EPISODES

In the United States, between 1850 and 1900, there were at least 11 episodes of speaking in tongues, occurring in New England, Ohio, Minnesota, South Dakota, North Carolina, Tennessee, and Arkansas. These were all isolated, however, and did not seem to have more than local significance. The following incidents are cited from the work of Stanley H. Frodsham, who seems to have obtained the most complete collection of charismatic manifestation data from the pre-1900 period.[26]

As early as 1875, R. B. Swan, a pastor in Providence, Rhode Island, reported manifestations of tongues in his services. He and his wife, with a few others, received the experience at this time. He reports, "In the year 1874-1875, while we were seeking, there came among us several who had received the Baptism and the gift of tongues a number of years before this, and they were very helpful to us."[27] Half a dozen people from five New England states are mentioned in this connection. This small group, centering in Providence, were known as the "Gift People." Evidently there was considerable local opposition to their practice, for they found themselves the object of social ostracism. Remarkable cases of divine healing were reported among the "Gift People."

In 1879, a young man who became a Baptist minister in Arkansas, W. Jethro Walthall, reported that he received the baptism in the Holy Spirit, speaking in tongues. He had no awareness of the Bible teaching on the subject, so at the time thought little of it. As the realization dawned on him, however, and he later began to proclaim the doctrines of the baptism in the Holy Spirit and divine healing, he was expelled from the Baptist ministry, eventually joining him-

---

[26]Stanley H. Frodsham, *With Signs Following* (Springfield, Missouri: Gospel Publishing House, 1946), pp. 7-30.

[27]*Ibid.*, p. 10.

self to a group known as "Holiness Baptists." A great Pentecostal effusion came upon this group in 1906, simultaneously with the Azusa Street revival in Los Angeles. Reverend Walthall later joined the new fellowship known as the Assemblies of God, and served for many years as superintendent of the Arkansas District Council.

In 1889, Daniel Awry, of Delaware, Ohio, was converted. Shortly afterward, on New Year's Day, 1890, at a prayer meeting, suddenly the Spirit fell on him and he began to pray in an unknown tongue. He reports that his wife received a similar experience 10 years later. While he was ministering in Benah, Tennessee, in 1899, a dozen persons received the experience. Later, when he found others who reported similar experiences, he joined their fellowship.

A Pentecostal outpouring came to the Swedish Mission Church in Moorhead, Minnesota, in 1892, where John Thompson was pastor. Frequently, while Pastor Thompson was preaching, the power of God would descend, people falling to the floor, speaking in tongues. Remarkable testimonies of divine healing were reported. Several other Minnesota communities nearby enjoyed a similar stirring, and the revival persisted for several years.

C. M. Hanson, a lay preacher, came walking through the fields to the farm home of H. N. Russum near Grafton, North Dakota, in 1896, asking if he could hold a meeting. Mrs. Russum, the maternal grandmother of G. Raymond Carlson, being a devout Christian, welcomed the request. For three days and nights the revival continued without interruption. In the course of the remarkable visitation, a girl appeared to have lost all signs of life. Alarm turned to bewilderment when someone identified the cataleptic state of the girl to be a trance. Upon hearing her speak in tongues, Brother Hanson exclaimed, "This must be that which the Prophet Joel described." Hanson himself began to seek the baptism in the Holy Spirit, and two years later received the experience. For some years thereafter, Brother Hanson and his daughter Anna traveled in evangelistic meetings. Later, when the Assemblies of God was formed, they were among the early members of that new Pentecostal fellowship. Brother Hanson was the first district superintendent of the North Central District when it was organized in 1922. Anna is better known as Mrs. Arthur Berg, who, with her husband, has exhibited true pioneer traits in the great Pentecostal Movement.

At the Shearer schoolhouse in Cherokee County, North Carolina, a revival meeting conducted by William F. Bryant in 1896 resulted in an unusual outpouring of the Holy Spirit. "The power of God fell and quite a number received the baptism in the Spirit with the speaking in tongues. There were many remarkable miracles of healing in this revival, and numbers of hardhearted sinners were converted."[28] A similar revival occurred through the ministry of Brother Bryant at Camp Creek, North Carolina, during this same period. Apparently without any connection with Bryant, a Baptist minister who had adopted the Holiness teaching, R. G. Spurling, witnessed similar manifestations in his meetings in Tennessee and North Carolina. The Pentecostal experiences, particularly in the southeastern United States, seem to have occurred principally in Holiness revival and camp meetings. Although the Pentecostal manifestations were isolated and episodic among them during these years, three of these Holiness bodies in the Southeast readily adopted the doctrine of the Pentecostal baptism, as a *third* work of grace, soon after the Great Revival swept across the country early in the 20th century. The Church of God (Cleveland, Tennessee), the Pentecostal Holiness Church, and the Church of God in Christ all followed a similar pattern.

A most remarkable evangelist in the last quarter of the 19th century was Mary Woodworth-Etter. She entered the United Brethren Church ministry in 1876, and subsequently preached in areawide tent meetings throughout the Midwest, centering principally in Indiana. She preached a Holiness message, and also prayed for the sick, reporting numerous spectacular healings. In the course of her ministry, numerous isolated individuals spoke with tongues, but, since none seemed to understand the significance of it, this was not in-

[28]*Ibid.*, pp. 16-17.

corporated into her ministry, though she did believe it to be of God.[29]

One other important influence on the Pentecostal revival was the unusual ministry of Dr. John Alexander Dowie, controversial revivalist of divine healing fame. Dr. Dowie was born in Edinburgh, Scotland, in 1847. After emigrating to Australia, he was converted and decided to enter the Christian ministry. In 1872 Dowie became pastor of a Congregational church. Shortly after his entry into the ministry, he became convinced of the scripturalness of divine healing. His zeal led him to conduct street meetings, for which he was arrested and imprisoned. His healing ministry drew large crowds, as many as 20,000 attending a single service. Dowie left Australia in 1888, moving to the United States. After conducting a series of healing missions, he eventually felt led to establish a headquarters for his operations in a new community near Chicago, called Zion. This new center was established in 1900, four years after the founding of his "Christian Catholic Church." Although there appears to be no organic connection between Edward Irving's earlier "Catholic Apostolic Church" in Great Britain and Dowie's movement, there are important similarities. Dowie sought to reestablish the office of apostle, and eventually engaged in dictatorial practices that led to his ouster by his own followers. The Dowie movement, like that of Irving, splintered amid excesses. Gordon Atter says of him: "Dr. Dowie did more to promote the doctrine of Divine Healing than possibly any other man. He was arrested 100 times for praying for the sick. Thousands were saved and healed under his ministry."[30] Donald Gee stated, "Critics made much capital out of some of the later phases of Dowie's work, but it is the testimony of all who knew him that he was, in the beginning, a man signally and genuinely used by God for some undoubted miracles."[31] The dissolution of Dowie's movement came at the very time the Pentecostal revival was in its opening stages. Many followers of Dowie left the pre-

---

[29]Brumback, *op. cit.*, p. 13.
[30]Atter, *op. cit.*, p. 20.
[31]Donald Gee, *The Pentecostal Movement*, enlarged ed. (London: Elim Publishing Company, 1949), p. 4.

Pentecostal movement to become early Pentecostal leaders. Dr. Dowie became for many an important stepping-stone to the Great Revival.

Summary

The United States in the years between the Civil War and the close of the century was in social and religious ferment. Moral, political, and economic corruption increased the stresses occasioned by urbanization, industrialization, and immigration. The great denominations, successful in Christianizing the frontier, had become complacent and sophisticated, lacking the vision and vitality to meet the changing needs of a distressed populace. Varying degrees of accommodation to popular ideas, newly imported from Europe, which assaulted orthodox Evangelicalism, further weakened the great communions. Against the erosion in the church world arose the Fundamentalist and Holiness Movements. It was largely out of the spiritual concern generated in this segment of the church that the yearning for a new Pentecost was born. Prior to 1900 there were charismatic manifestations, but these were isolated and episodic in nature. But the stage was being set for a great outpouring of the Holy Spirit which would quickly encircle the earth, bringing a great refreshing in the Latter Days. Let us turn now to the story of the Great Revival.

2

The Revival Begins: Topeka [1900-1901]

Charles F. Parham—Bethel Bible College—The Outpouring in Topeka —Significance of the Topeka Revival

On January 1, 1901, in Topeka, Kansas, a charismatic revival began that was to have far more than local implications. From this genesis can be traced a chain of circumstances that, more than any other stream, made the modern Pentecostal Movement worldwide. To be sure, there were other unrelated charismatic outpourings occurring spontaneously elsewhere in the world between 1905 and 1910, but it was the Topeka revival that was to become the primary avenue through which the spread of the movement would occur.[1]

Charles F. Parham

Donald Gee has observed: "The Pentecostal Movement does not owe its origin to any outstanding personality or religious leader, but was a spontaneous revival appearing almost simultaneously in various parts of the world."[2] However, even if it is not proper to title Charles F. Parham the "father of the Pentecostal Movement," one can scarcely overlook the role he played as a significant instrument in the Topeka revival.

Charles Fox Parham was born in Muscatine, Iowa, on June 4, 1873. At the age of nine, even before his conversion, he felt a call to the ministry. Four years later he professed

[1]Frodsham, *op. cit.* This volume contains several chapters describing the early spread of the Pentecostal message, citing spontaneous outpourings in India and Europe.
[2]Gee, *op. cit.*, p. 3.

salvation in the Congregational Church. However, the next year his denominational loyalty seems to have shifted, for at the age of 14 he became a lay exhorter in the Methodist Church. At 16 he enrolled at Southwestern College, Winfield, Kansas, to prepare for the ministry. During his student days he underwent a period of rebellion, considering for a time switching from ministerial preparation to the study of medicine. During this period of indecision he was afflicted with rheumatic fever. He came to believe that his illness was the result of his rebellion against the call to the ministry, so he earnestly sought God for healing, promising to return to his ministerial preparation if God would spare him. His health restored, Parham finished his course at the college, and at the age of 19 launched into active ministry in the Methodist Church in the state of Kansas.[3]

Parham seems to have had difficulty adjusting to ecclesiastical discipline. Frequent disagreement with church officials over what he considered to be narrowness and sectarianism led within three years to a permanent break with the Methodist Church. In 1894 he left his charge at Eudora, Kansas, and from then on championed nondenominationalism, although he did associate with others who proclaimed the Holiness doctrine.

In 1898 Parham moved to Topeka, Kansas, and opened a "faith home" to provide a hospitable environment for earnest seekers after divine healing. This institution seems to have been inspired by the example of Dowie in Zion, Illinois. Twice a month Parham issued a Holiness-slanted paper entitled *The Apostolic Faith*. In addition to these enterprises, the Parhams also conducted services in a mission associated with the faith home.

Word reached Parham of several outstanding spiritual ministries featuring divine healing and a deeper work of the Holy Spirit. Leaving the Topeka work in the hands of friends, Parham set out on a journey early in 1900 to learn what he could of the deeper things of God. His quest took him to Zion to see at first hand the work of Dr. Dowie; to Nyack,

---

[3]Sarah E. Parham, *The Life of Charles F. Parham* (Joplin, Missouri: Tri-State Printing Company, 1930). This volume is the chief source from which data are taken regarding the life of Charles F. Parham.

New York, and the ministry of Dr. Simpson; as well as other spiritual centers as far away as New England.

Bethel Bible College

Upon his return to Topeka, Parham opened an informal Bible school for Christian workers. It opened in October, 1900, in an elaborate, unfinished mansion known locally as "Stone's Folly." The purpose of Bethel Bible College was the intensive study of the Bible in a spiritual atmosphere for the developing of effective witnesses to Christ.[4] The school, which enjoyed but a single year of existence, opened with 40 students, all of mature years. The student body was composed of both married and single students; the single students being assigned to various rooms in the mansion; the married students occupying apartments in the building. Most were earnest lay people; about a dozen had already been engaged in the ministry. They represented a scattering of denominations, but the majority were from Holiness and Methodist bodies.

The program of Parham's school was threefold. The curriculum was quite simple, all the students studying a given Biblical topic, exploring together what the Bible teaches on the subject, then moving together to another topic. The Bible was the only textbook employed; the method a simple inductive approach. In addition to Bible study, considerable priority was given to prayer. One of the ornate towers that crowned the building was converted into a "prayer tower," where a continuous prayer vigil was maintained. Volunteers maintained three-hour watches. Occasionally a student would spend the night, waiting before the Lord.[5] The spiritual preparation of Christian workers was recognized by Parham as an essential part of the equipment for effective service. The third facet of Parham's school was practical service. The students participated in the services in Parham's mission and in home visitation throughout the city of Topeka.

Through the fall months, the students at Bethel Bible College had been studying the topics of repentance, con-

---

[4]Brumback, *op. cit.*, p. 22.
[5]Kendrick, *op. cit.*, p. 49.

version, sanctification, divine healing, and the second coming of Christ.[6] Late in December, just before his departure for a series of meetings in Kansas City, Parham assigned the entire student body the topic of the Biblical evidence of the baptism in the Holy Spirit. He suggested that they explore the Book of Acts. From his travels in the East earlier in the year he had become convinced that there was a supernatural experience available to believers in addition to regeneration and sanctification, yet he had run into considerable variety of opinion as to what constituted the evidence for such an experience. This question he left to his students to ferret out from the Scriptures.

Parham returned to the school on the morning of December 31, 1900. At 10 o'clock he rang the bell to call the students to the chapel to ascertain their findings from the three-day study they had engaged in during his absence. To his astonishment the students all had the same story, reporting that although different things occurred when the Pentecostal blessing fell in the various episodes recorded in Acts, the common denominator on each occasion was that they spoke with other tongues. This, they concluded, should be the Biblical evidence of a genuine baptism in the Spirit. In later years J. Roswell Flower concluded that this decision is what distinctively marked the birth of the modern Pentecostal movement.[7]

The Outpouring in Topeka

At once an air of expectancy charged the atmosphere of the little school in Topeka, for as yet none had received the experience which they had all come to believe was normative for the Apostolic Church. The first to receive was Miss Agnes N. Ozman. Stanley Frodsham quotes her own story:

> I had been a Bible student for some years and had attended T. C. Horton's Bible School at St. Paul, Minnesota, and Dr. A. B. Simpson's Bible School in New York. In October 1900 I went to this Topeka school, which was known as Bethel College. We studied the Bible by day and did much work downtown at night. Much time was spent in prayer every day and all the time.
>
> Like some others, I thought I had received the Baptism in the

[6] Frodsham, *op. cit.*, p. 21.

[7] J. Roswell Flower, "Birth of the Pentecostal Movement," *The Pentecostal Evangel*, November 26, 1950, p. 3.

Holy Ghost at the time of consecration, but when I learned that the Holy Spirit was yet to be poured out in greater fullness, my heart became hungry. At times I longed more for the Holy Spirit to come in than for my necessary food. We were admonished to honor the blood of Jesus Christ and to let it do its work in our hearts, and this brought great peace and victory.

On watchnight we had a blessed service, praying that God's blessing might rest upon us as the new year came in. During the first day of 1901 the presence of the Lord was with us in a marked way, stilling our hearts to wait upon Him for greater things. A spirit of prayer was upon us in the evening. It was nearly eleven o'clock on this first of January that it came into my heart to ask that hands be laid upon me that I might receive the gift of the Holy Ghost. As hands were laid upon my head the Holy Spirit fell upon me, and I began to speak in tongues, glorifying God. I talked several languages. It was as though rivers of living water were proceeding from my innermost being.[8]

For three days she could not speak in the English language, so overwhelmed was she. Her experience inspired others to believe for a similar experience. Miss Ozman urged them not to seek tongues, but to seek for the Holy Ghost. A large room was prepared for special prayer, and for three days the entire school remained in an attitude of intercession, praise and song punctuating periods of worship and supplication. On January 3 many received the baptism in the Holy Spirit, accompanied by "the initial, physical evidence." Within a short time, Parham himself received a similar experience. The revival was on.

Public reaction to the unusual events at the Topeka Bible school was immediate. The Topeka *Capital,* January 6, 1901, reported:

. . . strange goings on at the old mansion in the southwest part of town . . . thirty-five persons and they form a strange religious body. Whole days are spent with prayer. . . . But the really strange feature of the faith is the so-called "gift of tongues from heaven" . . . a sort of senseless gibberish . . . which they say is conveyed from God personally.[9]

Newspapers in Kansas City and as far away as St. Louis featured the revival in a number of articles. The result of

[8]Frodsham, *op. cit.*, pp. 19-20.

[9]"A Queer Faith," Topeka *Capital,* January 6, 1901, quoted in Mario G. Hoover, "Origin and Structural Development of the Assemblies of God" (unpublished thesis, Southwest Missouri State College, Springfield, Missouri, 1968), p. 8.

this publicity was a deluge of curiosity-seekers descending on "Stone's Folly" to see for themselves the strange goings-on. "Some of the visitors were favorably impressed; others extremely and openly critical."[10]

Further, within the school itself, there was some dissension. One student, S. J. Riggins, withdrew from the school on January 8, 1901, and renounced the institution as a fake. Some other students eventually left the school without having received the experience, but apparently Riggins was the only real defector. The rest who remained entered into the revival with enthusiasm, convinced of the genuineness of the experience and the scripturalness of the doctrine.[11] Within a month, an evangelistic crusade was launched by members of the Bethel Bible College family to spread the message across the nation. The school itself was closed within the year when the owners sold the old mansion. In December, 1901, a fire broke out in one of the tower rooms, and the old building was gutted.[12]

Significance of the Topeka Revival

THE INITIAL EVIDENCE

There are two aspects of the revival that began in Topeka that seem to be unique, distinguishing it from other previous charismatic outbursts. First, this seems to be the first time that the phenomenon of speaking with tongues, glossolalia, was related to the experience of the baptism in the Holy Spirit as the initial physical evidence. There had been episodes of tongues previously, and there was also the rather common teaching in a wide spectrum of American churches in the late 19th century of a baptism in the Spirit, but these two elements had not heretofore been so brought together. It is significant that this thought developed, not in a revival meeting, but in a Bible school, not in the midst of camp meeting excitement, but in a group of serious persons who were pondering thoughtfully the relationship of this experience to other events, attempting to give it theological substance.[13]

---

[10]Kendrick, *op. cit.*, p. 54.
[11]*Ibid.*
[12]Hoover, *op. cit.*, p. 10.
[13]Kelsey, *op. cit*, p. 70.

SURVIVAL!

Further, the Topeka revival was unique in its survival of the first wave of churchly reaction and the common tendency of such revivals to disintegrate amid extravagances. The adherents to Parham's revival were able to maintain sufficient kindred interests with the main stream of orthodox Christianity that in the years following World War II, the Pentecostals, in part at least, were assimilated into the ranks of the evangelical wing of Christianity.

This preservation of the Topeka revival seems to have both an ideological and a structural basis. First, even though the message of the Pentecostals sounded like a new doctrine to churchly ears, it was felt by the Pentecostals to be no new addition to the traditional teaching of the churches at all. Rather, it was felt to be that which gave substance to the creeds that affirmed belief in the Holy Spirit. Donald Gee, a leading Pentecostal scholar, evaluated this ideological kinship with mainstream Christianity in this fashion:

> The Pentecostal Movement adds nothing–it ought to add nothing–to the accepted fundamentals of the Christian Faith. It is in full and perfect fellowship with all others who are in Christ Jesus.[14]

The structural factor that preserved the revival was the willingness, howbeit reluctantly, of most of the Pentecostals to construct the necessary denominational apparatus needed for survival's sake. Reactions from various quarters of the church world forced the youthful movement out of the fold and into separate associations of like faith and practice. Although forced into isolation, it was such groups that developed, like the Assemblies of God, which refused to depart from orthodoxy, welcoming the opportunity to renew fellowship with evangelical Christianity many years later, especially in the decade of the 1940's.

[14]Donald Gee, *Why Pentecost?* (London: Victory Press, 1944), p. 51.

3

The Revival Spreads to Los Angeles [1901-1906]

Parham's Meetings in Kansas and Missouri—The Revival Spreads to Texas—The Great Los Angeles Revival—Early Characteristics of the Pentecostal Revival

A chain of events linked the initial revival at Bethel Bible College in Topeka, Kansas, with the great Azusa Street meeting in Los Angeles, the center from which the Pentecostal message rapidly spread around the world.

Parham's Meetings in Kansas and Missouri

KANSAS CITY

Three weeks after the first one received the baptism in the Spirit at Topeka, Parham took a group to Kansas City, a venture he hoped would be but the first stop on a tour to carry the new message of the Spirit's outpouring across the United States and Canada. For two weeks meetings were held in a small store building at 1675 Madison Avenue, with Sunday services conducted in the Academy of Music so more people could be accommodated. Some response was reported, but the traditional churches were not at all sympathetic, and the net result of this first venture was minimal. At first newspaper publicity was generous, but soon took on a critical tone. The early optimism with which the enthusiastic party of seven had left Topeka was considerably dampened by the disappointing response in Kansas City, so the missionary tour was canceled, and the group returned to Topeka. Parham permitted no public offerings to be taken in the meetings. He indicated that lack of funds, along with some persecution, were the reasons for the return to Topeka. The Bethel people would not experience much favorable support for their message for several years.[1]

LAWRENCE, KANSAS

In the middle of February, 1901, Parham took 20 of the Bethel Bible College students with him to nearby Lawrence, Kansas, to conduct meetings there, while the remainder of the school tarried behind to intercede for the venture. Meetings were conducted each night in the Music Hall. Door-to-door witnessing occupied the students during the day. Some were converted to Christ, and some testified to receiving the Pentecostal baptism, but the results were hardly overwhelming. Parham returned to Topeka, continuing the work of the Bible school on through the spring months. During the summer the school had to be closed, for the owners had sold the building. Parham decided to relocate in Kansas City.[2] The next months proved to be the most difficult in the entire ministry of Parham. He did remain in Kansas City long enough to conduct a four-month Bible school, but his tenure in that city was marked by public hostility and personal poverty. A quarter of a century later he reminisced that

> both the pulpit and the press sought to utterly destroy our place and prestige, until my wife, her sister and myself stood alone. Hated, despised, counted as naught, for weeks and weeks never knowing where our next meal would come from, yet feeling that we must maintain the faith once for all delivered to the saints. When we had car fare we rode, when we didn't we walked. When buildings were closed to us we preached on the street.[3]

Much of the following year, 1902, was spent by the beleaguered Parhams in Lawrence, Kansas. They conducted meetings in and around that city, but without much better success than in Kansas City the year before.[4]

NEVADA, MISSOURI

At the invitation of a Holiness preacher who had a mission in Nevada, Missouri, the Parham's went there to hold

---

[1]Kendrick, *op. cit.*, p. 55.

[2]*Ibid.*, p. 56.

[3]Charles F. Parham, "The Latter Rain," *Apostolic Faith*, July, 1926, p. 3, quoted in Kendrick, *op. cit.*, p. 56.

[4]Parham, *op. cit.*, p. 86.

a series of meetings in the spring of 1903. The meeting in Nevada was the first really successful episode since the initial Topeka outpouring, more than two years before. It had been a long, dry season, a most severe testing time, but at last the heavens were opened, and the Parhams' ministry and message seemed to be vindicated. For them this was a crucial turning point in their lives.[5]

EL DORADO SPRINGS, MISSOURI

Following the refreshing time at Nevada, Parham's party went to El Dorado Springs, Missouri, to conduct a campaign. This was in the summer of 1903. Possibly because the community was well known for the therapeutic quality of its local water supply and through this having become a refuge for many with numerous ailments, Parham sought to emphasize the ministry of healing. A most spectacular deliverance was reported by Mary A. Arthur, who had come to El Dorado Springs from nearby Galena, Kansas. Mrs. Arthur had had several serious ailments, chief of which was total blindness in one eye, and seriously impaired vision in the other, with accompanying intense pain. It was the custom of the Parhams to preach in a public park and to invite interested persons to join them in their home not far from the park where they offered to pray for those needing healing. One August afternoon Mrs. Arthur attended a prayer meeting in the home of the Parhams, and was prayed for. She removed her glasses, and upon stepping out into the sunlight, wondered how she would get home. A letter to E. N. Bell, dated December 7, 1921, describes what followed:

> I folded my handkerchief and held it over my eyes, took the hand of my little four-year-old daughter who led me to the spring. We went two blocks to get some cookies for her. Returning to my room, she let go of my hand to eat her cookies. Soon I spoke to her, but got no answer. I spoke again, but still no answer. Alarmed for her, I lifted the handkerchief off one eye—she was half a block behind me.
>
> Seeing that she was in no danger, I started to replace the handkerchief, when I realized that my eye was open to the light and yet—no pain! I looked on a white awning, at a white cloud, then, at the noonday sun. All of this brightness had formerly made me sick

[5]Kendrick, *op. cit.*, p. 57.

with pain, but now I was healed! And not only my eyes! His mighty healing power surged through my body from my head to my feet, making me feel like a new person.[6]

Mary Arthur's testimony created a sensation in Galena. A friend of hers ill with a cancerous tumor went to El Dorado Springs to learn more about the ministry of Parham, and she, too, returned to Galena claiming a miraculous deliverance through the prayer of Brother Parham. Enthusiastic citizens presented an invitation to the Parhams to visit Galena.[7]

GALENA, KANSAS

In October, 1903, the Parhams responded to the invitation, and began in Galena by conducting meetings in the home of Mr. and Mrs. Arthur. He was the town's leading hardware merchant.[8] The house could not contain the crowds, so after the second day a tent was erected on a vacant lot adjoining the Arthur home. The revival continued in the tent until Thanksgiving, when the cold weather and the crowds required a move to more adequate facilities. A renovated store building on Main Street, called the Grand Leader Building, which could seat 2,000, was secured to meet the growing need. Although this was the most commodious auditorium in town, it, too, proved to be inadequate, for the crowds spilled over into the streets. An eyewitness reports that "800 were converted and more than 1,000 were truly healed, while many hundreds were baptized in the Holy Ghost as evidenced by their speaking in strange tongues according to Acts 2:4."[9] This remarkable revival lasted until at least mid-January, 1904. During the months that the meetings continued, the influence of the revival touched numerous communities in the tri-state region of southeastern Kansas, northeastern Oklahoma, and southwestern Missouri. The Galena revival was, without doubt, an important reason for that region's becoming an early stronghold of Pentecostalism, with churches springing up in many towns within the next weeks and months.

[6]Quoted in Brumback, *op. cit.*, p. 26.
[7]*Ibid.*, p. 27.
[8]Ethel E. Goss, *The Winds of God* (New York: Comet Press, 1958), p. 11.
[9]*Ibid.*, pp. 12-13.

In the spring of 1904, Parham moved from the great triumph in Galena to hold meetings in some of the nearby communities. Although the crowds were not as great in Baxter Springs as they had been in Galena, yet a genuine revival was reported, with scores accepting the "full gospel" message, as Parham's doctrine was now being called. Parham evidently was much impressed by Baxter Springs, for he made it his permanent headquarters. His death occurred here in 1929. At another nearby town, Melrose, another meeting was conducted. Ten miles west of Baxter Springs, at a crossroads called Keelville, the first chapel erected as a Pentecostal church in the 20th-century revival was built.[10]

JOPLIN, MISSOURI

Joplin, Missouri, was the scene of the next of the Parham campaigns. In the fall of 1904, the campaign conducted in Joplin exhibited results comparable to the great Galena meeting. Again, visitors from as far away as Miami, Oklahoma, and Carthage, Missouri, responded to the Pentecostal message and the ministry of divine healing.[11]

Although there was great success, with numerous conversions, healings, and Pentecostal experiences being reported during the meetings of 1903 and 1904, opposition developed, as well. For example, the traditional churches in Galena rejected the Pentecostal message, and forced the new converts to establish their own separate meeting place. The first such Pentecostal gathering of a permanent nature in Galena was called the Third Street Mission. By 1905 there were established churches in Joplin, Missouri, and in Columbus, Melrose, Galena, and Baxter Springs, Kansas.[12]

THE REVIVAL SPREADS TO TEXAS

ORCHARD, TEXAS

Walter Oyler and his wife, whose hometown was Orchard, Texas, had received the Pentecostal baptism during the great Galena, Kansas, revival. Upon their return to Texas, they

---

[10]Kendrick, *op. cit.*, p. 60.
[11]*Ibid.*
[12]Goss, *op. cit.*, p. 29.

succeeded in obtaining one of Parham's helpers, Anna Hall, to conduct a series of meetings in March, 1905. However, the meetings were not producing much fruit, so the Oylers prevailed upon Parham himself to come. The invitation came while he was in Joplin. His health had failed and he felt a change might be beneficial. Consequently, Parham journeyed to Orchard, Texas, and on Easter Sunday, 1905, began his crusade there. Within two weeks, people were flocking to the meetings from a radius of 20 miles.

One of the visitors at the Orchard, Texas, revival was Mrs. John C. Calhoun, of Houston. She received the baptism in the Holy Spirit and returned with her testimony to her pastor, W. F. Carothers, of the Holiness Church in Brunner, Texas, a suburb of Houston. The pastor and his congregation studied the Scriptures, and became convinced that the new experience reported by Mrs. Calhoun was Biblical. The seedbed was being prepared for a great outpouring.[13]

HOUSTON, TEXAS

In May, 1905, Parham returned to Kansas to conduct some meetings that he had promised earlier, and to recruit workers for the anticipated campaign in Houston. On the tenth of July, 1905, Parham arrived in Houston with a party of 25 workers, following a week of meetings in nearby Orchard. The workers were mostly ordinary laymen, some of whom, like Howard Goss, had sold their earthly possessions to buy a train ticket to Houston, giving the rest into a common fund. The members of this "gospel band" were totally committed people who had experienced such a wonderful reality of the presence of the Lord that they were consumed with a passion to share the glorious message of the "full gospel." During the day they conducted meetings on the streets, and visited from house to house, then gathered to assist in the evening rally, conducted in Bryan Hall, a large dance pavilion which had been secured for $50 a week. The Holiness Church in Brunner formed the nucleus of the work, Pastor Carothers participating enthusiastically from the outset. Scores were converted, many embraced the Pen-

---

[13]Frodsham, *op. cit.*, p. 27.

tecostal experience, and numerous remarkable healings were reported.[14]

Goss reports: "The outstanding feature of the revival held in Houston's 'Bryan Hall' was the remarkable healings. One was a lawyer's wife, a Mrs. Delaney, who had been seriously injured in a streetcar accident and who, as a consequence, had had considerable publicity in the law courts of Houston, due to her resultant paralysis. When she was miraculously healed, she and her cure attracted the attention of the entire city."[15]

Following the summer crusade in Houston, Parham continued on for some time there making this his headquarters. The large band of workers was divided into smaller teams, and communities within a wide range of Houston were visited by Pentecostal "invasions."

At the end of this Houston Convocation all of us were separated and put into companies of five to eight workers with a man and his wife acting as chaperons for each company.

I was sent back to Alvin with a former Baptist minister, Brother Oscar Jones, of Kansas, as leader of our band. He rented the Opera House and we began our campaign. In a few days, the Lord Jesus began to manifest Himself and the town's people received us gladly.

Soon we needed a larger hall. We rented what had once been a storage building. We moved into this as the revival kept increasing in power and interest . . . and results.

There were many young people here who were filled with the Holy Ghost and had spoken in other tongues "for a sign." Many of these also received a call to the Lord's work. Among them were Walter Jessup, Hugh Cadwalder and his sister, Rosa, Hattie Allen, Millicent McClendon, and others.

The power of God was so great in the altar services here that seekers often fell as if they were dead, and would lie immovable for hours, only their lips whispering softly to God. Early in the morning they would have to be piled like cord-wood into the back of a delivery wagon and taken home to continue their solitary soul's search after God. These usually came through to a glowing experience right in their own homes. A thriving Pentecostal Church was the result of this revival. Alvin had now become another established revival center for us, for which we thanked God.[16]

---

[14]B. F. Lawrence, *The Apostolic Faith Restored* (St. Louis: Gospel Publishing House, 1916), pp. 54, 61.

[15]Goss, *op. cit.*, p. 30.

[16]*Ibid.*, pp. 30-31.

Similar churches were begun in Richard, Katy, Angleton, Needville, and Crosby. By wintertime, 1905, 25,000 had come under the influence of Parham's revival.[17] Most of these early leaders later identified with the Assemblies of God.

For the training of the growing number of workers and for stabilizing the spreading revival, Parham opened a "faith" Bible school in Houston, during the month of December, 1905. No tuition or other fee was charged, but the students were expected to take their turns at the domestic chores necessary to the operation of such an institution. The school was conducted much like the Bethel Bible College in Topeka, with the curriculum entirely an inductive Biblical study of selected topics, such as conviction, repentance, conversion, consecration, sanctification, healing, the Holy Spirit, and prophecy. Each day, Parham gave a lecture. As in Topeka, the students spent part of the day in street meetings, home visitation, and other types of practical service.[18] From this winter Bible school in Houston "about fifty preachers and workers went out into new fields and were soon having gracious revivals."[19]

A year after the initial revival in Orchard, Texas, a full-gospel convention was held there. This was in April, 1906. Stanley Frodsham describes an incident associated with this meeting:

> At the close of the convention a number who had attended were unsatisfied, as they had not received the Baptism in the Spirit as they expected. However, as they went to the railroad station to take a certain train they were full of expectation. The train was late and so while they waited the time was spent in singing, testifying, and preaching. When the train arrived the seekers were full of the joy of the Lord and in one hour twelve were filled with the Spirit. Three of these who received later became ministers of the gospel.[20]

A black Holiness preacher, W. J. Seymour, who was one of the students in Parham's Houston school during the winter of 1905-6, became in the providence of God the link between the Parham phase of the revival at Houston, and

---

[17]Kendrick, *op. cit.*, p. 63.

[18]*Ibid.*, p. 63.

[19]Lawrence, *op. cit.*, p. 64.

[20]Frodsham, *op. cit.*, p. 29.

Azusa Street, Los Angeles—the revival that transcended any individual human leadership.

THE GREAT LOS ANGELES REVIVAL

W. J. Seymour became convinced of the truth of the Pentecostal experience as he listened to the teaching of Parham, week after week, in the Houston Bible school. He came to believe that the initial evidence of speaking in other tongues as the Spirit gives utterance is the accompanying normative pattern. But, Seymour had not as yet received the experience himself. These were indeed days of preparation, however, for evidently God had a special mission for Seymour to accomplish.

ON THE EVE OF THE REVIVAL

Meanwhile, in Los Angeles an air of expectancy was being generated. In June, 1905, the pastor of the First Baptist Church, Joseph Smale, returned from an inspiring visit to the scene of the spectacular Welsh Revival.[21] Evan Roberts had encouraged him to pray for a similar outpouring for Los Angeles. Smale instituted regular prayer meetings in his church. "These prayer meetings ran for a number of weeks, and there was much spontaneous worship, also some very wonderful healings. But the burden that gathered volume daily, and the cry, was for a 'Pentecost' for Los Angeles, and for the world."[22] Several Holiness congregations were inspired to pray for revival, too, through these meetings. Pastor Smale's "enthusiasm" precipitated a disagreement with the church board. As a consequence, Pastor Smale resigned, with some of the people evidently going with him to form a "New Testament Assembly." Through the winter of 1905-6, prayer for a great outpouring continued at Pastor Smale's newly established fellowship, and in other cottage prayer meetings, as well.[23]

BONNIE BRAE STREET

A Holiness woman, Neeley Terry, associated with a small Negro Nazarene church in Los Angeles, visited Houston in

---

[21]See J. Edwin Orr, *The Light of the Nations* (Grand Rapids: Eerdmans, 1965) for an excellent account of the great Welsh Revival of 1904-05 and other related movements worldwide.

[22]Lawrence, *op. cit.*, p. 71.

[23]*Ibid.*

1905. On her return to Los Angeles, she told about a "very godly man" she had met in Houston, W. J. Seymour. The Nazarene group subsequently invited Seymour to Los Angeles to hold a meeting in their church. He spoke the first Sunday morning on the baptism in the Holy Spirit, using Acts 2:4 for his text, even though he himself had not yet experienced the Pentecostal manifestation. In the afternoon when he returned to the mission, he found the door locked. He was informed that the Holiness saints thought that he was preaching false doctrine, and that he was no longer welcome among them! His declaration that tongues is the invariable accompaniment of the baptism in the Holy Spirit was too much for them.[24]

Undaunted, Seymour moved his meetings to a private home owned by some Baptists, at 214 North Bonnie Brae Street. It was here, in this humble dwelling, that the first Pentecostal effusion came, the evening of April 9, 1906, to a company of black saints.[25]

> As though hit by a bolt of lightning, the entire company was knocked from their chairs to the floor. Seven began to speak in divers kinds of tongues and to magnify God. The shouts were so fervent—and so loud!—that a crowd gathered outside, wondering "What meaneth This?" Soon it was noised over the city that God was pouring out His Spirit. White people joined the colored saints, and also joined the ranks of those filled with the Holy Ghost, Lydia Anderson being one of the first white recipients. Seymour received the experience of Acts 2:4, which he had been preaching, on April 12. The home on Bonnie Brae Street could not begin to accommodate the congregation which spilled out into the street.[26]

AZUSA STREET

To accommodate the crowds that the excitement had attracted, an old, two-story frame structure in the industrial section of the city was secured as a meetingplace. The building, once a Methodist church, had more recently served as a livery stable and tenement house. Discarded lumber and plaster littered the large, barn-like room on the ground floor. "A space was cleared large enough to seat a score or two of persons. We sat on planks resting on old nail

[24]Lawrence, *op. cit.*, pp. 54-55.
[25]*Ibid.*
[26]Brumback, *op. cit.*, p. 36.

kegs. . . ."[27] (Eventually the debris was cleared away to make room for more people.) This was 312 Azusa Street, the mission soon to be heard of around the world.

The humble "Azusa Mission" was the home of a constant revival for three years. A witness to those events described the scene in the following fashion:

The news spread far and wide that Los Angeles was being visited with a "rushing mighty wind, from heaven." The how and why of it is to be found in the very opposite of those conditions that are usually thought necessary for a big revival. No instruments of music are used. None are needed. No choir. Bands of angels have been heard by some in the Spirit and there is heavenly singing that is inspired by the Holy Ghost. No collections are taken. No bills have been posted to advertise the meetings. No church organization is back of it. All who are in touch with God realize as soon as they enter the meeting that the Holy Ghost is the leader. One brother states that even before his train entered the city he felt the power of the revival. Travelers from afar wend their way to the headquarters at Azusa Street. There they find a two-story whitewashed store building. You would hardly expect heavenly visitations there unless you remember the stable at Bethlehem. But here they find a mighty Pentecostal revival going on from ten o'clock in the morning until about twelve o'clock at night. Pentecost has come to hundreds of hearts.

As soon as it is announced that the altar is open for seekers for pardon, sanctification, the baptism in the Holy Ghost, and healing for the body, people rise and flock to the altar. There is no urging. What kind of preaching is it that brings that? The simple declaring of the Word of God. There is such power in the preaching of the Word in the Spirit that people are shaken on the benches. Coming to the altar many fall prostrate under the power of God and often come out speaking in tongues. Sometimes the power falls on people and they are wrought upon by the Spirit during the giving of testimonies, or the preaching, and they receive the Holy Spirit. It is noticeably free from all nationalistic feeling. If a Mexican or a German cannot speak English he gets up and speaks in his own tongue and feels quite at home, for the Spirit interprets through the face and the people say "Amen." No instrument that God can use is rejected on account of color or dress or lack of education. That is why God has so built up the work.

Seekers for healing are usually taken upstairs and prayed for in the prayer room. Many have been healed there. There is a large room upstairs that is used for Bible study. A brother fittingly describes it this way: "Upstairs there is a long room furnished with

---

[27]Lawrence, *op. cit.*, p. 74.

chairs and three California redwood planks laid end to end on backless chairs. This is the Pentecostal upper room where sanctified souls seek the Pentecostal fullness and go out speaking in tongues."[28]

Another present in those wonderful days describes his visit to Azusa Mission in September, 1906:

I arrived at ten o'clock, and at that early hour found the house practically full, with many more coming later, some glad to secure standing room. I remained until one o'clock, returned at two and stayed until five, thus spending six solid hours on that one day. And I was more than ever persuaded that the movement was of God. . . .

One thing that somewhat surprised me at that first meeting I attended, and also subsequently, was the presence of so many persons from the different churches, not a few of them educated and refined. Some were pastors, evangelists, foreign missionaries, and others of high position in various circles, looking on with seeming amazement and evident interest and profit. And they took part in the services in one way or another. Persons of many nationalities were also present, of which Los Angeles seems to be filled, representing all manner of religious beliefs. Sometimes these, many of them unsaved, would be siezed [sic] with deep conviction for sin under the burning testimony of one of their own nationality, and at once heartily turn to the Lord. . . .

Of course some persons attending the meetings in those early days of the revival, mocked and cavilled, also as on the day of Pentecost, and are doing so at the present. But this is true of every mighty work of the Holy Spirit.[29]

The ostensible leader in this spontaneous, unstructured revival was, at least at the first, W. J. Seymour. His humility and simplicity seemed to invite the leadership of the Holy Spirit. God could have selected a more impressive person, but He used, rather, this relatively uneducated, obscure gentleman, afflicted with a noticeably defective eye.

Brother Seymour generally sat behind two empty shoe boxes, one on top of the other. He usually kept his head inside the top one during the meeting, in prayer. There was no pride there. The services ran almost continuously. Seeking souls could be found under the power almost any hour, night and day. The place was never closed nor empty. The people came to meet God. He was always there. Hence a continuous meeting. The meeting did not depend on the human leader. God's presence became more and more wonderful. In the old building, with its low rafters and bare floors, God

---

[28]Frodsham, *op. cit.*, pp. 33-34.
[29]Lawrence, *op. cit.*, pp. 77-78.

took strong men and women to pieces, and put them together again, for His glory. It was a tremendous overhauling process. Pride and self-assertion, self-importance and self-esteem, could not survive there. The religious ego preached its own funeral sermon quickly.

No subjects or sermons were announced ahead of time, and no special speakers for such an hour. No one knew what might be coming, what God would do. All was spontaneous, ordered of the Spirit. We wanted to hear from God, through whoever [sic] he might speak. We had no "respect of persons." The rich and educated were the same as the poor and ignorant, and found a much harder death to die. We only recognized God. . . .

We were delivered right there from ecclesiastical hierarchism and abuse. We wanted God. When we first reached the meeting we avoided as much as possible human contact and greeting. We wanted to meet God first. We got our head under some bench in the corner in prayer, and met men only in the Spirit, knowing them "after the flesh" no more. The meetings started themselves, spontaneously, in testimony, praise, and worship.[30]

B. F. Lawrence describes one episode that occurred in the early days of the Azusa Street revival when a newspaper reporter visited:

He had been assigned to "write up" an account of the meetings held by those supposed ignorant, fanatical, demented people. But it was to be from the standpoint of the comic or ridiculous,—the more highly sensational the better. It was doubtless supposed that this would the more freely meet the tastes of the readers of the paper. And the reporter went to the meeting with feelings in harmony with those of his employers. He was going to a "circus," as he and others would say, so far as genuine worldly amusement is concerned. But, fortunately for himself, he witnessed some very touching and solemn scenes, and heard the Gospel truth so powerfully presented in the Holy Ghost by different persons, that his frivolous feelings gave way to devout ones.

After a little while a Spirit-filled woman gave such a mighty exhortation and appeal to the sinner to turn to God that the reporter was still more greatly impressed. Suddenly she broke out, not voluntarily, but truly as the "Spirit gave utterance" (Acts 2:4), in a different language, one with which she was utterly unfamiliar. But it was in the native tongue of the foreign-born reporter, who was also proficient in the English language. Directing her earnest gaze upon him, she poured forth such a holy torrent of truth, by way of exposing his former sinful, licentious life, that he was per-

---

[30]Frank Bartleman, *How Pentecost Came to Los Angeles* (Los Angeles: by author, 1928), p. 58.

fectly dumbfounded, no one seemingly understanding the language but himself.

When the services were over, he at once forced his way to the woman, asking her if she knew what she had said concerning him while speaking in that particular foreign language. "Not a word," was her prompt reply. At first he could not believe her, but her evident sincerity and perfectly grammatical and fluent speech thoroughly convinced him that she absolutely knew nothing of the language. Then he told her that she had given an entirely correct statement of his wicked life, and that he now fully believed her utterances were exclusively from God in order to lead him to true repentance and the accepting of Jesus Christ as his personal Saviour. And he at once faithfully promised such a course. Going from the meeting he informed his employers that he could not give them such a report as they expected him to present. He added, however, that if they wanted a true and impartial account of the meeting he would gladly give it. But they did not want that, and also plainly told him that they did not need his services thereafter.[31]

It would not be fair to suppose that all that happened at Azusa Street was perfectly in order, nor would it be fair to suppose that there was no discipline, either. As is likely in any charismatic revival, some became fascinated by the sensational manifestations, rather than the God who energized, by the "tongues" rather than the Baptizer. However, an eyewitness observer, A. W. Orwig, commented:

In the first year of the work in Los Angeles I heard W. J. Seymour, an acknowledged leader, say, "Now, don't go from this meeting and talk about tongues, but try to get people saved." Again I heard him counsel against all unbecoming or fleshly demonstrations, and everything not truly of the Holy Spirit. Wise words, indeed. There had been some extremes, and still are in other places. But these things no more represent the real Pentecostal work than do the follies in various churches represent genuine Christianity. Bro. Seymour constantly exalted the atoning work of Christ and the Word of God, and very earnestly insisted on thorough conversion, holiness of heart and life and the fulness of the Holy Spirit.[32]

Frank Bartleman's concern over propriety and scriptural balance provided the needed correctives to keep the vigorous new revival in the proper channels. He writes:

In the beginning of the "Pentecostal" work I became very much exercised in the Spirit that Jesus should not be slighted, "lost in

[31] Lawrence, *op. cit.*, pp. 82-83.
[32] *Ibid.*, p. 86.

the temple," by the exaltation of the Holy Ghost, and of the "gifts" of the Spirit. There seemed great danger of losing sight of the fact that Jesus was "all, and in all." I endeavored to keep Him as the central theme and figure before the people. Jesus should be the center of our preaching. All comes through and in Him. The Holy Ghost is given to "show the things of Christ." The work of Calvary, the atonement, must be the center for our consideration. The Holy Ghost never draws our attention from Christ to Himself, but rather reveals Christ in a fuller way. We are in the same danger today. There is nothing deeper nor higher than to know Christ. Everything is given of God to that end. The "one Spirit" is given to that end. Christ our salvation, and our all. That we might know "the lengths and breadths, and heights and depths of the love of Christ, having a 'spirit of wisdom and revelation in the knowledge of Him (Christ).'" Eph. 1:17. It was "to know Him (Christ)," for which Paul strove. I was led to suddenly present Jesus one night to the congregation at Eighth and Maple. They had been forgetting Him in their exaltation of the Holy Ghost and the "gifts." Now I introduced Christ for their consideration. They were taken completely by surprise and convicted in a moment. God made me do it. Then they saw their mistake and danger. I was preaching Christ one night at this time, setting Him before them in His proper place, when the Spirit so witnessed of His pleasure that I was overpowered by His presence, falling helpless to the floor under a mighty revelation of Jesus to my soul. I fell like John on the Isle of Patmos, at His feet.

I wrote a tract at this time, of which the following are extracts: "We may not even hold a doctrine, or seek an experience, except in Christ. Many are willing to seek 'power' from every battery they can lay their hands on, in order to perform miracles, draw the attention and adoration of the people to themselves, thus robbing Christ of His glory, and making a fair showing in the flesh. The greatest religious need of our day would seem to be that of true followers of the meek and lowly Jesus. Religious enthusiasm easily goes to seed. The human spirit so predominates, the show-off, religious spirit. But we must stick to our text, Christ. He alone can save. The attention of the people must be first all, and always, held to Him. A true 'Pentecost' will produce a mighty conviction for sin, a turning to God. False manifestations produce only excitement and wonder. Sin and self-life will not materially suffer from these. We must get what our conviction calls for. Believe in your own heart's hunger, and go ahead with God. Don't allow the devil to rob you of a real 'Pentecost.' Any work that exalts the Holy Ghost or the 'gifts' above Jesus will finally land up in fanaticism. Whatever causes us to exalt and love Jesus is well and safe. The reverse will ruin all. The Holy Ghost is a great light, but focused on Jesus always, for His revealing."[38]

[38]Bartleman, *op. cit.*, p. 84.

It was stability and soundness of this order that paved the way for Bartleman to minister extensively during 1907 and 1908 among the Christian and Missionary Alliance people in the East, including several speaking engagements at Nyack, New York.[34] It would surely be a mistake to brush aside the Great Revival in Los Angeles as superficial enthusiasm.

The revival, in spite of the humblest of beginnings and mixed notices in the press, quickly attracted widespread attention. This was due in part to the considerable traffic flowing through Los Angeles, a major crossroads of the nation. Missionaries, evangelists, and other Christian workers were attracted, many of whom were convinced and filled with the Spirit.[35] Visitors from many parts of the nation and from every continent received the Pentecostal experience during the three years of the Great Revival, returning to their own localities to propagate the message. It was not uncommon for missionaries on their way to the field, embarking from the port of New York, to scatter the seed in meetings across the country as they journeyed eastward from Los Angeles. So it was that Elder Sturdevant, a Negro preacher on his way to the interior of Africa to serve as a missionary, brought the Pentecostal message to New York City in December, 1906.[36] Leaders of the Canadian Pentecostal Movement, A. H. Argue and R. E. McAlister, drank at the Azusa fountain.[37] Mrs. Rachel Sizelove carried the message to Missouri, Samuel Snell to Arizona, Glenn A. Cook to Indiana, C. H. Mason to Tennessee, G. B. Cashwell took the Pentecostal testimony throughout the Southland. A host of other men and women, destined to be stalwart figures in the years to come throughout the United States in a variety of Pentecostal denominations, first discovered the long-hidden truth of the New Testament Spirit-anointed church there in the humble stable. Others, like T. B. Barratt of Norway, spread the news further afield. It was not only by word of mouth and public ministry that the news spread, for short-

---

[34]*Ibid.*, p. 105.
[35]Kendrick, *op. cit.*, p. 68.
[36]Bloch-Hoell, *op. cit.*, p. 49.
[37]Goss, *op. cit.*, p. 36.

ly after the revival began, Seymour and his colleagues began to publish a small, four-page monthly pamphlet, *The Apostolic Faith,* the circulation of which increased from 5,000 to 20,000 within the first year.[38] And so the news spread, and the revival grew. The great significance of the Azusa Street revival is its role in transforming the embryo Pentecostal outpouring into a worldwide movement.

Early Characteristics of the Pentecostal Revival

Several distinguishing characteristics marked the movement by the time the Azusa Street revival was scattered across the land.

EXPECTANCY

Striking was the eschatological expectancy. Frank Bartleman was not alone in his anticipation of a ripeness of time for a "Latter Rain" outpouring. Premillennialist hope was a common denominator among many, and when news broke that Pentecost was being reenacted, it was not difficult for hungry hearts to attach prophetic significance to the revival. The sense that "Jesus is coming soon" gave a sense of urgency, of importance, of worth, to the burgeoning movement.

REALITY

One cannot come away from perusal of early documents describing the Great Revival without being awed by the sense of God's presence which the people felt. It was a worshiping community. There was intense awareness of "holy ground." It was only later that the sense of the holy was cheapened for some by raucous music and superficial services. They were a people much in prayer. Seeking God was the central passion of their lives.

HOLY LIVING

Holiness was more than a theological concept. To be sure, a fair proportion of the early Pentecostal seekers came out of the Holiness tradition, but pervasive among those in Azusa Street, regardless of what school of thought was entertained about the doctrine of sanctification, was a great concern about holiness of life. As Donald Gee stated, when

---

[38]Bloch-Hoell, *op. cit.*, p. 48.

asked to give briefly what the baptism in the Holy Spirit meant to him, "It has made the Lord Jesus intensely real."[39] In the face of such a burning reality, purity of thought and life becomes a central concern. "And when I saw him, I fell at his feet as dead" (Revelation 1:17).

EVANGELISTIC ZEAL

Although many who came in at the first were already strong Christian believers, many of them members of established denominations, there was a great sense of ministry to the unsaved, as well. Evangelism and missionary passion were important in the hierarchy of values of this early Pentecostal group from the beginning. It would be grossly unfair to label the revival as a proselyting enterprise, in spite of the fact that there was a conscious awareness that the participants did, as a matter of fact, have an important ministry to the church world, too.

OPENNESS TO CHANGE

Freshness, spontaneity, and rejection of form were part of the mood. At Azusa Street, the meetings were unstructured. No one knew who would be the speaker for that hour, nor what songs would be sung. No offerings were taken. There was a strong antipathy to anything that resembled organization, for fear that any intrusion of the human element would grieve the Holy Spirit. This, of course, permitted excesses and distortions on occasion, and required the watchfulness of mature teaching ministries.

FAITH

The fact that offerings were not taken is an indicator of the priority given to faith. These people believed God for the totality of life's needs. An important part of the early revival was the remarkable healing ministry that moved everywhere there was a Pentecostal outpouring. God was so real that He could meet any need, even the physical!

EQUALITY

That God was no respecter of persons was clearly demonstrated in the Great Revival. The color line was not apparent. Only later did the white saints move out of

---

[39]Donald Gee, *Pentecost* (Springfield, Missouri: Gospel Publishing House, 1932), p. 10.

Azusa Street and establish their own distinct congregations. There was no demarcation between male and female, for God inspired numerous godly women to testify and pray, along with the men. The rich and educated, the sophisticated and urbane, along with the uncouth and unlearned, all alike were humbled before the blazing fire of God's glory in the crude missions and tents in that early day. Surely God had visited His people with a wonderful refreshing!

BIBLICAL AUTHORITY

Some would have abused by overemphasis the spectacular features of the revival, but there were sufficient wise counselors who kept before the people the need for maintaining the centrality of Christ and the authority of the Word of God written. That the 20th-century Pentecostal revival has endured can likely be attributed to this fact, perhaps more than any other.

4

Revival and Reaction [1906-1914]

Rapid Spread from Azusa Street—Reaction and Rejection—Why the Revival Flourished

From 1905 to 1910, Pentecostal revivals erupted in widely scattered parts of the world: the United States and Canada, Great Britain, Holland, Germany, Norway, Sweden, Chile, and India. Some of these occurred without visible links with one another; others were the result of revival reports falling on fertile soil. A great yearning for renewal swept around the world in the first decade of the new century.[1] It would not be accurate to ascribe the entire story of the spread of the Pentecostal message to the Great Revival at Azusa Mission in Los Angeles, but without question it was that center that was the most significant instrument in the proliferation of the Latter Rain.

Rapid Spread from Azusa Street

THE SOUTH

In the United States the Pentecostal message spread swiftly after 1906, usually resulting in the formation of independent congregations. Opposition to the movement was already crystallizing in the established churches, including some denominations within the Holiness Movement. However, in the Southeast, at least four significant Holiness bodies were so engulfed by the overflow of the Azusa

---

[1]See J. Edwin Orr, *The Light of the Nations* (Grand Rapids: Eerdmans, 1965), pp. 230-41; Paulus Scharpff, *History of Evangelism* (Grand Rapids: Eerdmans, 1964, pp. 169-271; Nichol, *op. cit.*, pp. 18-53; Bloch-Hoell, *op. cit.*, pp. 5-52.

Street revival that, en masse, they adopted the Pentecostal experience as a distinct "third work of grace," thus becoming Holiness-Pentecostal denominations. Actually, this was the theology of both Parham and Seymour, as well as Frank Bartleman, another early leader in Los Angeles. Much of the yearning for a "new Pentecost" was generated in the dozen or so Holiness missions that had been spawned in Los Angeles by 1906 due to alienation from older, traditional denominations, which appeared to hungry seekers after God to have lost their interest in Holiness.[2] At least a thousand worshipers gathered at these Holiness missions on a given Sunday.[3] The great outpouring at the Azusa Street mission had a strong impact on these splinter groups.

> God suddenly shut up many little Holiness Missions, Tent meetings, etc., that had been striving with one another a long time for the pre-eminence. It would not work any more. They had to come together. God only could tame them. There was little going on anywhere else, but at Azuza [*sic*] St. All the people were coming. Even Pastor Smale finally came to "Azusa Mission" to hunt his people up. Then he invited them back to let God have His way. The fire broke out at his own Assembly also.[4] [Smale eventually rejected tongues, it must be noted, however.]

Before the end of 1906, news of the Azusa Street revival had spread over the nation, in large measure due to a variety of publications. Seymour's *The Apostolic Faith* was being distributed without charge to thousands of ministers and laymen. Holiness people in the South learned of the revival through the pages of *The Way of Faith,* an outstanding Holiness periodical edited by J. M. Pike in Columbia, South Carolina. During 1906 and 1907, Frank Bartleman contributed regular reports for publication. The prestige of Pike, who was regarded highly in Holiness circles, added weight to the reports of Bartleman.[5]

Tongue-speaking was not new to some of the Holiness people in the South. In 1896, more than 100 were reported to have spoken in tongues at a great revival at Camp

---

[2]Timothy L. Smith, *Called Unto Holiness,* pp. 112-21.

[3]Harold Vinson Synan, "The Pentecostal Movement in the United States" (unpublished Ph.D. dissertation, University of Georgia, Athens, Georgia, 1967), p. 115.

[4]Lawrence, *op. cit.,* p. 75.

[5]Synan, *op. cit.,* pp. 144-45.

Creek, North Carolina, among the Church of God people.[6] Although no connection was made between the experience and the doctrine of the fullness of the Holy Spirit at the time, it did precondition many for the doctrine of tongues as the initial evidence of the reception of the Holy Spirit when the report of the Azusa Street revival reached the Southland. Most Holiness people in the South who read of the Pentecostal revival in Los Angeles reacted favorably.[7]

G. B. Cashwell, a minister in the Holiness Association of North Carolina, left for Los Angeles in November, 1906, to see for himself the Azusa Street meeting. He was upset at first by some features of the revival, particularly the mixture of races in the mission. God softened him, however.

> At first deeply prejudiced against Negroes, he saw his prejudice fading as interest in speaking with other tongues began to overwhelm him. After a few services he "lost his pride" and asked Seymour and several Negro boys to lay hands on his head in order for him to be "filled." In a short time he received the Pentecostal experience and joyfully began to speak with other tongues.[8]

Cashwell, the "Apostle of Pentecost" to the South, returned home from his Los Angeles trip in December, 1906. He rented an abandoned tobacco warehouse in Dunn, and on the last day of the year launched a series of meetings that would approximate for the South what Azusa Street had been in the West.

> Before beginning the Dunn meeting, Cashwell had invited all the ministers of the Fire-Baptized Holiness Church, the Pentecostal Holiness Church, and the Free-Will Baptist Church to attend. The results far exceeded anything that had ever been seen in the Southern holiness movement. Thousands of people jammed the old warehouse to see and hear firsthand about the "tongues movement." Practically the entire ministerium of the Pentecostal Holiness Church and the Fire-Baptized Holiness attended, most of them going to the altar and receiving the pentecostal experience that Cashwell preached.[9]

---

[6]Charles W. Conn, *Like a Mighty Army* (Cleveland, Tennessee: Church of God Publishing House, 1955), p. 25.

[7]Synan, *op. cit.*, pp. 150-51.

[8]*Ibid.*, p. 152.

[9]*Ibid.*, p. 153.

After the meeting concluded in Dunn, early in 1907, Cashwell, bombarded with invitations, toured the Southland for two years, holding meetings in Tennessee, South and North Carolina, Virginia, Georgia, and Alabama. Wherever he went, "huge crowds gathered to hear him preach the new gospel of Pentecost and tongues."[10] During 1907 he began the publication of a paper called *The Bridegroom's Messenger,* which further broadcast the message among Southern Holiness people.[11] Most of the leadership of the Pentecostal Holiness Church and the much smaller Fire-Baptized Holiness Church joined the Pentecostal ranks by 1908, with the result that both of these bodies became thoroughly Pentecostal. In 1911 the Fire-Baptized group was absorbed by the larger denomination.[12] Many Free Will Baptist ministers, already Holiness-oriented, accepted the Pentecostal teaching of Cashwell, resulting eventually in the creation of a new organization in Dunn, North Carolina, the "Pentecostal Free Will Baptist Church."

In the spring of 1907, Cashwell conducted a revival meeting in Birmingham, Alabama. Two former Methodist clergymen, H. G. Rodgers and M. M. Pinson received the Pentecostal experience there. They later formed the "Pentecostal Association in the Mississippi Valley," a fellowship that was a progenitor of the Assemblies of God.[13]

While Cashwell was in Birmingham, word of his ministry reached the leaders of the Church of God in Cleveland, Tennessee. The General Overseer, A. J. Tomlinson, went to Birmingham in June to be with M. M. Pinson in a meeting. This was his first direct encounter with the phenomenon of tongues. When he returned to Cleveland, he discovered that many of his brethren had already received the experience. Consequently, he invited Cashwell to Cleveland to expound the way more fully to them. In January, 1908, Tomlinson received the baptism in the Holy Spirit during the annual General Assembly of the Church of God, while Cashwell was preaching. The Church of God, destined to

[10]*Ibid.*, pp. 156-57.
[11]*Ibid.*, p. 157.
[12]*Ibid.*, p. 164.
[13]Kendrick, *op. cit.*, p. 80.

become one of the largest American Pentecostal bodies, was swept into the Pentecostal Movement in that year.[14]

Elder C. H. Mason, leader of the Church of God in Christ, a Negro Holiness body of Memphis, Tennessee, and two of his associates, J. A. Jeter and D. J. Young, traveled to Los Angeles in March, 1907, to learn at first hand of the famous revival. They returned to Memphis after a five-week stay in Los Angeles, not only convinced of the doctrine, but professing the experience, as well.[15] A split in the leadership developed, some refusing to adopt the Pentecostal teaching. Mason succeeded in retaining the original name of the organization in the dispute that followed, and went on to lead the Pentecostal faction to become the largest Negro Pentecostal body in the nation.

> So great was Mason's prestige that many white Pentecostal ministers accepted ordination at his hands. From 1907 to 1914 his church was interracial, many whites joining it because as an incorporated denomination, the Church of God could obtain clergy permits for them on the railroads, and aid them in being bonded for weddings. Many of the men who founded the white "Assemblies of God" church in 1914, were thus ordained in the Church of God in Christ by Bishop Mason.[16]

And so it was that Pentecost invaded an important segment of the Holiness Movement. The Holiness-Pentecostal wing of the modern revival has remained largely a phenomenon of the American Southeast.

Elsewhere in the country, independent congregations were springing up. Several key centers seemed to be favored with unusual revival power.

THE MIDWEST

In the Midwest, a singular influence was William H. Durham, who was pastor of a Holiness mission on North Avenue in Chicago. In 1907 he visited the revival in Los Angeles, returning to his Chicago ministry a changed person. He had received the Pentecostal experience, and vowed never again to proclaim the traditional Holiness doctrine of sanctification. This led to a controversy in the

---

[14]Synan, *op. cit.*, p. 168.
[15]*Ibid.*, p. 170.
[16]*Ibid.*, p. 172.

Pentecostal ranks three years later, of which more will be said. When Durham arrived at his church in Chicago he discovered that already several of his parishioners had received the baptism in the Spirit. The North Avenue mission became the center of an outstanding move of the Holy Spirit, God using Durham there much as He did Cashwell in the South. Durham began to publish an effective paper, *The Pentecostal Testimony,* which succeeded in publicizing the work greatly. Friends came from great distances to participate in the services. A host of Pentecostal notables came into the experience in Pastor Durham's meetings, among them, A. H. Argue of Winnipeg, outstanding Canadian minister, and E. N. Bell, of Fort Worth, later to be the first Chairman of the Assemblies of God. William H. Piper, pastor of the newly formed Stone Church in Chicago, was influenced by Durham, and in 1907 that famous Pentecostal landmark was brought into the ranks.[17] Aimee Semple McPherson, for a time a member, was instantly healed of a broken foot in Durham's mission. Some of the students at Moody Bible Institute were inspired to seek for the baptism of the Holy Spirit.[18]

Just north of Chicago lay Zion City. As early as 1904 there was a Pentecostal penetration into Dr. Dowie's stronghold. A woman, fresh from the Lawrence, Kansas, revival meeting of Charles Parham, a Mrs. Waldron, moved to Zion, carrying her testimony with her. At least one person, Mrs. Hall, received the experience in a prayer meeting conducted in the Waldron home. Officers of Dowie's Christian Catholic Church, who controlled the entire community, succeeded in having the husbands of the women mentioned dismissed from their employment, forcing them to move from the community.[19] Two years later, Parham and a "gospel band" invaded Zion. Among those who were converted to the Pentecostal way were Fred Vogler, Harry Bowley, F. F. Bosworth, F. A. Graves, and Marie Burgess (later better known as the wife of Robert Brown, and for

---

[17]Brumback, *op. cit.*, pp. 68-69.

[18]Goss, *op. cit.*, pp. 123-25.

[19]Letter from Louise Albach to J. R. Flower, August 30, 1950, quoted in Brumback, *op. cit.*, p. 72.

many years co-pastor of the great Glad Tidings Tabernacle in New York City). These all became Assemblies of God leaders. Although Dowie sternly opposed the Pentecostal intrusion into his bailiwick, a church, known as The Christian Assembly, was formed.[20]

In Indianapolis, a Pentecostal revival broke out in the Christian and Missionary Alliance Gospel Tabernacle during January, 1907. Glenn A. Cook testified to the remarkable events occurring at Azusa Street, reporting that he had himself received the baptism in the Holy Spirit with the accompanying sign of tongues. Members of the congregation who sensed in this message an invitation from God appealed for "tarrying" meetings to be held in the church. In the absence of the pastor, who was vacationing at the time, permission was granted, but when the pastor learned what had taken place, he wired a church officer to deny the use of the church for such purposes. This resulted in a large contingent of the church retiring to other quarters where their plea for a personal Pentecost could be carried on without hindrance. It is interesting to note that the CMA pastor, Dr. G. N. Eldridge, later received the baptism in the Spirit, along with his wife.[21]

The Reynolds family were charter members of the Indianapolis Alliance Gospel Tabernacle. The youngest daughter, Alice, then but a teen-ager, received the Baptism on Easter Sunday, 1907.[22] It was during Cook's meetings that a young law student, J. Roswell Flower, was converted. Two years later he received the Pentecostal experience. In 1911, J. Roswell Flower and Alice Reynolds were united in marriage. This family was destined to have a place of singular influence on the burgeoning Pentecostal Movement. "Dad" Flower held almost continuous positions of leadership from the inception of the Assemblies of God until his retirement, exercising an important stabilizing ministry during formative years in the young fellowship. His death on July 23, 1970, was lamented far and wide, for a great leader had passed from this earthly scene. "Mother"

---

[20]Brumback, *op. cit.*, p. 73.
[21]*Ibid.*, p. 76.
[22]Alice Reynolds Flower, *op. cit.*, pp. 31-36.

Flower has contributed much in a variety of ways, particularly through her writing ministry. Their home produced three district superintendents, a missionary, and a pastor's wife. There is another important contribution to the Assemblies of God that came out of the Indianapolis Alliance Gospel Tabernacle. The mother of General Superintendent Thomas F. Zimmerman first heard the Pentecostal testimony in that revival!

Probably influenced by Parham and his "gospel bands," Glenn Cook inspired the young people in Indianapolis to a similar pioneer vision. As a result, even before J. Roswell Flower was married he was involved in extensive itinerant ministry as far away as Nebraska, sometimes in company with a team of eight or 10 other young people, sometimes as an associate of such men as Fred Vogler, Harry Bowley, B. F. Lawrence, and A. S. Copley.[23] In those days, it seemed that nearly all who received the baptism in the Spirit were impelled to tell the story abroad, many of them feeling a call to the ministry, launching out in faith, trusting God to supply every need.[24]

As early as 1907, Pentecostal revival fires burned in Des Moines, Iowa. The first Pentecostal mission was opened by the wife of Judge Scott Ladd, then on the State Supreme Court. In February, 1908, a "gospel band" composed of Mr. and Mrs. Howard Goss and four young people began meetings in the Presbyterian church in Lucas, Iowa. The result of this venture was the establishment of a small Pentecostal congregation, which the team left in the hands of a young convert from the Christian Church, a Mr. John Goben. A similar invasion by a gospel team headed by Stanley Bennett from D. C. O. Opperman's Bible school in Joplin, Missouri, resulted in a Holiness mission in Perry, Iowa, becoming identified with the Pentecostal Movement in the fall of 1910.[25] This "fly-by-night" invasion of communities, in which a nucleus would be formed and left behind as the task force moved on to other towns, seems

---

[23]*Ibid.*, p. 46.

[24]Interview with J. Roswell Flower, November 30, 1967.

[25]Eugene N. Hastie, *History of the West Central District Council of the Assemblies of God* (Fort Dodge, Iowa: Walterick Printing Co., 1948), pp. 23-25.

to have been typical of much of the Pentecostal evangelism in the central part of the United States in these years.

Much of the inspiration for the opening of Pentecostal missions in the northern Missouri-Iowa region seems to have stemmed from a camp meeting held on the farm of Jesse George, who lived four miles west of Mercer, Missouri. Mr. George, having heard of the Azusa Street revival, secured Glenn Cook and J. H. King to conduct the camp meeting in the late summer of 1907. It was so successful that a second camp meeting was held the next year at another farm, lasting the entire summer.[26]

THE NORTHWEST

In the Northwest region of the country, the most important contribution to the earliest period of Pentecostal revival was that of Florence Louise Crawford. She visited the revival in Los Angeles, receiving not only the Pentecostal baptism, but a remarkable healing as well. Impelled by these great experiences, Mrs. Crawford launched on a tour of the major cities in the Pacific Northwest, proclaiming the full gospel as far east as Minnesota. In December, 1906, she settled in Portland, Oregon, establishing the headquarters of an independent fellowship which she called the "Apostolic Faith," perhaps the oldest continuous Pentecostal organization in existence.[27]

THE NORTHEAST

Sporadic episodes of tongues had occurred in the Northeast, but there was no permanent Pentecostal work in that part of the nation until 1907. The first contact with the Azusa Street revival was the fleeting visit of Elder Sturdevant to New York City in December, 1906, but apparently no permanent work resulted.[28] In 1907, Marie Burgess, who had just recently received the baptism in the Holy Spirit in the revival at Zion, Illinois, was invited to conduct a meeting in a Holiness mission in New York City. The leader of the mission received the proclamation of the

---

[26]*Ibid.*, pp. 18-23.

[27]The most comprehensive authoritative account of the history of this group is *A Historical Account of the Apostolic Faith* (Portland, Oregon: The Apostolic Faith Publishing House, 1965).

[28]Bloch-Hoell, *op. cit.*, p. 49.

Pentecostal message coldly and after four weeks terminated Marie's meeting. She conducted prayer services in private homes for a time. Concluding that it was the will of God for her to remain in New York, she rented a building on 42nd Street, which she called "Glad Tidings Hall." Carl Brumback describes an interesting event that happened there:

> Robert A. Brown, a Methodist preacher, from Ireland, a former policeman, attended the services, and though he had misgivings about the "evidence theory," he felt the presence of God. One night Robert Brown was invited to preach. Never one to dodge an issue, Robert took as his text, Acts 2:4: "And they were all filled with the Holy Ghost, and began to speak with other tongues, as the Spirit gave them utterance." His mind was riveted upon the word, "all," the subject of both clauses (along with "they"). "A-1-1" he declared, "that means *all*—all that were filled—*all* spoke in tongues!" He preached conviction into his own heart, and was the first to get to the altar, announcing that he was a candidate for the Pentecostal experience. Such honesty and determination were not to be denied, and shortly thereafter the Lord met this son of Eire.[29]

And so Robert Brown received his "Pentecost." It was not long afterward that he wooed and wed Marie Burgess. They were married in October, 1909. "Glad Tidings Hall" was moved to Thirty-third Street, across from the Pennsylvania Railroad station, where it has been known ever since as "Glad Tidings Tabernacle," a great Pentecostal lighthouse in the metropolitan Northeast.[30] Marie Brown has continued as co-pastor of that great church many years now, even after the death of Robert some years ago.

An important early center of Pentecost was Rochester, New York. The Elim Faith Home, operated by Hattie Duncan and her sister, had from its beginning been attuned to the ministry of the Holy Spirit, including healing, but not until the spring of 1907 did the group there receive a Pentecostal visitation. It came about through reports of the Los Angeles revival and other subsequent outpourings, which drove the Faith Home people to their Bibles to search out the truth.[31]

---

[29]Brumback, *op. cit.*, p. 81.

[30]*Ibid.*, pp. 81-82.

[31]Letter of Hattie Duncan to E. N. Bell, January 19, 1922, quoted in Brumback, *op. cit.*, p. 82.

The Pentecostal revival in New England stemmed from Chelsea, Massachusetts, where a great Pentecostal visitation occurred in June, 1907. William J. Mitchell had left the Dowie movement in 1905, moving to Chelsea, where he started a mission in a building that had been previously used as a saloon. Late in 1906 they heard of Pentecost breaking out in Texas. It was not until the next summer that a real outpouring came.

On June 17, a local holiday, we held an all day meeting. At about 9:30 P.M. the Lord poured out His Spirit and baptized five or six. I was one of them! The Lord continued to bless all that summer with 30 or 40 receiving the Baptism. With the help of the brethren, I continued to carry on the meetings the rest of the year, besides working at my trade as a carpenter. The news spread that the Lord was blessing so that people came from everywhere, making it necessary for us to move into a larger building. On April 19, 1908 the great Chelsea Fire broke out, burning our building and half of the city, scattering the flock to different towns and cities, spreading Pentecost throughout New England.[32]

Throughout the East, and much of the Midwest, as far west as Ohio and Indiana, the story of the early spread of Pentecost is wrapped up closely with events taking place in the Christian and Missionary Alliance. Several great churches in the Alliance, and numerous outstanding ministers, reluctantly parted company with the parent body when the Pentecostal testimony was stifled by the Alliance leadership. Such "come-outers" provided a substantial proportion of early Assemblies of God leadership. For example, D. W. Kerr, Alliance pastor in Dayton, Ohio, later to be an important leader in the Assemblies, received the Pentecostal experience in 1907. In 1911, when he went to Cleveland to pastor the Alliance church there, he discovered that nearly all the members of the congregation had already received the baptism in the Holy Spirit. They voted to become the Pentecostal Church of Cleveland, Ohio.[33] It quickly affiliated with the Assemblies of God when that body was organized. It was very likely through the great missionary vision inculcated by Alliance leaders such as A. B. Simpson

[32]Letter of William J. Mitchell to J. R. Flower, May 7, 1956, quoted in Brumback, *op. cit.*, p. 83.

[33]Letter of Christine Kerr Peirce to Carl Brumback, September 15, 1959, quoted in Brumback, *op. cit.*, pp. 79-80.

that the Cleveland church through the years has developed an enviable reputation as one of the strongest supporters of the cause of foreign missions in the Assemblies of God.

From the time of the great Azusa Street outpouring in 1906, enthusiastic witnesses and published reports stimulated expectancy for similar happenings in communities all across the land. A Pentecostal movement was rapidly developing. Not all responses, however, were sympathetic to the reports of charismatic manifestations.

Reaction and Rejection

THE CHRISTIAN AND MISSIONARY ALLIANCE

Typical of the denominational reactions was that of the Christian and Missionary Alliance. In May, 1907, a remarkable Pentecostal revival swept over the student body and assembled ministers at the general convention at Nyack Missionary Training Institute in New York. Already several prominent Alliance ministers had received the Pentecostal baptism when this event occurred. Later that summer, two Alliance camp meetings were the scenes of Pentecostal visitations. "It seemed that the Christian and Missionary Alliance was well on its way to accepting the Pentecostal experience. Then it was discovered that this new movement was teaching that the baptism with the Spirit is always accompanied by speaking in other tongues."[34] Dr. A. B. Simpson appointed Dr. Henry Wilson to visit Alliance, Ohio, where there was a strong Pentecostal group. He was to study the meetings and bring back his evaluation. Wilson's statement is characterized by Tozer, longtime editor of the *Alliance Witness,* as the "crystallized utterance of the Society." He quotes Wilson as saying, "I am not able to approve the movement, though I am willing to concede that there is probably something of God in it somewhere."[35] The result of this report was that Simpson published a manifesto setting forth his position and renouncing the doctrine that all who receive the baptism in the Spirit must speak in tongues. This was the parting of the ways,

[34]*Ibid.*, p. 91.

[35]A. W. Tozer, *Wingspread* (Harrisburg, Pa.: Christian Publications, 1943), pp. 133-34.

and a number of prominent men in the Alliance withdrew to join the new movement.[36] The "seek not, forbid not" Alliance position effectively closed the door to Pentecostal phenomena within their ranks.[37]

OTHER HOLINESS BODIES

Other bodies within the Holiness tradition were not so charitable in their attitude, but the official position was much the same. The Pentecostal Church of the Nazarene, largest of the Holiness denominations, early became a citadel of anti-Pentecostal sentiment. Phineas Bresee, the leader of the denomination, was pastoring the mother church of the movement in Los Angeles in 1907. It is, therefore, not surprising that he and his church opposed the Azusa Street revival, since it posed a threat to his own congregation. The name of the organization, "Pentecostal" Church of the Nazarene, proved to be an increasing embarrassment, since many tended to confuse the group with the "tongues" movement. In 1919 the General Conference voted to delete the word "Pentecostal" from its title, seeking by this action to dissociate from any possible link in the public mind with "tongues."[38] "Following the lead of the Nazarenes, the Wesleyan Methodist Church, the Salvation Army, the Pilgrim Holiness Church, and the Free Methodist Church, also disassociated themselves completely from the pentecostal movement."[39]

FUNDAMENTALISM

Added to the rising chorus of criticism were the voices of leading Fundamentalists and other evangelical churchmen. Dr. G. Campbell Morgan, respected Bible expositor, referred to the Pentecostal Movement as "the last vomit of Satan," and Dr. Reuben A. Torrey, a leading evangelist of the times, claimed it was "emphatically not of God, and

---

[36]*Ibid.*

[37]Among those who withdrew from the Alliance, later becoming leaders in the Assemblies of God, were: G. F. Bender, J. T. Boddy, Frank M. Boyd, Herbert Cox, John Coxe, William Cramer, Minnie Draper, G. N. Eldridge, William I. Evans, Alice R. Flower, D. W. Kerr, J. E. Kistler, David McDowell, C. A. McKinney, D. W. Myland, Noel Perkin, Frederick Reel, E. F. M. Staudt, R. E. Sternall, W. W. Simpson, Joseph Tunmore, Louis Turnbull, John Waggoner, A. G. Ward, and J. W. Welch.

[38]Synan, *op. cit.*, p. 181.

[39]*Ibid.*

founded by a Sodomite."[40] H. A. Ironside repudiated the Pentecostal Movement as delusion and insanity.[41] It must be noted that much of this horrified reaction came about through limited contact with Pentecostals, hearsay and rumor generating at least some of the criticism. However, the volatility and instability of some within the Pentecostal ranks without question brought some justifiable reproach upon the adolescent revival.

THE LARGER CHURCH WORLD

A sampling of the reaction within the larger church world to the new phenomenon is the work of Professor Doremus A. Hayes of Garrett Biblical Institute, well-known Methodist theological seminary near Chicago. He identified the glossolalia of the Pentecostals as a common characteristic of aberrated Christianity throughout church history, explicable on purely naturalistic grounds. He dismissed the Pentecostal revival quite lightly as another of the recent wave of urban cults.[42]

There was some justification for the negative reaction to the Pentecostal revival in the early years, between 1901 and 1914. There were emotional excesses, frequently without adequate leadership to supply correction and guidance. Some unscrupulous persons invaded the churches, taking over, even absconding with funds. It was altogether too common for early Pentecostalists to attribute everything to the "leading of the Spirit." There was a danger of exaggerated emphasis on the distinctive truths which they felt God was restoring to the Church through them.[43] They gave the impression of impermanence. "The fly-by-night appearance of the movement continued even after the tattered tents were exchanged for the slightly more permanent (but not more sightly) missions."[44] Intent on spreading the message, going as they felt led of the Spirit, the first Pente-

---

[40]Synan, *op. cit.*, p. 179, and Frank J. Ewart, *The Phenomenon of Pentecost* (St. Louis: Pentecostal Publishing House, 1947), p. 7.

[41]H. A. Ironside, *Holiness, the False and the True* (New York: Loizeaux Brothers, n. d.), pp. 38-39.

[42]Doremus A. Hayes, *The Gift of Tongues* (New York: The Methodist Book Concern, 1913), p. 56.

[43]Interview with J. R. Flower, February 24, 1970.

[44]Brumback, *op. cit.*, p. 109.

costal preachers were not primarily concerned about establishing mature congregations. And, there were doctrinal tangents. Many of the preachers were laymen accustomed to working with plow and hammer. Few had the advantage of formal Bible or theological instruction. Their zeal frequently outstripped their understanding. There were some sad moral defections, as well, although it is not likely that the early Pentecostals were afflicted with a disproportionate number. Offensive, too, were the proselyting tactics of some and the sense of spiritual superiority which appeared to outsiders as arrogance.[45]

Sometimes the hostility generated against the Pentecostalists was more than vocal. Describing the kind of persecution that the itinerant evangelistic bands occasionally encountered, Goss writes:

> Some workers had been attacked, some had been beaten, some had bones broken, some were jailed, some were made to leave town, some were rotten-egged and some were shot at. . . . Tents, buildings, and sometimes residences were burned; drinking water was poisoned, windows were broken. . . . Often we had no protection; there were times when the police chose to close their eyes because we were the strangers, while the city paid them a salary.[46]

The Pentecostals not only faced criticism from without, but suffered from controversy within as well. Between 1906 and 1914 a doctrinal disagreement arose that polarized the movement into two rather distinct groupings. The issue was over sanctification as a "second work of grace." In the earliest stages of the revival, the Wesleyan view was overwhelming among the Pentecostals. It seemed quite natural for early leaders in the revival, most of whom came directly from Holiness bodies, to continue the terminology with respect to sanctification as a "second work of grace," understanding this "second blessing" to cleanse the individual from "inbred sin," this eradication experience thus preparing the seeker for the reception of the fullness of the Holy Spirit. Thus, the Pentecostal baptism for these people was understood as a "third work of grace."[47]

---

[45]Nichol, *op. cit.*, pp. 79-80.
[46]Goss, *op. cit.*, p. 87.
[47]Synan, *op. cit.*, p. 183.

A problem began to manifest itself when large numbers of people began to enter the ranks of the Pentecostals from non-Wesleyan backgrounds, notably the Baptists. The Baptists held an essentially Reformed view of sanctification, conceiving of sanctification not as a crisis experience, but as a process beginning at regeneration and continuing through the life of the believer. Thus, for them there were only two "works of grace," salvation and the baptism in the Holy Spirit. The individual most responsible for bringing this conflict out into the open was William H. Durham of Chicago. Durham repudiated the traditional Holiness sanctification view after his visit to the Azusa Street revival in 1907. Durham came to believe that the Holiness teaching of eradication was unscriptural. The vagueness of the Holiness experience, lacking the concrete verification factor of tongues, and the disappointment that some felt when they found themselves exhibiting traces of the old carnal nature after believing it to have been "rooted out," contributed to the support that Durham got in the succeeding controversy.[48]

The controversy really began with the preaching of a sermon by Durham at a Pentecostal convention in Chicago in 1910, in which he attempted to discredit the Wesleyan view of sanctification as a second definite work of grace. He had come to the conviction that what he had previously held as a private view now needed a public airing.

> I began to write against the doctrine that it takes two works of grace to save and cleanse a man. I denied and still deny that God does not deal with the nature of sin at conversion. I deny that a man who is converted or born again is outwardly washed and cleansed but that his heart is left unclean with enmity against God in it. . . . This would not be salvation. Salvation is an inward work. It means a change of heart. It means a change of nature. It means that old things pass away and that all things become new. It means that all condemnation and guilt is removed. It means that all the old man, or old nature, which was sinful and depraved and which was the very thing in us that was condemned, is crucified with Christ.[49]

In February, 1911, Durham carried his new message to the West Coast. By this time the leading Pentecostal center in Los Angeles was the Upper Room Mission, pastored by

[48] Brumback, *op. cit.*, p. 98.

[49] "The Pentecostal Testimony," June, 1911, quoted in Brumback, *op. cit.*, p. 99.

Elmer Fisher. When Durham's new emphasis was unveiled, he was asked not to return. Durham next went to the Azusa Street mission, by this time having become largely a Negro church, the white people drifting out to form their own churches. Durham's magnetic personality and powerful preaching resurrected some of the glamor of the earlier dramatic days in the famous mission. Crowds thronged the humble meeting place, practically emptying the other Pentecostal missions in the city. However, Brother Seymour, who had been in the East, returned, and upon discovering the doctrine that Durham was preaching, agreed with the trustees to lock him out. Frank Bartleman had responded to Durham's "message of grace," rejecting the old-line Wesleyan view through Durham's influence. Bartleman secured a mission on Kohler Street for Durham to preach in, but the crowds became too large to accommodate them. Durham rented a large building at the corner of Seventh and Los Angeles Streets. A thousand people attended the Sunday meetings; four hundred each week-night.

> Here the "cloud" rested. God's glory filled the place. "Azusa" became deserted. The Lord was with Brother Durham in great power. God sets His seal especially on present truth to be established. He preached a gospel of salvation by faith. He was used mightily to draw anew a clear line of demarcation between salvation by works and faith, between law and grace. This had become very much needed, even among the Pentecostal people.[50]

Opposition to Durham became intense because of the controversy he had generated. He was tempted to strike back. Feelings became intense and bitter. Even his publication *The Pentecostal Testimony* disclosed a strongly polemic temper at this time. He did not stay in Los Angeles long. He engaged in a speaking tour of the East, finally returning to Chicago, where he died within a few months. However, his teaching continued to spread rapidly over the nation. Almost without exception, the independent ministers and congregations that were emerging out of the Pentecostal revival, which later coalesced to form the Assemblies of God, adopted Durham's "Finished Work" view of sanc-

---

[50]Bartleman, *op. cit.*, p. 146.

tification.[51] Only those Holiness-Pentecostal bodies in the Southeast and the Apostolic Faith associations of Parham and Crawford preserved the traditional Wesleyan view.

Why the Revival Flourished

POPULAR APPEAL

Why, then, in view of the limitations of this movement, did it succeed in the first decades of its existence? There are several reasons. Evangelical believers had been conditioned to expect the supernatural, especially in the years just prior to the Pentecostal revival. This was especially true in the various Holiness bodies which were suffering from a process of fragmentation by the last decade of the century.[52] The Pentecostals emphasized an experience that transcended the boundaries of doctrinal systems or differences in polity. There was an undenominational character to the movement that gave it a widespread appeal. Yet, the Pentecostals skillfully adopted the methods successfully used by the denominations in the great 19th-century revival tradition. They went to the people. Evangelistic bands, mass meetings and conventions, and periodical literature disseminated their message across the land.[53] Between 1900 and 1908 no fewer than 34 periodicals came into existence, the first of which was Parham's *The Apostolic*

---

[51]Brumback, *op. cit.*, p. 100.

[52]Smith, *Called Unto Holiness*, pp. 16-21.

[53]The evangelistic bands were an integral and necessary part of the early evangelistic methodology. Goss reports: "Physically, the most attractive feature of our work was the newness of young people all on fire for God. . . . All of us lived entirely by faith, and would have been thought by the workers to be hopelessly backslidden had anyone mentioned a salary, or suggested a certain sum as desirable. . . . The vast majority of us went gladly anywhere God sent us, leaving it entirely up to Him for the supplying of our needs" (Goss, *op. cit.*, pp. 69-70).

The daily routine of the traveling bands went something like this: In the mornings, Bible study and prayer; noon preaching service to the factory workers; house-to-house visitation in the afternoons; street meetings nearly every evening prior to the night service. The day concluded with an evangelistic rally, which was terminated by a prayer meeting at the altar of the meetinghouse. Such a meeting is described by Goss: "Then came the after, or altar service of prayer and seeking God, which lasted until the last seeker had ceased praying. This could be anywhere from midnight to six o'clock the next morning. The girls usually stayed until the women seekers were gone. The boys remained with the men who were usually the last to leave. This altar service was the crowning climax to our day, the one in which we could really see all our labor and sacrifices bearing fruit. Converts made in this way were a replica of ourselves—earnest, sincere, devoted. These were the most rewarding hours which, I believe, ever came to any man or woman" (Goss, *op. cit.*, pp. 76-77).

Faith.[54] It was a democratic movement, drawing men and women of all estates, especially those whose needs were not being met in the churches of the day. And, they appealed to the youth. The "evangelistic bands" in that early period were composed of a ratio of youth to adults of six to one.[55]

PERSONAL NEEDS MET

As is true in revival movements, the preponderance of response was among the common people. The Pentecostals met the religious needs of the common people. They emphasized divine healing, a feature that drew large numbers to their meetings. They met the psychological needs of the people, providing in their music and worship for a high degree of participation and for emotional release. The rigoristic code of ethical standards they adopted was compensated for by "sanctifying" activity otherwise eschewed—dancing, shouting, clapping, enthusiastic singing, and instrumental music.[56] To many who were frustrated by their circumstances in the present world the Pentecostal message gave a shining new hope, bursting with vitality and enthusiasm.

SACRIFICIAL ENTHUSIASM

Not the least of its reasons for growth was the energetic, sacrificial, missionary spirit common among the Pentecostals. Their earnestness and radiance were winsome factors. In contrast to much of the church world which was then struggling to orient itself to turbulent social problems created by the newly urbanizing society and the theological crosscurrents occasioned by the New Theology,[57] the Pentecostals were consumed with overwhelming confidence born of fresh faith. They believed that God had commissioned them with an "end-time" message, the fulfillment of Joel's prophecy and of Peter's preaching in the Book of Acts.

THE BLESSING OF GOD

Surely the Spirit of God was with these people. One

---

[54]Nichol, *op. cit.*, p. 61.
[55]Goss, *op. cit.*, p. 69.
[56]Nichol, *op. cit.*, pp. 65-66.
[57]See Chapter 1 for a detailed description of the "New Theology."

cannot fully explain the phenomenon of the survival of the Pentecostal revival on any other ground than this. Charismatic revivals had punctuated the history of the Church, but never until this revival had such a spiritual eruption survived.

5

Call to Order: The Birth of the Assemblies of God [1914]

The Need for Organization—Early Steps Toward Organization—The Call for a General Council—The First General Council of the Assemblies of God

The Need for Organization

EXPULSION FROM THE CHURCHES

By 1914 the Pentecostals had been driven outside the framework of traditional, organized American Christianity. They were rejected by the Holiness Movement, as well as the Fundamentalists, to say nothing of the scorn with which they were viewed by the larger church world. Those who testified to a "tongues" experience found themselves very much alone. The reasons for this repudiation are various. Structured Christianity tends to be extremely conservative, looking askance at all revivals. Emotionalism was a common complaint from the quarter of conservative Christianity. There was also the onus of lack of social respectability. Gee observes, "Very few notable personalities were connected with the Movement in its beginning, and one looked in vain for any influential name that might have swayed multitudes among the masses of church members and pulpit admirers."[1] Another reason was the fear that was excited through exaggerated and garbled reports of what actually took place in Pentecostal meetings. To be sure, there was some fanaticism among enthusiastic, but poorly instructed, followers of the revival. "Truth must honestly admit that

[1]Gee, *The Pentecostal Movement*, p. 17.

there were scenes in the first rush of new spiritual enthusiasm and experience that no reputable Christian worker would now seek to defend or excuse."[2] Another charge leveled at the Pentecostals was that of divisiveness. In a given group, it was not uncommon for those who eagerly responded to the new message to charge the more reluctant ones with coldness and spiritual indifference. Churches were rent; hard feelings developed.

Gee points out an additional reason for the rejection of the Pentecostals.

> Finally, there seems to be a law which students are compelled to observe, that the last wave of spiritual revival in the Church nearly always seems to offer the greatest opposition to the new wave of oncoming blessing and advance. It must be remembered, and that with deep sympathy, that when the teaching and testimony of the Pentecostal Movement came to the front there were great numbers of Christian leaders who already were claiming to have been baptised in the Holy Spirit in connection with preceding revival movements.[3]

He concludes with the penetrating observation: "The history of the Pentecostal Movement might have been very different had the Church as a whole received it into its bosom forthwith. But the providence of God permitted otherwise, and the Movement therefore was compelled to develop as a separate entity."[4] So it was, then, that the embryonic revival movement would have to carve its own way in the world, painfully and hesitantly finding a way from adolescence to maturity without the benefit of interchange with established groups, whose counsel might have spared many a painful bruise.

Outside the Holiness-Pentecostal bodies in the Southland the bulk of the early Pentecostals were independent people, with but the loosest affiliations, if any were entertained at all. Advocates of organization found strong opposition from many who had undergone the painful experience of being ostracised from traditional denominations. Such bitter memories created a mood deeply resentful of anything that even remotely resembled formal organization. "We have been delivered from denominationalism,"

---

[2] *Ibid.*, p. 18.
[3] *Ibid.*, p. 19.
[4] *Ibid.*

was the common cry. However, it became increasingly apparent to growing numbers in the amorphous Pentecostal world that glaring needs were pressing for some kind of structured relationship, if the revival was to be preserved from disintegration.[5]

PRACTICAL NEEDS

An early practical need arose that Howard A. Goss resolved by securing ordination in 1907 from Bishop Mason of the Negro Church of God in Christ. That body, having been legally incorporated, was eligible for reduced clergy fares on the Southern railroads. To poverty-ridden Pentecostal preachers this was no small boon. As a consequence some joined that organization, particularly between 1910 and 1914, "mainly for purposes of business."[6]

PARTISANSHIP

Another problem that became increasingly a vexation was the emergence of strong personalities around which clusters of younger ministers gathered, producing a divisive and partisan spirit. Goss writes:

> I saw this happen over and over again. . . . Younger ministers, appraising the older ones, naturally grouped themselves around the more fatherly type of minister looking to him for counsel, example, and fellowship. These groups grew in ever-widening circles, until we really had an unwritten organization, with each group functioning separately, however much we had tried to avoid it.[7]

The partisan spirit became so evident that at a camp meeting or convention one could soon spot the followers of the various leaders, for the mannerisms and idiosyncrasies of a favorite were readily adopted by his following in a subconscious idolizing of that leader.

> Some might yell a quick "Amen" in a happy falsetto like Brother Pinson. Another might jerk his head a little to one side as Brother Durham did when the touch of God came upon him. Or some might have still more noticeable manifestations, if their leader happened to be of the spectacular type.[8]

---

[5]Goss, *op. cit.,* p. 163.

[6]*Ibid.*

[7]Goss, *op. cit.,* pp. 164-65.

[8]*Ibid.,* p. 166.

LOCAL ABUSES

Lack of structure occasioned other abuses. Local assemblies were sometimes invaded by confidence men who posed as Pentecostal preachers. Since ordination was virtually unknown, no one bothered to check credentials. It was common practice for one to walk into a church for a meeting whenever he felt so inclined. "The churches became so accustomed to it that they heartily welcomed anyone who claimed to be a Pentecostal preacher."[9] Tales began to circulate, however, of churches being "fleeced," as much money as possible being collected from the unsuspecting congregation, then the "marauder" leaving suddenly with a trail of debts in the community. Goss felt constrained to visit troubled congregations after such unfortunate episodes to "quiet the sheep, arbitrate if necessary, and assist in restoring the congregation's confidence in God and in their leader again."[10] Goss relates one particularly bizarre and hurtful episode that occurred while he was pastoring a small congregation in Hot Springs, Arkansas. Two strangers, claiming to be "Apostolic preachers," stopped at the home of one of Goss's parishioners. They reported in glowing detail the great achievements in previous meetings that they had conducted. Subsequently, when this good report became known, they were invited to participate in an evening street meeting which the Assembly had planned.

> That night the two men testified and did fairly well, until the last one, trying to impress their hearers with how much power they had, pointed to a telephone pole and said, "By this power I have I can climb that pole unaided," and proceeded to try. Of course, the workers were horrified, and started a song to cover up.
>
> Two policemen who often stopped and listened to the services had come up behind the large crowd, and had stopped in the shadow of a tall building, unseen by these speakers.
>
> They were alerted immediately. One went back to the Station house, only a few steps away, to refresh his memory. Just as the meeting was being dismissed, the two stepped out, arrested and handcuffed "our preachers" for horse-stealing in an Eastern state.[11]

---

[9]*Ibid.*, p. 167.

[10]*Ibid.*, p. 171.

[11]*Ibid.*, p. 169.

MISSIONARY COOPERATION

There were other needs. The fire of revival thrust zealous workers into the harvest, not only at home, but to mission fields abroad. There was a need for proper financing, legal representation, correlation of work, and endorsement for holding property in foreign lands. It was not long before it became all too apparent that some had gone out with more zeal than wisdom. And, too, the churches at home found themselves supporting a worker who had no credentials, lacked any supervision, and frequently made no accounting of the funds entrusted to him.

DOCTRINAL PROBLEMS

There were doctrinal problems, too. Enthusiastic lay people dropped their secular pursuits in the flame of evangelistic passion which their Pentecostal experience gave them. They had a glorious testimony to share. However, many found that without better tools for digging into the Bible, they were soon hard pressed to feed an established flock for very long. Some of the movement from congregation to congregation by such lay preachers was simply because they had run out of fresh soul-food for the saints. Some sought to make up for their lack by getting "new revelations," much of which produced confusion and disarray. Some means of providing a cooperative venture for the more effective training of workers became a pressing need early in the revival.

The barrage of periodicals emanating from diverse locations, sometimes with conflicting emphases, and the lack of uniformity in methodology and practice heightened the feeling of growing chaos as 1914 approached. Confusion in the bewildering array even of church names prevailed. Lack of discipline for unscrupulous persons, lack of standards, divisiveness, and unhealthy competition proved to be a high price for absolute independence.

Early Steps Toward Organization

Serving the Southeast were the Holiness denominations which had maintained their existing structures, simply tacking on the Pentecostal doctrine as an additional feature.

The largest of these bodies were the Church of God (Cleveland, Tennessee), the Pentecostal Holiness Church, and the Church of God in Christ, all of Methodist origin and episcopal in polity. However, spreading rapidly over the nation were independent congregations without formal cohesion, other than loose associations of some regional groups, such as Parham's Apostolic Faith movement.

EARLY CONVENTIONS

Parham was adamantly opposed to formal organization, although he may be credited with the first steps toward the organization of the Pentecostal Movement. In 1905 he was sponsoring conventions, the first interchurch associations of the new movement. By 1906, he was issuing credentials to new ministers, titling himself "The Founder and Projector of the Apostolic Faith Movement."[12] He furnished the name by which the early Pentecostal Movement was widely known, the Apostolic Faith.

APOSTOLIC FAITH GROUPS

In 1906, when Parham "invaded" the stronghold of Dr. Dowie in Zion, Illinois, he was successful in bringing a large number of Dowie's followers into the Apostolic Faith fold. He made no pretensions to "taking over" the crumbling movement of the tragic, eccentric Dowie, but such accusations were made. In October of that same year, Parham responded to the invitation of William J. Seymour to visit the great Los Angeles revival. At first he was looked upon as a kind of spiritual father. Parham was upset by some of the excesses he witnessed at Azusa Street, deploring "extremes . . . fanaticism and everything that is beyond the bounds of common sense and reason. . . ."[13] Parham assumed the role of disciplinarian, although he protested that he was not desiring to assert his authority. His reason for appearing on the West Coast was misunderstood by the independent-thinking people to whom he sought to minister. Referring to the Apostolic Faith leaders, notably Parham and Crawford, Frank Bartleman with some pique wrote:

---

[12]Parham, *op. cit.*, p. 159.
[13]*Ibid.*, p. 168.

> Why should they claim authority over us? We had prayed down our own revival. The revival in California was unique and separate as to origin. It came from Heaven, even Brother Seymour not receiving the "Baptism" until many others had entered in here. He did not arrive in Los Angeles until the "eleventh hour."[14]

This effectively ended the influence of Parham in the Pentecostal Movement. In 1907 he surprised many by "resigning" his position as "Projector of the Apostolic Faith Movement."[15]

Florence L. Crawford arrived on the Los Angeles scene about the same time as Parham. She adopted the name that Parham had popularized, Apostolic Faith, but there is no apparent connection between her work and Parham's. Parham's influence was chiefly in the Midwest and Texas; Mrs. Crawford's, in the Pacific Northwest. Her Apostolic Faith Mission in Portland, Oregon, gradually became the "mother church" to which other similar missions in the Northwest came to look for leadership. It was from Mrs. Crawford's Portland center, informally organized as it was, that the first Pentecostal missionaries were dispatched to the foreign field, occurring as early as 1907 or 1908.[16] The loose association of churches cooperated in the financing of these missionaries. Out of this grew a periodical that was circulated among the cooperating churches. The chief force that held the Apostolic Faith movement together, however, was the personality of Mrs. Crawford. Significant is the fact that out of a concern for effective missionary enterprise a semblance of interchurch structure was created. However, the cohesiveness of such associations up to that time depended on the strength and personality of a single individual.

A major stride toward formal organization was the development of a loose association of ministers and churches in Texas and neighboring states, beginning in 1908 or 1909. As early as 1905 "conventions" had been held in Texas, but apart from Parham's magnetism, there was no centralizing force to create an enduring fellowship. The meetings so conducted were fluid and disconnected, there

[14]Bartleman, *op. cit.*, p. 69.
[15]Parham, *op. cit.*, p. 176.
[16]Kendrick, *op. cit.*, p. 77.

being no continuity or planning from one to the next. By 1908, Parham was no longer actively on the scene, and other personalities emerged. Leaders in this loose association were E. N. Bell, H. A. Goss, Arch P. Collins, D. C. O. Opperman, and others.[17] They, like Parham and Crawford, employed the term Apostolic Faith. Without official written instruments as the basis of fellowship, it was held together by the confidence and trust of the cooperating churches and ministers in the leaders. Several periodicals began to appear, aiding in the strength of the fellowship considerably. A most important device that gave cohesiveness to the group was the annual camp meeting. The chief difference between this Apostolic Faith federation and the Parham-Crawford type was that this had no single dominant personality as its cohesive force.

CAMPS, SCHOOLS, AND PUBLICATIONS

The role of the camp meeting in stimulating cooperative fellowship can hardly be overestimated. By the summer of 1913 at least 15 camp meetings were publicly announced in one of the Pentecostal periodicals that had sprung up. These camps were located in Texas, Oklahoma, Arkansas, Missouri, Alabama, Kansas, Iowa, Indiana, and as far away as Cumberland, Maryland.[18]

Several valuable results accrued from this voluntary fellowship, informal and unstructured as it was. One was the curbing of theological confusion. And confusion did exist!

> For many years our preachers were far more afraid of compromising a message which they believed to be God than they were of backsliding. Walking in the light of God's revelation was considered the guarantee of unbroken fellowship with God. . . . Consequently, a preacher, who did not dig up some new slant on a Scripture, or get some new revelation to his own heart ever so often; a preacher who did not propagate it, defend it, and if necessary, was not prepared to lay down his life for it, was considered slow, stupid, unspiritual. All of them were more afraid of drifting back into "a form of godliness" or becoming "hide-bound," "legalistic," "dead," than they were of open sin, because so few fell into sin, I suppose. At least the possibility seemed remote. Calling

[17] *Ibid.*, p. 78.

[18] *Word and Witness*, June 20, 1913.

a man "a compromiser" killed his ministry far and wide. Because of this, no doubt, many new revelations began to cause confusion.[19]

At one of the conferences of the Apostolic Faith group in Texas, it was unanimously approved that every minister "who received a new revelation" was not to preach it until the next conference. There he was to submit it to his brethren publicly for criticism. "If none of his hearers could tear it to pieces scripturally, or 'shoot it full of holes,' and if it came through still in one piece, all preachers would be at liberty to preach it, if they wished."[20]

Such associations provided the basis for upgrading the quality of preaching through the introduction of training programs. Short-term schools were conducted, principally by Daniel C. O. Opperman. Such schools lasted only four or five weeks, usually, and were carried on entirely by "faith in God to direct and provide all needful things."[21] From December, 1908, to October, 1914, Brother Opperman conducted at least eight short-term Bible schools in Texas, Mississippi, Missouri, Alabama, Iowa, and Arkansas. He had been principal of the school system in Zion, Illinois, and had been ordained by Dr. Dowie. Out of his academic background he saw the need for training new workers who could proclaim the full-gospel message. Spiritual preparation was as important in these early schools as pursuit of book knowledge. Describing the Des Moines, Iowa, Bible school of October, 1911, Hastie writes:

> The lessons began with the beginning of the gospel of St. John, and when the school closed only a little more than the entire book had been covered. Brother Opperman himself directed the services and occasionally Brother Roselli [*sic*] would fluently speak out in tongues, which would be interpreted by Brother Anderson. These messages would have some bearing upon the scripture in question, and would be reverently regarded by the people as the voice of God through the Holy Ghost. At times there would be long periods of prayer; at other times silence would reign as the people waited before God. Once at least there was a confession meeting, in which the saints were urged to confess any grievance or feeling that they might have against a fellow brother or sister.[22]

---

[19]Goss, *op. cit.*, p. 155.
[20]*Ibid.*, pp. 155-56.
[21]Hastie, *op. cit.*, p. 31.
[22]*Ibid.*, p. 35.

Not only was intense spiritual development a major concern in these schools, but practical work also accompanied the busy day's activity. Various kinds of meetings were held, usually climaxed with an evening evangelistic rally. At the conclusion of the school, Opperman dispatched bands of workers to both new and old fields. Each team was accompanied by an experienced preacher. In this way many communities were successfully invaded with the Pentecostal testimony.[23] One peculiarity which Opperman carried over from the Dowie era was a legalistic bent, exhibited by such practices as the denial of the eating of pork. In time this faded away among his followers. Important was the role that such schools had in equipping, even if in elementary fashion, enthusiastic, faith-proclaiming witnesses. Inspiration outshone instruction, but it was a start.

D. Wesley Myland, a former Christian and Missionary Alliance minister in the Midwest, established a more permanent type of school in Plainfield, Indiana, not far from Indianapolis. Fred Vogler, Flem Van Meter, and J. Roswell Flower were among those who attended Myland's school. In a similar school at Hattiesburg, Mississippi, Ralph M. Riggs came into the Pentecostal ranks in 1909. In the same period, prior to the establishment of the General Council, three other schools came into existence in the East and received popular endorsement: Bethel in Newark, New Jersey; Elim in Rochester, New York; and Beulah Heights, in North Bergen, New Jersey.[24]

The growing cohesiveness of the fellowship furnished a ready market for periodicals. Important among these was *The Apostolic Faith,* first published in Houston, then in Fort Worth, and finally, in 1910, in Malvern, Arkansas. Eudorus N. Bell, a graduate of the Southern Baptist Seminary in Louisville, and sometime graduate student at the University of Chicago, assumed the editorship when the paper was moved to Malvern.[25] Another periodical with considerable appeal was the *Christian Evangel,* edited by J. Roswell Flower in Indiana. Flower, a law student, had

---

[23]*Ibid.*, p. 39.
[24]Kendrick, *op. cit.*, p. 79.
[25]Goss, *op cit.*, p. 122.

become enthusiastic about the Pentecostal Movement through his association with the remarkable revival in Indianapolis. Both of these early editors were to play a significant role in the formation of the Assemblies of God, to say nothing of the widespread influence that their papers had on the sprawling, disconnected fellowship scattered throughout the land.

In addition to these papers, there were others. The *Latter Rain Evangel* was published in Chicago; the *Way of Faith* in Columbia, South Carolina; and *New Acts* in Alliance, Ohio. Another paper entitled *The Apostolic Faith* originated in Los Angeles, but was finally issued from Portland, Oregon.[26]

By 1909 there were at least four regional associations of independent Pentecostal ministers and churches. Three of these employed the name "Apostolic Faith." These were Parham's original group in Kansas; the Crawford fellowship in the Northwest; and the Texas-Arkansas group headed by E. N. Bell and H. A. Goss. The latter had originated with the convention in Orchard, Texas, in April, 1906, but by 1909 had repudiated Parham, choosing to look to others for leadership. In addition to the three Apostolic Faith groups, a fourth association was forming in the Southeast, particularly Alabama and Mississippi, but extending its influence as far as Florida. H. G. Rodgers and M. M. Pinson, products of the Cashwell revivals, along with D. J. Dubose and J. W. Ledbetter, evangelized throughout Alabama and Mississippi, succeeding in establishing several churches. The believers gathered out of these evangelistic enterprises were holding associational meetings for fellowship and mutual inspiration by 1909. That year, Rodgers called a conference at Dothan, Alabama, and there they adopted the name "Church of God," without awareness that the same name was being employed by Tomlinson's Holiness-Pentecostal denomination in Cleveland, Tennessee. The new federation, listing as its only test of faith "the fruits of the Spirit," made preparation to license and ordain ministers, and to secure recognition from the Southern

---

[26]Hoover, *op. cit.*, p. 22.

Clergy Bureau for reduced railroad fares.[27] The second meeting of the new body was convened at Slocomb, Alabama, in 1911. At that meeting the association adopted a simple but definite structure, electing Rodgers as chairman and J. W. Ledbetter as secretary.[28]

Confusion developed because of similarity in the names used to designate the regional associations that were emerging. In 1911 the Texas-Arkansas fellowship dropped the name Apostolic Faith, and looked to Elder Mason's Church of God in Christ for credentials. The next year, Rodgers' group in the Southeast, discovering that their chosen name, Church of God, already was being used by the Cleveland, Tennessee group, and therefore was not suitable, chose to adopt a different one. Hardly relieving the problem, they cast their lot for Church of God in Christ. There were now three bodies employing that title.

The confusion that the names caused led to exploratory discussions between the Texas-Arkansas fellowship and the Alabama-Mississippi faction to seek a more fitting solution to the name problem. This was an important step toward the merger of these two associations. The consolidation of the two associations was consummated in June, 1913, at a convention held in Meridian, Mississippi. A ministerial list was issued at that meeting, containing the names of 352 ministers from both associations.[29] It must be observed that much of the impetus for this merger came out of dissatisfaction of the two white bodies with an uncomfortable relationship with Elder Mason's Church of God in Christ, almost entirely a Negro organization. The new white group continued to use the name Church of God in Christ, but issued credentials separately from Mason's group.[30]

---

[27]Flower, "History of the Assemblies of God," p. 18.

[28]C. C. Burnett, "Forty Years Ago," *The Pentecostal Evangel*, March 28, 1954, p. 12.

[29]"The Early History of the Assemblies of God," p. 7, contains the following observation: "Perhaps a few names of the better known men out of the 352 in the Church of God in Christ will indicate the influence the group had on the Assemblies of God: Clyde Baily [sic], 'Mother' Mary Barnes, Harry Bowley, Herbert Buffum, Hugh Cadwalder, A. B. Cox, W. T. Gaston, John Goben, C. A. Lasater, Agnes Ozman LaBerge, B. F. Lawrence, Fred Lohman, Burt McCafferty, Jacòb Miller, M. M. Pinson, L. E. Riley, J. W. Welch, and R. E. Winsett."

[30]Synan, *op. cit.*, p. 190.

In the course of the negotiations, it was agreed to merge the publications of the two associations. For some time M. M. Pinson had been publishing a paper entitled *Word and Witness,* which served as the chief organ of the Alabama-Mississippi association. The Texas-Arkansas body was served by *The Apostolic Faith,* edited by E. N. Bell. In the summer of 1913, at an interstate camp meeting held in Eureka Springs, Arkansas, it was agreed that the title of the Alabama-Mississippi paper be retained, and that Bell continue on as editor, producing the *Word and Witness* at his home in Malvern, Arkansas.[31] Subsequent issues of the periodical refer to the Church of God in Christ, and gradually omit reference to the Apostolic Faith group.

The Call for a General Council

Continuing ambiguity of relationship to Mason's Church of God in Christ and the frailty of the very tenuous association that had come into existence during the summer of 1913 led some of the more perceptive leaders to think of a bolder solution to the growing needs of the Pentecostal Movement.

Subsequent issues of the *Word and Witness* devoted considerable space to clarifying the issues which had been raised by the first formal call in the December 20, 1913, issue.

The difficulty with which formal organization came about is reflected in Goss's comments:

> As there was no apparent way to gather up the reins of the different cliques which each seemed in danger of galloping off in its own direction, Brother Bell and I worked privately together on some kind of solution. We later found that Brother Opperman saw this need, too, as did a few other leaders.
>
> We realized that great care was needed at this stage, as we had been strictly taught against *any* form of organization. Irresponsible brethren, if they heard too much, might immediately use the opportunity to poison the saints against us before we could explain, and call us "compromisers!"—a serious charge in those days.
>
> Of necessity, we secretly discussed calling a Conference to organize the work. So in November of 1913, Brother Bell and I ven-

[31]C. C. Burnett, "Forty Years Ago," *The Pentecostal Evangel,* March 28, 1954, p. 13.

tured to announce a Conference at Hot Springs, Arkansas, from April 2 to 12, 1914. We signed the original call ourselves.

I say "ventured" advisedly, because we knew that we were likely facing serious opposition, unless God worked mightily. But other leaders took their stand with us, and added their names to the call, which was being published month by month in *The Word and Witness*. I don't think any of us had many rigid ideas as to how all this should be worked out, but we all supported system against the threatened chaos of the moment. Among other leaders there still seemed to be apprehension as to our purpose. In spite of all, we stuck to our guns and prayed. This took courage, but it seemed we had a special filling of grace from the Lord, and we truly felt that He was leading.[32]

The December 20, 1913, issue of the *Word and Witness* carried the formal call for a "General Convention of Pentecostal Saints and Churches of God in Christ."[33] It was signed by M. M. Pinson, A. P. Collins, H. A. Goss, D. C. O. Opperman, and E. N. Bell.

The statement read:

We desire at this time to make this preliminary announcement of this general meeting so that workers far and near, at home and abroad, may sidetrack everything else and be present. Laymen as well as preachers are invited. . . . This call is to all the churches of God in Christ, to all Pentecostal or Apostolic Faith Assemblies who desire with united purpose to co-operate in love and peace to push the interests of the kingdom of God everywhere. This is, however, only for saints who believe in the baptism with the Holy Ghost, with the signs following. Acts 2:4; 10:46; 19:6; Mark 16:16-18; I Cor. 12:8-11. Neither is this meeting for any captious, contrary, divisive, or contentious person. But we leave for the body itself to take up any subjects it desires more than what is herein afterwards mentioned.[34]

Following were enumerated the five subjects to be considered at the forthcoming meeting, which constitute the reasons for proposing an organization.

First—We come together that we may get a better understanding of what God would have us teach, that we may do away with so many divisions, both in doctrines and in the various names under which our Pentecostal people are working and incorporating. Let us come together as in Act [*sic*] 14, to study the Word, and pray with and for each other—unity our chief aim.

---

[32]Goss, *op. cit.*, pp. 174-75.

[33]*Word and Witness*, December 20, 1913, p. 1.

[34]*Ibid.*

Second—Again we come together that we may know how to conserve the work, that we may all build up and not tear down, both in home and foreign lands.

Third—We come together for another reason, that we may get a better understanding of the needs of each foreign field, and may know how to place our money in such a way that one mission or missionary shall not suffer, while another not any more worthy, lives in luxuries. Also that we may discourage wasting money on those who are running here and there accomplishing nothing, and may concentrate our support on those who mean business for our King.

Fourth—Many of the saints have felt the need of chartering the Churches of God in Christ, putting them on a legal basis, and thus obeying the laws of the land. . . .

Fifth—We may have a proposition to lay before the body for a general Bible Training School with a literary department for our people.[35]

Many who read the invitation announcement in the paper reacted negatively, just as the sponsors had feared. A veritable storm of opposition arose, pen and pulpit decrying the proposal as unscriptural. Parham's influence created a strong antiorganizational mood:

Let us cease wasting time at this juncture in systematizing or organizing the work of God. Let each minister go forward doing his work, and leaving local Assemblies under local elders. . . .[36]

Editorials in sundry Pentecostal publications suddenly appeared, warning against the danger of ecclesiasticism and denominational pride. A witness to a debate on the subject, Walter C. Long, observed that one advocate of independence stated, "I feel before God that we are on the wrong track. God has brought us out of Popery, and for Jesus' sake, let's not go back in!"[37]

Regimentation was the thing that these refugees from denominationalism greatly feared. They had "come out" from creedal bondage and hierarchical denomination, and they were determined to resist any efforts to cheat them of their hard-won liberty. Voices were raised in protest against putting so much harness upon the Pentecostal horse that he could no longer pull (a well-understood metaphor in those days). It was alleged that reliance upon the might and power of ecclesiastical machinery would replace reliance upon the Spirit of God, that denominational pride would cause its members

[35]*Ibid.*
[36]Parham, *op. cit.*, p. 177.
[37]Brumback, *op. cit.*, p. 158.

to concentrate on building a "kingdom of this world," to the detriment of the spiritual kingdom.[38]

Opposition to the proposal for organization reached explosive dimensions in at least one instance. At Grand River, Iowa, "someone deliberately burned up the Church book, containing roster, minutes, records, etc."[39] To be sure, feelings ran high during the winter of 1913-14.

In the months that followed, the call was repeated twice, in February and in March. Considerable space was devoted to clarifying the issues that had caused such heat. One fourth of the March 20, 1914, issue of *Word and Witness* was so occupied, patient and careful explanation being supplied for the call for an organizational meeting. Editor Bell outlined the evils of uncontrolled independence within the Pentecostal Movement: doctrinal instability, cliques grouped about outstanding leaders, chaotic conditions in local assemblies, failure to conform to state laws regarding ownership of property, inequities in monetary support, and unscrupulous persons taking advantage of the simplicity and vulnerability of unorganized congregations.[40] It was further argued that through unified effort, not only could these abuses of fragmentation be corrected, but that positive good for the kingdom of God would come by pooling resources for establishing schools, publishing enterprises, and coordinating missionary work—none of which could be done as well by isolated churches. The fear of hierarchical authority was dispelled by articulating the principle of local church autonomy, the nature of the proposed organization being nothing more than a "cooperative fellowship," in which the integrity of the local assembly would be safeguarded. Standards of doctrine and practice would benefit all.

The appeal for organization was based on what advocates called "Bible order." They argued that God, by His nature, was a God of order. First Corinthians 14:40, "Let all things be done decently and in order," an injunction nestled in the heart of a favorite Pentecostal passage, served as a key

[38]*Ibid.*
[39]Hastie, *op. cit.*, p. 65.
[40]*Word and Witness*, March 20, 1914, pp. 2-3.

text in those crucial days. Advocates of organization pointed to the marshaling of Old Testament saints as they journeyed by cloud and fire through the Sinai wilderness. They argued that the arrangement of tribal units around the tabernacle, and in the line of march, was strong testimony to the inherent need for order in human affairs, even though there be divine direction. Through such methodological structure, the ragtag slaves of Egypt were transformed into a terrible army, triumphant as they marched in disciplined columns into the Promised Land. The New Testament Church, as well, was fashioned on an orderly plan. Acts 6 discloses the orderly choosing of personnel and the keeping of records. In Acts 15 a serious problem was resolved by an orderly interchurch assemblage, a "general council." The apostles served the need for supervision of young assemblies; churches were not expected to grow in haphazard fashion without the counsel, fellowship, and mutual support of more established churches and mature leadership.

The final call appeared in the March 20, 1914, issue of the *Word and Witness.* In spite of opposition, those who stood steady were prepared to go ahead.

> Everybody, all aboard for the Hot Springs convention. This is the final call for objects as previously specified. . . . Meeting is to be held in the old Grand Opera House, 200 Central Ave. All who can, come prepared to board yourself and pay your own fare to and fro. We will help, as far as God supplies the means, to supply meals and rooms for saints attending who cannot. No dead beats allowed. . . .[41]

In the meantime, while press and pulpit were heated with earnest argumentation pro and con, preparations were quietly going forward in Hot Springs. H. A. Goss, pastor in Hot Springs, secured a six-months' lease on the "Grand Opera House," an abandoned theater building located in the heart of the little resort community. Goss moved his mission congregation into the building during the winter, then left the church in the hands of faithful helpers while he journeyed northward on an extended evangelistic tour that took him as far as Milwaukee. Daniel C. O. Opperman, who had just concluded a short-term Bible school in Fort

---

[41] *Ibid.*, p. 1.

Worth, arrived in Hot Springs early in the spring. In the absence of Goss it was he who got things in readiness for the impending convention. When Goss arrived he was pleased to see that things were in order, and that Opperman "was full of faith that God would work out things for His glory."[42]

The First General Council of the Assemblies of God

They came from many parts of the nation, and from several foreign countries. Twenty states from coast to coast, but predominantly the Midwest, were represented by the 300-plus persons who attended that historic meeting.[43] Of these, 128 were registered as ministers and missionaries. They came in all manner of conveyances, some by automobile over Ozark mountain roads, some by train, others arrived on foot. Some came with strong antiorganizational feelings; others had a more open spirit. But they came.

Many of the great names in the early history of the Pentecostal Movement were present at the Hot Springs meeting. F. F. Bosworth, A. B. Cox, J. Crouch, R. E. Erdman, Cyrus B. Fockler, J. Roswell Flower, H. A. Goss, S. A. Jamieson, John G. Lake, B. F. Lawrence, T. K. Leonard, Jacob Miller, D. C. O. Opperman, M. M. Pinson, Fred Pitcher, E. N. Richey, and John Sinclair were there. Those present who would serve the fellowship sooner or later as Chairman (later the term was changed to Superintendent) were E. N. Bell, A. P. Collins, J. W. Welch, W. T. Gaston, and R. M. Riggs.[44]

The convention opened on Thursday, April 2, 1914. Because of the suspicion and tension that existed at the outset, no business was conducted until the following Monday, three days being devoted entirely to preaching, prayer, and fellowship. M. M. Pinson delivered the opening sermon, setting forth the purpose for the convention, citing Acts 15 as his text. Others followed with messages wonderfully anointed by the Holy Spirit, manifestations of the Spirit

[42]Goss, *op. cit.*, p. 175.
[43]General Council minutes, 1914, p. 3.
[44]"The Early History of the Assemblies of God," p. 9.

confirming the truth to the gathered company.[45] Testimonies from the delegates of the power of God being displayed throughout the land produced widespread rejoicing. Rich fellowship during those three opening days broke down much of the suspicion and animosity that seemed to threaten at the outset. "The meetings from the beginning were inspired of the Lord. Love and unity seemed to prevail from the first meeting."[46] Evidently the announced purpose of the convention to establish an organization had not, after all, grieved away the blessed Holy Spirit! This pattern of beginning General Council sessions with several days of prayer and devotions continued for years. It seemed a scriptural and successful pattern worthy of repetition.

One interesting feature, a sidelight of the opening days, was an impromptu parade. The entire group, all three hundred, marched down the main street of Hot Springs, Central Avenue. It must have been a stirring scene, but little notice was given in the local paper that a convention was in town. Two brief notes appeared on April 4 in the Hot Springs *Sentinel* to the effect that the "saints" were meeting in a conference entitled "the General Assembly of the Church of God in Christ."[47]

E. N. Bell, the acting chairman, opened the business session on Monday morning, April 6. The entire convention asked Bell to serve as temporary chairman for the duration of the convention. J. Roswell Flower was named temporary conference secretary.[48] With no agenda prepared, and no standing committees appointed, the first order of business was to select, on a regional basis, a resolutions committee. This committee was charged with the responsibility of receiving reports on pertinent subjects, and arranging and presenting them in suitable reports and resolutions for the benefit of the convention.

CRISIS

Generated out of concern lest the convention develop too rigid and authoritarian a structure, a smaller, unofficial

[45] *Ibid.*
[46] General Council minutes, 1914, p. 3.
[47] "The Early History of the Assemblies of God," p. 9.
[48] General Council minutes, 1914, p. 3.

committee, chaired by T. K. Leonard of Findlay, Ohio, met in secret. Goss observes, regarding this episode:

> One night a group of opposition ministers met privately and formed a resolution to be brought to the floor—a resolution which they hoped would forestall any move on our part toward rigid organization. Some of them knew that we wanted to incorporate with rules and regulations and this knowledge, perhaps had aroused their suspicion.[49]

Through the night the informal committee of eight toiled over a proposed resolution which they wished to present to the convention the following day. Toward morning Chairman Leonard dictated the distilled result of the night's argumentation and prayer to J. Roswell Flower, secretary of the clandestine committee.

Before the meeting opened the following day, word leaked out that an unofficial committee had been meeting secretly. The duly appointed committee invited representatives of the smaller group to meet with them, in an attempt to forestall any possible misunderstanding. It seemed as though the success of the entire convention lay under a cloud. However, when Leonard shared with the regular committee the results of the night's toil the electric atmosphere suddenly was dispelled, for the document revealed a high degree of unanimity between the thinking of both committees! The result was that the document was presented to the convention for consideration with the combined endorsement of both groups. The resolution carried the convention floor by a unanimous vote! Following is the text of that first declaration:

> 1. That God, our heavenly Father, sent His only-begotten Son into the world who built and established His church upon the foundation of the apostles and prophets, Jesus Christ Himself being the Head and Chief Corner Stone.
>
> 2. That the holy inspired Scriptures are the all-sufficient rule for faith and practice, and we shall not add to or take from them.
>
> 3. That Christ commanded that there should be no schism in His Body, the General Assembly and Church of the first born, which are written in Heaven.
>
> 4. That we recognize ourselves as members of said Assembly of God and do not believe in identifying ourselves into a sect or

[49]Goss, *op. cit.*, p. 176.

denomination which constitutes an organization which legislates or forms laws and articles of faith and has jurisdiction over its members and creates unscriptural lines of fellowship and disfellowship, which separates itself from other members of the General Assembly of the first born.[50]

This resolution was really a statement of intent, embodying the spirit of the convention, carefully limiting the restrictions that could be placed on the sovereignty of local assemblies.

Leonard's committee submitted a second resolution, providing a more positive note, setting forth the principle of "voluntary cooperation." The concept of legal incorporation is evident in this resolution:

Resolved, First, That we recognize that we have assembled as a general council of Pentecostal saints from local Churches of God in Christ, Assemblies of God, and various Apostolic Faith Missions and Churches, and Full Gospel Pentecostal Missions, and assemblies of like faith in the United States and foreign lands, whose purpose is not to legislate laws of government, nor to usurp authority over said various assemblies, nor to deprive them of their scriptural rights and privileges.

Second, to recognize scriptural methods and rules of unity, fellowship, work and business for God, and to disapprove all unscriptural methods and conduct, endeavoring to keep the unity of the faith and of the knowledge of the Son of God, unto a perfect man, unto the measure of the stature of the fulness of Christ, and to walk accordingly (Eph. 4:1-32).

Finally, That we recognize all of the above said assemblies of various names, and, when speaking of them, refer to them by the general scriptural name, i.e., "Assembly of God," and adopt it as soon as possible for the purpose of convenience, unity, fellowship, and to be more scriptural and legal in transacting business, owning property, and executing missionary work at home and foreign lands.[51]

Following the adoption of the second resolution, also by unanimous vote, a wave of great blessing swept over the convention. "Then it seemed that Heaven had opened. The power of God fell mightily upon us all. What a glorious time we had rejoicing and worshipping the Lord!"[52]

THE KEY DECISIONS

The crisis had been passed. Moderation and good sense carried the day. God's blessing seemed to be mightily evi-

[50]General Council minutes, 1914.
[51]*Ibid.*
[52]Goss, *op. cit.*, p. 176.

dent, in spite of the move to organize! These early resolutions paved the way for the adoption of the chief instrument that came out of the first General Council. The document entitled "Preamble and Resolution on Constitution" embodied much of the sentiment and content of the opening resolutions. However, the Preamble stood quite alone for many years, for no constitution was adopted until 1927! A statement of faith was not voted upon until 1916, two years later, and then only out of very evident necessity. Thus, the "Preamble" served a purpose far beyond its normal usefulness, since it stood alone as the outline of the principles of the new body for so long. It set forth the principles of equality, unity, and cooperation that underlay the fundamental relationship in the Assemblies of God, a "voluntary cooperative fellowship." The sovereignty of the local church was guaranteed, and a meaningful basis of fellowship for ministers and churches was spelled out. Because of its great importance, the entire text of the "Preamble and Resolution on Constitution" follows:

WHEREAS, God, our Heavenly Father, sent His only begotten Son, the Lord Jesus Christ, into the World, Who purchased and redeemed fallen man with His own precious blood, and called out of the world and saved a people, of whom He built and established His church (Assembly of God. Matt. 16:18), upon the foundation of the Apostles and Prophets, Jesus Christ Himself being the Head and Chief Cornerstone (Eph. 2:20), and organized and baptized it with the Holy Spirit, with its government upon His shoulders (Isaiah 9:6, 7), said "the gates of hell shall not prevail against it" (Matt. 16:18); and

WHEREAS, He gave the holy inspired Scriptures, (both old and new covenants, Heb. 8:6-13), as the all-sufficient rule for faith and practice (2 Tim. 3:16), as follows: "All Scripture is given by inspiration of God, and is profitable for doctrine, for reproof, for correction, for instruction in righteousness: That the man of God may be perfect, thoroughly furnished unto all good works," we therefore shall not add to nor take from it (Rev. 22:18); and

WHEREAS, He commanded that there should be no schism (Division, sectarianism) in His body, the GENERAL ASSEMBLY (Church) of the firstborn, which are written in heaven (Heb. 12:23); and

WHEREAS, We recognize ourselves as members of said GENERAL ASSEMBLY OF GOD (which is God's organism), and do not believe in identifying ourselves as, or establishing ourselves into, a sect, that is a human organization that legislates or forms laws and articles of faith and has unscriptural jurisdiction over its members and creates unscriptural lines of fellowship and disfellowship and which separates itself from other members of the General Assembly (Church) of the first born, which is contrary to Christ's prayer in St. John 17, and Paul's teaching in Eph. 4:1-16, which we heartily endorse:

THEREFORE, BE IT RESOLVED, First, That we recognize ourselves as a GENERAL COUNCIL of Pentecostal (Spirit Baptized) saints from local Churches of God in Christ, Assemblies of God and various Apostolic Faith Missions and Churches, and Full Gospel Pentecostal Missions, and Assemblies of like faith in the United States of America, Canada, and Foreign Lands, whose purpose is neither to legislate laws of government, nor usurp authority over said various Assemblies of God, nor deprive them of their Scriptural and local rights and privileges, but to recognize Scriptural methods and order for worship, unity, fellowship, work and business for God, and to disapprove of all unscriptural methods, doctrine and conduct, and approve all Scriptural truth and conduct, endeavoring to keep the unity of the Spirit in the bonds of peace, until we all come into the unity of the faith, and of the knowledge of the Son of God, unto a perfect man, unto the measure of the stature of the fulness of Christ, and to walk accordingly, as recorded in Eph. 4:17-32, and to consider the five purposes announced in the Convention Call in the February, 1914, issue of "Word and Witness:"

RESOLVED, Second, That we recognize all the above said Assemblies of various names, and when speaking of them refer to them by the general Scriptural name "Assemblies of God;" and recommend that they all recognize themselves by the same name, that is, "Assembly of God" and adopt it as soon as practicable for the purpose of being more Scriptural and also legal in transacting business, owning property, and executing missionary work in home and foreign lands, and for general convenience, unity and fellowship.[53]

An important decision arrived at during the first General Council was to incorporate under the name "The General Council of the Assemblies of God." Unwittingly, in spite of all the care the good brethren exercised to avoid the image of traditional denominationalism, that title moved them well along that road. J. Roswell Flower, reminiscing on the events of that convention, indicated that the insertion of "the" in the title negated the intention of the convention, for all they really thought they were doing was to convene an occasional meeting, called a "General Council," of autonomous churches. Hence, what they really

[53]General Council minutes, 1914, pp. 4-5.

intended was to say "The General Council of Assemblies of God."[54]

Continuing ambiguity regarding the chosen name followed the denomination until 1969, at which time the General Council in session at Dallas, Texas, sought to clarify the terminology. "General Council" was there defined as the denomination in its biennial session. "Assemblies of God" was set apart as the common designation of the constituent local churches; the denominational name. "The General Council of the Assemblies of God" was retained as the legal title of the corporation.[55]

Actually, the term "Assembly of God" was a rather common designation for local churches of evangelical persuasion at the turn of the century. The chief influence at Hot Springs that led to its adoption as the uniform name for churches in the newly created fellowship was T. K. Leonard. Leonard had employed this title in his work at Findlay, Ohio, for at least two years before the first General Council, records indicating that he had been ordained by "The Assembly of God, Findlay, Ohio," in April, 1912.[56]

They were determined, then, "not to organize a man-made church and to charter it as a new sect in the land."[57] "It was agreed by all not to organize or charter a church, denomination or sect, but to have an ANNUAL COUNCIL, made up from all Pentecostal Assemblies, Churches and individuals to meet once a year to advise scriptural methods of unity and to attend to business for God."[58] Their concept of what it was they were creating was an annual convention, to be held together between sessions by a small advisory body accorded very limited authority.

The problem of polity was resolved by the adoption of a congregational arrangement, a principle that has not been changed constitutionally through the years. Basic in the agreement was the autonomy of the local congregation. However, to administer the necessary affairs of missionary

---

[54]Interview with J. Roswell Flower, February 24, 1970.

[55]General Council minutes, 1969, p. 56.

[56]"The Early History of the Assemblies of God," p. 10.

[57]J. R. Flower, "History of the Assemblies of God," p. 21.

[58]*Ibid.*

and evangelistic enterprise, to serve as legal custodians of the corporation, and to furnish continuity from one annual convention to the next an Executive Presbytery of 12 men was elected. A General Chairman and a Secretary-Treasurer were to serve as officers of the body. Bell and Flower, who had served as convention officers, were elected to fill these posts, respectively. The resolution governing the formation of the Executive Presbytery arranged for its annual reappointment by the General Council, thus limiting it from self-perpetuation.[59]

No attempt was made to formalize a precise doctrinal statement. The Preamble outlined the general principles of common belief, basing the entire fellowship on the Bible as "the all-sufficient rule for faith and practice." It was not until doctrinal issues threatened to rend the unity of the fellowship that a sharply defined statement of faith was hammered out. Breadth and tolerance governed the opening session.

Other decisions were made by this monumental convention. Two current papers were designated as official organs of the newly formed fellowship. E. N. Bell's *Word and Witness*, edited in Malvern, Arkansas, was one of those selected. The other was the *Christian Evangel*, edited by J. Roswell Flower, in Plainfield, Indiana.[60]

Acknowledgment of two schools already in existence appears in the official minutes. R. B. Chisolm was operating a school near Union, Mississippi, which those interested in a "literary school" were instructed to consider. Attention was also called to T. K. Leonard's Gospel School in Findlay, Ohio.[61]

Credentials were to be supplied to "worthy ministers

---

[59]"The Early History of the Assemblies of God," p. 11, describes actually what took place regarding the selection of the initial Executive Presbytery: "By motion from the floor, twelve men were to become members, including T. K. Leonard, E. N. Bell, J. R. Flower, H. A. Goss, J. W. Welch, M. M. Pinson, C. B. Fockler, and D.C.O. Opperman. These later elected A. P. Collins, R. L. Erickson, and D. W. Kerr. Bell and Flower were named as 'permanent' members—at least until the next Council. Later, an issue of *Word and Witness* indicated John Sinclair of Chicago would serve instead of R. L. Erickson. The remaining member was to be selected on a sectional basis at a future date."

[60]General Council minutes, 1914, pp. 5-6.

[61]*Ibid.*

within the Pentecostal, Apostolic Faith and Church of God in Christ groups" in the name of the General Council of the Assemblies of God. Two men were assigned the task of dispensing such recognition. It was agreed that H. A. Goss be authorized to issue credentials to those requesting such recognition in the South and West; T. K. Leonard to furnish similar service for the North and East.[62]

A statement was adopted denying ministerial credentials to divorced and remarried persons. Provision for formation of district councils by local assemblies, within the principles of the General Council, was also cared for. Within months, several district councils were formed.[63] Finally, the Executive Presbytery was authorized to call a future General Council session.[64]

On April 12, 1914, the first General Council session came to an end, having transacted the incorporation of a new fellowship.[65] Out of diversity and independence, from all quarters of the land, and even beyond, those of like precious faith agreed together to join in a "voluntary, cooperative fellowship." From this humble, small beginning the work was destined to grow, until the combined influence of workers together would spread around the world. The Assemblies of God was on the way!

---

[62]"The Early History of the Assemblies of God," p. 15.

[63]Hastie, *op. cit.*, p. 59, describes the formation of the West Central District Council at a camp meeting in Davis City, Iowa, in August of 1914. John Goben was elected "Chairman," a term commonly employed on the district level until the current term "superintendent" displaced it on the General Council level.

[64]General Council minutes, 1914, pp. 6-7.

[65]The agreement to incorporate was actually consummated on October 13, 1914, with 58 men signing the historic document.

6

The New Issue [1914-1916]

The Second General Council, November, 1914—*The "New Issue" and the Third General Council, October,* 1915—*The "Statement of Fundamental Truths" and the Fourth General Council, October,* 1916

THE SECOND GENERAL COUNCIL, NOVEMBER, 1914

AFTERMATH OF THE FIRST COUNCIL

During the first General Council, T. K. Leonard offered the use of his small printing plant and school property in Findlay, Ohio, for the use of the new fellowship as a kind of headquarters location. Inadequate space and equipment at Plainfield, Indiana, and at Malvern, Arkansas, where the two official papers were being published, necessitated a move to Findlay, Ohio, in June, 1914. There, editors E. N. Bell and J. Roswell Flower carried on the publication of both papers throughout the summer, the *Word and Witness* as a monthly; the *Christian Evangel* as a weekly. Surprisingly, the editors discouraged patrons from subscribing to both, because "the editors of both papers are the same and it will not be profitable to take both."[1] By August the combined circulation of the two papers had risen to 25,000.[2] During this formative period these official papers were instrumental in consolidating and coordinating the work of the fledgling organization.

One of the important reasons that precipitated the formation of the Assemblies of God was the need for unifying and protecting missionary endeavors. At first, during the

[1]"The Early History of the Assemblies of God," p. 16.
[2]*Ibid.*

early years, up to 1917, there was little formal missionary policy, the activity of the General Council consisting largely of publicizing the needs of missionaries and forwarding what money was made available from freewill offerings received from the field. By the time of the creation of the General Council there were a goodly number of missionaries already abroad. These workers had a variety of buildings, homes, schools, and other facilities. Support for this sizable operation was generally sent direct to the field from interested friends and churches in the United States. Many of the missionaries joined the Assemblies of God and requested assistance. Bell and Flower faithfully forwarded 100 percent of all funds they received that had been designated for the field. Editor Bell wrote in the August 22, 1914, *Christian Evangel*:

> Because of this great circulation (25,000) our papers are enabled to be strong agencies for the use of missionaries, carrying the needs of the field direct to those in the homeland who have some of the Lord's money, who in turn respond to the need and send it to us to be forwarded, which we gladly do without charging a cent for postage, cost of drafts, or time consumed in taking care of this phase of the work. . . . We, therefore, urge upon our readers the necessity of laying aside a portion for the missionaries each week, even but a ten cent piece. . . . We will gladly forward, free, any sum whether it be great or small.[3]

In addition to their duties as officers of the fellowship and publishers of the official organs, E. N. Bell and J. R. Flower also taught that fall in T. K. Leonard's Gospel School in Findlay.[4] That these men could perform multiple functions is indicative of the simplicity of the new work during those first months.

However, during the early fall of 1914, the rapidly expanding administrative problems and the awareness that the facilities in Findlay would soon be outgrown prompted Bell and Flower to appeal for a second General Council. This action had been authorized by the initial meeting in Hot Springs. So, just seven months after that first historic gathering, the officers of the General Council announced a

[3]Quoted in "The Early History of the Assemblies of God," p. 17.
[4]Flower, "History of the Assemblies of God," p. 24.

second conclave "in order to lay a firm foundation upon which to build the fellowship of the Assemblies of God."[5]

The second General Council was announced for November 15-29, 1914, to convene at the Stone Church, then located on Indiana Avenue, in Chicago. Evidence of the prosperity of the new fellowship is the sizable increase in the ministerial list since the Hot Springs meeting. From 128 in April, the list had grown to 522 by the end of the second Council in November, representing 35 states, Canada, and 6 foreign countries.[6]

One should not assume, however, that all contention had been resolved by the establishment of the Assemblies of God earlier in that year. Following the Hot Springs convention,

> . . . sharp, pungent words were spoken. Caustic editorials appeared in Pentecostal papers. Prophecies foretold of ruin coming upon these men "who had dared place restriction on the moving of the Holy Spirit."[7]

Some of the opposition relented in time when they saw the fruit of such organized effort. Most reaction to the new fellowship was enthusiastic, and positive, farsighted individuals recognized the value of coming together in a cooperative venture. A letter from D. W. Kerr, pastor in Cleveland, Ohio, to E. N. Bell, represents the attitude of many Pentecostal leaders:

> I am glad steps are being taken, looking forward to a better understanding among all Pentecostal people. I have been notified through Brother Leonard of Findlay of my selection to act on the Council, which I have consented to do. . . . We should meet at the Council to go over the situation more thoroughly as a body and agree as to the methods of procedure in bringing this project clearly before the entire constituency. . . . *Cooperation without ecclesiastical centralization* has been the line of truth . . . which I have been advocating. . . . Organic cooperation and sympathetic relationship needs to be recognized and preached . . . between the members of the body of Christ and between assemblies of the same faith. One essential thing, in order to bring about this unity among Pentecostal saints, is the calling of conventions in different sections

---

[5]*Ibid.*
[6]"The Early History of the Assemblies of God," p. 16.
[7]*Ibid.*, p. 13.

and districts of the States and Canada, and the picking up of the questions which were considered at the Hot Springs convention in April.[8]

THE FALL CONVENTION

And so it was that, in the midst of hope and enthusiasm, the second General Council got under way on Sunday, November 15, 1914. After an initial day of enrolling delegates, the first major item of business was the election of officers. In spite of general appreciation and respect for E. N. Bell, he was not reelected as Chairman. Arch P. Collins, like Bell, a former Baptist minister from Fort Worth, was selected for that office. J. Roswell Flower was returned to office as General Secretary. Two new offices were created: D. C. O. Opperman was elected to serve as Assistant Chairman, and B. F. Lawrence, Assistant Secretary. (Bell was returned to executive office in 1918, serving in one of the top positions afforded by the Assemblies of God until his death in 1923.) Collins, although held in esteem by his brethren, "performed but few of the duties of his office and did not even appear at the opening of the next General Council."[9] The selection of the Assistant Chairman and Assistant Secretary was for the one Council only, and was not repeated until 1927, when a formal constitution was adopted. E. N. Bell was retained as Editor of Publications, and J. R. Flower was named Office Editor.

The Executive Presbytery was enlarged from 12 to 16 to broaden the base of responsibility. All the men elected in the previous Council were reelected, and the following were added: F. F. Bosworth, W. F. Carothers, George Chambers, Andrew L. Frazer, and David McDowell.[10] The duties of the Executive Presbytery were spelled out: they were to serve as advisers to the assemblies in their respective areas, and to furnish guidance for novice assemblies with a view to bringing them to a self-governing level. They were not permitted under any circumstances to intrude into the affairs of sovereign assemblies without official in-

[8]Quoted in "The Early History of the Assemblies of God," pp. 13-14.

[9]*Ibid.*, p. 18.

[10]The reason for there being five names was that the twelfth member of the original 12 had never been selected.

vitation. Local congregations were expected to care for the expenses of visiting presbyters.

A most significant decision at the second Council was the authorization for the purchase of printing equipment.

> . . . the Executive Presbytery is hereby authorized to take immediate steps in securing funds through voluntary offerings, subscriptions, or the sale of non-participating stock, or in any matter pleasing to God and the Executive Presbytery of an amount not less than $5,000.00 for publishing equipment to be owned and controlled entirely by the General Council and to be used for the glory of God.[11]

SUBSEQUENT DEVELOPMENTS

Following the Council, in the spring of 1915, this important resolution paved the way for the executive brethren to take action to move the Gospel Publishing House from Findlay, Ohio, to 2838 East Avenue, St. Louis, Missouri. Without much equipment in the printing plant and office in Findlay, the move was consummated with relatively little effort. A press originally purchased for government printing in Washington, D.C., was donated by a generous patron who lived in the nation's capital. To this gift was added a cutting machine. A secondhand linotype machine and a folding machine were purchased. The equipment was installed in the storeroom of the building in St. Louis, after the floor had been reinforced. The upstairs portion of the building became the headquarters offices of the Assemblies of God. For three eventful years this would be the "home" of the youthful Pentecostal fellowship.[12]

The sacrifice and hardship which early Pentecostal pioneers endured is exemplified by this vignette of courage and faith, written by Brother Flower:

> We had been authorized to establish a publishing house, but nothing had been given us to accomplish our purpose. In those early days, Brother Bell tried to live on $5.00 a week, which he took out of the funds for support of himself and family. Of course, he could not live on any such amount, and so he ran behind in his finances continually. Then after the move to St. Louis where increased rents were met and living expenses were higher (especially during war times), he accepted the munificent salary of $15.00 per

[11] General Council minutes, 1914, p. 10.

[12] "The Early History of the Assemblies of God," pp. 19-20.

week. . . . Only the utmost frugality could have brought into existence a publishing house under such conditions.[13]

To save all unnecessary expense, a large building on Garrison Avenue was leased from the Salvation Army. Here in quarters that once served as a children's home three apartments were established for the families of the headquarters workers, with some of the young women who aided in the office work housed in dormitory rooms in the commodious building.[14]

The "New Issue" and the Third General Council, October, 1915

In its second year of existence, the Assemblies of God was threatened with almost complete disaster. Even before the Hot Springs meeting, a doctrinal issue had erupted on the West Coast, which within a brief time was to sweep across the country, nearly carrying away the Assemblies of God with it.

OUTBURST IN THE WEST

In April, 1913, at a "worldwide" Pentecostal camp meeting being conducted at Arroyo Seco, near Los Angeles, a new "revelation" (not an uncommon thing in those days) received considerable emphasis. The main speaker at the camp meeting was Mrs. Mary Woodworth-Etter, but the speaker who unwittingly triggered the eruption was R. E. McAlister. At a baptismal service held near the main camp meeting tent, Brother McAlister casually observed that "the apostles invariably baptized their converts once in the name of Jesus Christ," and that "the words Father, Son, and Holy Ghost were never used in Christian baptism." When they heard this, "a shudder swept the preachers on the platform," one preacher even stepping over to whisper to Brother McAlister to refrain from emphasizing that doctrine or it would "associate the camp with a Dr. Sykes who so baptised."[15]

Reaction to this announcement was varied. One earnest preacher in particular, though, was deeply moved by the

[13]*The Pentecostal Evangel*, June 30, 1923.

[14]"The Early History of the Assemblies of God," pp. 20-21.

[15]Fred J. Foster, *Think It Not Strange, A History of the Oneness Movement* (St. Louis, 1965), quoted in Synan, *op. cit.*, p. 193.

significance of the "name of Jesus." John G. Scheppe spent much of the night in prayer. In the early light of morning he "was given a glimpse of the power of the name of Jesus." He jumped to his feet, ran through the camp grounds, startling early risers, and awakening those still asleep. Scheppe shouted his "new revelation" of the power in the name of Jesus. His enthusiasm caused many to spend the day searching their Bibles regarding "the name of Jesus."

The enthusiasm created at Arroyo Seco gained such momentum that it soon affected many Pentecostal churches up and down the West Coast. At Long Beach a large company of people were rebaptized in the new formula being advocated, "in the name of Jesus only." This rebaptism with the new formula was felt to be the gateway to new blessing. Attention was focused on the use of "THE NAME" invoked by the apostles in the Book of Acts in connection with the performance of miracles, exorcism of evil spirits, and, particularly, water baptism.[16] This emphasis led rapidly to the virtual denial of the Trinity, a type of Modal Monarchianism being espoused. Following the identification of the Holy Spirit with Jesus, the next step was the declaration of some that unless one had received the baptism in the Holy Spirit, accompanied by speaking with tongues, he was not truly saved.

This species of "Pentecostal Unitarianism" gained great strength chiefly through its promulgation by Frank J. Ewart, prominent West Coast Pentecostal leader who was present at the Arroyo Seco camp meeting. Ewart, originally from Australia, lately from Canada, and most recently from Portland, Oregon, had developed a reputation as a fearless Baptist preacher. In 1908 he accepted the Pentecostal message in Portland. His outspoken preaching of Pentecost led to his expulsion from the Baptist communion. Ewart joined William H. Durham in Los Angeles, serving as his assistant in the important mission at Seventh and Los Angeles Streets. When Pastor Durham died, Ewart fell heir to the pastorate, and by the time of the "Jesus Only" issue was recognized as one of the leading Pentecostals in the West.[17]

[16]Flower, "History of the Assemblies of God," p. 24A.
[17]Synan, *op. cit.*, p. 194.

Ewart spent nearly a year brooding over the implications of the new doctrine, and in April, 1914, the same month in which the Hot Springs convention was held, he preached his first "Jesus Only" sermon. This occurred at Belvedere, a suburb of Los Angeles. One of Ewart's first "converts" was Glenn A. Cook, the evangelist who had earlier been a pioneer promoter of Pentecost through much of the Midwest. On April 15, 1914, Ewart and Cook rebaptized each other "in the name of Jesus only" in a tank they had set up inside their evangelistic tent. From this time forward they both launched an aggressive campaign to convert the entire Pentecostal Movement to their way of thinking. Ewart began publication of a periodical dedicated to this objective, *Meat in Due Season.* Their forceful presentation, the appeal that the "new revelation" had been received in a supernatural manner, and the belief that great blessing was attached to the proclamation of this "truth" swayed many simple, earnest Pentecostal people.[18]

THE ENTHUSIASM SPREADS

The "New Issue," as it was commonly designated, was still largely a West Coast novelty until January, 1915, when Glenn Cook undertook an evangelistic tour eastward. He held a week of meetings in St. Louis, rebaptizing some of the saints in the waters of the Mississippi. J. Roswell Flower, already having relocated his family there from Findlay, was not overwhelmed by the new teaching, as were others. He wrote to G. T. Haywood in Indianapolis, one of the best-known Negro ministers in the Assemblies of God, warning him that Cook was on his way with disruptive doctrine. Haywood responded that the warning had come too late; he had already been rebaptized! Cook baptized nearly 500 of Haywood's followers, that church becoming a leading center of Jesus Only teaching for many years to come.

News of Haywood's defection, and rumors that the entire Executive Presbytery of the Assemblies of God had accepted the New Issue produced consternation and bewilderment throughout the fellowship. "The wildfire that

[18]*Ibid.*, pp. 194-95.

had been slow to start now began to leap from mission to mission, assembly to assembly, until it became *the* issue of the day."[19]

CONFRONTING THE ISSUE

In response to the hysteria that was being generated by the promulgators of the New Issue, editorials and articles appeared in the *Word and Witness,* beginning with the March 27, 1915, issue, stoutly defending the Trinitarian position, supporting the mode of baptism articulated in Matthew 28:19. An emergency meeting of the Executive Presbytery was called in May to convene in St. Louis. This urgent session drew up a document entitled "Preliminary Statement Concerning the Principles Involved in the New Issue."[20] The document was couched in conciliatory language, but maintained a firm Trinitarian position.

J. Roswell Flower, after study of Scripture and Church history, and following numerous interviews with advocates of the doctrine, concluded that the "new revelation" was nothing more than the resurrection of ancient heresy. He spoke out pointedly in the July 17, 1915, issue of *Word and Witness,* expressing the hope that the crest of the hysteria might already be passing. But Flower's optimism was premature.

The "Third Interstate Encampment of the Assemblies of God," a camp meeting hosted by H. G. Rodgers at Jackson, Tennessee, late in July, 1915, became the occasion for the most explosive scene in the entire "New Issue" episode. Bell, who but the month before had inveighed against the Jesus Only teaching, and Rodgers shocked the assembled saints by announcing that they were candidates for rebaptism! The camp evangelist, L. V. Roberts of Indianapolis, a leading proponent of the Oneness teaching, baptized not only Bell and Rodgers, but scores of others as well. Enthusiasm reached frenzied proportions, with more than 4,000 attending a single Sunday night's service during the camp.[21]

In the months that followed, headlines in Pentecostal

---

[19]Brumback, *op. cit.,* p. 193.

[20]*Word and Witness,* June 12, 1915.

[21]Brumback, *op. cit.,* pp. 195-96.

publications announcing Bell's defection jarred the stability of many. Wholesale defections now occurred in the ranks of the Trinitarians, nearly all the leaders of the Assemblies of God falling prey to the new enthusiasm in whole or in part. D. C. O. Opperman, L. C. Hall, G. T. Haywood, H. A. Goss, B. F. Lawrence, besides Bell and Rodgers, fell in line. R. E. McAlister and nearly the entire Canadian Pentecostal clergy were rebaptized. All 12 of the Assemblies of God ministers in Louisiana were carried away in the Oneness sweep.[22]

J. Roswell Flower, the great bulwark of stability in those turbulent weeks, stood his ground against the engulfing hysteria. He succeeded in gaining the consent of some of the Executive Presbyters to call a General Council. The August 14, 1915, issue of the *Christian Evangel* announced that the Third General Council would be held in St. Louis in October, in Turner Hall.

Neither the Chairman, A. P. Collins, nor the Assistant Chairman, D. C. O. Opperman, appeared at the opening session of the Council. Flower himself, the General Secretary, convened the meeting. According to the previously established pattern, the first three days of the meeting, October 1-3, were spent in prayer, praise, and testimonies, with the preaching pitched on a conciliatory note. A sense of great blessing moved over the assembled delegates on Sunday night, on the eve of the business session. In the absence of Chairman Collins, the convention chose J. W. Welch to serve as temporary Chairman, subsequently electing him as permanent Chairman, with William G. Schell being asked to fill the post of Assistant Chairman. Flower and Lawrence were continued as Secretary and Assistant Secretary, respectively.

The central concern of the Council was the agonizing issue that seemed about to destroy the Assemblies of God. Lengthy debate on the New Issue occupied much of the Council. Fortunately, the spiritual tone established during the opening days of the meeting persisted through the entire Council, tempering the spirit of debate so that courtesy

---

[22]*Ibid.*, p. 197.

and brotherly love prevailed. Both sides of the controversy were given a full and fair hearing. At the conclusion of the extended period provided for debate, the Resolutions Committee offered a six-point proposal which appealed for liberality of spirit and toleration of dissenting opinion on the question of the proper formula for baptism. Four of the points articulated careful safeguards for distinguishing properly the persons within the Trinity, so one must gather that the adoption of the resolution was something of a victory for the Trinitarian forces.[23] In effect, the adoption of this resolution staved off decisive action, allowing more time for reflection.

The worst appeared to be over. Apparently the tide was turning in favor of historic orthodox Trinitarian theology. Bell resigned as editor. J. W. Welch, the newly elected Chairman, was appointed to serve in that capacity for the coming year, in additon to his executive duties. None of those elected to the Executive Presbytery were strongly committed to the Jesus Only position. The flood had been stayed, but it was not a permanent solution.

One of the fundamental problems that complicated the actions of the Council was that at the Hot Springs convention no provision had been made for theological formulation, other than the broadly based commitment to the authority of the Bible. Out of fear of "creedalism" the Founding Fathers had assiduously avoided any attempt at articulating precise doctrinal statements as a test of faith. It would not be until clear agreement on specific doctrinal issues could be arranged that the controversy would be settled with finality.

However, it was not the ripeness of time for such precision. The air was still too emotion-laden in the fall of 1915 for such action to occur without threat of a fatal rift in the infant organization, still but 18 months old. The wisdom and tact of men like J. Roswell Flower saved the Assemblies of God from a collision course with disaster during those fateful October days.

---

[23]General Council minutes, 1915, p. 5.

The "Statement of Fundamental Truths" and the Fourth General Council, October, 1916

Although the 1915 General Council ended on an irenic note, afterward the controversy broke out anew with even greater intensity. Glenn Cook threatened Flower with disaster if he opposed the Oneness message; H. A. Goss in Texas soberly admonished E. L. Newby of Wichita Falls that if he turned down "this wonderful truth" he "would miss God."[24] Gradually, however, sentiment crystallized among more and more of the Assemblies of God brethren across the country that such a remarkable revelation seemed to be based more on subjective feelings than on the objective revelation of the Word of God written. More and more shied away from those, like Goss, who responded to the earnest challenge to "show it to me in the Bible," with such statements as "Oh, you'll never get this by studying it out like some other doctrine. This comes by 'revelation.' "[25]

Flagrant abuse by New Issue proponents of the time-worn General Council policy of avoiding public dissemination of novel teachings until they could be tested and proven by the brethren only further weakened the cause of the Jesus Only movement. This rule had been adopted by the entire fellowship, since it not only served to safeguard the Assemblies of God, but also acted as a check on impulsive individuals who might easily be led astray by ephemeral fascinations. The rule embodied the principle that there is safety in a multitude of counselors. Those who violated this principle, the militant Oneness people, appeared to be troublemakers, causers of dissension and discord. A growing cry went up for unity, for agreement on basic doctrines.

FINAL RESOLUTION OF THE PROBLEM

The feeling generated on the field pleading for a permanent resolution of the persistent conflict finally bore fruit. Chairman Welch, through the pages of the *Weekly Evangel*[26] (June 24, 1916), issued a call for a General Council to convene in October, 1916, with the express purpose of taking

---

[24]Brumback, *op. cit.*, p. 202.

[25]*Ibid.*

[26]The *Christian Evangel* and the *Word and Witness* were combined in 1915 to form the *Weekly Evangel.*

up doctrinal questions in a direct, conclusive manner. "The time has come for the interpretation of what scriptural teaching and conduct is. The time for sifting and solidifying is here. The time for great shaking has begun, and all that can be disturbed will be shaken into separation from that which is settled in God."[27]

The 1916 General Council opened at Bethel Chapel in St. Louis, in early October, amid an air of expectancy, for the focal point was the unresolved issue that had been carried over from the previous meeting.[28] There was considerable tension in the air, for the months preceding the controversy had been particularly acute. Every preacher and church was forced to take a stand on the New Issue. "Charges of 'Sabellianism' and 'oneism' were countered with accusations of 'three-Godism' and 'Popish slavery.'"[29] The Council began with the Trinitarians at a decided advantage. Flower, Welch, and Pinson had been able to regain some of the brethren who had been swept away in the first rush of the excitement generated in the previous year. A tremendous victory was the winning back of E. N. Bell, perhaps the single most influential man in the Assemblies of God.

In spite of the solemn vow expressed at Hot Springs that the Assemblies of God would never adopt a formal creed, a committee was appointed by Chairman Welch to prepare a statement of fundamental truths, and to present it to the floor. Named to the committee were T. K. Leonard, S. A. Jamieson, D. W. Kerr, S. H. Frodsham, and E. N. Bell. With Bell having repented of his dissimulation, acknowledging that he had been swept away out of fear of losing influence rather than out of Biblical conviction, he had been reinstated into fellowship among the Trinitarians with forgiveness and generosity. Thus, the entire committee appointed to draw up a statement of common belief was solidly orthodox.

The decision to formulate a body of approved doctrinal tenets was a far-reaching move in the direction of establishing a formalized denominational organization. Its justifica-

[27]*Weekly Evangel*, June 24, 1916.
[28]Flower, "History of the Assemblies of God," p. 27.
[29]Synan, *op. cit.*, p. 197.

tion was based on the Preamble provision arranging for the approving and disapproving of matters pertaining to doctrine and conduct. Vigorous debate ensued regarding the question of the right of the Council to draw up such a statement of faith. However, the majority ruled that the General Council was not violating its constitutional prerogatives, and so the proposed statement was considered section by section until the whole was adopted.[30]

Each member of the committee contributed to the eventual committee report, but the greatest contribution came from D. W. Kerr, pastor in Cleveland, Ohio. A former Christian and Missionary Alliance man, Kerr was a better-trained man than the average Pentecostal minister of his day. Deeply concerned about the New Issue, he had spent much time during the course of the previous year poring over his Greek Testament. He had even wavered somewhat at one point on the question of the Oneness issue, but a visit at the crucial hour from David McDowell helped to stabilize the earnest student of God's Word. This shy, somewhat retiring individual, hardly the image of a great contender for the faith, had already compiled a quantity of notes, and was well prepared for his assignment even before he arrived at the Council. Because of his careful preparation, the committee was enabled to furnish the Council with a statement of faith in a relatively brief span of time. It is remarkable that after all these years the Statement of Fundamental Truths, as it was called, has remained virtually unchanged, with but minor rewording for the sake of clarification in recent years.[31]

The doctrinal statement as adopted militated against the Oneness views, which resulted in the loss of some of the

---

[30]See Appendix A for the complete text of the Statement of Fundamental Truths.

[31]The General Council in 1927 made the Statement of Fundamental Truths Article V of the constitution which was adopted that year. In 1933 the section titled "The Adorable Godhead" was added to the section "The One True God." In 1961 a committee which had been assigned the task of suggesting revisions in the Statement of Fundamental Truths presented several minor changes, which were in no sense doctrinal changes, but intended to clarify and strengthen existing statements. The revisions were adopted and incorporated into the statement that year. In 1969 some changes in the Statement of Fundamental Truths were made. In that year, the articles governing the mission of the church were altered to conform to the statement on purpose produced by the Study Committee on Advance.

brethren, the 1916 ministerial roll dropping from 585 to 429.[32] During the Council, the Oneness people had sat together, voting en bloc against the whole idea of a "creed," for they knew that such an action would go against them. When that tactic failed, they voted solidly against the committee's proposed statement of faith, point by point, protesting all the way. Following the Council, there was considerable sadness as friends of long-standing but now separated by doctrinal cleavage shook hands and departed to go their separate ways. The decisive action of the 1916 General Council was an important milestone, not only in setting the course for the Assemblies of God, but in making it propitious for the disaffected Oneness men to organize their own Pentecostal Unitarian fellowship, several of these coming into existence shortly after this episode.[33]

After the initial pain of separation was past, the wisdom of the action taken seemed to be evidenced by a strong rallying of strength to the still-very-young Assemblies of God. The pattern of vigorous growth that began after the initial defections of 1916 were past, gained momentum, continuing for some decades at an impressive rate. The dangerous crisis had been successfully negotiated. Coming within a whisper of being completely engulfed by the New Issue, the infant fellowship rallied, and was spared the apparently inevitable tragedy of being swept out of the mainstream of historic orthodoxy into the eddy current of spurious doctrine. Wise were those who accepted the value of inter-

---

[32]Flower, "History of the Assemblies of God," p. 28.

[33]The Pentecostal churches in the American West and Midwest were hardest hit by the New Issue. Since the Assemblies of God was strong in these sections, it probably suffered the most from this episode of any established organization. The Holiness-Pentecostal denominations of the Southeast were able to fend off the invasion rather successfully. The phenomenon appears to be exclusively an American and Canadian issue, no evidence of it appearing in Latin America, Europe, or elsewhere.

Under the leadership of G. T. Haywood, a racially-mixed Pentecostal unitarian fellowship was created at a convention in Indianapolis shortly after the failure of the Oneness people to capture the Assemblies of God in 1916. This body was named "The Pentecostal Assemblies of the World." It continued as an integrated body until 1924, when the white ministers withdrew to form a separate organization. In 1945, two groups merged, forming "The United Pentecostal Church," largest of the Oneness bodies. A host of smaller, splinter groups exist, but information is fragmentary. The total number of Pentecostal Oneness adherents was estimated in 1964 to be about half a million in the United States, more than half of them Negroes (Kelsey, *op. cit.*, pp. 242-43.

preting Biblical belief, even in the face of the charge of "creedalism," when the times required clarity of expression.[34]

Another significant decision agreed upon in the 1916 General Council was the institution of a General Presbytery. The Executive Presbytery was reduced to five members, constituting an executive committee of the Assemblies of God, with its previously defined role unchanged. In recognition of the need for a more representative body to serve the judicial and executive needs between Council sessions, a General Presbytery was brought into being. Its authority was to be limited carefully so that it would not infringe on the ultimate authority of the General Council in session, itself.[35] Changes in the size and composition of the Executive Presbytery and the General Presbytery have been made periodically, but the structural relationships have not been changed. The bulk of the membership of the General Presbytery continues to consist of the leadership of the various district councils.[36]

And so the first two years in the existence of the Assemblies of God came to a successful conclusion. The greatest threat to the movement that it would encounter, to the time of this writing, was hurdled. The basic ingredients of successful and stable organization had been hammered out. With serious controversy resolved, the work of God could now proceed apace.

[34]Myer Pearlman, beloved Assemblies of God scholar, expressed the matured sentiment of the fellowship in an article which appeared in *The Pentecostal Evangel*, September 7, 1929: "Though the interpretation of Christianity contained in creeds is imperfect, sometimes inaccurate, sometimes one-sided, the creeds would not have arisen unless there had been someone and something to explain. Thanks be unto God that we know that Someone and possess that Something! As long as the Church has a Saviour to offer, it will find it necessary to explain who He is. As long as the Church has a real experience to offer to the world, it will need a form of words to describe it" (quoted in Brumback, *op. cit.*, p. 207).

[35]General Council minutes, 1916, pp. 5-6.

[36]The Executive Presbytery of the Assemblies of God has these functions: (1) It serves as trustee of The General Council of the Assemblies of God, (2) it supervises and exercises general oversight of all departments of the denomination, (3) it arranges for the biennial sessions of the denomination, which are called General Councils, and (4) the Executive Presbytery acts for the corporation between the biennial General Council sessions.

The General Presbytery of the Assemblies of God has these functions: (1) It serves as a court of appeal in matters of ministerial discipline, (2) it serves as an advisory body to the Executive Presbytery, and (3) it establishes policy on major issues between General Council sessions, as well as on matters referred to it by the Executive Presbytery.

7

Stabilizing Years [1916-1927]

The Move to Springfield—The Initial Evidence Controversy—Early Missionary Program—Coordination of Publications—Early Leaders —Christian Education—A Constitution Is Adopted

Following the momentous Council session of 1916, the Assemblies of God fellowship recovered rapidly. The clarification brought about by the adoption of the Statement of Fundamental Truths bred confidence in many who were undecided. Applications for membership in the denomination came from ministers and churches in all parts of the nation.[1] General Council rosters showed a sharp increase in the next years, climbing from 429 to 573 in 1917, and to 819 ministers and missionaries in 1918.

The Move to Springfield

A decision of far-reaching consequence was made with respect to the location of the organizational headquarters and publishing plant. Following the brief stay in Findlay, Ohio, modest quarters had been secured in St. Louis in 1915. These facilities were quickly outgrown, making either expansion or a move imperative. The 1917 General Council authorized the Executive Presbytery to proceed with relocation. In the spring of 1918, a friend provided a donation of $3,600 which was made available for the improvement of the printing operation. After a disappointing search for a suitable building in St. Louis, it was finally determined that an attempt should be made to look elsewhere. E. N. Bell

[1] J. R. Flower, "The Snare of Sectarianism," *The Pentecostal Evangel*, October 23, 1943, p. 9.

was commissioned to tour the region. His scouting expedition carried him to a number of towns in Missouri and Iowa, but his recommendation was that Springfield, Missouri, the "capital city of the Ozarks," be given top priority by the Executive Presbytery. Bell had discovered that real estate values in Springfield were depressed, and that several buildings were available which gave good promise for the expansion anticipated.[2]

Brother Flower was dispatched by the executive brethren to confirm the judgment of Bell. He returned to St. Louis with a positive report, and employed his influence for the purchase of a 45- by 90-foot, two-story brick building, located on the corner of Lyon and Pacific Street. The building had formerly been a grocery and meat market. Its first floor consisted of two large rooms with concrete floors ideal for the installation of heavy printing equipment. Upstairs the nine spacious rooms provided an ideal arrangement for the editorial and executive offices, with room for a large auditorium, as well. J. R. Flower was asked to go to Springfield to supervise the relocation.

Subsequent years of growth in the Assemblies of God necessitated five expansion programs, and eventually in 1961 the entire operation was moved to its present location at 1445 Boonville Avenue, but for many years, "434 W. Pacific Street" would hold a familiar ring to constituents. The building was purchased for approximately the same amount of money that had been made available for expansion purposes! A permanent home had been found for the General Council headquarters and the flourishing Gospel Publishing House.[3]

Not the least of the advantages of the move to Springfield was the fine reception afforded the young Pentecostal fellowship by civic leaders. Through the years a most wholesome relationship has existed between the city fathers and the citizenry and the Assemblies of God. Church members, workers at the headquarters offices and printing plant, and the faculty and students of Assemblies of God colleges in

---

[2]"The Early History of the Assemblies of God," p. 21 and Brumback, *op. cit.*, pp. 211-13.

[3]*Ibid.*

the community have developed a good reputation. Civic and commercial interests have been generous and warm in their response to the sizable Assemblies of God representation in the city.[4]

With the move to Springfield of the headquarters, an immediate impact was evident on the local Assembly.[5] The church had been meeting in a crude, frame tabernacle on East Central Street, opposite the Greene County Court House. With the sudden addition of numerous new members, the church was inspired to purchase a lot on the corner of Calhoun Street and Campbell Avenue, not far from the new headquarters building, for the erection of a permanent building. Fred Vogler, then pastoring a small church in Kansas, was invited to come to supervise construction of a 40- by 60-foot building, flanking Campbell Avenue. This structure was completed in 1920. It was in the basement of this building that Central Bible Institute[6] was begun.

Almost immediately after the move to Springfield was completed in the spring of 1918, the Executive Presbytery called for a General Council, the sixth, to convene at the new headquarters city. There, in an abandoned theater on Commercial Street, during the month of September, among important items of business cared for, a second major theological dispute was thoroughly aired.

The "Initial Evidence" Controversy

THE ISSUE IS RAISED

The distinctive doctrine that has characterized the Pente-

---

[4]*The Springfield News and Leader*, March 7, 1948, carried an editorial, of which this is an excerpt: "The Assemblies of God is one of Springfield's greatest industries—if you can call a church an industry—just as important to Springfield commercially as a great factory. It is an admirable industry—it creates no smoke or stench, it has no labor problem, it has no seasonal shutdowns, it never runs out of material and it never seems to have any difficulty meeting its payrolls. Its managers and employees . . . are substantial and respectable citizens engaged in an enterprise which requires no apology and needs no federal subsidy or supervision. . . ." (quoted in Brumback, *op. cit.*, p. 212).

[5]It was Rachel Sizelove who brought the Pentecostal testimony to Springfield, Missouri, from the Los Angeles revival, as early as 1913.

[6]The name of the Central Bible Institute was changed to Central Bible College in 1965. In this volume that institution is referred to in each case by the name prevailing at the particular time of reference, the abbreviations CBI or CBC sometimes being used.

costal Movement from the beginning is the belief that the Scriptures teach that the initial physical evidence of receiving the Spirit's baptism is speaking with other tongues. Many other evangelicals have accepted the concept of a filling with the Holy Spirit as an experience subsequent to conversion, but the Pentecostal touchstone has always been on the definition of the evidence. Assemblies of God people have expected tongues to be the initial physical evidence, but *also* that following the initial evidence of tongues, *further* evidences of a Spirit-filled life should be forthcoming, too. The various manifestations and fruits of the Spirit should be considered further "evidences" of a genuine baptism in the Spirit. The controversy has hinged not so much on the fruits of the Spirit, but on the *initial physical* evidence. Evangelical friends tended to emphasize that all that really matters is the ultimate fruit of being filled with the Spirit, the graces of the Spirit and *any* of the "gifts" of the Spirit being adequate testimony to a full New Testament experience. Pentecostals insisted—and still do—that a full Biblical experience is accompanied by evidential tongues. What this amounted to was that Pentecostals distinguished clearly between "evidential tongues" and "the gift of tongues," non-Pentecostalists not permitting such a distinction.[7]

Only once before the controversy of 1918 was there a question of any significance about this doctrine within the Pentecostal Movement. At a convention and short-term Bible school being conducted in Waco, Texas, in February, 1907, several questions respecting doctrine were raised, among them the matter of the evidence of the baptism in the Holy Spirit. Brother A. G. Canada suggested that *any* of the gifts could be the immediate, empirical evidence. Contending on the opposing side, W. F. Carothers "argued so conclusively for the orthodox Pentecostal position that the question was settled for most of those present once and for all."[8] It was determined that a test case should

[7]See Myer Pearlman, *Knowing the Doctrines of the Bible* (Springfield, Missouri: Gospel Publishing House, 1937), p. 310, and E. S. Williams, *Systematic Theology*, Vol. III (Springfield, Missouri: Gospel Publishing House, 1953), pp. 47-52.

[8]Brumback, *op. cit.*, p. 216.

be made. San Antonio had not yet received the Pentecostal testimony. Workers who went to San Antonio agreed not to mention anything about evidential tongues. Although seekers for the baptism in the Spirit at San Antonio, therefore, were not looking for tongues, when the outpouring came, seekers burst forth in other tongues, just as had happened elsewhere in the Great Revival. D. C. O. Opperman and L. C. Hall were among those who received the Pentecostal experience in the San Antonio awakening. Such "test cases" as this helped to confirm the worth of the "initial physical evidence" view among the early Pentecostals.[9]

No serious question erupted within the Pentecostal Movement over the initial evidence doctrine for 10 years. Even the very mild, moderate view of the Christian and Missionary Alliance precipitated wholesale defection to the Pentecostal camp. It was not until F. F. Bosworth, a highly respected, influential Pentecostal minister, challenged the doctrine that a genuine issue appeared, finally reaching the floor of the General Council in 1918.

As a young man in Zion City, Illinois, he had witnessed Marie Burgess (later Mrs. Robert Brown) receive such a remarkable infilling that he himself became so hungry that he, too, received that same night. The hand of God was upon him from the first. Bosworth was a sweet-spirited man, an avid student of the Scriptures, an eloquent

---

[9] *Ibid.*, pp. 216-17. A similar episode occurred in Pittsburgh, Pennsylvania, in 1921. An undenominational Bible school being conducted by Dr. Charles Pridgeon along the lines of teaching common to the Christian and Missionary Alliance became the scene of a tremendous revival. Pridgeon had gone to Dayton, Ohio, in the winter of 1920 to hear Aimee Semple MacPherson, who had invited ministers from all over the Midwest to see the power of God at work. She invited the ministers to assist her in praying for the sick. Pridgeon felt that he had received the fullness of the Spirit already, but when he came away from the MacPherson meetings, he was shaken. The school was closed to any who were attending Pentecostal meetings, or who professed the Pentecostal experience, so that a true test case might be demonstrated in Pittsburgh. Nightly "tarrying" meetings were conducted within the student body, except on Sunday nights when evangelistic meetings were held in the city. In the first week of April, a young business woman received the Pentecostal experience, evidenced by speaking in tongues. "This fine intelligent, young lady subsequently severed her business connections, attended Bible classes as a day student. She received a definite call to China as a missionary where she spent years of her life winning lost souls to Christ. Prayer for Revival was answered in many ways. A conservative estimate of those who received the baptism of the Holy Spirit was well over fifteen hundred in a two or three year period" (excerpt from a letter to the author from his mother, Mrs. W. E. Menzies, March 23, 1970). The author's mother was a student in the "Pittsburgh Bible Institute" at the time of the Great Revival, and the author's father was converted to Christ and received the baptism in the Holy Spirit in the revival, Easter Sunday, 1922.

speaker, and his healing ministry was outstanding. He had suffered for his Pentecostal testimony, and once was so destitute that he had been forced to gather gleanings from grain cars for food, and once was taken by a mob and tarred and feathered.[10]

Bosworth had been at the first Council in Hot Springs. He had served as an executive presbyter. As late as 1914 he was still evidently in solid agreement with the traditional Pentecostal view on the initial evidence. However, doubts began to appear.

His study of the lives and ministries of great men of God who had not spoken in tongues made him wonder about the correctness of the Pentecostal position. The shallow experience of some Pentecostal people seems to have been a major stumbling block, too.[11]

Apparently, too, he overreacted against the results of his own rather mechanical approach to seekers after the baptism in the Spirit. He ridiculed the idea of "tarrying" for the baptism, encouraging faith for immediate reception. Although there is great truth in this, for some it tended to be more an inducement to obtain a "tongues experience" than to be genuinely filled with the Spirit. Evidently some experienced some kind of motor phenomenon, possibly generated by hysteria or autosuggestion, but without really receiving the infilling of the Holy Spirit. It might have been salutary if Acts 2:4 had been thoroughly reexamined, with a fresh recasting of priorities according to the scriptural pattern. The infilling of the Spirit is *prior* to tongues, not the effect. It is perhaps because Bosworth was disappointed in the results of getting so many candidates to "speak with tongues" in this rather mechanical approach that he backed away from evidential tongues altogether.[12]

Bosworth adopted the view that tongues is but *one* evidence of the baptism in the Holy Spirit, a view quite similar to that which the Christian and Missionary Alliance had adopted in 1908. He disparaged the distinction Pentecostals had made between "evidential tongues" (Acts 2) and the "gift of tongues" (1 Corinthians 12-14), contending that *any* manifestation of the Spirit was sufficient evidence

[10]Brumback, *op. cit.*, p. 217.
[11]*Ibid.*, pp. 217-18.
[12]*Ibid.*, pp. 218-19.

of the Spirit's baptism. That Bosworth held such views was not in itself a serious problem to the young movement. But, he was not content to entertain such views quietly. He was a persuasive speaker, a forceful personality. First, in private argument he won three friends to his position, W. T. Gaston, M. M. Pinson, and A. P. Collins. Encouraged with this success, Bosworth began to proclaim his views publicly, both from the pulpit and by pen.[13]

During 1917, as Bosworth's views became more broadly publicized, letters of protest bombarded the executive offices in Springfield, challenging the propriety of his position. In spite of great reluctance by the executive brethren to institute any action on the matter, the controversy had reached such proportions that in the Council meeting of 1917, in St. Louis, a resolution was adopted denying credentials to any missionary who would not subscribe to the Statement of Fundamental Truths, the stated reason for the resolution being that some had called into question the doctrine of the initial physical evidence.[14]

During the course of the next year, a kind of informal debate ensued, with occasional articles on the subject appearing in the *Christian Evangel.* In the meantime, Bosworth was busy proclaiming his views, rallying some support for his position, just how much no one knew. The result of this agitation was that by late summer, 1918, it was announced that at the forthcoming General Council, to be held in Springfield, Missouri, in September, all the major doctrines of the fellowship would be openly discussed.[15] By this time Bosworth was aware that he had alienated himself from the Assemblies of God to such an extent that, out of a desire not to create embarrassment to the officials, he submitted his resignation, turning in his credentials on July 24.[16]

THE PROBLEM IS RESOLVED

The central issue of the 1918 Council was the initial evidence controversy. Vigorous debate occupied the central

[13]*Ibid.*, pp. 219-20.
[14]*Ibid.*, p. 220.
[15]*Christian Evangel*, August 24, 1918, and Brumback, *op. cit.*, p. 220.
[16]Brumback, *op. cit.*, p. 221.

stage of the Council, although in spite of the heat generated by the issue a spirit of courtesy and consideration governed the meetings. Robert Brown, Joseph Tunmore, J. T. Boddy, T. K. Leonard, W. H. Pope, and others spoke in defense of the traditional Pentecostal position, while W. T. Gaston and M. M. Pinson raised questions in behalf of the opposition. Bosworth was granted the courtesy of speaking from the floor, although he no longer was officially a member of the General Council fellowship. He was gracious enough not to seek to press his views on the Council, but did not retreat from his stated convictions. The issue was resolved by the wisdom and eloquence of D. W. Kerr, perhaps more than any other.

> Kerr not only marshalled all the truths presented by his brethren, but also drove home again and again that it is the Word of God, not the experiences of famous men, that is the touchstone for the Pentecostal belief concerning the immediate, outward evidence of the Baptism. The Scriptural record had not been twisted by Pentecostalists; no isolated case had been set forth as the sole basis for their belief; but in every case in which the results of the experience in Acts are recorded, each recipient spoke in tongues. Kerr also succeeded in answering conclusively Gaston's query about the difference between the evidence and the gift.[17]

Upon the conclusion of Kerr's able summarization, a firm resolution was presented to the Council:

> Resolved, That this Council considers it a serious disagreement with the Fundamentals for any minister among us to teach contrary to our distinctive testimony that the baptism of the Holy Spirit is regularly accompanied by the initial physical sign of speaking in other tongues as the Spirit of God gives the utterance, and that we consider it inconsistent and unscriptural for any minister to hold credentials with us who thus attacks as error our distinctive testimony.[18]

The resolution was adopted unanimously, all opposition being swept before it!

Bosworth, a gracious gentleman, accepted the decisive action of the 1918 Council, and departed with the good wishes and friendship of the Council, to take up his long association with the Christian and Missionary Alliance. His loss was felt keenly by the Assemblies of God, but he took

[17]*Ibid.*, pp. 222-23.
[18]General Council minutes, 1918, p. 8.

virtually no others with him. M. M. Pinson, A. P. Collins, and others who had been swayed, reaffirmed their allegiance to Council doctrine after the decision of the 1918 Council.[19]

Following the 1918 Council, Bosworth set down his crystallized ideas on the tongues controversy in a pamphlet, "Do All Speak with Tongues?" Although the pamphlet was given wide distribution for many years, there is no evidence that it caused more than a ripple in Assemblies of God circles. The controversy appears to have been ended decisively by the 1918 General Council. Bosworth, however, stoutly maintained his position throughout life.[20] He was mightily used of God in great healing campaigns for many years. Demonstrating the cordiality that existed between Bosworth and his former colleagues, Bosworth sometimes joined hands with Pentecostals in the conducting of great areawide revival crusades.

The 1918 Council is significant, not alone for the resolving of a potentially devastating crisis, but also for the principles upon which the solution was based. The authority of Scripture transcended sentiment. Out of conviction grounded in the Bible, the Council resolved a strategic matter of doctrine, rather than permitting the desire for harmony to override what was felt to be more than a peripheral matter. It was not mere sectarian narrowness that required clarity on the point of the initial physical evidence. The delegates felt that they were contending for the preservation of doctrine basic to a full-orbed New Testament church, without which the church would be immeasurably impoverished. That such firmness on an issue felt to be so urgent could be arrived at in the midst of openness of discussion, patience, and kindness, demonstrates that the embryonic fellowship, now but four years old, was already reaching a winsome level of maturity. "Truth held in love" could well be the appellation appropriate to the strategic General Council of 1918.

Early Missionary Program

Foreign missions had been one of the primary reasons

[19]Brumback, *op. cit.*, p. 224.

[20]Letter to the author from Mrs. F. F. Bosworth, February 3, 1953.

for the establishment of the Assemblies of God. So much money was being received and disbursed through the headquarters that it became too large a task for the Executive Presbytery to continue to handle unaided. In 1916, $4,879 had been received for forwarding to the field. By 1917 the amount had climbed to $10,223 and in 1918, $29,630 had come to headquarters for missions.[21] Just 15 missionaries had been listed in the 1914 roster, but by 1918 the number had climbed to 73, distributed in 14 different countries, including Alaska.[22] In 1919, to meet the growing need, J. Roswell Flower was appointed to fill a newly created post, Missionary Secretary.[23]

Need for a policy to govern the selection and appointment of Council-endorsed missionaries became apparent quite early. Such a policy was adopted at the 1921 General Council, although each missionary was still strictly on his own to secure what support he could muster from local churches and individuals.[24] The General Council did agree to disburse what funds were sent in; it did not endeavor to promise anything beyond this to those on the field. A resolution adopted in 1920 points to the strong dependence on faith in God in matters financial, for all missionaries were encouraged "to look to God alone for their needs."[25]

THE MISSIONS DEPARTMENT ESTABLISHED

A momentous act was the institution of the "Missionary Department" in 1925. It is significant that the first separate department established within the structure of the denomination was designed to expedite the work of missions. It would be many more years before any other specialized department or agency would be created.

In 1926 a young English missionary came to Springfield to assist in the department. Noel Perkin, tall, slender, and soft-spoken, quickly demonstrated his skill in management and his vision for the work of God. In 1927 this able young immigrant was appointed Missionary Secretary, a strategic

[21]General Council minutes, 1918, p. 4.

[22]Noel Perkin and John Garlock, *Our World Witness* (Springfield, Missouri: Gospel Publishing House, 1963), p. 29.

[23]General Council minutes, 1919, p. 19.

[24]General Council minutes, 1921, p. 61.

[25]General Council minutes, 1920, p. 42.

post he faithfully filled until his retirement in 1959. His long and capable tenure added much to the stability and depth of the Assemblies of God missionary endeavor during the formative years of the fellowship. His years of service span monumental world crises and cultural changes that have necessitated dramatic shifts in missions strategy. Typical of the leadership Perkin gave to the missions program of the Assemblies of God was his foresight in gathering missionaries together long before the end of World War II to map a campaign for the postwar world.

One of the important devices at the disposal of the youthful movement for the advancing of the cause of world evangelism was the printed page.

The Coordination of Publications

The weekly denominational organs, *Word and Witness* and the *Christian Evangel,* had a combined circulation of 25,000 at the outset of the organization of the Assemblies of God. In 1918, it was decided that *Word and Witness,* the monthly originally developed by Pinson and Bell, be discontinued, with the *Christian Evangel,* the paper Flower founded, a weekly, becoming the sole official publication of the Assemblies of God. Its name was changed to the *Weekly Evangel,* and shortly afterward, to its present title, *The Pentecostal Evangel.*[26]

From 1915 to 1919, J. W. Welch served in the dual capacity of Chairman of the fellowship and Editor, as well. Welch, however, did not feel that he had sufficient writing talent to do justice to that position. In 1916, Stanley Howard Frodsham, a young Englishman who had received the Pentecostal experience in the great revival at Sunderland in northern England in 1908, was approached by Welch to serve as an editorial aide. Frodsham had submitted several articles to *The Pentecostal Evangel,* but none had been published. Welch wrote to Frodsham, then pastoring a small work in California, "I read those three articles; they will be published later. They asked me to be editor of the

---

[26]General Council minutes, 1919, p. 24. This change was precipitated by the initial evidence controversy, a desire being expressed to speak out with conviction for the distinctiveness of the Pentecostal position.

Evangel, but I'm a misfit. We're praying for God's man for the *Evangel.* Are you that man? Will you come to the next Council meeting, starting October 1, 1916?"[27] "I was elected to serve as General Secretary of the Assemblies of God at my first visit to the General Council, many of the men there never having laid eyes on me previously," he reports whimsically. He held the position of General Secretary for three years, from 1916 to 1919, and for five years, from 1916 until 1921, he also served as an assistant to the Editor of *The Pentecostal Evangel.* In 1919, J. T. Boddy was elected to the post of Editor, but a terminal illness prevented him from fulfilling his duties, Frodsham, his assistant, practically covering his responsibilities for the last year of his term. In 1921, Frodsham was elected to the position of editorship of *The Pentecostal Evangel,* serving with distinction for nearly 30 years, until his retirement late in 1948. This long tenure was another important stabilizing force in the young movement.

Early Leaders

There were relatively few changes in leadership in the formative years of the Assemblies of God. The first Chairman of the General Council was 48-year old Eudorus N. Bell. Bell was one of the few well-educated men in the early days of the Pentecostal revival. Although he came from very humble surroundings in his native Florida, he succeeded in working his way through Stetson University in De Land. He went on to the Southern Baptist Seminary in Louisville, Kentucky. Upon graduation from seminary, the ambitious, scholarly young minister spent an additional three years in postgraduate work at the University of Chicago, before launching into a 17-year-long career as a pastor of Southern Baptist churches, chiefly in Texas. When he received the Pentecostal experience, he was disfellowshiped from his parent denomination, subsequently becoming a key instrument in the organization of the Assemblies of God, being elected to its highest office at the first Council in 1914. Bell was deliberate, thoughtful, an able articulator of Pentecostal issues. His insight and maturity were im-

[27]Interview with Stanley H. Frodsham, September 22, 1967.

portant factors in creating a climate in which the exuberant young fellowship could come to a proper birth.[28]

A tower of strength in the turbulent years of its greatest crisis was John W. Welch, who served as Chairman from 1915 to 1920. "Daddy" Welch, as his colleagues affectionately called him, had received the Pentecostal experience in 1910 in Muskogee, Oklahoma, where he had been conducting a revival on behalf of his parent denomination, the Christian and Missionary Alliance. While he was in Muskogee, a band of Pentecostal preachers led by A. B. Cox visited the community and succeeded in convincing Welch that he needed the Pentecostal experience. Within a few months, Welch had received the baptism in the Holy Spirit, and was soon in demand as a preacher in the Pentecostal world. He had been a lay worker in the state of New York for many years, opening Sunday schools for the American Sunday School Union, and conducting street meetings and mission services. While attending the Missionary Training Institute in Nyack, Welch, now 40 years of age, finally submitted to ordination, although he still insisted that he was too poorly qualified for such a high honor! Because of his more mature years, he generated the type of father image the burgeoning Pentecostal Movement so sorely needed, for most of the early Pentecostalists were surprisingly youthful. Noted for the strength of his convictions, his wisdom, and his impeccable integrity, Welch provided a strong, steadying influence on the Assemblies of God in its earliest years.[29]

At the 1920 Council, Secretary E. N. Bell and Chairman Welch exchanged positions. Welch resumed the office of Chairman in 1923 at the untimely death of Bell.

In 1925, W. T. Gaston was elected Chairman, serving two terms, until E. S. Williams assumed the office in 1929.[30] W. T. Gaston, tall and commanding in presence, filled a most important role, for it was during his administration that the General Council moved from a loosely operated

---

[28]Brumback, *op. cit.*, pp. 164-65.

[29]*Ibid.*, pp. 165-67.

[30]In 1921 it was decided to hold General Council sessions biennially thereafter. Office terms were therefore lengthened to two years.

fellowship to the formal adoption of a constitution. These were turbulent years, and it took one with the magnetism and leadership of such a man to hold the ship steady. A friendly person, broad in sympathy, Gaston was a skillful administrator who ably performed a most useful role. Arkansas can be proud of this son who contributed so much to the Assemblies of God.[31]

No man has been more intimately associated with the Assemblies of God than J. Roswell Flower, nor has served so long in positions of leadership. Flower was only 26 years old when the first General Council was held, the youngest of the leading lights in the early organization of the fellowship. Following his conversion in 1907, and his Pentecostal baptism two years later, Flower was ordained by D. W. Myland, receiving credentials from Myland's "World's Faith Missionary Association." This onetime law student pastored a mission in Indianapolis for a time, and also began the publication of a Pentecostal paper, the first weekly produced in the new movement. Flower's literary skill and his organizational ability admirably suited him for the position of General Secretary which he was to hold for a total of 27 years (1914-16) and (1935-1959). He served in a wide variety of ministerial posts in addition to his executive responsibilities at the headquarters offices. He served the Eastern District in every office on the district level, distinguishing himself for his able leadership during the decades of the twenties and the thirties, finally being recalled to Springfield for national office once again. He served as Missionary Secretary of the denomination from 1919 to 1925. Although he never was elected General Superintendent, his long and able influence on the affairs of the fellowship was deeply felt over the amazing span of more than fifty years! Flower had the distinction of being the only man who attended every General Council from 1914 to 1965, a period of over half a century! To many, this slight, alert, and forthright man of God was "Mr. Pentecost." Not the least of his contributions was his farsighted role in encouraging the Assemblies of God to

[31]Interview with J. Roswell Flower, March 25, 1970.

entertain dialogue with the evangelical world when overtures were made to the Pentecostals during the decade of the 1940's. He, perhaps more than any other single man, bridged that gap, helping to lead the Pentecostal Movement out of isolation.

It was through the inspiration and vision of such godly men that the Assemblies of God came through some of its most difficult and trying days. During the formative years, there were not only controversies to be resolved, workable missionary structures to be hammered out, but also there were great domestic educational and evangelistic needs to be met.

Christian Education

It had been one of the original purposes cited in the call to Hot Springs that conservation of the fellowship be provided for. Sunday schools were one means to this end, but it was not until the 1930's, and especially in the 1940's, that this phase of the work would blossom so dramatically. However, as early as 1919, Sunday school literature was being produced by the Gospel Publishing House. E. N. Bell wrote the first adult and intermediate level quarterlies. Mrs. J. Roswell Flower wrote the quarterlies for juniors and primaries. These early materials were supplemented in 1921 by a Sunday school take-home paper for children entitled *Our Pentecostal Boys and Girls.* By 1924 the Gospel Publishing House was advertising "a complete line of Sunday school literature." The combined circulation of Gospel Publishing House materials had reached 8,000,000 pieces annually by 1927.[32]

ESTABLISHMENT OF EARLY SCHOOLS

In the convention call to Hot Springs, one of the specific concerns mentioned was a "general Bible Training School, with a literary department."[33] Already at least ten Pentecostal Bible schools were in existence by 1914.[34] Most of these were in connection with local churches, and were at best informal in nature, designed to meet the basic needs

[32]"Development of Assemblies of God Literature," undated manuscript in Assemblies of God headquarters archives.

[33]General Council minutes, 1920, p. 43.

[34]Kendrick, *op. cit.*, p. 129.

of a constituency largely devoid of extensive formal education. At the first General Council, two schools were acknowledged and their support was encouraged, one of them being apparently a rough equivalent to a parochial grammar school, operated by R. B. Chisolm near Union, Mississippi. The other was the Gospel School of T. K. Leonard at Findlay, Ohio, which was designed for the preparation of Christian workers.

One of the most important early schools which had a most significant impact on the Assemblies of God was the Rochester Bible Training School, founded in 1895 by a Methodist minister, James Duncan. This school was operated in connection with the "Elim Faith Home" in Rochester, New York. During the early part of the Pentecostal revival, the Rochester school became a strong, independent, Pentecostal revival center, noted for inculcating a love for the Bible, a profound practical faith for the supply of daily needs, and a sacrificial spirit. Following the demise of the Rev. Duncan, his daughters continued to operate the Faith home and school. Although never more than 40 students were enrolled, this small school furnished the training for an impressive array of Assemblies of God leaders, including Ralph M. Riggs, Gayle F. Lewis, Charles W. H. Scott, Wilfred A. Brown, and Noel Perkin. Other distinguished alumni include J. Z. Kamerer, longtime general manager of the Gospel Publishing House, and missionaries Harry Waggoner, Jacob Mueller, Mrs. Nicholas Nikoloff, and Elsie Blattner. A gifted Bible teacher who ministered at Elim for a time was the godly John Wright Follette, whose devotional writings and spiritual pulpit ministry blessed the Pentecostal Movement for many years.[35]

Among some of the other early schools, which did not have a permanent character, was T. K. Leonard's Gospel School in Findlay, Ohio. In 1917 this school was merged with Andrew Fraser's Mount Tabor Bible School, conducted at Bethel Temple in Chicago. From 1912 to 1914, D. Wesley Myland and J. Roswell Flower maintained Gibeah Bible School in Plainfield, Indiana. Flem Van Meter

---

[35]Brumback, *op. cit.*, pp. 228-31.

and Fred Vogler assisted in the Gibeah enterprise.[86]

Another early school that made a great contribution to the youthful Assemblies of God fellowship was Bethel Bible Institute of Newark, New Jersey. This school was organized in 1916 by Allan Swift, pastor of Bethel Pentecostal Tabernacle in Newark, and two associates, Christian Lucas of Ossining, New York, and Minnie Draper, a prominent woman in the Christian and Missionary Alliance until her Pentecostal experience. W. W. Simpson, another CMA product, longtime missionary to China, was selected to serve as the principal of this school, which was dedicated to the training of ministers and missionaries. In 1918, when Simpson returned to China, Frank M. Boyd was asked to assume the office of principal, a post he held until 1923, when he left to accept a similar position at the new school in Springfield, Central Bible Institute. When Boyd left, William I. Evans became principal, holding that office until 1929, when Bethel was merged with Central Bible Institute in Springfield. It is interesting to note that all the men who served as leaders of "Bethel" were products of the Christian and Missionary Alliance. For many years Frank Boyd and William Evans served with distinction in the realm of Assemblies of God education, as writers, teachers, administrators, and camp meeting speakers. The impact of their lives on generations of Assemblies of God young people can hardly be measured adequately. At old "Bethel," and later at Central Bible Institute, literally hundreds of ministers and missionaries who have scattered to the ends of the earth have sat under the inspirational teaching and exhortation of such godly men as these. Someone has aptly said, "Central Bible Institute is the lengthened shadow of William Evans." A picture was taken on one occasion of four generations of Assemblies of God ministry: Frank Boyd, with his student Arthur Graves, next to his protege, Cordas C. Burnett, and lastly, Burnett's student, G. W. Hardcastle II!

A very early school in the East was Beulah Heights Missionary Training School, established in connection with a local church in North Bergen, New Jersey, in 1911. One

---

[86] *Ibid.*, pp. 226-28.

of the early leaders was E. L. Whitcomb. This school, never large, did maintain its existence for many years. In 1941 the name was changed to Metropolitan Bible Institute. Stanley Horton, famed Bible teacher and writer in the Assemblies of God, began his teaching career at this institution.[37]

On the West Coast, an early enterprise was the Pacific Bible and Missionary Training School at San Francisco. The 1919 General Council endorsed this school for those wishing ministerial preparation.[38] This school actually began as a class for new converts in the mission operated by Robert Craig. More elaborate facilities were secured, and the name of the school was changed to Glad Tidings Bible Institute. D. W. Kerr, Willard Peirce, J. Narver Gortner, J. Wesley Cooksey, T. J. Jones, and Leland Keys contributed much to the stature of the faculty of Glad Tidings. Later the school was moved to a lovely wooded acreage in the Redwoods country near Santa Cruz. At that time the name of the school was changed to Bethany Bible College. One of the early pioneers in the new field of radio, Glad Tidings instituted its own radio broadcast station in 1925, beaming the gospel over metropolitan San Francisco via KGTT.[39]

The earliest beginnings of what today is a fully accredited four-year liberal arts college, Southern California College, go back as far as 1921. While D. W. Kerr was at San Francisco, Harold K. Needham, pastor in Los Angeles, invited Kerr to launch a small Bible institute in the Southern California area. He offered the use of his home in Highland Park for that purpose. Bethel Temple of Los Angeles, pastored by G. N. Eldridge, helped to support the infant school. At first, Southern California Bible School was a summer school, enrolling about 30 students the first term. By 1923 the enrollment had climbed to 70 students. Later, men like John Wright Follette, Frank M. Boyd, and Irvine J. Harrison joined the faculty, contributing to the grow-

---

[37]Millard E. Collins, "Establishing and Financing of Higher Educational Institutions in the Church Body of the Assemblies of God in the U.S.A." (unpublished manuscript), pp. 45-46.

[38]General Council minutes, 1919, p. 23.

[39]Brumback, *op. cit.*, pp. 233-34.

ing stature of that outstanding citadel of learning.[40]

One other school that had early roots on the West Coast was the Berean Bible School, located in San Diego. This school, begun in 1923, closed its doors during World War II. An interesting feature of that school was its ministry to Latin Americans. Mrs. Alice Luce had begun a school in Los Angeles to minister to the Spanish-speaking people of the area in 1926. Her school was affiliated with the Berean Bible School, but after some years it was discontinued for lack of financial support.

At the same time that Mrs. Luce was launching her Latin-American school in Los Angeles, H. C. Ball engaged in a similar effort in San Antonio, Texas. Ball's Latin-American Bible School graduated its first students in 1928. Later that institution moved to Ysleta, Texas, where it continued under the direction of Kenzy Savage.[41]

P. C. Nelson, a former Baptist minister from Detroit, organized what became known as Southwestern Bible School at Enid, Oklahoma, in 1927. Brother Nelson is fondly remembered by many as one of the great scholars and educators of the Assemblies of God. Four years later, in Amarillo, Texas, Guy Shields founded another Bible school to serve the great Southwest. His school was named Shield of Faith Bible School. This institution included in its offerings an elementary and high school department, as well as a college-level program. Raymond T. Richey established Southern Bible College at Goose Creek, Texas, at about the same time. A series of mergers brought these institutions together, so that by 1941 one institution remained. Located at Fort Worth, the resulting school was named Southwestern Bible Institute. Two years later it moved to its present location, Waxahachie, Texas, about thirty miles from Dallas.[42]

A NATIONAL SCHOOL

It was in 1920 that the first Bible school was actually

---

[40]*Ibid.*, pp. 234-35.

[41]Collins, *op. cit.*, p. 54.

[42]Irvine J. Harrison, "A History of the Assemblies of God" (unpublished Th.D. dissertation, Berkeley Baptist Divinity School, 1954), p. 173; Brumback, *op. cit.*, p. 279; and the Bulletin of Southwestern Assemblies of God College, 1968-69, p. 14.

established by the Assemblies of God.[43] The new school, to be located at Auburn, Nebraska, lasted but one year. S. A. Jamieson was chosen to be the principal. It closed its doors in the spring of 1921. The Midwest Bible School, as it was named, was operated on a "faith" basis, with faculty salaries and other expenses cared for from freewill offerings, largely unsolicited.

This feeble effort may serve to indicate something of the lack of academic sophistication characteristic of the movement in those years. Many laymen who received the Baptism in those days received with that experience a call to preach. It was common practice for such enthusiastic witnesses to drop their secular employment and to launch out into the work without any formal preparation at all. Some did surprisingly well; others found themselves in difficulty. Some ridiculed the idea of the need for careful training; others quickly saw the need for guidance. A great fear common among Pentecostals in those days, and persisting for many years, was that education would produce carnal pride, and that if workers prided themselves in their own knowledge they would be less prone to depend on the operation of the Holy Spirit. This fear was not entirely unfounded, for it had not been so many years earlier that the great denominations had been infiltrated with Modernism, largely through seminaries which had become seedbeds of doubt. It had been the products of such checkered schools that had cast out many of the Pentecostal preachers from their midst. The memory was still fresh! And so it was that a kind of ambivalence developed; they felt need for solid, Biblical training for prospective Christian workers and at the same time a deep-seated fear of intellectualism.

In spite of the debacle at Auburn, however, a second attempt was made to establish a Bible school, this time on a more substantial basis. In 1921 the basement of Central Assembly in Springfield, Missouri, was remodeled for classrooms, dining room, kitchen, and offices. In the fall of 1922, Central Bible Institute opened its doors, with D. W. Kerr serving as the first principal and his son-in-law, Willard

---

[43]General Council minutes, 1920, p. 43.

Peirce, serving as an assistant. Approximately 40 students enrolled that first term. The school filled such an obvious need and grew so rapidly that it taxed the limited facilities at Central Assembly. A large, wooded tract of land north of the city was donated for a permanent school. The first building was erected and occupied in 1924. One hundred and six students enrolled that year.[44]

COORDINATION AND RECOGNITION OF SCHOOL

Meanwhile, in addition to Central Bible Institute, which was the only school actually owned and operated by the General Council, recognition was being extended to other institutions. By 1921 half a dozen schools, three in the Metropolitan East, two on the West Coast, and the ill-fated Nebraska school, had been granted General Council endorsement.[45] Steps were taken to coordinate the variety of programs being offered in the schools. At the 1923 General Council the Executive Presbytery was appointed to serve as a Bible school commission, with the charge that they supervise the schools and "effect as great a degree of standardization among the schools as possible."[46] A further step in this direction was taken at the 1925 Council with the request of the Executive Presbytery for representation on each of the governing boards of the schools, and the declaration that all schools whose work corresponded favorably with that given at Central Bible Institute should be considered equal to it.[47]

Through the accelerated printed ministries of the Gospel Publishing House and the development of a workable training program for ministerial and missionary candidates, the infant organization was well on its way to making a vigorous impact on both the domestic and foreign scene. It is hard to believe that this rapidly growing movement still was operating without a formal constitution when the 1927 Council opened.

A Constitution Is Adopted

As a final step in the formative phase of the Assemblies

---

[44]Harrison, *op. cit.*, p. 173.
[45]*Ibid.*, p. 172.
[46]General Council minutes, 1923, pp. 58-59.
[47]General Council minutes, 1925, pp. 36-37.

of God development, the heterogeneous collection of resolutions that had accumulated through the years was categorized into the orderly form of a constitution. This move did not occur without a storm of protest, however. There still lingered a horror of ecclesiasticism, from which many of the Pentecostals felt they had been emancipated. It was at the Eureka Springs, Arkansas, General Council of 1925 that J. W. Welch and J. Roswell Flower offered a recommendation that the accumulated resolutions be redrawn and codified into the form of a constitution. Such reaction erupted at the suggestion that neither was reelected! "Daddy" Welch assumed a pastorate in California, the chairmanship of the Assemblies of God passing to W. T. Gaston. The next ten years J. R. Flower spent in giving invaluable leadership to the Eastern District of the Assemblies of God.

By the time of the following Council, which met in Springfield, Missouri, in the fall of 1927, the heat had largely subsided from the controversy. The very same proposal, that a constitution be adopted, was presented again, but this time, in the short space of but two years, it was adopted—and it was by a unanimous vote![48] One of the changes wrought by this action was the substitution of the term "General Superintendent" for "Chairman" to designate the chief executive of the fellowship. For all practical purposes, the formative phase of the General Council of the Assemblies of God came to an end with the adoption of the constitution in September, 1927.

---

[48]General Council minutes, 1927, p. 73.

8

The Tranquil Time [1927-1941]

A Decade of Depression—Rapid Growth in the "Storefront" Era—Decisions During the Depression—Some of Those God Used

With roots deep in 19th-century revivalism, the Pentecostal Movement sprang into being early in the new century. Some Holiness bodies accepted Pentecostalism, but most of the newly formed congregations were quite independent, a few loose associations evolving in some regions to provide limited cohesion. Ostracism from the larger church world and internal problems evoked the call for a stronger federation. The Assemblies of God came into being reluctantly, but once created, soon achieved the posture of being the leading instrument through which the American Pentecostal revival was to be preserved. On one side stood the regional Holiness bodies; on the other, small independent-minded congregations and specialized associations. Drawing on a much more representative base than any of the other Pentecostal groups, the Assemblies of God quite early developed the image of being more or less the mainstream of the Pentecostal revival in the United States. Following the initial shock wave of the New Issue crisis, adherents were attracted rapidly from all parts of the country. By 1927, the basic character of the movement had been set, and it was gaining numerical strength swiftly.

A Decade of Depression

The years from 1927 to 1941 were years of relative tranquility for the Assemblies of God. The accession of Ernest

S. Williams to the office of General Superintendent in 1929 marked the beginning of an administration that was to last for 20 years, symbolizing the stability and harmony of the period. The denomination was relatively untroubled by internal conflict, and, isolated from the larger church world, forged ahead quite apart from the struggles afflicting the more traditional American churches. For example, the tremendous upheaval occasioned by the Fundamentalist-Modernist debate which rent the unity of several of the great denominations held but little concern for the Pentecostals. Few important changes were made in policy or structure. It was a period of "undifferentiated growth."

The mood of the "Roaring Twenties" in the United States was dramatically altered by the economic panic that began in 1929, ushering in the Great Depression. About the same time, the last strongholds of Fundamentalism were falling to the heavy artillery of Modernism in the great denominations. Theological barrenness in many of the great American churches during the ordeal of the Great Depression seemed to result in a distressing inability of these religious bodies to meet the needs of a sizable portion of the distraught populace.[1] The enrollment in American Sunday schools declined, and so did church membership in the larger denominations. Into this vacuum flowed the smaller revivalistic sects, including the Assemblies of God.[2] Symbolic of the stark contrast in growth rate were the numerous church buildings across the country, abandoned by the standard denominations, but eagerly purchased by the Pentecostals and relabeled "Full Gospel Tabernacles." To these were added countless storefront missions and roughly built temporary tabernacles, frequently boasting little more than sawdust floors. Many a family, bruised and wearied by the devastating Depression, found new hope and life in these "glory barns." The power of the living Christ to meet the needs of suffering humanity for them was intensely

---

[1]H. Shelton Smith, R. T. Handy, and Lefferts A. Loetscher, *American Christianity* (New York: Charles Scribner's Sons, 1963), II, p. 419.

[2]Samuel C. Kincheloe, *Research Memorandum on Religion in the Depression* (New York: Social Science Research Council, 1937), Bulletin 33. This volume points out the comparative vigor of the sects with respect to the traditional denominations. See pp. 136-37.

real. In this terrible decade of depression, sparkling stories of remarkable revivals punctuate the pages of Pentecostal history.

Rapid Growth in the "Storefront" Era

The domestic growth of the Assemblies of God during the 1930's was nothing short of phenomenal. It came about chiefly through intensive evangelism, but also by accessions to the fellowship of previously independent congregations that chose to identify with the Assemblies of God. In 1927 there were 1,353 churches, 72,143 members, and 1,457 ordained ministers in the Assemblies of God. Just six years later, in the General Superintendent's report at the 1933 General Council in Philadelphia, he stated that the membership total of 136,705 represented a net gain of 35 percent in just the previous biennium![3] Two years later, Superintendent Williams reported that there were now 2,606 ordained ministers (a gain of 25 percent in just one biennium), 3,149 assemblies (a gain of 23 percent) and 166,118 members (a gain of 22 percent).[4] In 1937, 10 years after the adoption of the Constitution, there were 3,086 ministers, 3,473 assemblies, and a membership of 175,362.[5] The 1939 statistics reveal that the Assemblies of God had a membership of 184,022, with an active constituency estimated at a quarter of a million.[6] In the intervening biennium, there were 470 new churches begun through home missions activity, 50 of these alone in the Southern Missouri District, 46 in Texas, 45 in the Central District, 37 in Oregon, and 31 in Arkansas. A striking indication of the prodigious growth in these years is the 1939 report on the opening of new Sunday schools. In the two years covered in that report, 2,080 schools were started![7] At the close of the period under study, 1941, the ministerial roll had climbed to 4,159, a gain of 15 percent over the previous biennial report, and a gain of 285 percent over the 1927 figure! The number of churches had grown to 4,348, a gain of 24 percent in the

[3]General Council minutes, 1933, p. 49.
[4]General Council minutes, 1935, p. 54.
[5]General Council minutes, 1937, p. 87.
[6]General Council minutes, 1939, p. 68.
[7]*Ibid.*, p. 89.

biennium, and 321 percent since 1927. Membership had climbed by 1941 to 209,549, a 14 percent gain for the biennium, and 290 percent for the period under study![8]

Two particular reasons for the amazing growth of the Assemblies of God in these years were listed in the 1941 minutes of the General Council. Superintendent E. S. Williams pointed out that approximately 50 percent of all Bible school graduates were engaging in active Christian work. "It is known that 1200 graduates have entered the ministry in home fields and about 250 have entered foreign service."[9] A ready supply of workers being equipped for service seemed to be a major factor in this rapid occupation of new territory.

Another important factor in the development of the home base was the adoption of a world missions strategy. At first the Assemblies of God forwarded all funds denotated for the foreign field to the parties designated, with no provision for the maintenance of a missions office, nor of providing for domestic mission work. In 1926 a young missionary from Minnesota got an idea while sailing in a dugout canoe on Lake Kivu in eastern Belgian Congo. Young Arthur F. Berg conceived the notion that a portion of the undesignated funds received should be returned to the home district from whence the gifts came, so that new works could be encouraged at the home base. His rationale was simple: if there were more churches in the homeland, there would be more potential for foreign missions! On his return to Minnesota later that year, Berg succeeded in winning support for his idea in the North Central District. Using the imagery of a beehive, Berg's idea, now labeled the "Busy Bee Plan," quickly caught on. Henry H. Ness's church in Fargo, North Dakota, and Frank Lindquist's church, the Minneapolis Gospel Tabernacle, were the first churches to adopt the world missions program for giving. Small model beehives were distributed widely to promote the program. The result was a sudden acceleration in missionary giving. By 1929 the General Council was reporting that 18 districts

---

[8]General Council minutes, 1941, pp. 73-75.

[9]General Council minutes, 1939, pp. 48-49.

were cooperating with the Busy Bee Plan for church extension.

As a feature of the world missions concept, in addition to the Busy Bee Plan, the Executive Presbytery set up a "Church Extension Fund," according to the 1939 General Council minutes. This fund, established with the modest capital of $5,000, was to be made available to needy churches in amounts up to $300 to each congregation, for a nominal interest charge.

The work on foreign soil began with less spectacular growth during the period from 1927 to 1941, but it has since continued to accelerate at a rate greater than the domestic growth. In 1927 there were 277 missionaries serving in 17 countries and regions. The great majority of the missionaries were located in China, India, Japan, Africa, and Latin America. Giving for the fiscal biennium reported in 1927 amounted to $400,000.[10] The Great Depression made a mild dent in the pattern of missionary growth during the early 1930's. A staff of 259 missionaries was reported in 1933, with the following poignant commentary added: "Since the depression a conservative missionary policy has been necessary, and while no missionaries have been recalled because of shortage of funds, a number of new applicants for missionary appointment have been restrained from going forth."[11] Part of the problem seems to have been the rather limited base on which the foreign missions program was erected. "The trouble has been that 30% of our people have been doing almost our entire giving for Missions, the other 70% giving almost nothing."[12]

To stimulate interest in the foreign missions program, some of the personnel at the Springfield headquarters arranged for a series of missionary conventions during the winter of 1932-33. This methodology was so successful that the practice of encouraging missionary conventions throughout all the districts became a standard policy thereafter.[13] The tide had been turned, evidently, for

[10]General Council minutes, 1927, pp. 34, 48-49.

[11]General Council minutes, 1933, p. 53.

[12]*Ibid.*, p. 59.

[13]*Ibid.*

by the time of the 1935 General Council, the number of foreign missionaries had climbed to 287, and missionary giving was moving ahead without the restrictions lamented earlier.[14]

By 1937 there were 346 missionaries registered, serving in 34 fields. A total of $672,000 had been disbursed during the biennium, $41,000 of which was distributed without charge to non-Council missionaries.[15] Giving reached $1,000,000 for the first time in the biennium reported in 1941, and nearly 400 missionaries were on the field.[16]

During the 1930's the churches consistently at the top of the list of those contributing to world missions were: Glad Tidings Tabernacle, New York City; The Pentecostal Church, Cleveland, Ohio; Bethel Temple, Los Angeles, California; Highway Mission Tabernacle, Philadelphia, Pennsylvania; The Gospel Tabernacle, Minneapolis, Minnesota; The Pentecostal Tabernacle, Tacoma, Washington; The Assembly of God (Central), Springfield, Missouri; The First Pentecostal Church, Lancaster, Pennsylvania; and the Church of the Four Fold Gospel, Battle Creek, Michigan.

Decisions During the Depression

OFFICERS

There were relatively few personnel changes effected by General Council elections during the 1927-1941 era. The office of General Superintendent changed hands but once. In 1927 W. T. Gaston was reelected as General Superintendent, but in 1929 the General Council selected Ernest S. Williams to fill that post, a position he continued to hold until 1949.

Other decisions of the 1927 General Council included the selection of David H. McDowell as Assistant Superintendent, J. R. Evans as Secretary-Treasurer, and Harold H. Moss, Missionary Field Secretary. Two perennials, Noel Perkin and Stanley Frodsham, were elected to serve as Missionary Secretary and Editor of *The Pentecostal Evangel,* respectively. Throughout the entire period under consideration, these last two retained their positions.

[14] General Council minutes, 1935, p. 55.
[15] General Council minutes, 1937, p. 88.
[16] General Council minutes, 1941, p. 88.

The 1929 General Council, in addition to the change in the office of the General Superintendent, replaced David McDowell as Assistant Superintendent with a new man, J. R. Evans.

Two years later, at the 1931 Council in San Francisco, J. Roswell Flower was elected to serve as Assistant General Superintendent, an honorific position not requiring a move to Springfield from his pastorate in Pennsylvania. J. R. Evans was elected to fill the post of Secretary-Treasurer. The position of Missionary Field Secretary was dropped.

No changes occurred in 1933, all officers being returned to office. In 1935, with the retirement of J. R. Evans, J. R. Flower was elected to fill both the office of Assistant Superintendent and General Secretary-Treasurer. This action required Flower's move to Springfield from the Eastern District, where he had been serving as District Superintendent. Flower continued as General Secretary until his retirement in 1959.

At the 1937 General Council in Memphis, Fred Vogler, able home missions leader from Kansas, was elected to fill the office of Assistant General Superintendent, all other offices remaining intact. In 1939, all officers were reelected.

ISSUES

At the 1927 General Council, some sought to change the name of the fellowship to *The Pentecostal Evangelical Church,* a name that was felt to be more clearly descriptive of the distinctive position of the fellowship than the term Assemblies of God. It was agreed to defer action until the following Council session.[17] In spite of J. Narver Gortner's persuasive appeal, the 1929 Council decided to table the matter of a change of name indefinitely.[18]

The 1929 General Council increased the size of the Executive Presbytery from six to nine, six of whom were to be residents of Springfield.[19] Another structural change was effected in 1933, with the agreement that the manner of election of the General Presbytery and the composition of that body be altered. Previously considerable time had to be

[17]General Council minutes, 1927, p. 69.
[18]General Council minutes, 1929, p. 80.
[19]*Ibid.*

taken at the General Council sessions for the election of General Presbytery personnel by caucus of each district. Now it was agreed that by virtue of his office, the district superintendent should be accorded a place on the General Presbytery, and each district should elect two other representatives in a manner of their choosing, thus freeing the General Council from that time-consuming responsibility.

By the mid-thirties Sunday school enthusiasm was being reflected by the notices evident in the General Council minutes. A young minister, pastor of Central Assembly in Springfield, Missouri, was secured to give part-time service in the work of promoting Sunday schools. Superintendent E. S. Williams noted, regarding Ralph M. Riggs, "He has written a splendid book entitled 'A Successful Sunday School.' . . . Another remarkable book just recently published is that written by Myer Pearlman, entitled 'Successful Sunday School Teaching.' "[20] The 12-point standard for good Sunday schools recommended by the Sunday School Committee was enthusiastically endorsed in 1935.

The year 1937 was a momentous one. The growing need for oversight of the educational institutions that were now appearing in various parts of the country led to the adoption of a far-reaching resolution. A Department of Education was authorized, following the recommendation of the Committee on Institutions, chaired by Fred Vogler. It was then decided to combine the newly created department with the Home Missions portfolio, producing a Department of Home Missions and Education.[21] In addition to the schools that had already begun by 1927, five new ones appeared during the 1930's. These were Southwestern Bible Institute, of Waxahachie, Texas; Southeastern Bible Institute, Lakeland, Florida; Eastern Bible Institute, Green Lane, Pennsylvania; North Central Bible Institute, Minneapolis, Minnesota; and Northwest Bible Institute, Seattle, Washington. A host of willing workers poured from these schools during the Depression years, carrying the Pentecostal banner not

[20]General Council minutes, 1935, p. 61.

[21]General Council minutes, 1937, p. 61.

only to new fields at home, but manning an increasing proportion of the missionary posts until the day would come when 90 percent of the missionary force would be graduates of the Bible schools.[22]

The only theological ripple on the rather placid horizon of the 1930's appeared in the 1937 Council in Memphis. Some differences of opinion regarding eschatology had caused a minor degree of unrest, resulting in the adoption of the following resolution with respect to the "post-tribulation rapture view."

> Whereas, the General Council has declared itself in the Statement of Fundamental Truths that it holds to the belief in the imminent coming of the Lord as the blessed hope of the church, and
>
> Whereas, The teaching that the Church must go through the Tribulation tends to bring confusion and division among the saints; therefore,
>
> We recommend that all our ministers teach the imminent coming of Christ, warning all men to be prepared for that coming, which may occur at any time, and not to lull their minds into insecurity by any teaching that would cause them to feel that certain events must occur before the Rapture of the saints.
>
> Furthermore, we recommend that should any of our ministers hold to the post-Tribulation doctrine, they refrain from preaching and teaching it. Should they persist in emphasizing this doctrine to the point of making it an issue, their standing in the fellowship will be seriously affected.[23]

There were other developments during the 1930's, some of which will be alluded to in the latter part of this book at appropriate junctures, but the decisions sampled here reflect the temper of the times, the relative tranquility of the Depression years internally within the Assemblies of God.

Some of Those God Used

During the burgeoning years of the 1920's and the 1930's, a cavalcade of heroic pioneers paid a sacrificial price to carry the Pentecostal message across the nation. Energized by the Holy Spirit, inspired by the presence of the living Christ, and moved with compassion over the multitudes suffering in sin, these stalwarts of the faith heralded the Good News in spite of poverty and, not infrequently, in the

[22]Brumback, *op. cit.*, p. 311.

[23]General Council minutes, 1937, pp. 69-70.

face of outright persecution. Strong conviction of Biblical truth heavily outweighed the taunts and epithets of anti-Pentecostal critics. No, it was not popular to be Pentecostal in those decades. But, they were days of glorious revival, nonetheless! Space does not permit a complete catalog of the Pentecostal pioneers, but the sampling that follows reflects the mood and spirit of a great host to whom younger generations owe a large debt.

LEADERS AND PASTORS

A name that epitomizes the temper of the times perhaps as well as any other is E. S. Williams. He was born in San Bernardino, California, on January 7, 1885, to charter members of the First Holiness Church. At 19, Ernest surrendered his life to Christ in Los Angeles, and at once set out on a lifetime of ministry. Another youthful companion and he became caught up in personal evangelism, living on odd jobs. When funds ran low, they sometimes lived on 10 cents' worth of food a day and slept in the great outdoors. They traveled over much of eastern Colorado on bicycles, distributing Christian material as colporteurs. Occasionally schoolhouses were opened to them for ministry, but their limited preaching material made it difficult for them to preach more than once or twice in the same location!

News reached the itinerant evangelists of a great outpouring of the Spirit at Azusa Street in Los Angeles. They went home to investigate the reports, attending the meetings night after night, until both received a personal Pentecost. E. S. Williams received the baptism in the Holy Spirit on October 2, 1906. Young Ernest was ordained by the Apostolic Faith people shortly thereafter and launched into Pentecostal ministry as pastor of a mission in San Francisco in 1907. For two years he preached on the streets and in the rented hall, seven nights a week. He lived in a shed at the rear of a house, with an old quilt for a mattress. The lessons in faith he learned in those days established the tone of his entire future ministry. From 1909 to 1911, he ministered in Colorado, Oregon, Washington, and British Columbia. In Oregon he met Laura Jacobson, an immigrant from Denmark, whose interest in the Lord's work attracted his attention. They were married in 1911, and the next year accepted the pastorate of a small work in Conneaut, Ohio.

Through reading the *Word and Witness*, Brother Williams learned of a new Pentecostal fellowship that was being formed. In April, 1915, E. S. Williams received certification as a minister of the young Assemblies of God organization.

Ministry in Conneaut was followed by a call to Bradford, Pennsylvania. In 1917 the Williamses were invited to Newark, New Jersey, where a new phase of ministry opened. For three years Brother Williams served as pastor of the church in Newark and also as a teacher in Bethel Bible Institute. They were happy years in Newark. Their apartment was in the students' dormitory, and their association with the students was delightful. Frank Boyd served as principal of the school, and W. I. Evans was one of the instructors. Brother Williams helped to organize an aggressive evangelistic program, involving the talent and enthusiasm of the young people in Newark.

The effective ministry of Brother Williams attracted the attention of the friends in nearby Philadelphia. In 1920 when the Union Highway Mission, one of the strongest Pentecostal churches in the East, was looking for a pastor, the invitation was extended to E. S. Williams. At once a vigorous outreach program was launched in that great city. Meetings in homes, on the streets, and in hospitals and jails were conducted. A "gospel car" served as a portable platform. Youth services were started. A 30-piece orchestra was organized under the direction of Nicholas Nikoloff. The resulting crowds required three additions to the building in the course of the next several years. Eventually, the thriving work led to the erection of a lovely new sanctuary, Highway Mission Tabernacle.

Brother Williams made a practice of writing synopses of his better sermons and submitting them to *The Pentecostal Evangel*. His helpful articles, reflecting spiritual insight and maturity, began to appear with some regularity in the denominational weekly. In addition to this pastoral and writing ministry, he was an executive in the Eastern District and also served on the General Presbytery. In this fashion he became acquainted with the larger dimensions of the rapidly growing fellowship. In 1927 he was elected to the Executive Presbytery. Few were surpised when he was elected to serve as General Superintendent of the Assemblies of God in 1929. It took weeks of prayer, however, before he was willing to leave his delightful pastoral ministry to assume executive responsibilities in Springfield. His humility, wisdom, and godly life served as a tower of stability during the Depression years, as he traveled extensively from coast to coast ministering in conventions and camp meetings. His life deeply influenced students and teachers at Central Bible Institute, leaving a stamp on innumerable lives, through his association as president (by virtue of his office as General Superintendent) and, later, as teacher of theology. Now retired, aged and beloved Brother Williams continues to extend his influence on the Assemblies of God through his question-and-answer column read weekly in *The Pentecostal Evangel.*[24]

Although Ernest S. Williams' ministry was truly national, yet it was largely centered in the metropolitan East. Other pioneers in that part of the country included Robert and Marie Brown, whose names are inseparable from Glad Tidings Tabernacle in New York City. Harry L. Collier founded the great Full Gospel Tabernacle in Washington, D. C. For 39 years Ralph Jeffrey was pastor of the Bethel Assembly in Hagerstown, Maryland, during which time more than a dozen other churches were started in the neighboring communities.

A leader in the Assemblies of God in a wide range of ministries was Ralph M. Riggs. He was born June 16, 1895, at Coal Creek, Tennessee, but spent most of his boyhood days in Meridian, Mississippi. He was present at the organizational meeting of the Assemblies of God in Hot Springs, Arkansas, in 1914, and was ordained to the ministry of the

[24]"The E. S. Williams Story" (unpublished manuscript prepared by the Central Bible College Alumni Association).

new fellowship just two years later. Brother Riggs attended Elim Bible Training School in Rochester, New York. Following a three-year term as pastor of Grace Tabernacle, Syracuse, New York, he journeyed to South Africa as a missionary. This was in 1920. Later that same year, the young missionary married Lillian Merian, a missionary already in the field. For six years the young couple served Christ in Africa.

Following their term of missionary service, the Riggs family resumed pastoral responsibilities for a time and engaged in some Bible school ministry. Concurrently, while serving as pastor of Bethel Church in Newark, New Jersey, Riggs taught at the Bethel Bible Training School during the 1928 term. The next year he was invited to join the faculty of Central Bible Institute in Springfield, Missouri, the beginning of 30 years of service in that city. In 1931 Riggs was elected pastor of Central Assembly. Eight years later he was elevated to the post of district superintendent of the Southern Missouri District Council. Four more years and he was elected to serve as Assistant General Superintendent of the denomination. After 10 years of service in that capacity, Ralph M. Riggs was chosen by the General Council in Milwaukee, in 1953, to fill the post of General Superintendent, a position he occupied for six years. Upon his retirement from active leadership, Riggs returned to the classroom, serving for 10 additional years on the faculty of Bethany Bible College. On January 13, 1971, at the age of 75, this pastor, administrator, missionary, teacher, and writer went to be with his Lord.

A man of many interests, skills, and achievements, perhaps the single greatest contribution of his long life was in the sphere of education. It was in considerable measure through his influence that Sunday school work became so quickly a dominant enterprise in the fellowship, and likewise, through his forward-looking vision, he encouraged the establishment of Evangel College.[25]

A young Canadian from the great Montreal Pentecostal Church, Charles W. H. Scott, went to the Elim Bible In-

[25]News Release, Public Relations Office, January 14, 1971.

stitute in Rochester, New York, to prepare for ministry. His first pastorate was in Trenton, New Jersey, from 1924 to 1926. Early in 1927, the Scotts moved to the industrial city of Altoona, Pennsylvania, where they pioneered an Assembly. Not only was a church started in Altoona, but through the vision and energy of Scott, the nearby towns of Roaring Spring, Tyrone, and Lebanon also received their initial glimpses of Pentecostal power. Successive pastorates in Atlantic City, New Jersey, and Flint and Battle Creek, Michigan, were followed by election to the office of district superintendent. After he had spent twelve fruitful years in that position in Michigan, the fellowship honored Brother Scott by elevating him to Assistant General Superintendent, a post he still occupies.

In the Pittsburgh, Pennsylvania, area, a series of Pentecostal revivals around 1920 succeeded in sending out a significant number of ministers into the Pentecostal work. In nearby McKeesport, James Menzie and Frank Lindquist were converted, later coming under the influence of Will and Frank Casley, "rough-and-ready" independent Pentecostal revivalists. The Casleys were instrumental in the conversion of Ben Mahan, revered pastor in the East for many years, and Ben Hardin, one of the sparkling evangelists of the 1930's. Ben Mahan pioneered the First Pentecostal Church in Jeannette, Pennsylvania, which he served for 19 years, before serving 17 years at the Full Gospel Tabernacle in Washington, D. C.

Upon the return of Ben Hardin to McKeesport after one of his evangelistic tours, James Menzie asked, "Where is the neediest field you know?" Brother Hardin indicated that Minnesota was just such a place. Forthwith James Menzie disposed of his material goods, giving nearly all his assets to the work of the Lord, and set out in 1921 for Minnesota with Frank Lindquist, who joined him as song leader. These two men, assisted by Ben Hardin, soon had works established in Brainerd, Crosby, Ironton, Pillager, Casino, and Motley, Minnesota. On one occasion, the tent these youthful evangelists used was splattered by acid in the night by local antagonists, while they were asleep inside! Out of the work of these men must be attributed the organization of the North Central District Council, which was brought into being late in 1922. James Menzie returned East to engage in long and prosperous pastorates in Canton, Ohio, Gary, Indiana, and New Castle, Pennsylvania, but Frank Lindquist remained in Minnesota, serving for a quarter of a century as district superintendent and president of North Central Bible Institute, besides pastoring the Minneapolis Full Gospel Tabernacle for more than 40 years!

A Norwegian immigrant who was ordained to the Assemblies of God ministry in Minnesota was Henry H. Ness. He first pastored in Brainerd, then pioneered the assembly in Fargo, North Dakota. During his seven-year stay in Fargo, Ness was effective in establishing other churches in the adjacent region. In 1933, Ness accepted a call to Calvary Temple in Seattle, Washington. Under his leadership the membership grew from 75 to 700. In 1934, he took the lead in establishing Northwest Bible Institute, a school he served as president for 15 years. Ness, particularly in his later years, had a most remarkable ministry with the upper echelons of international political life.[26]

A young man converted in one of James Menzie's campaigns in Casino, Minnesota, was Bartlett Peterson. Young Bartlett launched into full-time ministry in 1927, engaging in evangelistic work for several years, traveling as far afield as Indiana, Tennessee, and Florida. Following successful pastorates in Sauk Center, Minnesota, and Sisseton, South Dakota, Peterson returned to evangelistic work, covering much of the United States. In 1936, he accepted the pastorate at Fergus Falls, Minnesota, remaining there until his election as field secretary for the district in 1940. Brother Peterson successively served as district superintendent, then president of Central Bible Institute for ten years, and, finally, succeeded J. Roswell Flower as General Secretary of the Assemblies of God, a position he has held now since 1959. Of special interest has been the role Brother Peterson has played in radio ministry. While pastoring in Sisseton,

---

[26]*The Pentecostal Evangel*, March 22, 1970, p. 28.

South Dakota, in 1930 he became one of the first Assemblies of God pastors to conduct a local radio broadcast.

One of the great revivals to touch Minnesota occurred in 1933. E. Elsworth Krogstad, a young evangelist who had been holding campaigns in the upper Midwest and the Pacific Northwest, was invited to Willmar, Minnesota, to conduct a series of meetings. He stayed 11 years! A great church was the outgrowth of that outpouring, and a host of gospel workers flowed forth from that revival.

In 1926 Charles S. Price came to Minneapolis to hold a union campaign. A lad suffering from anemia joined the healing line. Prostrated by the power of God, Howard S. Bush not only received physical healing, but was wonderfully converted in that great meeting! Bush began to attend the Full Gospel Tabernacle, which had suddenly mushroomed in size as the direct result of the Price campaign. Frank Lindquist tutored the budding preacher, and sent Bush on his way to pioneer in North Dakota and Minnesota. Bush, still unmarried, made a practice of going out for eight months or so, long enough to start a church, then returning to his parents' home for a respite. He succeeded in beginning four churches between 1928 and 1931 in this fashion. In 1931 he felt a definite impression that God wanted him to go to Florida. Miracles of faith attended his ministry in Tampa and St. Petersburg. This godly Northerner was recognized as one with singular spiritual leadership by his Southern colleagues, and in 1942 was elected district superintendent. In 1960 he moved to Springfield as Assistant General Superintendent, where he served with distinction until his untimely death nine years later.

In a great revival in northwestern North Dakota in 1925, G. Raymond Carlson found the Lord. Evangelist Blanche Britton was a mighty instrument in that move of the Holy Spirit from which many churches were started, and more than 100 ministers entered the ranks of the Lord's army. Brother Carlson received his first credentials in 1937 and was ordained to the Assemblies of God ministry in 1941. Two years later he moved to Minnesota, serving for many years in various executive capacities in the district, eventually leaving his position as president of North Central Bible College in 1969 to assume national responsibility as Assistant General Superintendent.

A student at Oklahoma State College received the baptism in the Holy Spirit in 1925, and immediately dropped everything to respond to the call to preach. Bert Webb spent a year or more in evangelistic work in Oklahoma and Arkansas, then, at the age of twenty, put up a tent in September, 1927, in Granada, Minnesota. Within a year, a church building had been erected—and paid for! When he arrived in Granada, residents could not point to an identifiable conversion in that community in 25 years; in four weeks of Pentecostal revival 60 or 70 found the Lord! Webb remarked about revivals of this quality: "In every instance, in which I have been involved, the catalyst was a God-given hunger. Protracted, almost endless, demanding prayer preceded these moves. Courting the favor of God is the key to the situation." Webb held other remarkable meetings throughout Wisconsin, South Dakota, and Minnesota for several years, with vigorous churches frequently being the product. In 1934, Webb was invited by the Pickthorn Brothers, William and Albert, to hold a meeting in Memphis. During the five-week campaign there, nearly 100 were converted and 60 received the Pentecostal experience. This great stir was the real beginning of that great Pentecostal citadel of the South, First Assembly of Memphis.

Perhaps the most remarkable visitation came in Webb's ministry at Hope, Arkansas. When he went to Hope in 1935, there were 12 members, with perhaps 30 attending Sunday school. For five months they preached without much visible result, but daily Webb and his wife prayed and visited from house to house and from farm to farm within a radius of half-a-dozen miles of the community. After some months without a genuine "break," the Webbs invited James Hamill, a youthful evangelist from Mississippi, to hold special services for them. The Sunday before Hamill arrived the "break" came; two dozen were saved that day, with the meeting running through the afternoon. During the week others found the Lord in their homes. Eight or nine had received the Baptism before Hamill arrived! In three weeks, 140 were converted and 90 received the baptism in the Spirit. The leading businessmen of the community became ardent disciples of the Lord. In 1939, when the Webbs left Hope, the Sunday school was averaging over 400, and there were 130 Christ's Ambassadors in that little city! In July of 1939, Webb accepted the pastorate of Central Assembly in Springfield, the first church he served in which he followed another pastor!

Many of the successful pioneers of the earlier decades were very young. Few, however, were as young as Theodore Gannon. He received the Pentecostal baptism at 12, near his home in north central Missouri, not far from the Iowa line, and started preaching at once! At first he preached on weekends, on holidays, and during summer vacations. Even as a teen-ager he spoke at camp meetings. He entered full-time ministry at 16. Not until after he was married did Brother Gannon take time to finish high school! During the 1930's this youthful firebrand for God pastored small pioneer churches in Kentucky, interspersing pastoral ministry with evangelistic meetings. By 1940 he was pastoring in Louisville, and serving as assistant superintendent at the same time. A succession of pastorates and district positions, including the superintendency of two districts, Kentucky and the West Central District, led eventually to Springfield in 1965, with his election as Assistant General Superintendent.

Wesley Rowland Steelberg, 1902-1952, as a youthful evanlist, signed his name to a gospel songbook he used in his meetings, and beneath his signature penned what seems to have been the motto of his life, "All for Jesus." Brother Steelberg's life, brief as it was, exhibited the finest qualities of Pentecostal ministry, and so endeared him to his colleagues that at a relatively youthful stage in life he was projected into prominence. He was born in the home of a Scandinavian Methodist "lay preacher" in Denver, Colorado. At the age of eight Wesley was saved and filled with the Spirit. About this time, he was remarkably healed of brain fever and spinal meningitis. His deliverance brought the whole family into the Pentecostal ranks. Shortly afterward they moved to Los Angeles. After graduation from school, young Steelberg left his employment as mechanic and carpenter to launch into full-time ministry. Already by the age of 16 he had begun to preach. From the age of 17 he was fully active in the ministry, traveling extensively throughout the western United States, featured as the "Boy Preacher." In 1919, after some months of evangelistic ministry, he became assistant pastor of Victoria Hall, an early Pentecostal church, in Los Angeles. There he met and married Ruth Fisher, daughter of the pastor of one of the missions in Los Angeles where the Spirit fell in the early days. The young couple launched into pioneer work in Arizona shortly afterward. Before long Steelberg was called to Stockton, California, to pastor the Assembly there. While in Stockton, Steelberg provided the leadership that brought into being the "Pentecostal Ambassadors for Christ," the embryo organization from which the present national Christ's Ambassadors program has grown.

Happy years of pastoral ministry in Stockton were succeeded by equally fruitful terms in Sacramento, and, later, at Philadelphia. While in Philadelphia, Steelberg was elected superintendent of the Eastern District. Only in the district office a brief time, Steelberg was elected to the post of Assistant General Superintendent in 1945. Four years later, upon the retirement of E. S. Williams, the Assemblies of God fellowship called upon this able and spiritual young man to fill the office of chief executive.

His energetic and conscientious service through the years had taken a toll of his physical resources. In office less than three years, he suffered a serious heart attack. It was the spring of 1952. Instead of allowing time for adequate recuperation, as medical advice prescribed, he continued to fulfill his duties as much as he was able, continuing to record sermons for the newly launched "Revivaltime" ministry, in addition to his other responsibilities. While in Cardiff, Wales, engaged in ministry, he suffered a second attack in June. He lingered for several weeks, lying bedfast in Cardiff, but on July 8, 1952, Wesley R. Steelberg died. He had given "All for Jesus." Those who remember him well continue to recall the sweet and Christlike spirit of this outstanding Pentecostal leader.[27]

Gayle F. Lewis was born in Elgin, Pennsylvania, late in 1898. As a boy, he and his family were faithful participants in the services of the local Methodist Protestant Church of Youngstown, Ohio. About 1915, while Gayle was courting a young lady from the church, her mother began to attend Pentecostal services. First the daughter "came in," and she, in turn, led her husband-to-be, Gayle, into Pentecost! In those days nearly all the young people who received the baptism in the Holy Spirit felt a call to preach. Gayle, who married very young, began as a lay preacher. To support his growing family he worked, first as a plasterer, then later in a grocery store. All the while he was absorbed in ministerial work. From 1921 to 1924 he pastored the little congregation in Austinburg, Ohio, where services were first held in the living room of the home of Charles Woolever, who later went to India as a missionary. Virginia, the Lewis's daughter (now the wife of J. Philip Hogan, Assistant General Superintendent), recalls those days of commuting from Youngstown to Austinburg in an old Model-T Ford, with the children wrapped in army blankets to fend off the piercing cold!

The tiny beginnings in Austinburg led to full-time ministry at Conneaut, Ohio, and later, in Canton, Ohio. During his pastorate in Canton, Gayle Lewis served as secretary-treasurer of the Central District Council, as well. Then, in 1930, Brother Lewis was elected by his brethren to the office of district superintendent, a position he held for 15 years. In 1945 the General Council in session chose him to fill the post of Assistant General Superintendent. For 20 years Brother Lewis filled that position, with the exception of a brief period in 1952 and 1953, when his colleagues asked him to fill the unexpired term of General Superintendent, that office having become vacant due to the untimely death of Brother Wesley R. Steelberg. One of the

---

[27]*The Pentecostal Evangel*, August 10, 1952, pp. 3, 4, 10, and Lester Sumrall, *All for Jesus* (Springfield, Missouri: Gospel Publishing House, 1955).

outstanding characteristics of the ministry of Brother Lewis has been his pulpit ability. Even in the golden years of retirement, he has been in demand as a speaker at ministers' institutes and camps.[28]

On August 9, 1969, one of the truly great pioneers of the South in the Assemblies of God went to be with the Lord. James O. Savell enjoyed a varied and profitable ministry as a pastor, evangelist, and executive officer for many years. He was ordained in 1914 at San Antonio, Texas, and began to exercise his ministry by witnessing to his own relatives in Mississippi. For eight years he labored in Mississippi, during which time he established three churches. After two additional pastorates, he was elected as district superintendent of Mississippi, a position he filled from 1922 to 1926. Until 1948 Brother Savell pastored a succession of churches in Alabama, Louisiana, Texas, Georgia, and Ohio, with extensive evangelistic activity interspersed, as well. In 1948 Brother Savell was elected district superintendent of the Texas District. Four years later the fellowship honored him with elevation to the office of Assistant General Superintendent. For five years, from 1952 to 1957, Brother Savell served the Assemblies of God as an executive, but then he felt impressed of God to return to pastoral ministry. He pastored in Houston, Texas, from 1957 to 1960. In that year he resigned his pastorate to launch on a wider sphere of pulpit ministry as a camp and conference speaker. For nine years J. O. Savell traveled extensively, delivering from the pulpit the fruit of a life of rich experience with God, with the Word, and with needy humanity. His life made an indelible impression on the Southland.[29]

In Seguin, Texas, Kermit Reneau received the baptism in the Holy Spirit when he was 18 years old. A year later, when he graduated from high school, this young Texan launched into full-time ministry. Over the course of years, Reneau pastored churches in Stockdale, Nixon, Bruni, Bay City, and San Antonio, all in Texas. In 1953, Reneau was elected district superintendent, but returned to San Antonio

[28]Interview, Virginia Hogan, July 28, 1970.

[29]*The Pentecostal Evangel*, September 28, 1969, pp. 6-7.

to pastor in 1961. The Assemblies of God honored him in Dallas, in 1969, by electing him Assistant General Superintendent. He had served as a nonresident Executive Presbyter prior to the 1969 election.

Reneau, in reminiscing about the 1930's, adds a dimension of realism as a practical check on the tendency to cast a halo around the past. He remembers that in the midst of much of the burning zeal for evangelism current in the pre-World War II days many overlooked the ministry of establishing churches. "We were sometimes too busy to pastor!" Reneau states. He recollects that too often the fruit of evangelism was lost because of impatience with the need for nurturing new converts and shepherding young flocks. He also remembers that, while not overemphasizing the ministry of the Holy Spirit, there was not always a commensurate emphasis on getting people to read the Scriptures. "People who do not read the Bible lose much of the value of the impact of the Holy Spirit," he admonishes. With a note of some concern, Reneau observes, "While we have taken the proper attitude toward building churches, we have lost some of that evangelistic fervor."[30]

Martin B. Netzel, General Treasurer of the Assemblies of God since 1957, was born in San Felipe, Texas, not far from Houston. To the community where he was born a band of independent Pentecostal workers came, late in the summer of 1913. Following this campaign, cottage prayer meetings were conducted under the direction of Brother Netzel's mother. A year later, when another campaign was conducted in San Felipe, Martin, then a boy of six, was converted and received the infilling of the Holy Spirit.

Brother Netzel recalls a healing he experienced as a very young Christian. "As a lad, I had severe attacks of croup, resulting in very severe coughing and breathing. My parents feared to take me to the regular meetings which were being held three times a week, but persisted in doing so, and in answer to prayer, God completely delivered me in the winter of 1914."

The independent group that brought the Pentecostal mes-

[30]Interview, Kermit Reneau, April 9, 1970.

sage to San Felipe identified themselves as "Apostolic Faith" people, but were not connected with other groups with a similar title. They were well-meaning people, but adhered to several ideas that were either heretical or fanatical, among which was the belief that to fully follow the Lord, one must sell all and live in a communal center located at Houston. "The fallacy of this became apparent within a couple of years, and, providentially, a believer baptized in the Spirit prior to our coming into Pentecost informed us of the recently organized movement, the Assemblies of God." In 1918, the Netzel family came under the stabilizing influence of the still-new General Council.

Brother Netzel felt a call upon his life from early years, but during his teen-age years, resisted the whispering of the Holy Spirit. "My resistance to the idea of being a preacher was not a matter of rebellion but of feeling that others could express themselves so much more fluently than I." But, finally in 1927, while managing a grocery store, he applied for a license with the Texico District (Texas and New Mexico), in order to assist another minister in gospel work. It was not until five years later, after having been ordained, that this very humble servant of God would accept credit for being a preacher!

By 1932 Brother Netzel had cut loose from the business world and was launched into full-time ministry, engaging in evangelistic and pastoral ministry in Texas. In one of his early meetings, 70 were converted, three of whom subsequently entered the ministry. Evidently this modest young man had the divine seal upon him, after all! Out of this revival, a pioneer church was built, the Netzels staying on in that community for an additional 18 months.

Happy years of successful ministry led eventually to Brother Netzel's election as superintendent of the North Texas District Council. He served in this position for four years, from 1953 to 1957, when the fellowship called upon him to become the General Treasurer of the Assemblies of God.[31]

Another of those men who by election to high office

---

[31]Martin B. Netzel (unpublished manuscript) July 30, 1970.

represent the kind of people who are the backbone of the Assemblies of God is J. Philip Hogan. Brother Hogan began life on a ranch on the western slopes of Colorado, near a village named Olathe. Pentecost came to that part of the country about 1920. The Martin Sisters from Southern Missouri were the first evangelists to bring the message. About 1922 two young men came, conducting a tent meeting. Shortly afterward, a permanent congregation was established, meeting at first in the homes of members, one of which was the Hogan home. Young Philip was saved in this Pentecostal revival in 1922, giving his heart to the Lord at one of the cottage meetings. In 1923, the congregation bought an abandoned Presbyterian church building. In due course the congregation became affiliated with the young Rocky Mountain District of the Assemblies of God. It was in the year that the church was formally organized, in 1923, that Philip received the baptism in the Holy Spirit. Ten years later, Mother and Dad Hogan moved to Springfield, Missouri, so their two sons, Philip and Gene, could attend Central Bible Institute.

The ministry of Brother Hogan began even while he was a student. The last year of his Bible school days, 1935-36, he pastored the little Assembly at nearby Republic, Missouri. Philip spent a year in evangelistic work after his graduation, while he waited for Virginia Lewis (daughter of Gayle Lewis) to finish her course at CBI. When she graduated, the newlyweds were asked by Bert Webb, then pastor of Central Assembly, to assume the responsibility for a branch church which was being established, Eastside Assembly. For two years the Hogans pastored this new work. In 1941 they journeyed to Painesville, Ohio, and later, on to Bethel Assembly (now located in Lincoln Park, Michigan) near Detroit. It was while the Hogans were conducting a missionary convention in their church that they themselves responded to the ringing call to missions delivered by Leonard Bolton of China, the guest speaker. They answered their own missionary appeal!

A new phase of ministry was thereby thrust upon them. During 1945-46, just at the conclusion of World War II, they studied the Chinese language and culture at the University of California. In 1947 they finally arrived in China. They were difficult, turbulent years in that troubled land. The Hogans stayed until they were forced to leave, as the Red Chinese swallowed up the country. They moved their missionary operations to nearby Formosa, becoming, with the Garland Benintendis, the first American missionaries to establish a gospel witness on that island in modern history. Virginia was evacuated from Formosa in 1949, but Philip stayed on an additional six months to train national leadership for the infant church. He left shortly after the first baptismal service, a triumph in that new field.

The Hogans engaged in pastoral ministry upon their return to the homeland in 1950, enjoying a brief period of ministry in Florence, South Carolina. Meanwhile, Noel Perkin was looking for additional staff members for the Springfield office to aid in correlating the burgeoning work of Assemblies of God missions. He invited Philip to join him in Springfield as director of promotions. Upon the retirement of Noel Perkin in 1959, the fellowship selected J. Philip Hogan to assume the responsibility of directing the vast army of Assemblies of God missionaries. He has won the respect, not only of Assemblies of God people who have continued to return him to office since then, but of observers of the missions scene across denominational lines, as well. In 1969 he was elected president of the Evangelical Foreign Missions Association, the first time a Pentecostal was so honored.[32]

A real "war-horse" of the Assemblies of God has been Aaron A. Wilson. A successful businessman, Wilson felt the call of God on his life shortly after receiving the baptism in the Holy Spirit. In those days it seemed that nearly all who received the Pentecostal effusion felt impelled to launch into full-time work for the Lord! In 1921 businessman Wilson went to Puxico, Missouri, serving that church until the district elected him superintendent, four years later. In 1930, Wilson went to Kansas City, pastoring for 31 years what came to be known as Evangel Temple, one of

---

[32]Interview, J. Philip Hogan, July 28, 1970.

the great churches of the Assemblies of God. Wilson ranged far and wide during those long years, a favorite camp meeting speaker, and honored for years as a nonresident Executive Presbyter of the fellowship. During the 1960's, following his "retirement," "War-Horse Wilson" launched into one additional pioneer venture. In his seventies, he pioneered a new Assembly in Springfield, Missouri.

District superintendents who made way for fledgling Bible school students were Fred Vogler and V. G. Greisen of the Kansas District. In 1930, Fred Vogler visited the nearby campus of Central Bible Institute in Springfield, extending an invitation to students to use the 12 tents purchased by the district for summer ministry, promising that none would starve before the beginning of the fall term! The warm, fatherly interest of men like Vogler and Greisen resulted in a veritable army of graduates marching into the wheatfields of Kansas over the next several years. There a sizable contingent of loyal CBI alumni still hold forth the Pentecostal message!

Time permits but the merest mention of some of the other giants of faith who have left a worthy heritage. There were George Bowie and D. P. Holloway in Cleveland, John Waggoner in Warren, A. B. Cox in Dayton, and O. E. Nash in Cincinnati that belong in the Ohio hall of fame. J. R. Kline in Detroit, John Kolenda in Flint, and Alvin Branch of Battle Creek were some of the valiant warriors in Michigan. Elsewhere in the central states, Howard Osgood, C. A. McKinney, and Richard Carmichael were but some of the host of workers who stood tall during the Depression years.

Herman Johnson, first superintendent of North Dakota, and Elmer Trygg of Montana were among the prominent names in the upper Midwest. To the southwest, beginning in Arkansas, the names of T. J. Gotcher, E. J. Bruton, W. D. Burris, and C. A. Lasater must be inscribed. W. F. Garvin, Dexter Collins, and W. T. Gaston are names that blessed Oklahoma. A host of men like F. D. Davis, A. C. Bates, E. L. Newby, Kermit Reneau, E. N. Richey, W. B. McCafferty, E. R. Foster, Harry Bowley, E. C. Crump, H. M. Cadwalder, H. C. Ball, and Albert Ott go down in Texas annals. Farther west, L. H. Hauff helped pioneer in New Mexico and Arizona, as did S. S. Scull. Colorado enjoyed the ministry of W. M. Stevens, F. C. Woodworth, Eric Booth-Clibborn, H. B. Garlock, and John McConnell. The West Coast boasts such names as Wesley R. Steelberg, Carl Hatch, Louis Turnbull, Minnie Draper, A. S. Osterberg, and Lloyd and Harold Persing. To the Pacific Northwest must be added Fred Snyder, O. R. Cross, Lester Carlsen, Will C. Trotter, Wesley F. Morton, Frank Gray, J. E. Rasmussen, Carl G. Carlson, D. W. Raines, and J. E. Secrist.[33] And to this list so many others should be added!

EVANGELISTS

There were great evangelists during the 1920's and 1930's who contributed enormously to the success of many local Assemblies throughout the land. Aimee Semple McPherson, although a member of the Assemblies of God for only three years, from 1919 to 1922,[34] nonetheless in city after city where she conducted her great citywide meetings was responsible for the real establishment of strong Assemblies. What were struggling missions when she came to town were transformed overnight into thriving churches in such places as Washington, D. C., Baltimore, Philadelphia, Rochester, Akron, Dayton, Tampa, Miami, St. Louis, Chicago, Tulsa, Denver, Dallas, San Diego, Los Angeles, and San Francisco.[35]

Dr. Charles S. Price, onetime prominent Methodist minister, and more lately a Congregational minister on the West Coast, went to San Jose to join battle with Mrs. McPherson over the doctrine of divine healing. He was stunned to learn that the pastor of the First Baptist Church

---

[33]Brumback, *op. cit.*, pp. 267-70.

[34]Interview with Rolf McPherson, August 21, 1967. See also Sister McPherson's autobiography, *This Is That* (Los Angeles: Echo Park Evangelistic Association, 1923). Sister McPherson parted company with the Assemblies of God because of a difference of opinion on matters of ministerial discipline. Rolf McPherson said of his mother, "Aimee tolerated anyone who could claim forgiveness. The Assemblies of God set standards of fellowship which prevented her from associating with the denomination." He feels that if this difference between his mother's latitude on such issues as divorce and remarriage and the stricter views held by the Assemblies of God could have been resolved back in the early 1920's, there might not have been such a group as the Foursquare Gospel Church developing as a separate entity.

[35]Brumback, *op. cit.*, pp. 271-72.

of Oakland, Dr. William Towner, had received the Pentecostal experience, and was sponsoring Mrs. McPherson's meeting in San Jose! In due course, sophisticated Dr. Price accepted the message of God's power. He could do little else, for he saw with his own eyes the wonderful works of God being performed night after night! In 1922 Dr. Price launched into his own evangelistic ministry, traveling extensively throughout the United States, frequently erecting sawdust-floored wooden tabernacles seating more than one thousand people. Older saints will recall the phenomenal healing ministry of Dr. Price. Through his great crusades, many families were swept into the Kingdom and found their way into local Assemblies. During the Depression years, Dr. Price was one of the strong voices proclaiming God's power to deliver.[36]

An Englishman who made repeated visits to the United States during the 1920's and 1930's was Smith Wigglesworth, renowned for his amazing faith. A humble, almost unschooled plumber, his powerful ministry touched many lives for God.[37] To this list of dynamic, and yet deeply godly, evangelists should be added Raymond T. Richey, John H. Bostrom, Harvey McAlister, Guy Shields, and the women God used, Dr. Lilian B. Yeomans and Hattie Hammond. Rich ministries these have been, blessing an innumerable company of people, strengthening local Assemblies everywhere.

EDUCATORS

The ministry of teaching during the Depression years complemented the great revival and evangelistic meetings, producing not only a virile, but a stable and well-grounded fellowship. The pulpit and pen ministry of revered Donald Gee of the British Assemblies of God ranks on the highest level of contribution to the American Pentecostal Movement. His sound, yet warm and vibrant, counsel packs the pages of numerous volumes printed by the Gospel Publishing House in the 1930's.

---

[36]See Charles S. Price, *The Story of My Life* (Pasadena: Charles S. Price Publishing Co., third edition, 1944).

[37]See Stanley H. Frodsham, *Smith Wigglesworth: Apostle of Faith* (Springfield, Missouri: Gospel Publishing House, 1951).

Another staunch bulwark in Pentecostal teaching was P. C. Nelson. A well-trained Baptist minister, Nelson was brought into the Pentecostal ranks as the result of a personal healing in the city where he pastored, Detroit. His inspiration and vision led to the establishment of a Bible school in Enid, Oklahoma, which in the course of time became Southwestern Assemblies of God College in Waxahachie, Texas. The book *Bible Doctrines* represents the mature, stable wisdom of a godly man, held in high esteem by numerous students who sat in his classes, and the larger numbers who sat in rapt attention in conventions to hear him expound the Scriptures.

A most impressive contribution to Assemblies of God literature and Bible education was made by Myer Pearlman. Pearlman was born in Edinburgh, Scotland. He emigrated to the United States early in the new century, locating on the West Coast. He had been steeped in Judaism through attendance in Hebrew schools as a boy, learning to hate Christianity through his intensive studies. However, the Holy Spirit touched his heart.

> Standing one evening outside Glad Tidings Mission in San Francisco, Pearlman listened to the congregation sing, "Honey in the Rock," composed by his father-in-law-to-be, F. A. Graves. He felt himself irresistibly drawn inside this mission where the people were singing so joyfully.[38]

And so it was that this immigrant Jewish lad found Christ. Following this, he spent a brief time studying at Glad Tidings Bible Institute, but shortly transferred to Central Bible Institute in Springfield, enrolling for the first full term of CBI in 1922. Pearlman, already well-versed in several languages, and obviously adept in serious study of the Bible, was asked to join the faculty when he graduated from CBI in 1925. Pearlman distinguished himself quickly in the classroom, eventually developing a Bible-teaching reputation that took him during the summers to some of the largest camp meetings in the fellowship, where he was a favorite interpreter of God's Word. But, perhaps even more than by his teaching ministry in classroom and at camp,

[38]Brumback, *op. cit.* p. 237.

Pearlman endeared himself to the fellowship with his ready pen. For many years he prepared the *Adult Teacher's Quarterly,* as well as the *Adult Student's Quarterly*. In this fashion his name became a household word in the Assemblies of God. A monumental achievement was his great outline of theology, still one of the finest in Pentecostal circles, *Knowing the Doctrines of the Bible.* Shortly before his untimely death in 1943, Pearlman's versatile and prolific pen cheered the hearts of literally millions of American servicemen. During World War II he edited *Reveille,* a publication that ran to a total printing of 14 million copies by war's end!

William I. Evans is a name that two generations of students at Central Bible Institute can never forget. An ardent champion of solid Christian character, the towering influence of this great and godly man extends wherever his students have carried the gospel of Christ. Of particular concern to Brother Evans was the oversight of the chapel services. His insight into the gentle movings of the Holy Spirit enabled him to lead large groups of worshipers into delightful cooperation with the divine will. Out of such sessions in God's presence, many young people learned invaluable lessons in leading in true Pentecostal worship.

LAYMEN

A layman whose important contribution to the General Council during the early years of the movement must not be overlooked was J. Z. Kamerer. Brother Kamerer went to Springfield in September, 1919, to supervise the growing printing activity of the General Council. He had been in the printing business in Findlay, Ohio. It was there that his uncle, D. W. Kerr, suggested to E. N. Bell that Kamerer might be just the man to fill the need in Springfield. In Kamerer's words, "I joined the working staff of the Gospel Publishing House for the primary purpose of helping in the publishing and printing of our first Sunday school literature." He never lost sight of the vision of "getting the gospel to the children."

In 1927, Kamerer was named General Manager of the Gospel Publishing House, the first to hold such a position. The scope of his activities ranged far beyond the printing establishment itself, for his counsel was sought in a wide area of decision-making. He was responsible for the purchasing and supervision of equipment, and served as personnel manager, as well. He was considered the "good right arm" of E. S. Williams, working closely with him for many years.

Before the creation of the Sunday School Department, Brother Kamerer also had the oversight of the promotion of literature used in Sunday school work. It was his idea to have the first Sunday school convention to train workers in better methods. He had the foresight to develop a promotional staff for Sunday schools, beginning with the hiring of Marcus Grable, a layman, to serve as the beginning of what grew into the Sunday School Department. His retirement in 1951 was felt keenly by the host of workers who had come to esteem him highly as a man sent from God.[39]

These, then, were some whom God used to carry forward the Pentecostal revival during the 1920's and 1930's. To this sampling could be added so many others, but, after all, it is the Lord of history who keeps the Final Record, and that is what really matters! How many unsung heroes of cottage meetings and all-night vigils there are who prayed whole churches into being only Eternity will reveal.

Summary

And so the period of "undifferentiated growth" comes to an end. The years of tranquility that span the Great Depression gave way to the turbulent times ushered in by World War II. Only with the advent of that great holocaust would the youthful denomination encounter problems of sufficient magnitude that profound changes would be wrought in the character of the Assemblies of God. Following the period of simplistic development, there would be a period of "analytical proliferation" in which a host of service agencies would be created to meet the growing needs of a new generation. This, in turn, was to be followed by an attempt to synthesize the dispersed energies of the movement. And this story of the dramatic changes in the Assemblies of God following Pearl Harbor is the burden of the chapters that follow.

---

[39] Unpublished notes of Mrs. J. Z. Kamerer.

PART II

THE RECENT YEARS [1941-1970]

9

Cooperation: From Isolation to Evangelical Identification

Withdrawal into Isolation—Alignment with the Pentecostal World —Pentecostal Cooperation—Opposition to Ecumenism—New Relations with Older Churches—Summary

Withdrawal into Isolation

The early Pentecostals felt that they had been commissioned with a life-giving apostolic message for the entire Christian church; they disclaimed any intention of creating new denominations. Almost immediate, sometimes violent, reaction from virtually all quarters of the church world changed that position. Separate Pentecostal organizations sprang into existence. Gradually a wall of separation isolated Pentecostal groups from the rest of the church world and even from each other.

REJECTION BY THE HOLINESS GROUPS

Although the Holiness Movement contributed more than any other segment of church life to the initial development of the Pentecostal revival, the Holiness bodies reacted quite negatively almost at once. A few entire Holiness bodies, regionally located in the Southeast, were captured quickly by the Pentecostals, but apart from these, the traditional Holiness groups manifested varying degrees of rejection, ranging from the relatively mild position of A. B. Simpson, enunciated in 1907, to the quite vitriolic denunciation by such groups as the small body in the National Holiness Association known as The Pillar of Fire. Following is a sample of their antipathy:

> When "Tongueism" is sifted down, it will be found that the cunning craftiness of depraved humanity figures in it to a greater degree than any one has yet dreamed. I have no doubt that there is much demon manifestation in the "Tongues" meetings for I have seen it with my own eyes, but many learn the art of copying others.[1]

J. H. Smith, noted Holiness theologian of the early part of the century, disclaimed any relationship either in doctrine or practice between the Holiness Movement and the Pentecostal Movement, which he labeled the "Tongues Movement." The latter he viewed as "neither Scriptural, Sensible, nor Spiritual," and he considered some of its fruit as "sensual, sinful, and often Satanic."[2] Leaders of the National Holiness Association branded "twentieth-century Pentecostalism as fanatical, unscriptural perversions of the doctrine of the baptism with the Holy Spirit."[3] This revulsion led Holiness people to lay aside, for the most part, the word "Pentecostal," and to use "Holiness" or "full salvation" to describe the theological position and to label their meetings in which they advocated the Wesleyan interpretation of holiness.[4] In 1919 the Pentecostal Church of the Nazarene quietly dropped the word "Pentecostal" from its title.[5]

The Church of the Nazarene, apparently quite typical of the Holiness tradition, in 1928 revised its statement of faith, "shoring up its denominational position in opposition to modernism *and* fundamentalism, including Pentecostalism."[6] The wall of separation was practically complete by the end of the 1920's.

REJECTION BY THE FUNDAMENTALISTS

The Niagara Bible Conference of 1895, alarmed at the directions being taken by the New Theology, set forth five anchor points which it felt must be safeguarded at all

---

[1]Alma White, *Demons and Tongues* (Zarephath, New Jersey: Pillar of Fire Publishers, 1919), p. 77.

[2]Delbert R. Rose, "The Theology of Joseph H. Smith" (unpublished Ph.D. dissertation, The University of Iowa, 1952), p. 279.

[3]*Ibid.*, p. 10.

[4]*Ibid.*

[5]Nichol, *op. cit.*, p. 72.

[6]Smith, *Called Unto Holiness*, p. 320.

costs.[7] This position was given classic defense in the 12-volume work edited by R. A. Torrey and A. C. Dixon, *The Fundamentals.* Through the generosity of wealthy concerned businessmen, three million copies of this 1910 publication were eventually distributed throughout the land.[8] The Pentecostals readily accepted the label of Fundamentalism without reservation.[9] There was no question where their loyalties lay.

But, the Fundamentalists repudiated any association with the Pentecostals. There are perhaps three reasons for this. First, within the broad term "Pentecostalism" there were emerging undisciplined groups that bordered on the cultic.[10] Not all those who stood outside made the necessary distinctions that would identify orthodox Pentecostals from the aberrated forms. The bizarre fringe without doubt cast a shadow over the whole. Even within the Assemblies of God the characteristic emotional worship was not palatable to many of the Fundamentalists.

There was another reason. Fundamentalism had been captured by Scofieldian dispensationalism. On hermeneutical grounds the dispensationalists denied the possibility of genuine gifts of the Spirit, such as speaking with tongues, to the post-apostolic age. According to their view, the baptism in the Spirit is accomplished at regeneration for all believers, and has nothing to do with the manifestations described in the Book of Acts occurring at Pentecost. The tongues manifestation at Pentecost was but a sign to authenticate the advent of a new dispensation and was to cease, as were all the other sign gifts.[11] For the dispensationalists, then, Pentecostalism was theologically absurd.

---

[7]Bruce Shelley, *Evangelicalism in America* (Grand Rapids: Eerdmans, 1967), p. 62. The five points enumerated were: (1) verbal inerrancy of Scripture, (2) the deity and virgin birth of Christ, (3) the substitutionary atonement, (4) the physical resurrection of Christ, and (5) His bodily return to earth.

[8]*Ibid.*, pp. 61-62.

[9]Brumback, *op. cit.*, pp. 130-31.

[10]Nichol, *op. cit.*, pp. 147-51. For example, the "Snake Handlers" of eastern Tennessee came into existence in 1909; "Sweet Daddy Grace," United House of Prayer for All People, in 1919. Groups like these are considered cults by the Assemblies of God.

[11]Merrill F. Unger, *The Baptizing Work of the Holy Spirit* (Wheaton, Illinois: Van Kampen Press, 1953), p. 63.

There was yet another reason for the alienation. Fundamentalism was engaged in a desperate struggle with Modernism. The struggle parallels in time the period in which the Pentecostal Movement came into being. In the 1920's the battle reached its crest. For the Fundamentalists it was a disastrous decade, for they lost the battle on nearly all fronts to the Modernists.[12] The battle had been lost on a political level, not necessarily by theological debate, but it had been lost.[13] Increasingly on the defensive, the Fundamentalists developed an image to match. The last stages of the debate descended to the level of rancor and recrimination, giving the Fundamentalists a pugnacious and disruptive reputation.[14] Along with the Modernists, the Pentecostals, also considered by now a threat to orthodox Christianity, were included in the castigation. The World's Christian Fundamentals Association, brought into being in 1919 as the chief Fundamentalist voice, passed sweeping judgment on the Pentecostals at their convention in the spring of 1928.[15] The resolution as adopted reads:

> Whereas, The present wave of Modern Pentecostalism, often referred to as the "tongues movement," and the present wave of fanatical and unscriptural healing which is sweeping over the country today, has become a menace in many churches and a real injury to sane testimony of Fundamental Christians,
>
> Be it Resolved, That this convention go on record as unreservedly opposed to Modern Pentecostalism, including the speaking in unknown tongues, and the fanatical healing known as general healing in the atonement, and the perpetuation of the miraculous sign-healing of Jesus and His apostles, wherein they claim the only reason the church cannot perform these miracles is because of unbelief.[16]

In response to this painful action, the editor of *The Pentecostal Evangel,* Stanley Frodsham, supplied a turned-cheek attitude: "Although we Pentecostal people have to be without the camp, we cannot afford to be bitter against those

---

[12]Calvin Carmen, "The Posture of Contemporary Pentecostalism in View of the Crucial Issues of the Fundamentalist-Neo-Evangelical Debate" (unpublished M.A. thesis, Central Bible Institute, 1965), p. 19.

[13]Sidney E. Mead, *The Lively Experiment* (New York: Harper and Row, 1963), p. 186.

[14]Carmen, *op. cit.*, p. 30.

[15]Norman F. Furniss, *The Fundamentalist Controversy*: 1918-1931 (Hamden, Connecticut: Archon Books, 1963), pp. 51-56.

[16]*The Pentecostal Evangel*, August 18, 1928, p. 7.

who do not see as we do. . . . So our business is to love these Fundamentalists and to pray, 'Lord, bless them all.' "[17] It is generally conceded that the 1928 action slammed the door to meaningful dialogue with Fundamentalists for many years to come.

THE LIBERAL CRITIQUE

The basic attitude of the larger church world was simply an ignoring of the Pentecostals. The occasional notices prior to 1930 exhibit a patronizing posture, in which Pentecostalism was stereotyped by the pejorative term "Holy Rollers."[18] During the 1920's the few volumes written on Pentecostalism appeared to be unsympathetic. Alexander Mackie said: "Christendom has waited long and patiently to see whether this thing—this gift of tongues—is of God. It is of sickness, of poverty, of fatigue, of disease, of crime. It is not of God."[19] George B. Cutten, president of Colgate University, wrote critically, but not bitterly, of the Pentecostals, concluding that the common denominators between Christian glossolalia and non-Christian manifestations indicate that the phenomenon could be explained on psychological, not religious, grounds.[20]

PENTECOSTAL RESPONSE

Between 1926 and 1936 when the last major government religious census was undertaken, the record shows that the traditional churches *lost* 2,000,000 members, or 8 percent of their total.[21] During the same period, the revivalistic sects demonstrated surprising vigor, led by the Pentecostals. The Assemblies of God had a 208.7 percent increase in membership; the Church of God, 92.8 percent.[22] Unquestionably some of the 2 million lost sheep found their way into the tabernacles and missions that had sprung up during

---

[17]*Ibid.*

[18]Jules Bois, "The Holy Rollers, the American Dervishes," *Forum*, LXXIII (February, 1925), pp. 145-55.

[19]Alexander Mackie, *The Gift of Tongues* (New York: George H. Doran Company, 1921), p. 275.

[20]George B. Cutten, *Speaking with Tongues* (New Haven: Yale University Press, 1927).

[21]John L. Sherrill, *They Speak with Other Tongues* (New York: McGraw-Hill, 1964), p. 50.

[22]*Ibid.* Assemblies of God membership by 1936 was 170,000.

the Great Depression. When the Pentecostals volunteered to explain why they were reaping such a harvest they succeeded in antagonizing all too frequently.[23] Oliver, quoting an undated pamphlet published by the Gospel Publishing House, states: "The denomination has defended strongly speaking in tongues by saying that those who oppose it are the 'servants of Satan,' and reject a power and necessity in the Christian life."[24]

The walls were going up. Pentecostalism had entered a period of isolationism, standing aloof from the rest of Christendom.

PENTECOSTAL FELLOWSHIP

Within the world of Pentecostalism several streams had been emerging, many of them sharing much in common. Deeply regretting the divisions that existed, the 1921 General Council passed a significant resolution deploring the many factions within the Pentecostal Movement, and appointed a committee to seek means of promoting closer bonds of fellowship.[25] Unfortunately, this high resolve died by default, for the committee did not find it convenient to meet.[26] Apparently the time was not propitious, for it would be many years before the possibility of genuine fellowship among the various strands of American Pentecostalism would ripen into fruition.

ALIGNMENT WITH THE EVANGELICAL WORLD

EMERGENCE OF EVANGELICAL COOPERATION

The idea of Bible-believing Christians forming a cooperative association has roots that go back at least as far as the Evangelical Alliance, organized in Britain in 1846.[27] An American branch was formed in 1867, but it never was a vigorous enterprise on this side of the Atlantic. In 1886, Josiah Strong became the first full-time general secretary of the branch, but 10 years later he resigned to participate in the formation of a new association oriented to a more

[23]Sherrill, *op. cit.*, p. 50.

[24]John B. Oliver, "Some Newer Religious Groups in the United States: Twelve Case Studies" (unpublished Ph.D. dissertation, Yale University, 1946), p. 235.

[25]General Council minutes, 1921, pp. 59-60.

[26]General Council minutes, 1923, p. 61.

[27]Shelley, *op. cit.*, p. 74.

liberal brand of theology.[28] In 1908 the Federal Council of Churches of Christ in America was formally organized, with 31 constituent American denominations as members.[29] "The Council's preamble and plan of federation (1908), as well as 'The Social Creed of the Churches' issued in 1912, revealed clearly the spirit of the liberal social gospel."[30] This defection from the Evangelical Alliance destroyed its effectiveness in the United States.

By the time of the American entry into World War II, it had become apparent to many conservative Christians that not only was the unity offered on the FCCCA platform not acceptable, but that the Fundamentalist type of unity was undesirable, as well. In September, 1941, the American Council of Christian Churches was brought into being by separatist Fundamentalists, headed by Carl McIntire.[31] Its purpose was "to coordinate some of the multifarious and overlapping associations and institutions and to combat what they considered the nefarious ecumenicism of the National Council of Churches (dominated by the mainline liberals)."[32] By 1965 the ACCC claimed to speak for 15 denominations and more than a million and a half Fundamentalists.[33] This figure seems much too high, a more likely figure being nearer 200,000.[34] However, its basic stance of militant reaction, breathing much of the belligerent spirit of the defeated Fundamentalism of the late 1920's and 1930's, did not appeal to the majority of conservative evangelicals.

As early as October, 1941, McIntire was invited to present the objectives of the ACCC to evangelical leaders gathered in Chicago.[35] McIntire urged the Evangelicals who were gathered there to join ranks with his group, maintaining

[28]*Ibid.*, p. 76.

[29]*Ibid.*

[30]*Ibid.*

[31]Carl McIntire, editorial, *Christian Beacon*, December 17, 1942, p. 1.

[32]William G. McLoughlin, "Is There a Third Force in Christendom?" *Daedalus*, XCVI (Winter 1967), p. 57.

[33]*Ibid.*

[34]Shelley, *op. cit.*, p. 118.

[35]*Ibid.*, p. 81.

his priority in the field.[36] But the Evangelicals there were reluctant to do this, feeling that the ACCC would not properly express the ideals they shared for a more positive evangelical witness.[37] As late as 1944 a serious attempt was made to combine the two bodies, but for various reasons the efforts failed. In effect, the Pentecostal churches were partially responsible for the maintenance of the separate identity of the newer and larger association that had come into being in the interval, the National Association of Evangelicals. What apparently happened was that the leaders in the American Council, unhappy that the newly formed National Association of Evangelicals had several Pentecostal bodies in it, did not wish an outright merger, but asked rather that the individual member bodies in the NAE apply separately for admission into the ACCC. This was demanded specifically as a means of barring the Pentecostal churches from membership in the proposed merger. The NAE leadership chose not to forsake their Pentecostal friends, and so the merger was never effected.[38]

The last attempt of the militant Fundamentalists to capture the leadership of Evangelicalism by seeking a merger with the NAE was at the second annual convention of the NAE in Columbus, Ohio, in April, 1944. Immediately following the failure of that attempt, McIntire launched a bitter tirade against the NAE, assailing it for permitting Pentecostals to participate. An excerpt from that volley is supplied as a sample of the attitude in the ACCC:

> "Tongues" is one of the great signs of the apostasy. As true Protestant denominations turn from the faith and it gets darker the Devil comes more into the open, and people who are not fed in the old line denominations go out to the "tongues" movement, for they feel that they have some life.
>
> The dominance of the "tongues" groups in the NAE "denominations" and their compromise in regard to the Federal Council will not, we believe, commend this organization to those who desire to see a standard lifted in behalf of the historic Christian faith.[39]

---

[36]Charles W. Conn, *Like a Mighty Army* (Cleveland, Tennessee: Church of God Publishing House, 1955), p. 258.

[37]Shelley, *op. cit.*, p. 81.

[38]Conn, *op. cit.*, pp. 258-59.

[39]Carl McIntire, editorial, *Christian Beacon*, April 27, 1944, p. 8.

Disappointed with cooperative enterprises to the left (the FCCCA) and to the right (the ACCC), a moderate force was emerging, seeking to form an association that would have positive purposes, not negative criticism, as its foundation. It was in this spirit that the National Association of Evangelicals came into being.[40]

The National Association of Evangelicals came to birth largely through the efforts of a regional group formed in 1929 known as the New England Fellowship.[41] This group was formed to effect cooperation among theologically conservative people in the area. Its activities centered in a series of annual Bible conferences at Rumney, New Hampshire. The conferences of 1939, 1940, and 1941 adopted resolutions calling for a national fellowship of Evangelicals.[42] Following preliminary correspondence by several of the leaders, Dr. J. Elwin Wright, director of the NEF, toured 31 states during 1941, seeking to ascertain the strength of interest in the proposed national association. As the result of this groundwork, about 20 evangelical leaders gathered for an exploratory meeting in Chicago, in October, 1941. The group unanimously agreed to issue a call for "a national conference of evangelicals, including leaders of various denominations, mission boards, colleges, seminaries, Bible institutes, the religious press, and interdenominational organizations."[43] It was at this meeting that the decision was made to reject the invitation of the leaders of the ACCC.

Response to the call brought about 150 leaders together at St. Louis in April, 1942. The importance of this meeting for the Pentecostals was that it was the first time any evangelical body had extended an invitation for participation. This was the crack in the wall of isolation for the Assemblies of God. Official delegates from the Assemblies of God to this constitutional convention were General Superintendent Ernest S. Williams, General Secretary J. Roswell Flower, and Missionary Secretary Noel Perkin. A

---

[40]Shelley, *op. cit.*, p. 83.
[41]*Ibid.*, p. 72.
[42]*Ibid.*, p. 73.
[43]J. Roswell Flower, *The Pentecostal Evangel*, June 19, 1943, p. 8.

young pastor from nearby Granite City, Illinois, Thomas F. Zimmerman, came as an unofficial observer. Zimmerman, currently the General Superintendent of the denomination, has not missed a meeting of NAE since. From 1960 to 1962 he served as president of the group.[44]

At the St. Louis meeting, Dr. Harold John Ockenga, pastor of Boston's Park Street Church, was elected to serve as the president of the new organization, and a constitution was adopted. The National Association of Evangelicals had been born. By 1967 it would claim representation of 29,000 churches and two and a half million Christians. Through its 12 affiliated agencies it would render a united evangelical witness for several million more.[45]

The response of the Assemblies of God to the overture from NAE was immediate. Although the biennial General Council would not be meeting until 1943, the General Presbytery at its September, 1942, meeting adopted a historic resolution:

> Resolved, that this session of the General Presbytery of the Assemblies of God hereby express sympathy with the general purpose and policy of the NAE for United Action as the purpose and policy have been outlined to this body and hereby authorize the Executive Presbytery to appoint delegates to the meeting of this association to be held at Chicago, Illinois, April 27-29, 1943, who shall be empowered to represent this body and to bring back a report to the General Council to enable us to determine whether or not the Assemblies of God should be represented in this association for united action.[46]

The resolution was adopted unanimously.

About 600 delegates, representing 65 denominations and agencies, gathered in Chicago for the 1943 NAE meeting. "Interest in the movement became so great that no less than one hundred and six members of the Assemblies of God attended the Chicago meeting."[47] Among those present were Calvinists, Arminians, Holiness people, and Pentecostals who "found a common bond in their love for the Lord Jesus and their belief in the fundamentals of the

[44]Interview, Thomas F. Zimmerman, December 8, 1967.
[45]Shelley, *op. cit.*, p. 86.
[46]General Presbytery minutes, 1942, p. 2.
[47]J. Roswell Flower, *The Pentecostal Evangel,* June 19, 1943, p. 8.

Christian faith."[48] Two Pentecostal bodies, the Assemblies of God and the Church of God, were included by representation on the 22-member Board of Administration.[49]

The February issue of the "Quarterly Letter," official voice of the executive offices to the ministers of the Assemblies of God, had carried a lengthy explanation of the NAE and urged prayer for and cooperation in the enterprise.[50] At the General Council that convened in Springfield in September, 1943, a resolution was adopted affiliating the Assemblies of God with the NAE and authorizing financial support for it.[51]

However, the alliance was still somewhat tenuous. The Pentecostals were not sure that the friendly association would endure—they had been accustomed to repeated rejections previously. This first venture into interchurch cooperation was characterized by sensitivity and timidity, a feeling that persisted among Pentecostals for years.[52] A crisis occurred at the Columbus, Ohio, meeting in April, 1944, that nearly ended the venture. A well-known Biblical expositor and radio personality had taken exception from the pulpit to a musical presentation by a Pentecostal girls' trio at one of the sessions. He seemed to use the occasion to question the propriety of permitting Pentecostals to participate at all. His remarks came at the very time when McIntire was making his final bid to get an alliance with the NAE. It was obvious that a major obstacle standing in the way of such a move was the presence of Pentecostals in NAE. And the Pentecostals were quite sensitive about all this. J. Roswell Flower, on behalf of the Pentecostals, offered to withdraw from active participation in NAE, expressing their willingness to sit in as observers only.[53] However, Dr. Ockenga, President of NAE, tipped the scales in favor of Pentecostal fellowship. He made it plain that the leaders wished to repudiate the personal remarks and views of the offending speaker, and disclaimed responsibility for

---

[48]*Ibid.*
[49]*Ibid.*
[50]"Quarterly Letter," February 15, 1943.
[51]General Council minutes, 1943, p. 8.
[52]Interview, Clyde Taylor, July 17, 1967.
[53]*Ibid.*

them. Ockenga rebuked the gentleman for abusing the privileges of the platform to which he had been invited to preach the gospel.[54] The crisis was passed and the tide turned.

For what reasons had the Evangelicals extended the invitation to the Pentecostals to share in the development of the NAE? There are several contributing factors. One was the role of the Assemblies of God in World War II. Assemblies of God men were thrown together with others in the military services, creating a mutual feeling of respect between Evangelicals and Pentecostals. Without question, the contact of Pentecostals with the larger church world occasioned by the grim circumstances of the war broke down many barriers on both sides. Another avenue of openness occasioned by the conflict was the service of Assemblies of God ministers for the first time in the army chaplaincy corps, a venture the pacifist-oriented denomination had not engaged in heretofore. Thirty-four Assemblies of God men served as chaplains, all in the army.[55]

Of special significance was the selfless ministry of the Assemblies of God in the publication of millions of copies of *Reveille,* a devotional and inspirational paper for servicemen, made available to 3,500 chaplains of all faiths without cost. The name of the denomination did not even appear on the paper; no attempt was made to capitalize on it for propaganda value, and yet the Assemblies of God constituency raised over $450,000 during the war years to supply the paper around the world, without consideration for the cost.[56] The Evangelicals took notice of this labor of love.

Another reason for the new openness of the Evangelicals was the rather impressive missionary work of the Assemblies of God, and that of other Pentecostals, too, around the world. By 1941 the Assemblies of God was engaged in missionary work in 43 countries, with nearly 400 appointed missionaries and 1,230 national workers.[57] In some parts of

---

[54]Carl McIntire, *Christian Beacon*, April 27, 1944, p. 8.
[55]General Council minutes, 1945, p. 45.
[56]Harrison, *op. cit.*, p. 245.
[57]General Council minutes, 1941, pp. 87-88.

the world the growth of Pentecostal missions was leading other groups. The role of the Assemblies of God in pioneering indigenous practices was already beginning to be an object of considerable interest.[58]

Still another reason was simply that it had become apparent that the Pentecostals were here to stay. The image of permanence, missing in the earlier days, was emerging. Perhaps this was strengthened by the recognition by leading Pentecostals of past evidences of isolationism, exclusivism, and even fanaticism within the ranks, failures they deplored.[59]

For these reasons, and possibly others, the Assemblies of God was received into the fellowship of moderate Evangelicalism. From 1942 onward there followed a thoroughgoing identification with the spirit and practice of this wing of the Christian church.

NAE-ASSOCIATED EVANGELICAL ENDEAVORS

Within the framework of the National Association of Evangelicals, three of the twelve affiliated organizations have had special importance for the Assemblies of God. These have been the National Religious Broadcasters, the National Sunday School Association, and the Evangelical Foreign Missions Association.

The National Religious Broadcasters. The role of the NAE in championing religious liberty is epitomized in the story of the National Religious Broadcasters. By late 1943 it looked as though the Federal Council of Churches had largely succeeded in persuading the networks that it alone should speak for all Protestantism. The issue had been the abuse of the airwaves by "religious racketeers," independent revivalists who were frequently identified as Fundamentalist or Pentecostal. Conservatives feared that their freedom to use American radio would be cut off should the FCCCA gain such a proprietary role. Cognizant of this danger, the NAE invited evangelical broadcasters to Columbus, Ohio, in April, 1944, where the second annual NAE convention was to meet. One hundred and fifty broad-

[58]See Chapter 10, Communication.
[59]Nichol, *op. cit.*, p. 209.

casters responded, and the National Religious Broadcasters was organized on April 14.[60] The following September in Chicago, the group adopted a formal constitution, elected officers, and developed a code of ethics, signed by each NRB member.[61] It sought to safeguard responsible evangelical broadcasters from religious racketeers on the one hand and ecclesiastical limitation on the other.[62] Diligent efforts followed in the presentation of the case for evangelical broadcasting to the commercial world. By 1946 the apparent threat to religious liberty had been erased. Freedom to purchase radio time on the networks was assured.[63]

On the original executive committee in 1944 was Thomas F. Zimmerman.[64] His interest in radio continued through the years, contributing greatly to the development of the NRB.[65] He has held several leadership positions, including the presidency of the group. Bartlett Peterson, C. M. Ward, D. V. Hurst, and Lee Shultz have also contributed in various ways to the NRB through the years. In return, the Assemblies of God has had the advantage of counsel and encouragement in developing its national network broadcast, "Revivaltime."

The National Sunday School Association. Sunday school literature was another area of special evangelical concern in the early days of the NAE. Between the World Wars, the strength and influence of the Sunday school movement had deteriorated, 19.6 percent of American children being enrolled in Sunday school in 1916, but only 17.6 percent in 1945.[66] Many conservatives felt that a factor in the decline of the Sunday school had been the theological erosion within the International Council of Religious Education which had assumed the control of the interdenominational Sunday school movement in 1922.[67] "The Council's uniform les-

---

[60]Shelley, *op. cit.*, p. 91.

[61]"National Religious Broadcasters, Incorporated" (undated pamphlet).

[62]Shelley, *op. cit.*, p. 91.

[63]*Ibid.*, p. 92.

[64]Letter from B. L. Armstrong, Executive Secretary, NRB, October 24, 1967.

[65]Interview, Bartlett Peterson, October 5, 1967.

[66]Shelley, *op. cit.*, p. 93.

[67]J. D. Murch, *Christian Education and the Local Church* (Cincinnati: Standard Publishing Company, 1943), p. 86.

sons presented liberal theology and the social gospel with little if any reference to the Bible."[68]

In June, 1943, the NAE executive committee appointed a group to study the possibility of developing a series of uniform Sunday school lessons.[69] It was in New York City in December, 1944, that J. R. Flower offered to the group the benefit of the experience of the Assemblies of God in curriculum development. As early as 1937 the Assemblies of God had broken away from the ICRE and had launched its own pioneer series of uniform lessons under the direction of Editor Stanley Frodsham.[70] Apparently the Assemblies of God was the first denomination in the evangelical orbit to venture in this direction. Consequently, the committee adopted a recommendation that the NAE Commission for Church Schools make use of Flower's generous offer.[71]

Exploration into the curricular problem led to the proposal that a whole new Sunday school agency be created for the promotion of evangelical Sunday school work. Such discussion began as early as April, 1944.[72] A year later, the National Sunday School Association was formed.[73] On the original executive committee of the NSSA were Ralph M. Riggs and Loine Honderick from the Assemblies of God. Early in October, 1946, the NAE Board of Administration formally received the NSSA as an affiliated organization, contingent upon the ratification of the proposed NSSA constitution at the first national convention of NSSA, scheduled for later in the month.[74] And in this fashion the National Sunday School Association came into being.

Through the years Assemblies of God personnel have participated actively in the NSSA program, notably Bert Webb who served as president in 1960, and Ralph Harris who has served since 1956 as chairman of the Curriculum Commission. In 1947, William E. Kirschke of the Assem-

---

[68]Shelley, *op. cit.*, p. 93.

[69]Minutes of the NAE Executive Committee, June 17-18, 1943.

[70]Interview, Ralph Harris, November 15, 1967.

[71]Minutes of the NAE Executive Committee, December 13, 1944.

[72]Shelley, *op. cit.*, p. 94.

[73]Minutes of the NSSA Executive Committee, April 30-May 1, 1945.

[74]Minutes of the NAE Board of Administration, October 1-2, 1946.

bles of God filled the position as Executive Secretary.[75] There has been a strong and mutually beneficial relationship between the Assemblies of God and the NSSA from its inception.

The Evangelical Foreign Missions Association. A development in the area of missions parallel to that in Sunday school work has been the story of the Evangelical Foreign Missions Association. Anxiety about the implications of the growing propensity for ecumenism in existing intergroup missionary agencies was already developing when the NAE was formed. Consequently the NAE established a Department of Home and Foreign Missions in 1943.[76] An office was opened in Washington, D.C., with Dr. Clyde Taylor, currently the Executive Director of NAE, serving as a representative in government matters. However, missions leaders felt that a separate organization was needed so that a constituency somewhat broader than NAE-member agencies could benefit.

A call was issued to 75 mission boards for a conference to be held in Chicago in May, 1945. With the full approval of NAE, the Evangelical Foreign Missions Association came into existence at that meeting.[77] A constitution was adopted in September. The following spring the first annual EFMA convention was held. The purposes and functions of EFMA have been manifold, but particularly outstanding have been the achievements of the Washington office. Effective government representation, headed by Clyde Taylor, has expedited the acquisition of visas, cared for numerous diplomatic matters, and represented the needs of evangelical missionaries to the United States government.[78] So effective have been the efforts of EFMA that by 1966 it was serving over 100 mission boards and 14,000 missionaries, directly or indirectly.[79]

The Assemblies of God has eagerly participated in the EFMA from its beginnings. Noel Perkin, and later Philip

---

[75]Interview, William Kirschke, October 12, 1967.

[76]Shelley, *op. cit.*, p. 100.

[77]*Ibid.*

[78]Interview, Clyde Taylor, July 17, 1967.

[79]Shelley, *op. cit.*, p. 100.

The "Apostolic Faith" band, with Rev. Charles F. Parham, at the Bryan Hall meeting in Houston, Texas, July 6 to August 10, 1905.

"Stone's Folly," the home of Parham's Bethel Bible College, Topeka, Kansas.

"Apostolic Faith" camp meeting, Houston, Texas, in 1906 or 1907.

The Azusa Street Mission, Los Angeles, California

It was in the back of this general store in Malvern, Arkansas, that E. N. Bell printed the "Word and Witness," forerunner of "The Pentecostal Evangel."

Pentecostal camp meeting, Eureka Springs, Arkansas, midsummer, 1912. E. N. Bell was director of this camp meeting, which proved to be a significant step in the formation of the Assemblies of God.

The Opera House in Hot Springs, Arkansas, site of the First General Council of the Assemblies of God, April 2-12, 1914.

Visitors and delegates at the First General Council of the Assemblies of God, Hot Springs, Arkansas, April 2-12, 1914. Kneeling across the front are the eight men elected as the initial Executive Presbytery.

Students at the Full Gospel School, Findlay, Ohio. T. K. Leonard, the director of the school, is at the extreme right.

The first Executive Presbytery of the Assemblies of God, elected in Hot Springs, Arkansas, April, 1914. Front row (left to right): T. K. Leonard, E. N. Bell, C. B. Fockler; back row (left to right): J. W. Welch, J. R. Flower, D. C. O. Opperman, H. A. Goss, and M. M. Pinson.

The General Presbytery, elected at the 1919 General Council, Stone Church, Chicago: Front row (left to right): J. R. Flower, S. A. Jamieson, E. N. Bell, J. W. Welch, J. T. Boddy, S. H. Frodsham, Ellis Banta; second row (left to right): Frank Gray, J. R. Kline, John Goben, D. H. McDowell, R. A. Brown, Joseph Tunmore, F. A. Hale; third row (left to right): O. P. Brann, E. R. Fitzgerald, E. N. Richey, John Coxe, D. W. Kerr, R. J. Craig, Orville Benham, A. P. Collins, T. K. Leonard.

The Gospel Publishing House on West Pacific Street, Springfield, Missouri, as it appeared shortly after it was purchased, 1918.

Inside the Gospel Publishing House, Springfield, Missouri, 1918. Third from right is Stanley Frodsham; fifth from right is E. N. Bell; sixth is J. W. Welch.

The employees of the Gospel Publishing House, 1926

The Gospel Publishing House, 434 W. Pacific Street, Springfield, Missouri, a familiar address for many years.

Ground-breaking ceremony for the new printing plant, 1948. From left to right: J. Z. Kamerer, J. R. Flower, Wesley R. Steelberg, J. O. Harrell, Stanley Frodsham, and H. B. Garlock.

Placing the cornerstone at the dedication of the new administration building, February, 1962. Watching the two workmen are (left to right): C. W. H. Scott, M. B. Netzel, J. R. Flower, T. F. Zimmerman, G. F. Lewis, E. S. Williams, Bert Webb, Howard S. Bush, J. Philip Hogan.

The Assemblies of God headquarters complex, 1445 Boonville Avenue, Springfield, Missouri. 1. Warehouse (1980). 2. International Distribution Center (1971), and Assemblies of God Graduate School (1972). 3. Gospel Publishing House printing department (1949). 4. Administration building (1962). Not shown, Radiant Book & Music Center (1978), and Conference Center (1977).

Stanley Frodsham and Charles E. Robinson pictured in the editorial office of the Gospel Publishing House, 1928.

An early camp meeting scene. Potomac Park Camp, Falling Waters, West Virginia.

Rocky Mountain District Camp, Littleton, Colorado.

General Council officers in conference about 1927. From left to right: S. H. Frodsham, Arthur Graves, William Faux, J. Z. Kamerer, J. R. Evans, David McDowell, W. T. Gaston, Noel Perkin.

The Executive Presbytery of 1970. Front row (left to right): C. W. H. Scott, Bartlett Peterson, T. F. Zimmerman, M. B. Netzel, T. E. Gannon. Second row (left to right): G. W. Hardcastle, N. D. Davidson, Roy Wead, Edgar Bethany, E. M. Clark, Kermit Reneau, G. Raymond Carlson, and Paul Lowenberg.

E. N. Bell
Chairman (1914; 1919-1923)

A. P. Collins
Chairman (1914-1915)

J. W. Welch
Chairman (1915-1919; 1923-1925)

W. T. Gaston
Superintendent (1925-1929)

E. S. Williams
Superintendent (1929-1949)

W. R. Steelberg
Superintendent (1949-1952)

G. F. Lewis
Superintendent (1952-1953)

R. M. Riggs
Superintendent (1953-1959)

T. F. Zimmerman
Superintendent (1959-   )

First Assembly of God, Wheaton, Illinois. This structure, completed in 1961, was an early "Breakthrough" project of the Assemblies of God. Cooperative ventures, such as this, have enabled new congregations to move forward more rapidly than if they had to struggle entirely on their own. Wayne Kraiss served as the founder of this church.

Titled "The Ambassador," this World War II B-17 bomber was purchased with "Speed-the-Light" funds and served as an important means of shuttling missionaries to and from the field in the years immediately after the war.

The mammoth Eleventh National Sunday School Convention attracted more than 10,000 people to Kiel Auditorium, St. Louis, Missouri, in the spring of 1954.

Heard "across the na-
ion and around the
world" for many years
has been the "Revival-
time" preacher C. Morse
Ward.

The Assemblies of God in recent years has been reaching into the urban world with such ministries as Teen Challenge. Pictured above is a scene in "The Hidden Manna," a coffeehouse in Philadelphia. At the right is the founder of the original New York City Teen Challenge Center, David Wilkerson.

The library at Evangel College. Evangel College is the senior liberal arts college owned and operated by the General Council of the Assemblies of God.

Dedicated in 1970 to E. S. Williams is the new chapel at Central Bible College, the ministerial training institution operated by the General Council.

Hogan, served on the Board of Directors of EFMA. Hogan completed a term as president of EFMA in 1970.

OTHER EVANGELICAL ENDEAVORS

In the years following 1941 a host of evangelical enterprises flourished. Among those not organically related to the National Association of Evangelicals that had special significance for the Assemblies of God were the Accrediting Association of Bible Colleges, the Evangelical Theological Society, and the Evangelical Press Association. The Wheaton and Berlin congresses on evangelism also had special importance to the Pentecostals.

The Accrediting Association of Bible Colleges. The origin of the Accrediting Association of Bible Colleges goes back to 1944.[80] At that time the National Association of Evangelicals, through its Education Commission, sponsored the development of the North American Association of Bible Institutes and Bible Colleges.[81] It became apparent almost at the outset that many non-NAE institutions wished to be served by such an agency. At the 1946 NAE convention in Minneapolis, Dr. Howard W. Ferrin appealed for the establishment of an independent agency that could furnish an accrediting service for all evangelical institutions.[82] Invitations were dispatched to a large number of Bible institutes in the United States and Canada for an exploratory conference. The Accrediting Association of Bible Institutes and Bible Colleges was formed at that conference, held in October, 1947, at Winona Lake, Indiana. Dr. Samuel Sutherland of the Bible Institute of Los Angeles was selected to serve as the first president of the new organization. Twelve schools were accredited in 1948, and soon afterward the agency received recognition by the United States Office of Education as the one accrediting agency in the field of undergraduate theological education.[83]

The Assemblies of God was represented at the Winona

---

[80]The title of the agency was originally the Accrediting Association of Bible Institutes and Bible Colleges (AABIBC). It was later changed to the Accrediting Association of Bible Colleges (AABC), the term by which it is now known.

[81]Letter from C. C. Burnett, September 28, 1967.

[82]S. A. Witmer, *Education with Dimension* (Manhasset, New York: Channel Press, 1962), p. 46.

[83]*Ibid.*

Lake meeting by Ralph M. Riggs, Secretary of the Assemblies' Education Department, and by J. Roswell Flower, General Secretary.[84] Riggs and Arthur Graves, then the president of South-Eastern Bible College, Lakeland, Florida, were appointed to serve on the first executive committee of AABIBC, two out of the eight thus being from the Assemblies of God.[85] In addition to these men, Bartlett Peterson, Paul Emery, and C. C. Burnett have served on the executive committee in years since.[86]

Immediately the denomination urged full participation in the new accrediting association. By 1951 all the schools operated by the Assemblies of God enjoyed either full or associate membership.[87] The beneficial results derived by the Assemblies of God schools from this association with AABIBC may be detected in the following excerpts from a 1956 report by J. Robert Ashcroft, then National Secretary of Education for the denomination.

> In 1947 12% of the faculty members of the average school had advanced degrees. In 1955 34.6% had advanced degrees. Five of the 12 schools in 1947 had *no* teachers with advanced degrees. The highest school in that year had 33%. . . .
>
> In 1955 the lowest school had 10% with advanced degrees; the highest school had 62%. . . .
>
> A strong trend toward more faculty members with advanced degrees can be seen. This is part of the trend to upgrade standards to receive accreditation on the collegiate level. When the AABIBC issued its first list of accredited schools in 1948, 3 of our then 13 schools were accredited on the collegiate level. In 1955 5 of our 9 Bible schools were accredited on the collegiate level and two others were applying for this recognition.[88]

Few external associations have so directly and dramatically made an impact on the Assemblies of God.

The Evangelical Theological Society. In the years immediately following World War II an important new phenomenon began to manifest itself in the world of Amer-

---

[84]Interview, Ralph M. Riggs, August 24, 1967.

[85]*Ibid.*

[86]Letter from C. C. Burnett, September 28, 1967. C. C. Burnett has been particularly active in evangelical affairs. He has served as secretary of the NAE since 1956 and is chairman of the committee that arranges all the conventions.

[87]Kendrick, *op. cit.*, p. 135.

[88]Minutes of the Board of Education, September 8, 1956.

ican evangelical Christianity. A rising chorus of criticism from within the evangelical quarter attacked the schismatic and negative spirit of Fundamentalism, challenging the right of its exponents to represent the concerns of genuine orthodox Christianity in the postwar world. "The movement's 'wowser' worship, its cultural isolationism, its sectarian separatism, its monastic ethics, its theological hair-splitting—these and other characteristics were relentlessly exposed."[89] The basic objectives of the "new evangelicalism" were a quest for academic respectability, social involvement, and denominational redirection.[90] Although Assemblies of God involvement in this new mood has been sketchy, it appears to be gaining ground.[91] The one area in which there has been a degree of Pentecostal participation from near the beginning has been the Evangelical Theological Society.

Faculty members of the Gordon Divinity School, Beverly, Massachusetts, proposed that conservative scholars gather periodically for Biblical and theological discussion as a means of stimulating evangelical scholarship.[92] Notable among these were Dr. Burton Goddard, sometimes called "the father of the Evangelical Theological Society," and Dr. Edward Dalgleish, now at Baylor University.[93] As a result of the proposal of the Gordon men, 60 scholars from a wide variety of schools and fellowships gathered at the YMCA in Cincinnati, Ohio, December 27-29, 1949, to form the Evangelical Theological Society.[94] Its birth came just two years after the publication of Carl F. H. Henry's *The Uneasy Conscience of Modern Fundamentalism,* which appears to be the genesis of the new Evangelicalism.[95] From its beginnings in 1949, the ETS has steadily grown year by year, claiming 400 full memberships (requiring at least a Th.M. degree) and 200 student memberships by 1967.[96] Its primary function

[89]Shelley, *op. cit.*, p. 112.

[90]*Ibid.*, p. 113.

[91]Carmen, *op. cit.*, p. 54.

[92]"The Evangelical Theological Society" (undated pamphlet).

[93]Interview, Burton Goddard, July 20, 1967.

[94]"The Evangelical Theological Society" (undated pamphlet).

[95]Shelley, *op. cit.*, p. 111.

[96]Interview, Burton Goddard, July 20, 1967.

is to provide a forum, both nationally and regionally, for theological and Biblical discussion, but it has also published several volumes prepared by members.

The most conspicuous Assemblies of God representative through the years of ETS has been Dr. Stanley Horton, chairman of the theology department at Central Bible College. Largely through his influence, and that of the late Dr. T. A. Kessel, former dean of CBC, there has been a rather strong liaison with the Midwest Region of the ETS. In 1969 Dr. Robert Cooley, dean of Evangel College, was elected president of ETS, the first Pentecostal to bear this distinction.

Evangelical Press Association. Another facet of postwar evangelical activity has been editorial interchange. James DeForest Murch, editor of *Action,* felt that the mutual stimulation of evangelical editors would result in a more effective ministry for each periodical. He was largely responsible for the calling together of evangelical editors to a meeting in Chicago in January, 1948.[97] This was the origin of the Evangelical Press Association. More than 150 member publications are served by the EPA.[98] In addition to providing a means of upgrading the quality of evangelical journals and magazines, since 1951 it has also operated a news service.

The Assemblies of God has been a vigorous participant since the first session of EPA in 1948. Wildon Colbaugh was present at that first meeting.[99] Each year since there has been representation, sometimes outnumbering that of any other single group.[100] Robert Cunningham, current editor of *The Pentecostal Evangel,* has served as president. Ralph Harris, Gwen Jones, and Harris Jansen have also occupied offices in the association.[101] In 1970 the Assemblies of God had seven periodicals registered with the EPA with a total circulation of over 400,000.[102]

The Wheaton Conference. A historic event in evangelical

[97]Interview, Robert Cunningham, September 13, 1967.
[98]"EPA Membership Directory," 1970.
[99]Interview, Robert Cunningham, September 13, 1967.
[100]*Ibid.*
[101]*Ibid.*
[102]"EPA Membership Directory," 1970.

Christianity was the Congress on The Church's Worldwide Missions, which met on the campus of Wheaton College during the week of April 9-16, 1966. One hundred and fifty mission boards sent 938 delegates representing more than 13,000 American missionaries.[103] A joint enterprise of the Interdenominational Foreign Missions Association and the Evangelical Foreign Missions Association, this great convocation assembled to redefine their task of world outreach in the light of the changing cultural, political, and theological milieu. It was remarkable for its breadth of participation, unthinkable a generation ago, especially respecting the participation of Pentecostals. "The Spirit of God has shown them their common unity based upon a commitment to an authoritative Bible, a conviction of the lostness of men, and of their need for personal regeneration."[104]

Of the ten major papers read at the conference, one, entitled "Mission and Church Growth," was presented by Melvin Hodges of the Assemblies of God. Participation on this level had not been known before.

The Berlin Conference. Following the Wheaton Congress by several months was the mammoth Berlin Congress, a similar evangelical enterprise, but on an international scale. Sponsored by *Christianity Today* as its tenth anniversary project, it brought together 1,250 delegates from 104 countries to rethink the mission of the church in the contemporary world.[105] There had not been such a gathering since 1910, at Edinburgh, embracing such a wide representation of evangelical leaders from throughout the world. Over 200 speakers were listed on the Congress program, including several Pentecostals. T. F. Zimmerman participated in a panel on eschatology, presenting an address entitled "Eschatology and Evangelism." Jose Maria Rico of Bolivia, an international evangelist of the Assemblies of God, served

---

[103]Harold Lindsell, *The Church's Worldwide Mission* (Waco, Texas: Word Books, 1966), p. 4.

[104]*Ibid.*, p. 8.

[105]"World Congress on Evangelism," *The Pentecostal Evangel*, January 29, 1967, pp. 14-15.

on another panel. All told, there were 38 Assemblies of God delegates and observers.[106]

Carl Henry, principal sponsor of the great Berlin Congress, considers it to be a major step in the generating of a climate of good feeling between the evangelical world and the Pentecostals. To him it was evidence that the Pentecostal Movement had matured.[107]

A NEW CLIMATE OF GOODWILL

Chiefly as the result of the association of Holiness and Pentecostal leaders precipitated by the NAE, a perceptible, if not radical, change has been occurring within the Holiness tradition respecting the Pentecostals and their theological position. Delbert Rose, historian of the National Holiness Association, has distinguished two strands within the Holiness Movement, one maintaining the older—and quite negative—stance; the other developing a considerably more tolerant perspective.[108] He cites Donald Metz and Kenneth Geiger as examples of the persistence of the older, somewhat inflexible, antipathy.[109] However, the National Holiness Association now admits into membership those professing entire sanctification as a second definite work of grace, but who also profess to have had an experience of speaking in tongues. An example of such a body now participating in the National Holiness Association is the Bethany Fellowship, Incorporated, with headquarters in Minneapolis.[110] Dr. Frank Bateman Stanger, president of Asbury Theological Seminary, supports the contention that there is a new climate of understanding emerging between Holiness and Pentecostal people, and that this has been occasioned in large measure by the associations engendered through common participation in evangelical agencies and enterprises.[111]

---

[106] *Ibid.*, p. 14.

[107] Interview, Carl F. H. Henry, July 14, 1967.

[108] Letter from Delbert Rose, July 10, 1967.

[109] See Donald Metz, *Speaking in Tongues: An Analysis* (Kansas City, Missouri: Nazarene Publishing House, 1964), and Kenneth Geiger, ed., *The Word and the Doctrine* (Kansas City, Missouri: Beacon Hill Press, 1965).

[110] Letter from Delbert Rose, July 10, 1967.

[111] Letter from Frank Bateman Stanger, June 30, 1967.

There appears to be a persisting, inflexible antipathy to Pentecostalism, however, among dispensational Fundamentalists.[112] No change is evident from this quarter.

Pentecostal Cooperation

INFLUENCES

In the years prior to 1941 the Assemblies of God had been isolated not only from evangelical bodies, but also from other American Pentecostal groups. The Pentecostal Movement was badly fragmented. A major reason for this proliferation was undoubtedly disagreement on theological interpretation, especially revolving around the doctrine of sanctification.[113] Two streams of influence, each developing in the post-1941 era, produced a marked change in this unfortunate situation. By 1948 the Pentecostal Fellowship of North America had become a reality.

One of the major influences in creating a better climate of feeling within the American Pentecostal Movement was the National Association of Evangelicals. Here it was that Pentecostal leaders were thrown together for the first time. They discovered that their differences were not so great as they had imagined.[114] As a direct consequence of the NAE fellowship, the Pentecostals decided to hold an exploratory meeting in conjunction with the NAE convention in Chicago in May, 1948.[115] An examination of the constitutions of the NAE and the PFNA discloses a striking evidence of NAE influence.[116] The PFNA statement of faith, part of the constitution, is a verbatim reproduction of the NAE statement, with the single exception that an additional article has been added to specify Pentecostal distinctives.

The other important stimulus to American Pentecostal fellowship came from Europe. In 1947, at Zurich, Switzerland, the World Pentecostal Fellowship was created, large-

[112]Letter from Merrill F. Unger, September 25, 1967. Also, this unchanging dispensational attitude is reflected by a representative of the "Radio Bible Class," founded by M. R. De Haan, in a letter from Robert E. Roush, Executive Administrator of the "Radio Bible Class," September 13, 1967.

[113]Harrison, *op. cit.*, p. 277.

[114]Interview, J. Roswell Flower, June 26, 1967.

[115]"Quarterly Letter," November 20, 1948.

[116]"Constitution and By-laws of the Pentecostal Fellowship of North America" (undated pamphlet), and "Constitution of the National Association of Evangelicals" (undated mimeographed pamphlet).

ly through European efforts that had been germinating through the years.[117] At this conference a challenge was issued to the American groups that if they expected unity among European Pentecostals they should first make an effort of their own to bring about cooperation among Pentecostals in the United States.[118] As early as January, 1921, a European conference had been held in Amsterdam, with leaders of several countries meeting for the first time.[119] It proved to be unsuccessful owing to the attempt of the Germans to dominate the convention with a theological fad current among them.[120] Through the continued encouragement of Donald Gee of England, Pastor Lewi Pethrus of the huge Filadelphia Church in Stockholm succeeded in calling another European conference together. Delegates from about 20 European countries gathered in June, 1939, in Stockholm. Prince and Princess Bernadotte of the Royal House of Sweden attended the great Sunday morning service in a large tent. More than 15,000 attended the convocation.[121]

The war interrupted further gatherings, but in September, 1946, a planning session was held in Paris for another great international Pentecostal conference, scheduled for Zurich in May, 1947.[122] Leonhard Steiner, pastor of the Basel Church, acted as Organizing Secretary. Following the great Zurich conference, when the World Pentecostal Fellowship was organized, an international clearinghouse was established in Basel for the purpose of European relief work and evangelism. Its main task was to facilitate the recovery of Pentecostal churches that had suffered in the recent war.[123]

The Zurich meeting had been so promising that a second conference was scheduled for Paris in May, 1949. One hundred and fifty-six delegates and 320 observers from 32

---

[117]Harold A. Fischer, "Progress of the Various Modern Pentecostal Movements Toward World Fellowship" (unpublished M.A. thesis, Texas Christian University, 1950), p. 22.

[118]"Quarterly Letter," November 20, 1948.

[119]Donald Gee, *The Pentecostal Movement*, p. 122.

[120]*Ibid.*, pp. 122-23.

[121]*Ibid.*, p. 181.

[122]*Ibid.*, p. 180.

[123]Fischer, *op. cit.*, p. 22.

countries attended the meeting.[124] The important achievement of the Paris meeting was the decision agreed upon regarding a permanent basis of fellowship that would not offend the consciences of the ultracongregational-minded Scandinavian Pentecostals who feared formal organization.[125] Successive meetings were held triennially thereafter. Three have been held in the Western Hemisphere: in 1958 the conference met in Toronto, and in 1967 in Rio de Janeiro. The Ninth World Pentecostal Fellowship conference met in the United States in 1970 in Dallas, Texas.

The purpose of the World Pentecostal Fellowship is strictly spiritual fellowship; no formal legislation or organic unions have been intended.[126] One concrete by-product was the appointment of Donald Gee to serve as editor of a quarterly Pentecostal review entitled *Pentecost.* Seventy-seven issues were published between September, 1947, and November, 1966. Gee's untimely death on July 20, 1966, ended the existence of the informative periodical.[127] His penetrating insight into the worldwide dimensions of Pentecostalism was a fruitful contribution to the entire Pentecostal Movement. Percy Brewster of Wales was asked to begin a new journal at the Dallas meeting in 1970.

THE PENTECOSTAL FELLOWSHIP OF NORTH AMERICA

So it was that through the instigation of the World Pentecostal Fellowship and the National Association of Evangelicals, the Pentecostal Fellowship of North America came into being. Leaders of eight American Pentecostal bodies met on May 7, 1948, in Chicago, immediately following the NAE convention to explore the possibility of a structured fellowship. Selected to serve as temporary chairman and secretary were John C. Jernigan of the Church of God and J. Roswell Flower of the Assemblies of God.[128]

A second exploratory conference was held in Chicago on August 3 and 4, with 27 representatives from 12 denomina-

---

[124]*Ibid.*, pp. 23-24.
[125]*The Pentecostal Evangel*, June 25, 1949, pp. 8-11.
[126]Interview, Thomas F. Zimmerman, December 8, 1967.
[127]*The Pentecostal Evangel*, August 8, 1966, p. 3.
[128]*The Pentecostal Evangel*, June 19, 1948, p. 11.

tions.[129] An important action of this session was the appointment of a committee to frame a tentative constitution for presentation to a constitutional convention that was scheduled for October. The committee consisted of J. Roswell Flower, chairman, E. J. Fulton of the Open Bible Standard Church, Howard P. Courtney of the Foursquare Church, and H. L. Chesser of the Pentecostal Holiness Church.[130]

Nearly 200 representatives from about a dozen Pentecostal bodies gathered in Des Moines, Iowa, October 26 to 28, 1948, for the constitutional convention. It was estimated that the delegates and leaders who attended represented nearly a million Pentecostal believers.[131] Elected to serve the new fellowship were John C. Jernigan, chairman; E. J. Fulton and Howard P. Courtney, vice-chairmen; and J. Roswell Flower, secretary. The chief task of the convention was the formation and adoption of a constitution. This was accomplished easily and quickly owing to the warm spirit of brotherhood and mutual confidence that pervaded the meeting.[132] The purposes of the new fellowship as set forth in the constitution can be distilled in this fashion:

1. To provide a vehicle of expression and coordination of effort in matters common to all;
2. To demonstrate to the world the essential unity of Spirit-baptized believers;
3. To provide services to its constituents which will enable them to accomplish more quickly and efficiently their responsibility for the speedy evangelization of the world;
4. To encourage the principles of comity for the nurture of the body of Christ, endeavoring to keep the unity of the Spirit until we all come to the unity of the faith.[133]

Assemblies of God reaction to the new fellowship was favorable from the beginning. Seven of the 24 who met at the May, 1948, meeting were from the denomination.[134] In September the General Presbytery adopted a resolution encouraging the effort being made for closer cooperation

[129] *The Pentecostal Evangel*, August 28, 1948, pp. 6-7.
[130] *Ibid.*, p. 7.
[131] *The Pentecostal Evangel*, November 20, 1948, p. 13.
[132] *Ibid.*
[133] "Quarterly Letter," November 20, 1948.
[134] *The Pentecostal Evangel*, June 19, 1948, p. 11.

among the Pentecostal bodies.[135] The Executive Presbytery during the course of the following year made formal application for membership in the PFNA, a course of action approved by the General Presbytery of 1949 with the recommendation that it be presented for adoption to the General Council.[136] Subsequently the 1949 General Council in session approved the application for membership.[137] In this fashion the Assemblies of God joined its support for Pentecostal unity.

By 1969 the PFNA claimed 17 denominations in its fellowship, with slightly over a million total membership and 16,000 local churches. Of this, the Assemblies of God, with 625,000 members and 8,500 churches, constituted more than half the total strength of the association.[138]

However, much of the leadership and enthusiasm have come from the smaller groups in the fellowship, notably E. J. Fulton and R. Bryant Mitchell of the Open Bible Standard Church, Howard P. Courtney of the Foursquare Church, John Jernigan and James Cross of the Church of God, Walter McAlister of the Pentecostal Assemblies of Canada, and A. J. Synan of the Pentecostal Holiness Church. From the Assemblies of God, Thomas F. Zimmerman, J. Roswell Flower, and Gayle F. Lewis have made a sizable contribution.

The chief success of the PFNA has been the bringing together of the leadership of previously isolated disparate Pentecostal groups. On the local level there has been far less accomplishment. In spite of the adoption of a comity agreement in 1962, there have been few locations where strong local fellowship has developed.[139] Notable exceptions are Portland, Oregon; Toledo and Dayton, Ohio; and Chicago, Illinois.[140]

Since 1941, then, the Assemblies of God has gravitated strongly to an involved association with moderate evangelical Christianity, as opposed to militant Fundamentalism.

[135]General Presbytery minutes, 1948, p. 7.
[136]General Presbytery minutes, 1949, p. 8.
[137]General Council minutes, 1949, p. 29.
[138]"Pentecostal Fellowship of North America, Official Statistics" (July, 1969).
[139]PFNA Business Session minutes, November 1, 1962, p. 6.
[140]Interview, R. Bryant Mitchell, February 7, 1968.

It has also entered into a promising relationship with other Pentecostal bodies. At the same time, the denomination has moved further from the Ecumenical Movement, as expressed by the National Council of Churches and the World Council of Churches.

Opposition to Ecumenism

Prior to 1941 the Assemblies of God participated, on an unofficial basis, in several agencies subsequently gathered into the 1950 organization of the National Council of Churches of Christ in America. As early as the year 1919, J. Roswell Flower, then Missionary Secretary of the Assemblies of God, attended the conventions of the Foreign Missions Conference of North America. It was helpful at that time to bear some kind of relationship to a large, well-known body, inasmuch as the Assemblies of God was new, unknown, and in need of recognition so that missionaries could have their papers expedited.[141] In addition, through the years, the Assemblies of God participated informally in such ventures as the Department of Church World Service, the Missionary Research Library, and the Associated Missions Medical Office.[142] In the 1950's representatives of the Assemblies of God participated in the stewardship seminars conducted by the National Council of Churches.[143]

By 1963 all these associations had been terminated. On August 31, 1962, the General Presbytery unanimously adopted a resolution, subsequently ratified at the General Council of 1963, also by a unanimous vote, condemning the Ecumenical Movement and disapproving of "ministers and churches participating in any of the modern ecumenical organizations on a local, national or international level in such a manner as to promote the Ecumenical Movement. . . ."[144] The reasons for this decisive action were stated in the form of a series of propositions:

> 1) We believe said movement to be a sign of the times and contrary to the real Biblical doctrine of spiritual unity in the church of Jesus Christ, and

[141]Interview, J. Roswell Flower, June 26, 1967.
[142]Interview, Robert J. McGlasson, October 9, 1967.
[143]Interview, Curtis W. Ringness, October 10, 1967.
[144]General Council minutes, 1963, pp. 41-42.

2) We are opposed to ecumenicity based on organic and organizational unity, and

3) We believe that the combination of many denominations into a World Super Church will probably culminate in the Scarlet Woman or Religious Babylon of Revelation. . . .[145]

The resolution, however, did seek to safeguard participation of ministers on a local level in such interdenominational activities as ministerial alliances.[146]

The basic reason for this withdrawal is theological. As early as 1950, at the time of the formation of the National Council of Churches, an editorial in *The Pentecostal Evangel* expressed for the first time apprehension about the rising ecumenical thrust. It likened the movement to the gathering of weeds referred to in Matthew 13. "Our Lord said that the bundling would be for the burning."[147] The same article, while eschewing relationship with the newly created National Council of Churches, specifically endorsed the NAE and the PFNA as examples of "cooperation in worthy projects without compromising on those truths which distinguish them from other Christians and which are dear to their hearts."[148]

Fears regarding the possible loss of religious liberty were a factor in the march away from the Ecumenical Movement. It had been but a short time before that the National Religious Broadcasters had organized to combat what was felt to be a threat of a monopoly of religious broadcasting on American networks, a monopoly by ecclesiastical powers. Fresh alarm recurred when it appeared that the radio agency of the National Council of Churches, RAVEMCCO, was displaying a similar restrictive attitude toward gospel broadcasting in Latin America.[149] Such episodes seemed to confirm the belief among the Pentecostals that the Ecumenical Movement posed a threat to their unrestricted freedom.

New Relations with Older Churches

Although there was a definite turning from the Ecu-

[145]*Ibid.*, p. 41.
[146]*Ibid.*
[147]"Unity—False and True," *The Pentecostal Evangel*, December 17, 1950, p. 2.
[148]*Ibid.*
[149]Interview, Robert J. McGlasson, October 9, 1967.

menical Movement, in recent years events have occurred that have brought the Assemblies of God into communication with representatives of a wide range of denominations in the larger church world.

THE RISE OF NEO-PENTECOSTALISM

Statistical data indicate that there was a revival of interest in religion in the United States in the 1950's, but commentators seem to agree that it did not make a profound impact on American society. [150] One interesting religious phenomenon that arose in that period which seems to have persisted in Neo-Pentecostalism was the appearance of glossolalia and associated manifestations in the historic churches. Prior to the late 1950's it was standard practice for laymen and ministers of other communions who received the Pentecostal experience to withdraw from their respective fellowships and seek association with denominations in the Pentecostal orbit.[151] Variously dated from 1955 to 1960, a change in this pattern became apparent. Those receiving the experience no longer felt it necessary to leave their parent churches. It is still too early to assess the full significance of this recent development in American church history, but it is possible to trace some of its origins and to establish some tentative implications for the Assemblies of God.

In 1951 two events occurred that seem to mark the earliest moments in the rise of Neo-Pentecostalism. In that year Robert Walker, editor of the popular evangelical monthly *Christian Life*, visited the Assemblies of God headquarters in Springfield, Missouri. He became interested in the Pentecostal message, subsequently received the experience, and gradually reoriented the editorial policy of the magazine so that it became a sounding board for the present-day ministry of the Holy Spirit. This changing mood in the periodical dates from the appearance of a penetrating

[150]See Rachel Jean Taylor, "The 'Return to Religion' in America After the Second World War: A Study of Religion in American Culture, 1945-1955" (unpublished Ph.D. dissertation, University of Minnesota, 1961), p. 279, and William G. McLoughlin, "Is There a Third Force in Christendom?" *Daedalus*, XCVI (Winter 1967), pp. 44-45.

[151]A typical testimony of a minister who felt constrained to leave his denomination upon receiving the Pentecostal experience is found in *The Pentecostal Evangel*, March 1, 1953. See Hazen G. MacDonald, "How a Baptist Minister Was Baptized with the Holy Spirit," pp. 6, 7, 15.

article in the April, 1953, issue that challenged the evangelical community to reassess its assumption that the miracles recorded in the Book of Acts were not for our day.[152] Walker sought to lead his staff and his readership into a responsive posture to the winds of the Holy Spirit which he felt were blowing afresh.[153] For the next decade the editorials and articles in *Christian Life* were punctuated with accounts of the work of the Holy Spirit in diverse circles of the religious world.

In 1951, David du Plessis, a South African Pentecostal leader who had moved to the United States, became acquainted with Dr. John A. Mackay, then president of Princeton Seminary. Mackay introduced du Plessis to leaders in the World Council of Churches.[154] The warm response he received precipitated an extensive itinerant ministry lecturing among church leaders in the historic churches.

Through Pentecostal influence a Methodist layman, a Mr. Dunscombe, received the baptism in the Holy Spirit in 1955 in a small Ohio town near Fort Wayne, Indiana. As a result of a series of informal prayer meetings led by Dunscombe in Oak Park, Illinois, Father Richard Winkler, rector of Trinity Episcopal Church in Wheaton, Illinois, received the experience on April 26, 1956. Winkler believes he is the first Episcopalian clergyman to receive the Pentecostal experience.[155] His church in Wheaton has been a major center of Episcopalian Pentecostal influence. A diocesan inquiry, commissioned by Bishop Burrill of the Chicago diocese, gave a permissive report in December, 1960.[156]

It was not until the episode at Van Nuys, California, however, that the Neo-Pentecostal Movement attracted nationwide attention. On April 3, 1960, Father Dennis Bennett, rector of St. Mark's Episcopal Church in Van Nuys gave public testimony to the events of the preceding months. Through association with a Pentecostal couple, Mr. and Mrs. John Baker, Episcopalian lay people, had received

---

[152]Myrddin Lewis, "Are We Missing Something?" reprinted from *Christian Life* in *The Pentecostal Evangel*, July 29, 1956, pp. 6-7.

[153]Interview, Robert Walker, April 26, 1963.

[154]Letter from James McCord, September 8, 1967.

[155]Interview, Richard E. Winkler, April 25, 1963.

[156]*Chicago Daily Tribune*, December 20, 1960.

the Pentecostal experience. They in turn led Father Bennett into a similar experience in the fall of 1959. Father Bennett quietly witnessed to individuals in his congregation through the winter months, with about 100 receiving.[157] The public announcement in April touched off sizable reaction, both positively and negatively, with the result that considerable publicity was given to the incident. Sufficient interest was generated in the new controversial movement that a series of pastoral letters emanated from the offices of Bishop Francis Bloy of Los Angeles and Bishop James Pike of San Francisco.[158] In spite of intense negative reaction, the appearance of Pentecostal phenomena spread rapidly from that time, giving commentators the impression that the Van Nuys incident of 1960 was the true birth of the Neo-Pentecostal Movement.[159]

By 1961 the American Lutheran Church was experiencing similar episodes of Pentecostal manifestation.[160] Baptists, Presbyterians, Methodists, Mennonites, and people from the Churches of Christ and Disciples were similarly visited. Most striking of all has been the appearance of glossolalia within the Roman Catholic Church in sufficient profusion in more recent years for Father O'Connor, theologian at Notre Dame University, to refer to it as a "movement" within Catholicism.[161]

At least ten periodicals, in whole or in part, have been instrumental in promoting Neo-Pentecostalism. The Full Gospel Businessmen's Fellowship, International, was originally intended as a means of encouraging laymen within the traditional Pentecostal Movement when it was organized in 1951, but it rapidly changed character. It began to promote the charismatic renewal theme by February, 1955.

One of the important factors in the promotion of Neo-Pentecostalism has been the new appraisal by prominent churchmen of the role of Pentecostalism in the total life

[157]Joan Baker, "The Baker Story," *Trinity*, II (Trinitytide, 1962), pp. 5-6.

[158]*Los Angeles Times*, March 17, 1963.

[159]Sherrill, *op. cit.*, p. 64.

[160]Interview, Dr. Lowell Satre, April 20, 1963.

[161]Edward O'Connor, C.S.C., "A Catholic Pentecostal Movement," *Ave Maria*, June 3, 1967, p. 6. See also Kevin and Dorothy Ranaghan, *Catholic Pentecostals* (New York City: Paulist Press, 1969).

of the modern church. Lesslie Newbigin's *The Household of God,* published in 1953, was a contributing factor in the new appraisal.[162] As early as 1954, President Henry P. Van Dusen of Union Theological Seminary was giving serious acknowledgment to the place of Pentecostalism.[163] This was followed in 1958 by the now famous article in *Life* which popularized the term, "the Third Force."[164] Such recognition, although possibly not representing more than a small fraction of church world opinion, has nonetheless stimulated interest in Neo-Pentecostalism.

IMPLICATIONS FOR THE ASSEMBLIES OF GOD

Neo-Pentecostalism has been viewed with mixed feelings in the Assemblies of God. Anxiety has been expressed over the excesses frequent in Neo-Pentecostal circles, excesses common in the early days of the traditional Pentecostal Movement. Although the Neo-Pentecostal Movement had its origins largely in the older Pentecostal Movement, it has been growing up quite apart from direct association with the parent movement. Traditional Pentecostalists view this aloofness with disappointment, for they see an unnecessary repetition of errors in the new group, yet see little opportunity for providing counsel from their vantage point of fifty years of experience. Why should there be such a gap? It appears to be principally a cultural issue. Many of the new charismatics recall the "holy roller" image of traditional Pentecostalism and are loath to bridge the gulf between.[165]

The Assemblies of God has engaged in several activities endeavoring to make its resources available to the Neo-Pentecostal Movement. Significant is the resolution adopted at the 1963 General Council in Memphis, expressing sympathy wth the new movement and authorizing all possible assistance.[166] The Public Relations Office at General Council headquarters has carried on extensive correspondence with inquirers, the volume of such traffic reaching sizable pro-

---

[162]Letter from Dr. Eugene Smith, December 8, 1967.

[163]Henry P. Van Dusen, "Caribbean Holiday," *Christian Century*, August 17, 1955, pp. 946-48.

[164]Henry P. Van Dusen, "The Third Force in Christendom," *Life*, June 9, 1958, pp. 113-24.

[165]Interview, David du Plessis, June 28, 1967.

[166]General Council minutes, 1963, p. 41.

portions by 1965.[167] Again, in the fall of 1967 *Paraclete*, a new journal designed for the assistance of Neo-Pentecostals, was instituted by the denomination. Instructive is the statement of purpose for the new journal, articulated by General Superintendent Zimmerman:

> With a delightful disregard of denominational barriers, the present Holy Ghost revival touches people in many denominations outside the older Pentecostal churches. And contrary to the earlier pattern of rejection, many of these people are being retained within their denominational groups. This places a responsibility upon us who have enjoyed the Pentecostal outpouring for more than half a century.[168]

The single most dramatic feature of the Neo-Pentecostal revival for the Assemblies of God has been the series of encounters with the Protestant Episcopal Church. During 1962 and 1963 three meetings were held by members of a committee appointed by Presiding Bishop Arthur C. Lichtenberger of the Episcopal Church and the Executive Presbytery, along with others from the Assemblies of God. Not intended to come to theological agreement nor any ecclesiastical arrangement, the talks were to learn from each other about Christian life and faith in the spirit of spiritual fellowship. The occasion was the appearance of Pentecostal manifestations within the Episcopal Church. After the second meeting, held at Grace and Holy Trinity Cathedral in Kansas Cty, Missouri, a joint statement was released on January 16, 1962, which contained among other statements:

> We discussed the things of God without tension or ambitions. There emerged a deep sense of Christian understanding and mutual trust. We found ourselves a fellowship, open to the leading of the Holy Spirit to a degree which we had hardly dared to expect.[169]

In addition to opening new avenues of conversation with individuals and groups within the historic churches, the Neo-Pentecostal revival has also furnished a sobering challenge to the Assemblies of God. In a sermon delivered at the Sixteenth Annual Pentecostal Fellowship of North America convention in Montreal in November, 1963, Gen-

---

[167]Letter from Carl Conner, November 1, 1967.

[168]Thomas F. Zimmerman, "Introducing Paraclete," *Advance*, October, 1967, p. 15.

[169]"Joint Statement Issued by Episcopalians and Assemblies on Manifestations of the Spirit," *The Pentecostal Evangel*, January 20, 1963, p. 4.

eral Superintendent Zimmerman listed the symptoms of complacency within the Pentecostal Movement which the Neo-Pentecostal revival was pointing up. Among the warning signs of unwarranted ease he cited less dependence on the moving of the Holy Spirit, de-emphasis on the ministry of divine healing, less dependence on God for meeting needs, less militant preaching of the Word of God, and a breakdown of the necessary separation to God's will.[170]

SUMMARY

In the years before the entrance of the United States into World War II, the Assemblies of God found itself isolated, not only from the Fundamentalist and Holiness quarters, but from the larger church world and even from other Pentecostal bodies. From 1942 and onward, the Assemblies of God rapidly entered into a whole series of alliances with moderate evangelicalism, an invigorated form of conservative Christianity that made its appearance in the early 1940's. The steady move toward identification with the evangelical world was paralleled by continued rebuffs from militant Fundamentalism and by a withdrawal from the very tenuous connections with the National Council of Churches.

Association with Evangelicalism and stimulus from European Pentecostalism led to the formation of the Pentecostal Fellowship of North America. The walls of separation within the world of Pentecostalism were coming down, at least on the higher levels, if not at the grass roots.

The advent of Neo-Pentecostalism in the late 1950's served to elevate the image of the Pentecostal Movement, although fear of the Ecumenical Movement and cultural differences have limited the amount of cross-fertilization between the Assemblies of God and the larger church world.

Evangelical association has served to create a new climate of goodwill between the Assemblies of God and a variety of groups that were previously quite aloof, notably the Holiness bodies. Militant Fundamentalism has remained adamant in its opposition to the Pentecostals.

---

[170]Thomas F. Zimmerman, "The Pentecostal Movement's Responsibility to the Present-day Outpouring," *The Pentecostal Evangel*, March 1, 1964, p. 3.

10

Communication: The Evangelistic Outreach

Home Missions—Foreign Missions—Radio—Summary

The missionary impulse has been an important characteristic of the Assemblies of God from its earliest years. Three of the five stated reasons for the calling of the first General Council were directly or indirectly related to the church as a missionary enterprise.[1] A basic tenet of the denomination is the belief that the baptism in the Holy Spirit has been made available to believers as an enduement of power for the special purpose of effective witnessing, according to Acts 1:8.[2]

At home, missionary zeal produced profound enthusiasm for a kind of pioneering anchored deep in the 19th-century American tradition of voluntaryism. Poorly trained and ill-equipped, but filled with boundless faith, lay preachers scattered into the hamlets and cities of the land to open storefront missions and tent-churches, often at enormous personal sacrifice and occasionally in the face of considerable religious opposition.[3] Prior to 1941 home missions was largely understood as the opening of new churches, almost exclusively a grass roots activity demanding little assistance from a central headquarters. In the years since, church extension has been joined by a variety

[1]*Word and Witness*, IX (December 20, 1913), p. 1.

[2]"Statement of Fundamental Truths," Article V, Section 7, of the "Constitution of the General Council of the Assemblies of God in the United States of America and Foreign Lands, Revised to August 26, 1969," in the *General Council Minutes*, 1969, p. 98.

[3]See Brumback, *op. cit.*, pp. 107-47, for a good description of early pioneering in the Assemblies of God.

of vigorous new enterprises designed to reach previously neglected segments of modern society, enterprises coordinated increasingly on the district and national levels. This is the story of the Home Missions Department of the Assemblies of God.

Pentecostal missionaries were going abroad at their own charges even before the convening of the First General Council. An important function of the young organization was the collection and disbursing of funds for these early pioneers. The work grew rapidly, expanding into a coordinated missionary program demanding the selection and sending of workers and the administration of a growing network of national churches springing up in many parts of the world. By 1925 the infant denomination had found it necessary to create a separate department to care for the needs of missions. In the years prior to World War II, Assemblies of God missionaries dispatched reports to their colaborers at home glowing with testimonies of great gains matching the impressive statistics of domestic church extension. The prewar years required but a small office staff and few major strategy changes from the national headquarters level. However, in the closing days of World War II, the energetic leadership of the Foreign Missions Department developed plans for the increasingly complex postwar world. The growing differentiation of missionary activity and the development of new strategy in postwar Assemblies of God missions is the concern of the pages that follow.

Alert to new avenues for communicating the gospel, local Assemblies of God ministers were engaged in experimentation with religious broadcasting as early as 1930.[4] It was not until the post-World War II era that the denomination itself launched an aggressive national and international radio ministry. The radio has been one of the most effective instruments for evangelism both at home and abroad in recent years. The story of evangelistic outreach would be incomplete without consideration of this significant activity.

---

[4]Interview, Bartlett Peterson, October 5, 1967.

Home Missions

THE DEVELOPMENT OF THE HOME MISSIONS DEPARTMENT

When the General Council in session in 1925 authorized the establishment of a distinct Missionary Department, the burden of home missions was included in the assignment.[5] However, for many years the central organization concerned itself little with the home missions feature of the task.[6] The problem of establishing new churches in the homeland was a matter of local responsibility. Specialized ministries, particularly ministry to the foreign language groups within the continental United States and Alaska, assumed sufficient proportions that the General Council of 1937 authorized the creation of a separate Home Missions Department. Actually, the newly created department was set up to serve two areas, education and home missions. This arrangement was based on the argument that the work of home missions furnished the chief opportunity for the graduates of the Bible schools. Newly elected Assistant General Superintendent Fred Vogler was invited to supervise the work of the new department.[7] It was not until 1945 that a separate Education Department was established. During the interval, the interest of education remained subordinate to the burgeoning ministries of church extension and specialized outreach.

Fred Vogler served as executive of the Home Missions and Education Department until 1943. At the 1943 General Council session, Ralph M. Riggs replaced Vogler as Assistant General Superintendent and also assumed the portfolio of the department. With the creation of a separate Education Department in 1945, Riggs became the Secretary of that new office, and Fred Vogler assumed the assignment of the Home Missions Department once again, a post he continued to hold until 1953. Gayle Lewis held the executive directorship from 1953 until his retirement in 1965. Charles W. H. Scott has served since then in executive capacity.

---

[5]Perkin, *op. cit.*, p. 43.

[6]Kendrick, *op. cit.*, p. 102.

[7]General Council minutes, 1937, p. 61.

CHURCH EXTENSION

The Home Missions Department was originally charged with the responsibility of encouraging the starting of new churches in the homeland as its primary function.[8] This was part of an overall world outreach strategy that recognized the importance of a strong home base for overseas operations. Immediately after the end of World War II, there was some debate about priorities, some championing the urgency of overseas ministries, others arguing for a longer-range view which would give attention to a strong home base. As evidence that the latter view prevailed, the General Council of 1947 outlined for itself a 10-year plan of domestic expansion, anticipating 10,000 churches in the United States by 1957.[9]

Limited assistance was made available on the national level for the establishment of new churches before World War II. In 1935 a Committee on Church Buildings reported to the General Council that the committee would be available for consultation with any ministers interested in construction guidance.[10] In 1939 the General Secretary reported that a Revolving Loan Fund had been established in the amount of $5,000 for the assistance of needy congregations.[11] More important, in 1939 a plan was adopted whereby a portion of the net earnings of the Gospel Publishing House was distributed on a pro rata basis to the various districts for assisting struggling new churches. The distribution to the weaker districts was augmented by special appropriations. By 1941, $50,000 had been turned over to the districts in this fashion.[12]

Important new programs for church extension have been instituted since World War II. New funds were established to replace the Gospel Publishing House earnings distributions to the districts. The last such distribution was made in 1946, when it became apparent that the decision to build a new publishing plant would require all available re-

[8]Harrison, *op. cit.*, p. 211.

[9]*Ibid.*

[10]General Council minutes, 1935, p. 92.

[11]General Council minutes, 1939, p. 76.

[12]General Council reports, 1941, pp. 76-77.

sources.[13] In 1947 the "Store House Plan" of missionary giving was instituted by the General Council in session, by which 20 percent of all undesignated missionary offerings were to be returned to the districts in which such offerings originated.[14] A "Needy District Fund" was created from 5 percent of missions offerings, serving as a resource for special appropriation to areas of pressing need.[15] A special revolving loan fund was created out of a permanent non-interest bearing loan from industrialist Henry Krause.[16] From this fund, amounting to about $300,000, $5,000 loans at low interest are made to pioneer churches.[17] The original Revolving Loan Fund created back in 1939 continued to be administered through the office of the General Treasurer, amounting to $500,000 by 1969.[18] A special fund for purchasing real estate in promising areas, known as "Sites for Souls," established in 1963, had accumulated to more than $47,000 by 1969, as well.[19] More than $150,000 was transferred from the youth department's "Speed-the-Light" offerings in the biennium of 1967-69 for the opening of new churches.[20]

In addition to vastly increased financial help for erecting new churches, the Home Missions Department appointed a Church Building and Planning Commission in 1956.[21] Architectural plans for small church buildings were prepared by a special commission. More than 200 sets of blueprints have been distributed since the beginning of the service, and several thousand "Plans for Pioneers," a book with building suggestions and drawings, also have been distributed.[22]

GROWTH PATTERNS

The distribution of Assemblies of God churches has remained substantially the same since World War II. In 1945, Ralph M. Riggs, executive in charge of home missions,

---

[13]Interview, Evelyn Dunham, September 30, 1967.
[14]Harrison, *op. cit.*, p. 213.
[15]*Ibid.*
[16]"Branch Out," Home Missions Department pamphlet (1967), p. 8.
[17]General Council reports, 1969, p. 64.
[18]*Ibid.*, p. 30.
[19]General Council reports, 1969, p. 34.
[20]*Ibid.*, p. 102.
[21]General Council reports, 1957, p. 26.
[22]Home Missions Department statistics.

reported that "We have made the least progress east of the Mississippi River and the greatest progress in four southern and southwestern states."[23] A report by General Superintendent Zimmerman, based on figures available in May, 1967, indicates much the same geographical distribution, but with a generally increased ratio of Assemblies of God membership to the population as a whole.

> Using the estimated 1965 population as a base, 30 districts show a substantial rate of growth over the last two decades. Twelve districts have held the same ratio, while only three districts show a slight decrease. . . . The highest ratio of Assemblies of God members to population is in West Florida and Arkansas where it is 13 to 1,000; Oklahoma is next with 12, North Texas has nine, and Southern Missouri and Oregon seven. In 1951 eight areas had a minus-one ratio—less than three areas which do not have at least one member for each 1,000.[24]

The penetration of the urban areas has been significant. In the same report Zimmerman referred to Home Missions Department statistics of 1951 in which 179 cities of 10,000 population or more had no Assemblies of God work. This had grown to more than 300 cities by 1970, owing to population shifts.[25] Thirteen cities over 50,000 were still unoccupied.

Coordinating efforts to evangelize the world, as an outgrowth of the Council on Evangelism and the Study Committee on Advance, the year 1970 was designated "Impact '70: Go and Tell." The domestic dimension of this program has been the planning of concentrated "invasions" of seven American cities, in which a literature-saturation campaign is coupled with a carefully planned citywide evangelistic thrust. The cities chosen for this concentrated activity for 1970 were: Albuquerque, New Mexico; Charlotte, North Carolina; Minneapolis-St. Paul, Minnesota; New York, New York; Omaha, Nebraska; San Francisco, California; and Seattle-Tacoma, Washington. The program has been so successful that it is expected to continue for years to come.

In 1916 the average number of adult members per church

[23]Ralph M. Riggs, *The Pentecostal Evangel,* June 9, 1945, p. 8.

[24]Thomas F. Zimmerman, "A Full Day's Work," *The Pentecostal Evangel,* February 11, 1968, p. 12.

[25]Home Missions Department statistics.

was 57.[26] In 1970 it was still only 72.5, possibly indicating that the proportion of young churches is quite high.[27] The growth in the number of new churches prior to World War II was largely spontaneous, with but a minimum of assistance available to the pioneer in the field. However, it was an era of spectacular growth, nonetheless. The growth rate continued into the postwar era in an unbroken line until 1957. In the biennium ending that year, a net gain of 605 new churches was reported.[28] In spite of greatly increased assistance on the national level, and on the district level as well, the denomination entered into a period in which the net increase in churches rapidly tapered off, dwindling to a net gain of only 54 churches in the biennium ending in 1967, a gain of less than 1 percent for the 8,506 churches reported.[29] Some small increase appeared in the 1969 report, with a net gain of 64 churches reported.[30] This is far below the average growth rate of 162 churches *per year* throughout the denomination's 55-year history.[31] A study of statistical data reveals a similar plateau experience in Sunday school membership, church membership, and number of ordained clergymen, although there are some encouraging signs of fresh growth in the last two categories.[32] For example, a gain of 8.6 percent in membership was reported for the biennium ending in 1969. Possible reasons for this plateau experience will be reviewed in another section.

SPECIAL MINISTRIES

By 1941 the Home Missions Department had under its purview not only church extension, but also the care of Assemblies of God work in Alaska. Work among the Jewish people, the American Indians, and the servicemen stationed in domestic military bases completed the assign-

[26]Perkin, *op. cit.*, p. 36.

[27]Statistics derived from General Secretary's office, dated May 1, 1970.

[28]General Council reports, 1967.

[29]*Ibid.*

[30]General Council reports, 1969. It should be observed that in citing figures for net gain in number of churches, the actual number of new churches started remained fairly high. The number of churches that were closed during these years was substantial, making the net increase quite small. Only in one year, 1965, did the actual number of new churches begun drop below 100. Most of the church closings were occasioned by shifts in population from rural to metropolitan areas.

[31]General Council reports, 1967, p. 113.

[32]*Ibid.*, pp. 16, 148.

ment. Ministry to military personnel was eventually committed to the Christ's Ambassadors (youth) Department, hence it will be treated there. Since 1941 several additional special ministries have been added to the responsibilities of the department. More than 300 home missionaries serve in special areas under Home Missions Department appointment. Of these, approximately two-thirds minister to the American Indians. Others were serving in various capacities including Alaska, the deaf, the blind, the urban enterprise of Teen Challenge, the Jewish, the Spanish Eastern Branch, Hawaii, the Chinese, the American gypsies, and prisoners.[33] The Home Missions Department also supervises 54 institutions, including 17 Bible schools.[34]

The American Indians. Work among the American Indians was undertaken by concerned individuals without official denominational appointment or support as early as the 1930's. Among such hardy pioneers were B. K. Davis and LaVerne Stellrecht.[35] In 1943 the Home Missions Department organized the American Indian division to correlate the work.[36] Two hundred and eighty tribes scattered on 300 reservations, many of which are small and isolated, have made this a difficult and challenging ministry. The Indian population has been growing rapidly, with about half of the 600,000 population still living on the reservations.[37] The Assemblies of God is reaching 100 tribes on 80 reservations.[38] This accounts for 80 percent of all such work being undertaken by denominations affiliated with the National Association of Evangelicals.[39]

An important step in the Indian ministry has been the opening of the American Indian Bible Institute in Phoenix, Arizona, in the fall of 1965.[40] It is sponsored jointly by six western districts of the Assemblies of God and by the National Home Missions Department. The purpose of the

---

[33]Home Missions Department statistics.
[34]Interview, Curtis W. Ringness, July 21, 1970.
[35]Harrison, *op. cit.*, p. 218.
[36]Interview, Curtis W. Ringness, October 10, 1967.
[37]"Reaching Our American Indians," Home Missions Department pamphlet.
[38]Home Missions Department statistics.
[39]"Branch Out," HMD pamphlet, p. 12.
[40]General Council reports, 1966, p. 119.

school, which ministers to representatives from tribes across the nation, is to provide an indigenous leadership among the Indian population.[41] Two district-operated Indian Bible schools, located in Mobridge, South Dakota, and Fayetteville, North Carolina, are in process of establishment, as well.

Alaska. Assemblies of God ministry in Alaska dates back to 1917. Charles C. Personeus and his new bride went to Juneau, the capital city, trusting the Lord to meet their needs.[42] They were followed by others willing to accept the challenge of the Far North. Alaska was one of the first enterprises taken under the supervision of the Home Missions Department. By 1941, the work was well developed. In the postwar years it continued to grow until the Assemblies of God work there became one of the largest of all evangelical groups.[43] In 1965, following the entrance of Alaska into the family of states, the Alaska District Council of the Assemblies of God was created, with the Home Missions Department retaining supervision only of remote stations and the native ministry.[44] There were 90 missionaries under appointment when the transition was made. In 1970 nearly 40 native churches and outstations remained under the guidance of the Home Missions Department.[45] Seventeen churches are self-sustaining.

Eleven Home Missions Department personnel staff the Children's Home in Juneau, ministering to 50 children.[46] Since 1962, the Reverend and Mrs. Arvin Glandon of Fairbanks have conducted an unusual short-term mobile school to assist pastors and missionaries to improve their skills. Traveling by air to remote points, the Far North Bible School also seeks to develop leadership in lay personnel for establishment of an indigenous Alaskan church.[47]

The Deaf. Ministry to the deaf has been one of the dramatic evangelistic enterprises of the Assemblies of God.

41"Presenting the American Indian Bible Institute," HMD pamphlet.
42"Alaska Evangelism," HMD pamphlet.
43"Branch Out," HMD pamphlet.
44*Ibid.*
45Home Missions Department statistics.
46*Ibid.*
47News Release, Public Relations Office, September 19, 1967.

To reach the deaf, in 1969 there were 130 groups ministering in as many cities, more than 20 of these having developed in the recent biennium.[48] The Christian Deaf Fellowship was organized in Tulsa, Oklahoma, at a convention held in the Church of the Silent Sheep, in 1947.[49] The next year Central Bible Institute offered for the first time a course in the sign language. Miss Lottie Riekehof, now on the staff of Gallaudet College, pioneered this program.[50] In 1952 the Assemblies of God Deaf Fellowship became a division of the Home Missions Department, with Earl Walpole serving as the first national representative.[51] Three years later, the work had grown to such proportions that the first full-time coordinator was appointed. Miss Maxine Strobridge served in that capacity for 10 years, being succeeded in 1965 by Harry Brotzman upon Miss Strobridge's appointment as missionary to the deaf in Korea.[52]

It was in California in 1951 that the first deaf summer camp was conducted. This aspect of the work has developed well, seven states conducting such camps in 1969, with total attendance approximating 900.[53] A unique activity in the evangelical world has been the School for the Deaf, a separate department of Central Bible College begun in 1962. It consists of a three-year Bible course for the deaf.[54] In 1964 the Home Missions Department placed the first chaplain ever to be appointed at Gallaudet College, the world's only college for the deaf.[55]

The Deaf Ministries Division of the Assemblies of God Home Missions Department publishes tracts for the deaf and a monthly newsletter, *Signs of Life,* for ministers and workers for the deaf.[56] The work of the Assemblies of God among the deaf is more developed than that of any other evangelical group in the United States.[57]

---

[48]Home Missions Department statistics.
[49]*The Pentecostal Evangel,* March 1, 1947, p. 11.
[50]*The Pentecostal Evangel,* December 4, 1955, p. 7.
[51]*The Pentecostal Evangel,* May 18, 1952, p. 7.
[52]*The Pentecostal Evangel,* February 26, 1967, p. 31.
[53]Home Missions Department statistics.
[54]*Slant,* October, 1966, p. 26.
[55]"Branch Out," HMD pamphlet.
[56]General Council reports, 1967, p. 117.
[57]Interview, Curtis W. Ringness, October 10, 1967.

The Blind. In March, 1961, Mrs. E. W. Whitney of Waukesha, Wisconsin, became the first appointee of the Home Missions Department to minister to the blind.[58] She had been preparing gospel literature for several years on a Braillewriter provided by the Home Missions Department, chief of which has been *The Pentecostal Digest,* which is circulated throughout the United States and in 15 foreign countries.[59] In addition to Braille literature, a tape service has been provided since 1960 (reel-to-reel tapes and now cassettes). This tape library and a new Braille library is sponsored by the Home Missions Department.[60]

Inner-city Evangelism. A project in its formative stages in the Home Missions Department of the Assemblies of God is Inner-city Evangelism, an effort to encourage the establishment of evangelistic centers in the heart of our great metropolitan areas. The initial pilot effort has been in the Harlem district of New York City. A Negro, Thurman Faison, valedictorian of his class at Eastern Pentecostal Bible College in Peterborough, Ontario, was instrumental in developing such a center under the direction of the Home Missions Department. Currently he is pastoring an inner-city church in Chicago. The denomination is investing more than $100,000 in the New York operation.[61]

Teen Challenge. A much more developed effort to minister to the needs of urban America is Teen Challenge. Twenty-seven Teen Challenge Centers serve the delinquent youth and teen gangs in major metropolitan areas.[62] Each of the centers has its own constitution and bylaws, but all operate under the oversight of the executive director of the Home Missions Department and the superintendent of the district in which the center is located. The permanent staff of each center is augmented each summer by students from Bible schools.[63]

The New York Center was the original from which other centers have been initiated. It came into being through the

[58]General Council reports, 1961, p. 94.
[59]General Council reports, 1967, p. 118.
[60]"Blind Evangelism: Filling the Dark Emptiness," *Advance,* March, 1968, p. 12.
[61]Interview, Curtis W. Ringness, October 10, 1967.
[62]HMD statistics.
[63]*Ibid.*

burden and vision of a young Pennsylvania minister who felt impressed to do something for the youthful gang members he had read about in the news. David Wilkerson's dramatic story is recounted in a series of books, the best-known being *The Cross and the Switchblade.*[64] In February, 1958, Mr. Wilkerson went to New York City to the trial of a young gang member on an impulse he believed to be from God. His eviction from the courtroom and the subsequent publicity accorded it became a means of winning the confidence of some of the gang members. In July he began a series of rallies in the St. Nicholas Arena and succeeded in reaching several gang leaders for Christ. That October, "Dave," as he is called, opened an office on Staten Island as a kind of local headquarters for his street-witnessing program. By this time he had resigned his pleasant pastorate in Pennsylvania and had moved his family to New York. In 1959, just a year after the first encounter with the gang world of New York, through the backing of local ministers and churches, Dave purchased a building in Brooklyn as an inpatient center for dope addicts on withdrawal therapy. In 1962 the Teen Challenge work expanded by turning a farm near Rehrersburg, Pennsylvania, into a "Teen Challenge Training Center," a 200-acre rehabilitation school for addicts. The next year, the rapidly growing sphere of teen ministries included the purchase of an estate on the Hudson River at Rhinebeck, New York, for the training of workers. Former alcoholics, drug addicts, and prostitutes follow an intensive trimester program that packs three years of Bible training into two calendar years of study.[65]

In 1964 three additional buildings were purchased on Clinton Street in Brooklyn near the original Center. One of these serves as a residence for workers, the others as "re-entry" residences for former addicts who are being oriented to normal useful living. In 1965 a half-million-dollar "Spiritual Therapy Clinic" was built which serves as the nerve center of the New York operations. Another acquisition has been an estate at Garrison, New York, with

[64]David Wilkerson, *The Cross and the Switchblade* (New York: Bernard Geis, 1963).

[65]Interview, David Wilkerson, January 9, 1968.

sufficient acreage for a summer camp, intended for the rehabilitation primarily of delinquent girls.[66] The Chicago Teen Challenge Center operates a home for girls at Silver Lake, Wisconsin. The latest Teen Challenge institution that has been opened is the Mid-America Teen Challenge Center, Cape Girardeau, Missouri.

Prison Ministry. Another Home Missions Department outreach is to those behind prison walls. Isolated individuals were attempting to minister to prisoners before 1941, but only one Assemblies of God minister was actually serving as a state-appointed prison chaplain, Arvid Ohrnell of Walla Walla, Washington.[67]

Pastor Paul Markstrom of Newburgh, New York, had been apprised of the need for denominational assistance in correctional institutions by Clifford Scrimshaw, Methodist chaplain at the Elmira Reformatory. Markstrom journeyed to Springfield, Missouri, in August, 1950, to share his burden with the executive officers of the Assemblies of God. As a result of that informal meeting, Markstrom was invited to return the following month to present his proposal to the assembled General Presbytery. The outcome of that encounter was that Arvid Ohrnell was invited to move to Springfield to develop a denominational prison ministry. It is interesting to note that Ohrnell, entirely without knowledge of developments in Springfield, had resigned from 16 years of service at the prison in Walla Walla just hours before the call came from Springfield, early in September, 1950! Ohrnell had spent 6 months planning a national prison program, but had communicated this to no one.[68]

Ohrnell spent much of his time visiting prisons, working with chaplains and inmates. Recognizing that the correspondence materials offered by the denomination through the Berean Correspondence division were not tailored to the special needs of prisoners, Ohrnell began to prepare a series of courses of his own, the first appearing in 1955. Eight such courses were completed by 1962. By 1969 nearly 200,000 courses had been mailed to inmates across the

---

[66]*Ibid.*
[67]Interview, Paul Markstrom, September 25, 1967.
[68]*Ibid.*

country, located in 240 federal, state, and county prisons. All of these materials have been nondenominational in nature.[69]

Ohrnell suffered a fatal coronary attack while he was visiting the Louisiana State Penitentiary at Angola in March, 1963. Paul Markstrom, then pastoring in Coldwater, Kansas, was invited to step into the office to replace Ohrnell as National Prison Representative. He has served since July, 1963.[70]

The number of Assemblies of God men serving as prison chaplains has increased sharply in recent years. In 1963 there were only six full- and part-time chaplains; in 1969 there were 30.[71] The prison ministry of the Assemblies of God, particularly its correspondence work, is more extensive than that of any other evangelical group, with the possible exception of the Southern Baptists.[72]

Foreign Language Groups. A segment of the American population posing special problems for evangelism is the sizable immigrant group beset with barriers of language differences. To provide an effective means of conducting church work among the foreign language populations, the Executive Presbytery arranged for the creation of foreign language district councils. As early as 1929, this principle was implemented. In that year the Latin-American District Council was established to coordinate the domestic Spanish-speaking activity of the Assemblies of God.[73] Based on ethnic rather than geographic boundaries, through the years six such district councils have come into being. The single exception to the nongeographic principle is the Spanish Eastern District, created to care for the very rapid increase of Spanish-speaking work east of the Mississippi River.

In 1954 the six foreign language districts were brought under the supervision of the Home Missions Department. Church membership in the five groups—German, Italian,

---

[69]Interview, Paul Markstrom, September 25, 1967, and Home Missions Department statistics.

[70]Interview, Paul Markstrom, September 25, 1967.

[71]Home Missions Department statistics.

[72]Interview, Curtis W. Ringness, October 10, 1967.

[73]General Council minutes, 1929, p. 86.

Latin-American, Spanish Eastern, and Ukrainian, totals more than 32,000, with more than 960 ministers holding credentials.[74] A large proportion of the 670 churches, especially the Spanish-speaking, are of recent origin, making this segment of the Assemblies of God one of the fastest-growing in the whole movement. The Spanish Eastern District is the largest of the six major Spanish Pentecostal groups working in New York City, with 52 churches and a membership of approximately 7,000 in the five boroughs.[75] Particularly impressive is the fact that more than 150 students are graduated each year from the 14 Spanish-speaking Bible schools, equipped to aid in the extension of Spanish work both at home and abroad.[76]

While church extension in the Assemblies of God has lagged somewhat in the last decade compared with previous years, the special domestic evangelistic enterprises of the Home Missions Department have had a most colorful and encouraging history. It is noteworthy that much of this specialized ministry has first been generated at the grass roots level, receiving coordination and support from the national level only as needed.

Foreign Missions

The story of missionary enterprise in the Assemblies of God is a massive study all its own. The purpose of this presentation must be limited to a brief consideration of major developments and overall strategy, particularly as they affect the home base in the United States.

ACHIEVEMENTS PRIOR TO 1941

Only 32 missionaries were on the original roster at the first General Council in April, 1914. The number had grown to 195 by September, 1919, requiring the installation of a Missionary Secretary to care for the increased volume of funds flowing into headquarters.[77] J. Roswell Flower served as the first Missionary Secretary, a position he held for four years.[78] In 1925 the General Council authorized the establishment of a separate department for missionary super-

[74]HMD statistics. [75]*Ibid.* [76]*Ibid.*

[77]*The Pentecostal Evangel*, October 25, 1964, p. 14.

[78]Harrison, *op. cit.*, p. 208.

vision. Following a brief tenure by William Faux, Noel Perkin became secretary of the Foreign Missions Department in 1926, an office he held until his retirement in 1959. Since then J. Philip Hogan has served in that office.

Original missionary policy was established by a small committee appointed by the 1917 General Council. Amplifications of policy disclosed that by 1921 the establishment of strong national churches, not simply the winning of isolated converts, was the chief objective of Assemblies of God missions.[79] Already by 1919 a resolution had been adopted urging the establishment of schools "for the education of duly accredited Native Workers, in the various fields where practicable. . . ."[80] The first such long-term school appears to have been set up in North China as early as 1922, although the first permanent school still in existence was established in South India by John Burgess in 1927.[81]

Further strengthening the concept of indigenous missions was the early institution of district councils on the field. Although consisting almost entirely of missionary personnel at first, they gradually were displaced by national leadership, a process still developing.[82] In 1936, Nicaraguan missionaries M. L. Hodges and Ralph D. Williams established the first national conference, governed by nationals.[83] This was a milestone in the creation of autonomous national Assemblies of God groups throughout the world, a vision first given expression in a 1921 General Council resolution.[84]

Faith has always been a basic ingredient in missionary work in the Assemblies of God. The individual missionary was responsible for securing his own support, the national office only guaranteeing to forward to him 100 percent of the funds received that were designated for him.[85] The nature of the Assemblies of God as a voluntary cooperative fellowship of sovereign local churches has made the prin-

---

[79]Perkin, *op. cit.*, p. 42.

[80]General Council minutes, 1919, p. 22.

[81]*The Pentecostal Evangel*, November 29, 1964, p. 18.

[82]*Ibid.*, p. 13.

[83]*The Pentecostal Evangel*, August 22, 1965, p. 22.

[84]*The Pentecostal Evangel*, November 29, 1964, p. 17.

[85]General Council minutes, 1919, p. 13. (It should be noted that 2 percent is deducted for the individual's emergency fund.)

ciple of assessments on local congregations for any purpose, including that of missions, an incongruous arrangement which has never received serious consideration.[86] One important result of this concept has been a sense of missionary responsibility at the grass roots level of the denomination.

Promotion of missions at home began very early through the pages of the official publications of the denomination. *The Pentecostal Evangel* carried a relatively heavy proportion of missionary news from its origins. By 1925, in a resolution adopted at the General Council, the sessions of that body were required to feature foreign missions prominently.[87] During the 1930's missionary conventions were being conducted in local churches and in district meetings. And, because of the individual responsibility resting on each missionary to secure his own support, the public was continually being informed about missionary matters through itinerating missionaries home on furlough.

The Great Depression made little impact on the work of missions. The work grew so that five full-time workers were needed in the office before the end of 1935.[88] Finally, in the Memphis General Council of 1937, the home missions portion of the responsibility was cared for by the creation of a new department for that task, allowing the Foreign Missions Department to concentrate on the overseas work.[89] By the fall of 1940, just on the eve of Pearl Harbor, 38 fields outside the United States were being occupied by 400 General Council missionaries and ministers residing in 204 mission stations, supervising the work of 1,231 nationals and 1,131 preaching points.[90] Nineteen Bible schools, 16 elementary schools, and nine orphanages were in operation at the outset of the war.[91] Reported at the 1941 General Council was an overseas constituency of 60,000, roughly a

---

[86]Perkin, *op. cit.*, pp. 31-32.

[87]*Ibid.*, p. 45.

[88]Harrison, *op. cit.*, p. 209.

[89]General Council minutes, 1937, p. 61.

[90]*The Pentecostal Evangel*, October 12, 1940, p. 13.

[91]*Ibid.*

quarter of the domestic membership.[92] In that biennium missionary giving reached $1,000,000 for the first time.[93]

POSTWAR EXPANSION

World War II curtailed missionary activity somewhat. Twenty-nine missionaries were interned in the Far East, most of whom where expatriated during the war. Anna Ziese in North China never returned home and contact with her was lost for many years.[94] However, eight new countries were entered during the war in spite of severe restrictions.[95]

A unique conference was called in April, 1943, for the purpose of considering strategy for world-outreach so that the Assemblies of God would be prepared when the war should end. More than 60 missionaries from 18 countries gathered in Springfield, Missouri, to counsel together with Foreign Missions Department personnel.[96] Five important goals were established: (1) appointment of field secretaries for all major areas; (2) recruiting of 500 new missionaries; (3) providing for additional training for missionary candidates and missionaries on furlough; (4) establishing of conventions in strategic centers to present various phases of the missionary enterprise to the constituency; and (5) raising of a reserve fund of $5 million for a great advance at the conclusion of hostilities.[97] Much of this was implemented in the immediate postwar period, 1945 through 1949 being years of considerable structual and methodological change.

Already in 1942 the first field secretary had been appointed. H. C. Ball, veteran Latin American missionary, was appointed to cordinate all Latin American work.[98] By 1944, H. B. Garlock to serve the needs of Africa, and Gustav Kinderman for Europe had been added.[99] Howard Osgood became the first Far East field secretary in 1945.[100] It became apparent that such supervision, providing for closer con-

---

[92]General Council minutes, 1941, p. 88.
[93]*Ibid.*
[94]*The Pentecostal Evangel,* September 19, 1965, p. 11.
[95]*Ibid.*
[96]*Ibid,* p. 12.
[97]*Ibid.*
[98]Harrison, *op cit.,* p. 210.
[99]*The Pentecostal Evangel,* July 1, 1944, p. 11.
[100]General Council minutes, 1945.

tact with missionaries on the field, was meeting a great need.

In the home office, Glenn Horst came in to coordinate transportation and itineraries of missionaries, serving as the forerunner of the Promotions Division in 1944.[101] In that same year, Borneo missionary Kenneth Short spent his furlough time to launch the first major missionary department publication, the *Missionary Challenge*.[102] The title of this promotional monthly was changed to the *World Challenge* in 1956 and continued under that title until 1959, when the magazine was discontinued. In 1959 a new promotional magazine was launched, this time not as a subscription item, but for free distribution. *Global Conquest* became the symbol of vigorous missionary outreach, designed in part to compensate for the increasing competition from independent missions agencies originating in the "Salvation-Healing" orbit.[103] The name of this periodical was changed in September, 1967, to *Good News Crusades* to avoid the militaristic connotation of the previous title.

An important structural change was the creation of a series of advisory bodies to enlarge the scope of counsel for the now mammoth operation of world missions. In 1955 the Foreign Missions Board was created by the General Council, consisting of representatives of the national office and missionaries, for the formulation of policy.[104] In 1957 the General Council in session authorized the establishment of a Foreign Missions Advisory Committee, to consist of "six consecrated, Spirit-filled men from among our fellowship, known for their spirituality, good judgment and faithfulness, as an advisory committee to work in cooperation with the Foreign Missions Board in the promotion of World Missions. . . ."[105]

One of the goals enunciated at the historic 1943 conference was the improving of the training of missionary

---

[101]*The Pentecostal Evangel*, July 1, 1944, p. 11.

[102]*Ibid.*

[103]See Chapter 13, Controversy, for a discussion of the problems engendered by the "Salvation-Healing" movement.

[104]General Council minutes, 1955, p. 23. Pastors were added to the Board by action of the 1957 General Council

[105]General Council minutes, 1957, p. 51.

personnel. A preliminary means to that end was a second missionary conference held in Springfield in June, 1948, with over 100 missionaries in attendance.[106] The concept of such a gathering as an annual event matured so that by 1957 the General Council gave approval to the "School of Missionary Orientation."[107] Each year since that time all missionaries on furlough who are free to attend join with new candidates for two weeks of intensive study, prayer, and fellowship in Springfield. Through the years the general level of training of the missionary staff has increased so that by 1967 fully half of all furloughed missionaries were attending graduate schools of various kinds.[108] In the period from 1914 to 1949, 74 percent of the missionary force were trained in Bible schools; from 1949 to 1953 the figure climbed to 93 percent having at least this degree of preparation.[109]

Another of the goals envisioned in 1943 was the raising of a large sum for availability at war's end for strategic deployment. In the years that followed, several auxiliary agencies created within the General Council structure provided large sums of money for special missionary projects to supplement the regular support by the churches of missionary personnel. Most striking of such harnessed resources within the fellowship was "Speed-the-Light," the special project of the youth department which was a fund for purchasing vehicles, radio, and printing equipment for missionary use. Several millions of dollars have been turned into aids for missionaries in this fashion.[110] Speed-the-Light funds purchased a twin-engine C-46 transport plane which began a shuttle service for missionary personnel to and from various foreign fields in August, 1948. Christened the "Ambassador," it attracted considerable attention for its novel employment of modern means to the communication of the gospel. In 1950 the first plane was succeeded by a four-engined converted B-17, the "Am-

[106]*The Pentecostal Evangel*, October 24, 1965, p. 22.
[107]*The Pentecostal Evangel*, December 19, 1965, p. 20.
[108]Interview, Philip Hogan, September 30, 1967.
[109]General Council reports, 1953, p. 34.
[110]National CA Department statistics. See Chapter 11, Conservation, for a detailed account of the history of the CA Department.

bassador II."[111] Its frequent stops at exotic ports of call made the work of Assemblies of God missions widely known. As commercial carriers improved their service, the use of such planes was no longer so important, and missionaries were then transported by conventional means within a few years.

Another auxiliary agency that has been a significant source of aid to the cause of missions is the "Boys and Girls Missionary Crusade," a project of the Sunday school, designed to furnish material for Sunday school and training literature in missionary territories. More than $2 million has been raised by Assemblies of God children in this way.[112] In its 17-year history the Women's Missionary Council has given more than $24 million, much of it related directly to the work of missions.[113] The Men's Fellowship project, "Light for the Lost," has been the supply of evangelistic literature for overseas crusades. Since its inception as a General Council program in 1961, nearly half a million dollars has been furnished to the Missions Department.[114]

Giving to missions on the local church level was refined by the adoption of the "World Missions Plan," a means of distributing undesignated funds into priority categories.[115] Funds specified for individual missionary support have still been forwarded to the field in toto, the costs of maintenance of the Foreign Missions Department coming from undesignated funds and other sources. A report by the auditing committee assigned to investigate the operations of the Foreign Missions Department in 1961 commended the department for its efficiency of operation, spending only 4.9 percent of the total income on administrative expense, apparently among the lowest of any church body in the country.[116] In addition to auxiliary funds previously enumerated, the denomination contributed $8 million to world missions in 1969, more than half of the total receipts of the General Council.[117]

---

[111] *The Pentecostal Evangel*, November 21, 1965, p. 19.
[112] General Council reports, 1969, p. 121.
[113] *Ibid.*, p. 125.
[114] General Council reports, 1969, p. 106.
[115] *The Pentecostal Evangel*, December 19, 1965, p. 19.
[116] General Council minutes, 1961, p. 80.
[117] "Key," 1969 Annual Report of the Foreign Missions Department, p. 5.

RECENT STRATEGY

In 1957, "Global Conquest" was born. Previous to this the general policy had been to scatter missionaries to the ends of the world, a noble program, but geared primarily to the rural and remote spots in the world.[118] The Assemblies of God missionary force had been widely dispersed from early years, many of the missionaries having already been under appointment by various mission boards when they received the Pentecostal experience. The new program, instituted in the closing days of Noel Perkin's farsighted administration, sought to focus attention on the rapidly urbanizing character of the world. To do this a three-pronged emphasis was detailed: (1) increasing the distribution of gospel literature, (2) increasing efforts to train a national leadership through Bible school programs, and (3) emphasizing the evangelization of key metropolitan centers.[119] The magazine *Global Conquest,* introduced in 1959, became the chief instrument for informing the constituency of the advances on this new front. In keeping with this new thrust, goals were announced at the 1957 General Council, anticipating 60 new missionaries by 1960, 10,000 national workers, and 600,000 members in foreign lands. At that time there were 758 missionaries, 8,005 national workers, and 574,653 members of the Assemblies of God congregations overseas.[120] By 1960 there were only 788 appointed missionaries, but there were 12,657 national workers and the membership in foreign lands had jumped to 745,446.[121] Since the institution of the Global Conquest strategy, the emphasis has not been to seek new fields, this policy being underscored by the Foreign Missions Board in 1958, which recognized that the forces were spread quite thinly.[122] However, new fields have been entered since then, but by the appeal of the nationals for assistance from the Assemblies of God Foreign Missions Department.

In practice, the first thrusts of Global Conquest were in

[118]Interview, David Womack, January 11, 1968.
[119]*The Pentecostal Evangel,* December 19, 1965, p. 20.
[120]*Ibid.*
[121]*Ibid.*
[122]Interview, Robert McGlasson, October 9, 1967.

the areas of literature and the creation of urban "evangelistic centers." Gradually, the Boys and Girls Missionary Crusade and the Light-for-the-Lost programs became the instruments for implementing the literature feature of the new strategy. By 1965 the Light-for-the-Lost program became formally the literary agency of Global Conquest. In the meantime, urban evangelistic centers were being developed in several major cities, Seoul, Korea, being the pilot project, well underway by 1960. It was not only the first, but also the most successful of the evangelistic centers, having 7,000 adherents by 1967. By 1965 half a dozen other such centers were launched. It was the hope that these centers would be scenes of continuous urban evangelism, serving as "feeders" for multiplied small churches in the regions around them. However, this hope was not realized, and the evangelistic centers tended to become simply great metropolitan churches. Some of the efforts described here were located in Manila, Dakar, and Managua.[123]

Between 1963 and 1965 a significant shift was made. Global Conquest made way for "Good News Crusades," an emphasis on mass evangelistic crusades in which personnel and funds from the United States were to be employed, but in close cooperation with the missionaries and nationals on the field. The objective was to be a stimulation of work already existing, and through intensive follow-up campaigns to follow the mass meetings, to conserve the fruits of evangelism. No plans for crusades were contemplated unless adequate follow-up could be undertaken. Support of such undertakings by the local people has proved to care for two-thirds of the cost. It appears that this new thrust, geared to the strengthening of indigenous churches, is the prevailing philosophy.[124] The initial campaigns which seemed to point in the direction of mass evangelism as an effective urban technique were undertaken by several specially appointed Assemblies of God evangelists as early as 1950.

The third prong of the original Global Conquest strategy,

---

[123]Interview, David Womack, January 11, 1968.

[124]*Ibid.*

the training of nationals, has also been receiving special attention. The number of Bible schools for the training of national leadership grew from 19 in 1941 to 91 by 1969, more than with any other denomination or agency in Protestantism.[125] This phase of the work grew quietly, receiving little notice. However, late in 1967 a bold new supplement was inaugurated. Headed by Dr. George Flattery, the International Correspondence Institute seeks to coordinate the various programs of correspondence work currently in operation on many mission fields. At its inception there were about 200,000 enrolled in the existing courses, but it is anticipated that through adequate promotion this will rapidly climb to 1 million.[126] This appears to be particularly strategic in areas of the world where conventional evangelism is restricted.

Functioning as part of the Good News Crusade program is the dynamic forward thrust growing out of the denominational self-study undertaken in 1967-68. A spiritual "invasion" of key world metropolitan centers was launched. The initial phase of this venture began with the theme "Impact '70: Go and Tell," concentrating intensive evangelistic campaigns in seven overseas cities. The cities scheduled for 1970 were Bahía Blanca, Argentina; Djakarta, Indonesia; Kinshasa, Congo; Mexico City, Mexico; Noumea, New Caledonia; Salisbury, Rhodesia; and Teheran, Iran.

The Mobilization and Placement Service (MAPS), an outgrowth of the Memphis General Council of 1963, is directed by General Superintendent Zimmerman. Coordinator Charles Denton and Representative John Ohlin assist him in this new enterprise. MAPS is a means for coordinating the efforts of lay personnel who contribute their services in such helpful activity as construction projects at mission stations. Teams assisting missionaries on location in such fashion have already been active in Jamaica, Honduras, Costa Rica, Alaska, and the Bahamas. Vocational volunteers, laymen who serve overseas and who assist missionaries, are also supervised by MAPS. A feature of this latter program

[125]"Key," 1969 Annual Report of the Foreign Missions Department, p. 3.

[126]"Our Campus Is the World," Foreign Missions Department pamphlet, 1968.

is the work of the college interns who spend their summers giving aid to missionaries. During 1970 alone, college interns served in 25 foreign countries around the world. Ambassadors in Mission, the Christ's Ambassadors overseas ministry, is coordinated through the MAPS office.

MISSIONARY DYNAMIC

In 1941 there were about 400 missionaries under appointment; by 1970 the number had climbed to 1,018. From half a million dollars given in 1941 to missions, giving topped $10 million in 1969, counting the auxiliary funds supplied to foreign missions. The foreign constituency in 1941 was 60,000; in 1969 it had passed the 2,800,000 mark. Work was being undertaken in 38 fields when Pearl Harbor arrived; in 1970 there were 82 countries outside the United States with Assemblies of God work.[127] In the same interval Assemblies of God domestic membership increased from just over 200,000 to 625,000, an impressive gain, but overshadowed by the spectacular growth overseas.[128] What have been some of the factors in this rapid growth?

The Pentecostal emphasis on each member being a candidate for an enduement of power is central in this story, a view supported by Noel Perkin.[129] Everyone is considered a potential preacher; the laity are integrally related to the evangelistic activity of the church. Participation is basic to an understanding of the theology and practice of the Pentecostal.

The sense of personal missionary responsibility has been projected from early days, penetrating to nearly all Assemblies of God churches, and most individuals, from the children on up. The nature of the fellowship, a voluntary cooperation of sovereign churches, has pressed considerable initiative on both missionary and local people for the support of the work. The personal visits of itinerating missionaries, the prominent featuring of heroes of the faith in the publications, and the centrality of world-outreach even in the biennial national conventions of the denomination

---

[127]Statistics derived from "Key," 1970 FMD publication, and the General Council reports, 1969.

[128]*Ibid.*

[129]Interview, Noel Perkin, October 10, 1967.

have kept the message ever before the people. Lillian Trasher, famous as the "Nile Mother" of Egyptian orphanage fame; "Ma" Steidel, founder of the great leprosy center at New Hope Town, Liberia; rugged pioneer of Tibet, Victor Plymire, first missionary to trek across the wastelands of that forbidden Asian country; and J. W. Tucker, martyr for Christ in the Congo—these and others have served as a noble challenge to sacrificial dedication to Christ and the extension of His kingdom. Every nine churches send one missionary.[130]

The indigenous pattern of missions, particularly applicable to the Pentecostals and their practices, was already well developed when the great wave of natonalism surged over the world in the wake of the war. The transfer of church control to national leadership has been an important means of multiplying the work.

Growing literacy and rapid urbanization have been not only challenges but great opportunities. New strategy has sought to reach the people in the cities, and a great harvest has been following.

At home increased prosperity has been reflected in additional resources for overseas work. Although not at the top of the list of per capita giving, still the Assemblies of God constituency has maintained a strong sense of missionary responsiblity financially.

Another important factor in the growth of missions is the nearly unique manpower resource available. There are still more candidates available than funds with which to send them, a phenomenon almost without parallel in the country today.[131] With such a ready supply of dedicated candidates a careful screening process has been possible which has made the dropout rate among the lowest in evangelical circles.[132]

According to observers of evangelical missions, such as Clyde Taylor and Arthur Climenhaga, the Assemblies of God has been blessed with astute leadership. The ability to coordinate into a team the energies of multitudes of ag-

---

[130]"Key," FMD pamphlet.

[131]Interview, Philip Hogan, September 30, 1967.

[132]*Ibid.*

gressive, pioneering spirits, each charged with his own special sense of God-given mission, is a circumstance demanding the most skillful administration.[133] Men like Noel Perkin and Philip Hogan command considerable respect in the evangelical world.

Radio

EARLY EFFORTS

It was in 1933 that the General Council authorized a program of radio ministry. By a resolution adopted that year the Executive Presbytery was commissioned to negotiate for a single-station outlet "to broadcast the glorious full gospel message that God has entrusted to us."[134] Three years later the Assemblies of God launched its first broadcast series over KWTO, a new station beginning operations in Springfield, Missouri.[135] Nothing further developed until World War II.

In 1943 the General Presbytery established a committee to investigate the possibility of a national network broadcast.[136] Two years later the General Council authorized the establishment of a Radio Department and accepted the offer of Pastor Leland Keys of San Francisco to take over the 34-station network arrangements he had pioneered on the West Coast.[137] On January 6, 1946, "Sermons in Song," a 15-minute service was aired for the first time on a network now grown to 72 stations. E. S. Williams was the speaker, T. F. Zimmerman the narrator, and Les Barnett served as music director.[138]

In the course of the next several years "Sermons in Song" was accorded a series of honors by the National Religious Broadcasters, but it never did quite capture the public imagination. The Radio Department launched a children's broadcast in 1948, called "The Gospel Rocket," which won the NRB award in 1949 as the best children's broadcast of the year.[139]

---

[133]Interviews, Clyde Taylor, July 17, 1967, and Arthur Climenhaga, June 21, 1967.
[134]General Council minutes, 1933, p. 109.
[135]Brumback, *op. cit.*, p. 318.
[136]General Presbytery minutes, 1943, p. 11.
[137]General Council minutes, 1945, pp. 14-18.
[138]"Revivaltime: Ten Years on the ABC Network," Radio Department pamphlet.
[139]*Ibid.*

With a new format, the broadcast went on the air on April 9, 1950, as "Revivaltime." General Superintendent W. R. Steelberg became the regular speaker. That year "Revivaltime" became an international ministry with the addition of powerful stations in Luxembourg and Lorenco Marques to the log.[140] The sudden death of General Superintendent Wesley R. Steelberg in June, 1952, necessitated a change in personnel. Bartlett Peterson was the speaker for nearly a year, and then he was followed by Wilfred Brown. It was still a 15-minute broadcast, made available to local stations through a transcription service.

COMMERCIAL NETWORK RADIO

The 1953 General Council was one of the most important events in the history of the Assemblies of God, for it brought into being a wide range of sweeping changes in the structure of the denomination. One of its notable achievements was the resolution adopted respecting radio broadcasting. It was agreed to appoint a full-time speaker for the broadcast, and to produce it "live," seeking for release through a major network.[141] It was recognized that the budget of $116,000 currently being expended would now require at least triple that amount. It was a bold venture.

On December 20, 1953, C. M. Ward, the unanimous choice of the Executive Presbytery, delivered his first sermon on the new half-hour ABC network release. Aided by the "Revivaltime Choir" composed of students from Central Bible College, C. M. Ward has served continuously as the speaker of the program. In spite of being launched at the very outset of the "dark ages" of radio when television seemed to be gaining the ascendancy, "Revivaltime" has demonstrated consistent growth. By 1969 it was being released over 601 stations, including 97 foreign outlets.[142] More than 10,000 letters a month are regularly received, opening the door to a vast literature program. Nearly 8 million pieces of gospel literature have been mailed, all upon request.[143]

---

[140] *Ibid.*

[141] General Council minutes, 1953, p. 30.

[142] General Council reports, 1969, p. 117.

[143] Interview, Leland Shultz, October 13, 1967, and General Council reports, 1969, p. 117.

The purpose of "Revivaltime" has been consistently evangelism, not denominational promotion. Any benefit accruing to the denomination has been strictly a by-product; no promotional announcements for specific denominational emphases are permitted.[144] Yet it is certain that the familiar sound of "Revivaltime" to its weekly audience of 12 million has been instrumental in acquainting multitudes with the Assemblies of God.

Summary

Evangelism was understood by the founders of the Assemblies of God to be primarily the communication of the gospel to the unconverted. Their task was also understood to carry with it the responsibility of sharing with the rest of the church world the blessing of the "full gospel," the message that Pentecostal power had been restored in the latter days.

In the homeland in the period prior to World War II this energy found expression chiefly in the establishment of new congregations. Following 1941 a variety of new avenues for reaching specialized segments of the population have been exploited with considerable success. However, in spite of additional resources available for aiding the work of church extension, the growth rate of new church development has fallen off noticeably since 1957.

Overseas outreach has displayed from the beginning of the denomination a pattern of almost continuous expansion, outstripping the growth of the church at home. In the years before World War II the chief objective was to reach the uttermost parts of the earth, a vision that led pioneers to the hinterland of remote countries. Developing strategy since 1941 has sought to shift the focus to the urban and literate populations of the world. Although the home base has not grown in proportion to overseas expansion, financial support and available candidates for missionary service have continued to furnish resources for the work abroad.

---

[144]Interview, Leland Shultz, October 13, 1967.

11

Conservation: The Multiplication of Service Agencies

Evolution in Education and Literature—National Christ's Ambassadors Department—Women's Missionary Council—Men's Fellowship —Department of Benevolences—Additional Service Agencies—Summary

In January, 1941, the beginning of the era under consideration, there were a total of 125 people serving the needs of the denomination at the national headquarters. Of this number, 79 were engaged in the printing operations of the Gospel Publishing House. Twenty were engaged in editorial work, with another seven working in the Sunday school division. Noel Perkin and his aide Jacob Mueller were assisted by 12 others in the Foreign Missions Department. The Executive Offices were manned by five people: E. S. Williams, the General Superintendent; Fred Vogler, the Assistant Superintendent; J. Roswell Flower, the Secretary-Treasurer; and two office helpers. There were only two departments, as such, at that time. The Foreign Missions Department had been in existence since 1925. In 1937 the Home Missions and Education Department had been established. The editorial and Sunday school work was all considered a part of the overall task of the Gospel Publishing House. It was a simple structure, and for the size of the denomination, which by then had grown to more than 200,000, a relatively small staff.[1]

From 1943 to 1953 a process of proliferation characterized the denomination, with the authorization by the General Councils of these years of a host of new departments and

[1]*The Pentecostal Evangel*, January 11, 1941, p. 14.

agencies. By 1957, 486 people were employed at the national headquarters and publishing plant. The last decade has disclosed a more gradual increase in personnel, the total number of workers being 692 in April, 1969.[2] The General Council in Milwaukee in 1953 was the great climax of this decade-long process of multiplication of services. Following that year new programs have been added only infrequently. The mood has changed since 1953 from proliferation to coordination; from analysis to synthesis.

Why did the Assemblies of God create this array of new enterprises in the decade following the war? There are at least two reasons. First, a new generation was emerging that did not share the same perspective as the original founders of the denomination. The early Pentecostals had been nourished in denominations that had communicated to them many values, some of which they wished to pass on to their children. They also wished to communicate to their children the distinctive values of the Pentecostal faith. Such communication, they discovered, required the erection of structures designed for such purposes. Conservation of the youth was the principal concern behind the creation of the various educational enterprises launched in that period.[3] There was another reason. During the rise of the second generation during the 1930's, it became increasingly apparent that the church was composed not just of an undifferentiated mass of people, but rather of distinct subgroups, each of which had special needs—and opportunities. Much of the elaboration of specialized structures that took place in the 1940's and early 1950's must be seen as an attempt to mobilize the men, the women, the youth, the boys and girls for increased effectiveness in world-outreach. Such auxiliary functions from a financial standpoint alone contributed large sums to the cause of missions when challenged in this fashion.

Evolution in Education and Literature

PUBLICATIONS DEPARTMENT

In January, 1947, the Publications Department was

[2]Public Relations Office news release, April 12, 1970.
[3]Interview, Charles W. Denton, September 8, 1967.

created by recommendation of the General Presbytery after considering a proposal of a committee on constitutional revision.[4] The new department was to supervise not only the printing plant operations, but also the editorial staff of *The Pentecostal Evangel* and a new, separate division, the editorial staff of church school literature. Previously all such editorial work had been administered by Stanley Frodsham, the editor of *The Pentecostal Evangel,* a task now too large to be handled in this fashion. Hart Armstrong was brought in to serve as the first editor of the new Church School Literature division, relieving Stanley Frodsham of the heavy workload entailed by this rapidly growing arm of the editorial work. J. Z. Kamerer, General Manager of the Gospel Publishing House since 1921, continued to serve until his retirement in 1952.[5]

The Pentecostal Evangel. In 1941 the circulation of *The Pentecostal Evangel* was 75,000. By 1969 it had climbed to 194,217, making it one of the largest religious weeklies in the nation.[6] Through the years it has served as the official denominational organ and news medium. Its editorial policy has been controlled by the Executive Presbytery and has remained constant through the years in spite of personnel changes.[7]

Stanley Frodsham had been serving for many years as editor of the periodical by the time Robert Cunningham joined the staff in 1937 as an editorial assistant. Upon the retirement of Frodsham on September 30, 1949, Cunningham assumed the editorship, a position which he has held ever since.[8] After 25 years of service as associate editor, beloved Charles E. Robinson died in March, 1954.[9] Continuity has been the hallmark of *The Pentecostal Evangel,* underscored by stability of editorial policy and longevity of personnel.

---

[4]General Council reports, 1947, p. 6.

[5]Interview, J. O. Harrell, October 24, 1967.

[6]General Council minutes, 1941, p. 96, and General Council reports, 1969, p.114.

[7]General Council minutes, 1957, p. 53. (Actually, an Editorial Policy Board was created at this council, to be appointed by the Executive Presbytery, and amenable to it.)

[8]*The Pentecostal Evangel,* October 15, 1949, p. 4.

[9]*The Pentecostal Evangel,* April 18, 1954, p. 12.

Church School Literature. A large proportion of the total production of the printing done in the Gospel Publishing House is Sunday school material. More than 60 publications are prepared by the staff, serving nearly 20,000 churches, more than half of whom are Sunday schools of other denominations. Sales receipts totaled over $6 million in 1969.[10]

In 1926, Stanley Frodsham expressed anxiety about the drift in theological content in the curricular materials provided by the International Council of Religious Education.[11] Ten years later the Assemblies of God withdrew from association with that body and began to develop its own uniform lesson series. In January, 1937, the first Assemblies of God series was introduced, scheduled to carry the adult and youth student through the Bible in seven years.[12] It was actually completed in six years, as it turned out, and a second cycle was launched in 1943.[13] This was a five-year cycle which terminated at the end of 1947. At that point, considerable discussion arose about the direction that curricular materials should take for the future, some advocating a continuation of uniform lessons, some advocating the development of a graded series for the various age-levels. In 1946 Ralph Riggs, whose portfolio assignment as Secretary of Education included the oversight of church school literature and Sunday school promotion, engaged in an intensive study of graded materials, hoping to see such literature supplement the older uniform pattern.[14] This concept was not adopted at that time, but gradually became the policy of the editorial department after 1955, with all age-levels having specialized courses by 1967 except the junior-high and adult groups, which still follow the uniform pattern.[15]

An important supplement to the regular curricular ma-

---

[10]General Council reports, 1967, pp. 130-33, and General Council reports, 1969, p. 23.

[11]Interview, Ralph Harris, November 15, 1967.

[12]Interview, Robert Cunningham, September 13, 1967.

[13]Interview, Ralph Harris, November 15, 1967.

[14]*Ibid.*

[15]Interview, Ralph Harris, November 15, 1967. See also Ralph Harris, "The Development of Church School Curricula of the Assemblies of God During the Period 1954-1966" (unpublished M.A. Thesis, Central Bible College, Springfield, Missouri, 1969).

terials has been the introduction of a series of undated manuals for teen-age and adult use. Twenty-four such courses have appeared since 1958, offering specialized study of important Biblical and theological topics.[16] A new seasonal schedule, conforming to the school year which begins in September, was adopted in 1970.[17]

Gospel Publishing House. In November, 1914, the second General Council authorized the raising of $5,000 for the purchase of printing equipment. Following a brief tenure in St. Louis, the publishing facilities of the embryo organization were removed to a modest building in Springfield, purchased for $3,600.[18] That location, an abandoned market, was remodeled and enlarged five times, serving the needs of the fellowship as executive offices and printing plant until 1948.[19] By unanimous vote at the 1945 General Council, the fellowship authorized construction of a new publishing plant and an office building to house administrative offices.[20] The old White City Ball Park, a choice site of five acres in downtown Springfield on its main street was purchased that year for $35,000. The first unit to be erected was the concrete and brick structure to house the printing facilities. Begun in 1947, this phase of the construction was completed and the building occupied in 1949 at a cost of $1,500,000.[21] Within 4 years this building was occupied to capacity and the urgency of expanding office facilities demanded action. The 1953 General Council, famous for its far-reaching authorizations, granted permission to complete the headquarters building project by the erection of a new office building at the front of the printing plant.[22] Almost as long as a city block, the modern four-story office building was completed in January, 1962, at a cost of $3 million.[23]

In the last several years the printing operations have evolved rapidly, moving from 100 percent letterpress to 95

---

[16]*Ibid.*

[17]Interview, Ralph Harris, March 4, 1970.

[18]"The Building" (unpublished manuscript in General Council files).

[19]*Ibid.*

[20]General Council minutes, 1945, pp. 27-29.

[21]Harrison, *op. cit.*, pp. 256-57.

[22]*Ibid.*

[23]Derived from file material in office of the General Manager, October 19, 1967.

percent offset lithography. Each day from 10 to 11 tons of printed matter is mailed from the self-contained printing operation, complete with its own editorial staff, 16 full-time artists, and 311 printing plant employees.[24] The publishing house is operated as a nonprofit enterprise, and the net earnings are used to subsidize the various departmental operations of the denomination. Supervising the activities of the Gospel Publishing House from the time of J. Z. Kamerer's retirement in 1951 until his own retirement in 1965 was J. Otis Harrell, who first entered the service of the Gospel Publishing House in 1925, 40 years before.[25]

The Music Division is a recent addition to the services provided by the Gospel Publishing House, having been established in 1956 to provide materials and guidance to the churches.[26] By 1963 the Music Division was sponsoring National Music Conferences, designed to furnish assistance to local church music program directors.[27] In addition to hymnals and songbooks, sheet music and an increasing number of recordings are distributed. A million and a half hymnals alone have been produced since 1957.[28]

To promote the sales of Gospel Publishing House materials several interrelated agencies cooperate with a variety of materials and literature. The basic unit is the Merchandising Division of the Gospel Publishing House. This agency furnishes a catalog each year, featuring not only Assemblies of God materials, but also a variety of materials and literature from other publishers.

On the basis of dollar volume, there has been a steady increase through the years, with church school literature accounting for the greater proportion of sales, and books printed by the Gospel Publishing House second, followed by materials from other publishers.[29] More than half of the customers are outside the Assemblies of God.

To make Gospel Publishing House materials more readily

---

[24]*Ibid.*

[25]Interview, J. Otis Harrell, October 24, 1967.

[26]Edwin Anderson, "Music in the Assemblies of God Tradition," *Church Music in Dimension*, II (Second quarter, 1966), pp. 4-5.

[27]*Ibid.*, p. 5.

[28]Interview, David Johnston, September 22, 1967.

[29]*Ibid.*

available a bookstore and mail order operation were established in Pasadena, California, in 1954.[30] That outlet was closed in 1968, but other outlets are now located in Santa Ana, California, and Seattle, Washington, in addition to the store and mail order operation in Springfield. In 1967 a special agency was created to supervise the promotion of Sunday school materials. This activity was, in 1970, merged with other operations to form the Marketing and Services Division. Magazine circulation is coordinated and promoted through the office of the Public Relations Office.

THE DEPARTMENT OF EDUCATION

A discussion of significant trends in the realm of education is reserved for a later chapter.[31] Our purpose here concerns only the establishment of structures by the denomination for the management of education.

As early as 1923 the need for coordination of the various Bible school programs for the training of the Pentecostal ministry was already apparent. A committee of the General Council in that year recommended the creation of a Bible School Commission to supervise and coordinate existing Bible school programs.[32] By resolution in 1925, Central Bible Institute was established as the norm for judging the quality of offerings of other schools, and General Council representation was requested for each of the boards of directors of the schools endorsed by the fellowship.[33] The 1935 General Council appointed a special committee to restudy the matter of standardization of programs and to draft a new criterion for institutional endorsement. The recommendation of this committee included an appeal for a national department with a secretary to implement the coordination of the educational enterprise.[34] The Memphis Council in 1937 did authorize the creation of a new department, but broadened its scope to include not only education but home missions as well.[35] This council recommended that no new schools be started without approval

---

[30] *The Pentecostal Evangel*, July 11, 1954, p. 13.
[31] See Chapter 14.
[32] General Council minutes, 1923, p. 58.
[33] General Council minutes, 1925, p. 37.
[34] General Council minutes, 1935, pp. 100-110.
[35] General Council minutes, 1937, pp. 62-65.

of the newly created department, and that no privately owned schools be endorsed by the General Council. Until the conclusion of World War II the home missions portion of the department's responsibility preoccupied its attention, but the campuses of the various Assemblies of God schools were visited occasionally.[36]

In 1941, 12 schools were endorsed by the Department of Education with a total enrollment of 1,754 students. Approximately 1,200 graduates of the schools had entered the ministry of the Assemblies of God by that time, and an additional 250 had been appointed to tours of duty as foreign missionaries.[37] All of the schools except one were Bible institutes, offering three-year courses or less, with the specific purpose of preparing church-related workers. The single exception was Southern California Bible College, which had become a four-year degree-granting institution in 1939.[38] It, too, was primarily designed for the training of ministers.

The war created a veritable avalanche of interest in post-high school training in the Assemblies of God. To care for the expanding operations the General Council in 1945 authorized the separation of the interests of education from home missions, and a separate Department of Education came into being. The Executive Presbytery was constituted a standing committee on education.[39] Fred Vogler, who had served as the executive in charge of the department since 1937, was replaced in 1943 by Ralph M. Riggs. At the next General Council, when the functions of home missions and education were separated, Riggs was given the oversight of education and Vogler once again supervised home missions. Upon Riggs' election as General Superintendent in 1953, a position he held until 1959, the executive oversight of education fell to J. Roswell Flower. Later Charles Scott and T. E. Gannon served in that capacity. Currently G. Raymond Carlson is the executive director.

---

[36]Interview, Ralph M. Riggs, August 24, 1967.

[37]General Council minutes, 1941, p. 58.

[38]Millard E. Collins, "Establishing and Financing of Higher Educational Institutions in the Church Body of the Assemblies of God in the U.S.A." (unpublished manuscript, 1959).

[39]General Council minutes, 1945, pp. 23-24.

Riggs served as both executive director and secretary from 1943 to 1953. Since 1953, a series of national secretaries have been appointed to work under the supervision of the executive directors. J. Robert Ashcroft, C. C. Burnett, and Hardy Steinberg have so served.

To establish policy governing the functions of the Department of Education, a standing committee, consisting of the Executive Presbytery, existed from 1945 until 1955. At the General Council in 1955 the standing committee was reconstituted, henceforth being elected by the General Presbytery from the six geographical regions of the country.[40] This committee in 1959 was renamed the Board of Education.[41]

In addition to oversight of ministerial training schools, the Department of Education was given the supervision of several other types of educational activity. Its initial responsibility, established in 1945, called for the creation of three divisions: the Church School Division, the Academic, and the Bible Institute. Church school responsibility gave way rapidly to an emerging division within the Gospel Publishing House called the Sunday School Department, which was given formal departmental status at the General Council of 1953. Included in the "Academic" division was the care of the various parochial day schools that were beginning to appear, and also the implementation of the mandate of the General Council of 1953 for the establishment of a liberal arts college. Bible training, as a category of departmental responsibility, included by 1947 not only the supervision of the ministerial training schools of the denomination, but also a correspondence program launched that year by Frank M. Boyd. The Berean School of the Bible, the name by which the correspondence program is known, continues to be the basis of a required ministerial training program in several districts for candidates who have not completed a standard Bible college course at an accredited institution. The Berean School of the Bible offers 12 correspondence courses. Each year a total of about 2,000

---

[40] *Educator*, September-October, 1958, p. 1.

[41] General Council minutes, 1959, pp. 34-35.

are sold. Nearly 26,000 courses have been completed since the beginning of the correspondence school.[42]

To serve as a coordinating link among the college personnel in the denomination, National Secretary J. Robert Ashcroft inaugurated a publication entitled the *Educator*, in May, 1956. Each succeeding secretary has continued to edit the bimonthly periodical.

THE NATIONAL SUNDAY SCHOOL DEPARTMENT

Beginnings. In 1919 the General Council authorized the new printing plant to prepare Sunday school materials for the denomination. This was an important milestone in the direction of the eventual creation of a national structure for the promotion of local church educational programs. However, it was not until the decade of the 1930's that the value of the Sunday school to the local church really "caught on." It was not uncommon for pastors to be suspicious of Christian education, some considering it to be a substitute for Pentecostal evangelism and revivalism.[43] When it became apparent that the Sunday school was being employed effectively as an instrument of evangelistic outreach into the community, the antipathy faded rapidly. As a new generation within the fellowship arose, thoughtful leaders recognized the urgency of furnishing a methodical teaching agency for the indoctrination of the youth.

The early 1930's seem to have been a turning point. In 1933, Pastor Ralph M. Riggs of Central Assembly in Springfield, Missouri, wrote *A Successful Sunday School*, a manual that quickly found its way into the hands of church workers throughout the fellowship.[44] At the General Council that year it was reported that "Sunday school interest has become almost a revival in our assemblies since the last General Council, resulting in larger enrollments and an addition of approximately six hundred new Sunday schools."[45]

The year 1935 was an important one. Oklahoma created the first district Sunday school office that year. More impor-

---

[42]Interview, Hardy Steinberg, September 7, 1967, and statistical data from the Department of Education, July 17, 1970.

[43]Kendrick, *op. cit.*, p. 118.

[44]Harrison, *op. cit.*, p. 263.

[45]General Council minutes, 1933, p. 50.

tant was the appointment of Marcus Grable, a layman from Springfield, Missouri, by General Manager Kamerer of the Gospel Publishing House, to set up a promotions office to stimulate interest in Sunday school and to publicize Assemblies of God Sunday school literature.[46] This was the real beginning of the Sunday School Department, although it continued to be a division of the Gospel Publishing House until the General Council of 1953 voted to make it a separate department.[47] The growing feeling of need for a national program to provide continuity and consistency found expression in the adoption of the first national efficiency plan, called "The First-Class Sunday School."[48]

By the time of the outbreak of World War II, the Sunday school had become a strategic force in the Assemblies of God, both as an evangelistic tool and as a means of conserving the results of evangelism. One thousand new schools were being opened annually by the late 1930's.[49]

The Great Sunday School Conference Boom. Marcus Grable had visited the last great International Sunday School Convention, which had been held in Kansas City in 1924. In the late 1930's, Grable and his wife, together with two young ladies from the editorial staff of the Gospel Publishing House, Misses Zella Lindsey and Dorothy Morris, conducted weekend conferences featuring Sunday school methodology in the metropolitan centers within driving distance of Springfield.[50] The conference concept on a local basis was sufficiently successful that Grable laid plans for a national conference, designed to gather Sunday school leaders together for inspiration and sharing of methodological ideas. In February, 1940, the first such convention was held. About two dozen district leaders gathered in the library of the publishing house.[51] Two sessions were held in Springfield through the war years, and were not particularly impressive, although attendance increased. As late as 1944 there was little to indicate that a boom would develop that

[46]Interview, Marcus Grable, October 24, 1967.
[47]Kendrick, *op. cit.*, p. 120.
[48]*The Sunday School Counselor*, February, 1964, p. 2.
[49]General Council minutes, 1939, p. 89.
[50]Interview, Marcus Grable, October 24, 1967.
[51]Harrison, *op. cit.*, p. 270.

would overshadow even the great International Sunday School Convention Grable had visited twenty years before.

Following the 1945 convention, it was decided to hold the meetings annually. The 1946 convention featured a variety of departmental conferences to supply helpful information and inspiration to special interest groups. The next year several thousand enthusiastic Sunday school workers descended on Springfield to attend the Fifth National Convention.[52] By 1948 the convention, having outgrown the facilities of any single church building in the city, moved to the largest auditorium in southwestern Missouri, the Shrine Mosque, in Springfield. A gigantic parade, estimated to be over three miles long, complete with floats and banners, was staged. The public schools of the city were dismissed for the occasion.[53] The 1952 Tenth National Sunday School Convention, held in Springfield, taxed the limit of Springfield's facilities. Attendance exceeded 10,000, with representatives from every state, several countries, and more than 30 denominations.[54] Twenty-nine separate departmental conferences in addition to gigantic mass meetings created a mood of intense enthusiasm.

Having grown too large for Springfield, the conference concept in 1953 was carried to the various regions of the country. A team of 15 Sunday school specialists conducted six conventions in six strategically located cities across the nation. Aggregate attendance totaled more than 26,000.[55]

The great climax came in the spring of 1954 at the Eleventh National Sunday School Convention in St. Louis. Total attendance exceeded the goal of 11,000 that had been set, making it the largest Sunday school convention of any kind ever assembled. More than 100 booths in the Exposition Hall displayed materials of interest to Sunday school enthusiasts. The mass rallies at Kiel Auditorium featured the theme, "Set Your Sunday School Aflame."[56]

Although 28,600 attended the regional conventions con-

---

[52]*Ibid.*, p. 271.
[53]*The Pentecostal Evangel*, March 20, 1948, p. 11.
[54]*The Pentecostal Evangel*, April 27, 1952, p. 7.
[55]General Council reports, 1953, p. 55.
[56]General Council reports, 1955, p. 70.

ducted in 1955, the great boom was over.[57] In 1956 a new policy was adopted in an effort to take Sunday school evangelism to the grass roots. In that year an effort was made to encourage conventions on the district level.[58] The regional conventions scheduled by the denomination for 1957 were not for the purpose of emphasizing Sunday school, but focused attention on world missions. They were not as successful as had been the Sunday school conventions. The trend toward "all-church" conventions continued, in an effort to create a more balanced attention to the other facets of church life. Perhaps the Fiftieth Anniversary Convention, conducted in Springfield in April, 1964, best symbolizes the trend toward the effort to bring Sunday school emphasis more in line with other aspects of the life of the church. After the great boom days of the large Sunday school conventions, a comparable level of enthusiasm was not registered by the fellowship in large convention-type meetings until the 1968 Council on Evangelism at St. Louis.

Why were the great conventions so successful and why did the boom falter? Perhaps the single best reason for the prodigious growth of the Sunday school conventions is that the time was ripe. In the years immediately after the war, travel was easy for the first time in five years. And, more important, Sunday school furnished a greater opportunity for the involvement of the laymen in church work than any other facet of church life in the Assemblies of God. It was something that everyone could participate in, even more so than such enterprises as missions, in which participation was largely vicarious for the many. And, further, Sunday school had been demonstrated as a highly successful evangelistic tool. It worked. Enthusiasm was readily kindled by sharing testimonies of local church growth through deployment of lay people in Sunday school endeavors. Statistics attested a spectacular growth in the Assemblies of God, much of which was being attributed to the Sunday school emphasis. In 1955, General Secretary J. Roswell Flower reported a gain in the number of new churches

[57]*Ibid.*

[58]General Council reports, 1957, p. 37.

in the previous 10-year period of 38 percent, a membership gain of 65 percent, and an increase in the number of ordained ministers of 70 percent.[59] Membership since 1941 had almost doubled.

Why, then, did the boom come to an end? There are several possible reasons. The most obvious reason for cutting back the Sunday school convention emphasis was financial. The year 1953 was the high-water mark for the proliferation of service agencies in the Assemblies of God, a number of new undertakings being authorized in that year. It became apparent that the General Councils had been in a spending mood, but that this was not matched by means for securing revenue to support new ventures. After 1953 it took several years to digest the programs that had been adopted. It was discovered that the budget of the Sunday School Department had climbed rapidly during the heyday of the great conventions. A mood of conservatism displaced the expansive mood of previous years when it became obvious that the denomination was overspending. The budget for the National Sunday School Department in 1955 was reduced sharply from $245,000 in 1954 to $177,276 in 1955, and the number of office personnel from 35 to 28.[60] No longer would there be unlimited funds to prepare spectacular conventions.

Another reason for the decline of convention enthusiasm is that such endeavors seem to lose their appeal after limited repetition.[61] The denomination was responsive to such an enterprise in the postwar period, but the novelty of mass conventions seemed to wear off. Even the General Council sessions, the denomination's biennial business convention, have not demonstrated unusual growth in recent years. Some have argued that redirecting the nature of the great conventions toward a broadened "all-church" emphasis has cost the individual appeal to the layman who readily identifies with the Sunday school but who has a much more vague sense of personal involvement in less tangible areas of church life, but not all agree with this opinion.

---

[59]General Council reports, 1955.
[60]General Council reports, 1957, pp. 42-43.
[61]Interview, Bernard Bresson, December 7, 1967.

There does seem to be a correlation between the decision to cut back continued advancement of the big convention concept and the growth rate of the Sunday schools in the Assemblies of God. It seemed that the Sunday school goal enunciated in 1957 of "On to a Million" would easily be reached by 1960, but the rapid leveling off of new growth at that point prevented the attainment of that goal until 1963.[62] It is noteworthy that the membership in Assemblies of God Sunday schools is roughly twice the membership in the churches, reflecting much more accurately the true dimensions of the denomination's actual influence, and, quite possibly, the significance of the Sunday school as the single greatest resource for church growth.

The Sunday School Standard. The first standard for measuring the quality of a local Sunday school program was developed in 1935. This was elaborated in 1941 by the adoption of the Lighthouse Plan, a 12-point standard of excellence employed for seven years. A series of changes were made in the years that followed, with the most extensive revision being made in 1961. Since 1942, Assemblies of God Sunday schools have been evaluated by means of an annual report form submitted to the national office.[63] More than 75 percent of the Sunday schools in the denomination cooperate, 6,845 schools reporting in 1969.[64] Edith Denton has supervised the Standards Division for many years.

Workers Training. To provide for the education of local Sunday school teachers, January was established by the denomination to be National Training Month in 1952. In that year a manual for Sunday school teachers, *Administration and Organization,* written by Hart Armstrong, became the first in a series of annual study books.[65] Although a book each year has been featured for the National Training Month, additional books have been added to the library available to Sunday school workers. By August, 1969, there were 46 such manuals. In 1948, 30,000 copies of such books

[62]General Council reports, 1967, p. 148.
[63]*Counselor,* February, 1964, p. 2.
[64]Sunday School Department statistics.
[65]Interview, Jerry Sandidge, January 10, 1967.

were distributed by the Gospel Publishing House, but in the latest Sunday school year, ending September 31, 1969, 65,000 manuals had been sold.[66] This seems to indicate a growing concern for the quality of local church school education as well as sheer quantitative concern.

In 1954 an additional training feature was added. To make it possible for district directors, sectional representatives, Christian education directors, and Sunday school teachers to receive specialized training an annual Advanced Christian Training School was instituted on the campus of Central Bible Institute.[67]

The Sunday School Counselor. The magazine with the largest paid circulation in the Assemblies of God, outside *The Pentecostal Evangel,* is *The Sunday School Counselor,* with a circulation in 1969 of more than 51,000. This monthly is the official organ of the Sunday School Department. Through the years the *Counselor,* as it is known, has channeled inspiration and information to local leaders, teachers, and workers. In the course of its history it has been the recipient of several awards for excellence by the Evangelical Press Association.[68] Of special interest was the inauguration of a feature in the October, 1948, issue in which the monthly attendance of local Sunday schools was listed. This seems to mark the beginning of an emphasis on statistics, a self-conscious awareness in the denomination of its rapid growth. It has come to be the custom in the denomination to measure the strength of a local church, not by its membership, but by its Sunday school attendance, a circumstance without doubt supported by the *Counselor*'s monthly attendance listing.

National Christ's Ambassadors Department

YOUTH DEPARTMENT ORIGINS

The National CA Department was given formal authorization at the General Council of 1943, but organized youth ministry in the Assemblies of God dates from 1925.[69] On May 30, 1925, about 300 young people from 13 churches

[66]General Council reports, 1969, p. 123.
[67]General Council reports, 1955, p. 74.
[68]*The Sunday School Counselor,* April, 1964, p. 2.
[69]General Council minutes, 1943, pp. 24-26.

in the northern and central parts of California gathered at Glad Tidings Assembly in Oakland for fellowship and inspiration. A second rally was planned for October, in Stockton, at which the "Pentecostal Ambassadors for Christ" was organized, with Wesley R. Steelberg elected as president. Meanwhile, Pastor A. G. Osterberg of Fresno Full Gospel Tabernacle was organizing a similar group, which he called "Christian Crusaders." This southern group in California spread rapidly through the San Joaquin Valley. At Bethel Temple, Los Angeles, Youth Director Carl Hatch suggested the name "Christ's Ambassadors" for the youth group developing in his church. Across the country, David Burris, later to be district superintendent, was elected the first state youth leader in Arkansas.[70]

Carl Hatch began the publication of a young people's paper, *The Christ's Ambassadors Herald,* as a district periodical, but after 1931 it took on national scope. At the Memphis General Council in 1937, the youth committee recommended that the denomination assume responsibility for Hatch's paper. Consequently, beginning in January, 1938, the *CA Herald,* with Robert Cunningham as editor, became a denominational enterprise.[71] It was only 10 years prior, in 1927, that the General Council had first recognized the importance of youth work by appointing a committee to study its role in the fellowship.

The next major step toward the creation of a national office was the calling of a series of National Christ's Ambassadors Conferences.[72] The first such national gathering met on the campus of Central Bible Institute in June, 1940, with 342 participants registered. Bert Webb, pastor of Central Assembly in Springfield, was the conference director. Each year thereafter similar conferences met in Springfield, with a peak registration of 650 being reached at the fourth and last conference in June, 1944.[73] Considerable credit for the calling of these conferences goes to

---

[70]"Historic Highlights" (mimeographed, undated publication of the National CA Department).

[71]*Ibid.*

[72]The name "Christ's Ambassadors" very quickly was adopted throughout the Assemblies of God to designate the youth activity of the denomination.

[73]"Historic Highlights"

Dorothy Morris and Zella Lindsey, who caught a vision of the value of organized youth activity from their visit to the Southern Baptist youth conference at Ridgecrest, North Carolina.[74]

At the first conference, representatives of the youth leaders met informally several times with Assemblies of God executives, and following these meetings an appeal was made for the establishment of a national office. As a result of this appeal, William Pickthorn, then a pastor in Memphis, was called to Springfield to lay the groundwork for such an office. In 1942, Ralph Harris, pastor in Clio, Michigan, and director of the Christ's Ambassadors for that district, offered to prepare a chronicle for the conference, much as he had done at the summer conventions in Michigan. This editorial work brought Harris to the attention of the executives in Springfield, who were looking for the right man to head the proposed youth department. Ralph Harris arrived in Springfield in February, 1943, to open the office. It was in September of that year that the General Council formally approved the new enterprise. And so the CA Department was born.

SPEED-THE-LIGHT

One month after Ralph Harris arrived in Springfield the idea of "Speed-the-Light" came to him. In the spring of 1943 the Foreign Missions Department had conducted its historic planning session for postwar expansion. The turning point had come in the war, and farsighted strategists, such as Noel Perkin, were looking to the future. Harris developed the concept of the youth of the movement raising funds for airplanes—which had played such a vital part in the war—to speed the work of the missionaries. General Superintendent E. S. Williams liked the idea and lent it his full support. The idea was officially launched at the 1944 National Youth Conference, at which more than 40 district youth leaders were present. The name "Speed-the-Light" was adopted at that meeting, and a goal of $100,000 was announced.[75]

---

[74]Interview, Dorothy Morris, November 16, 1967.
[75]Interview, Ralph Harris, October 19, 1967.

The concept of Speed-the-Light caught fire among the young people. By the end of 1969 more than $9 million had been appropriated for the Foreign Missions Department to provide vehicles, printing equipment, radio equipment, and for the construction of evangelistic centers.[76] Verne MacKinney has served as the office clerk for Speed-the-Light from its beginning.

MINISTRY TO SERVICEMEN

At the General Council in 1941 a resolution was passed committing to the Home Missions Department the responsibility of devising means for ministering to military personnel.[77] During the war years this ministry became the outstanding contribution of the Home Missions Department. The first effort in this direction was the preparation of a small devotional paper, without denominational overtones, called *Reveille*. Edited by Myer Pearlman until his death in 1943, the paper apparently filled a need not met by any other agency. During the war years alone 14 million copies were supplied to thousands of chaplains of all faiths for distribution to servicemen, all costs being supplied by Assemblies of God contributors.[78]

The work had grown so rapidly that in 1944 a separate Servicemen's Department was created. A bustling office was quickly established, with a staff of 24 full-time and 28 part-time workers handling the enormous volume of private correspondence and printed mailings to servicemen.[79] The department coordinated the efforts of 11 field representatives who ministered at military bases, hospitals, and in communities adjacent to them. Forty-one Victory Service Centers were operated by the department, the Long Beach center alone in one year having a quarter of a million visitors.[80] Contact was maintained with the 34 Assemblies of God chaplains serving the United States Army.

In June, 1946, a "Reveille Reunion" was held in Springfield, when many of the chaplains and men who had served

[76]News Release, Public Relations Department, January 16, 1970.
[77]General Council minutes, 1941, p. 64.
[78]Harrison, *op. cit.*, pp. 242-43.
[79]*Ibid.*, pp. 243-44.
[80]General Council minutes, 1945, p. 84.

in the war gathered for a last get-together. At this time the Servicemen's Department was disbanded and the work of ministering to servicemen was assumed by the National CA Department. During the Korean conflict and more recently during the Vietnam war, the activity of the Servicemen's Division has increased greatly. At the end of 1969, 15,000 servicemen were on the mailing list of the Servicemen's Division, with an estimated 34,000 Assemblies of God men in uniform around the world. Forty-five chaplains, more than at the peak of World War II, were in military service. A total of more than 17 million copies of *Reveille*, in 33 editions, had been distributed.[81] Robert Way served as coordinator of the Servicemen's Division from 1964 to 1969.

CAMPUS MINISTRY

In February, 1949, J. Robert Ashcroft, a member of the National CA Department staff, introduced a resolution to the National Sunday School Convention meeting in Springfield, challenging the denomination to develop a program for ministering to Assemblies of God youth attending colleges outside the fellowship. The CA Department in the fall of 1948 began the publication of a duplicated paper, *The College Fellowship Bulletin,* issued free, four times during the school year. By the 1951-52 school year, 338 names were on the mailing list.[82]

In the fall of 1952, the paper was renamed *Campus Ambassador.* When J. Robert Ashcroft assumed new duties as secretary of the Education Department in 1954, J. Calvin Holsinger became the editor of the paper and also developed a new phase of the program, the guidance of campus youth groups, called Chi Alpha chapters. William Menzies, instructor at Central Bible Institute, served as part-time director of the college program following Holsinger, from 1958 to 1962. The first full-time director was Lee Shultz who spearheaded the first national Chi Alpha conference in 1963. Chi Alpha activity was reported at the beginning of 1970 on 70 campuses, with several boasting

[81]National CA Department statistics.

[82]Rick Howard, *Chi Alpha Manual* (Springfield, Missouri: Gospel Publishing House, 1966), p. 6.

student centers. The circulation of the *Campus Ambassador* magazine reached 14,000 as the new decade began.[83]

DEPARTMENTAL DEVELOPMENT

To coordinate the work of the various local and district youth activities, a national leaders' conference was instituted in 1946. In July of that year, the first issue of a monthly publication designed for the informing of district leaders appeared. Since then, annual "D-CAP" (District CA Presidents) Conferences have been an important function in the operation of the national program.[84]

In 1955 a standard of excellence was adopted for local CA groups.[85] Known as "GOAL," the standard has been a means of upgrading the quality of youth work. About half of the churches in the fellowship submit an annual checkup form each fall to the national office.

In 1962 a Bible quiz program was introduced, featuring intensive study of a Bible book each year. In the same year a "Talent Search" program was launched with the objective of encouraging young people to develop skills in church music. These programs have led to a revival of national youth conferences, where regional quiz and talent winners compete for national honors. Ten thousand young people participated in these ventures in 1969.[86]

Important publications of the National CA Department are *Youth Alive* and the *CA Guide*. *Youth Alive* (previously known as the *CA Herald*) reached a circulation of over 25,000 by 1969, and the *Guide*, a quarterly designed for youth leaders, had a circulation of about 8,700.[87]

Summer camp activity has been one of the important features of Assemblies of God youth ministry. Begun during World War II, specialized camps for youth have had a vigorous growth, with 76 camps being reported for 1969, enrolling more than 15,000 young people. Study courses, organizational guidance, and a standard of excellence are provided by the national office.[88]

---

[83]National CA Department statistics.
[84]General Council reports, 1947, p. 38.
[85]Interview, Verne MacKinney, September 27, 1967.
[86]National CA Department statistics.
[87]General Council reports, 1969, p. 80.
[88]Interview with Dale Harmon, April 15, 1970.

In 1966 the Christ's Ambassadors Department launched a new program which has rapidly captured the imagination of youth. Now titled "Ambassadors in Mission," (AIM), the new program is a summer evangelistic activity in which teams of carefully-screened young people, between 16 and 24 years of age, conduct intensive house-to-house witnessing, both in continental United States and abroad. AIMers pay their own way for the privilege of participating in the program. Light-for-the-Lost furnishes the literature used in the foreign phase of the ministry, and Evangelism Literature for America provides stateside assistance. The first year, 12 young people spent 25 days in Jamaica and British Honduras. Seven hundred conversions were reported in that initial venture! Seventy-four went in 1967, scattered in 10 teams through six countries from Latin America to Alaska. In 1968, 129 participated, registering nearly 2,500 decisions for Christ! The following year 90 invaded six Latin American countries. More than 6,700 accepted Christ through their efforts, and nearly 200,000 pieces of literature were distributed! The domestic phase of AIM in 1969 had 10,000 youth involved in organized witnessing! More than 400 "AIMers" ministered in 12 countries in 1970. A new feature of the 1970 AIM program was an invasion of Europe, as well as several Latin American countries. Testimonies of the young people who have participated reveal that such experiences have indeed made a profound impact on their priorities and values in life.[89]

The men who have led the National CA Department through the years have made a sizable contribution to the conservation of Assemblies of God youth. Following Ralph Harris as National Secretary have been Harry Myers, Don Mallough, Dick Fulmer, Owen Carr, Russell Cox, and currently, Norman Correll.

Women's Missionary Council

The story of the Women's Missionary Council begins with Etta Calhoun, a prominent Women's Christian Temperance Union leader in the state of Texas who received the Pentecostal experience in 1905. Mrs. Calhoun felt that

[89]NCAD statistics.

Spirit-baptized women, properly organized, could accomplish much more for the kingdom of God than if their individual efforts remained uncoordinated. Having received permission from the district presbyter of the Houston section, Mrs. Calhoun organized the first Women's Missionary Council at Morwood Mission in February, 1925.[90]

Several other churches in the area quickly adopted the idea, and by August of 1925 at the Texas-New Mexico District Council a resolution was passed acknowledging the existence of this auxiliary function. Mrs. Calhoun became the first District WMC President.[91]

Women's Missionary Council groups developed in state after state, in spite of considerable reluctance to encourage such activity expressed by ministers in some sections of the fellowship. The development of a "Ladies Aid" type of organization was a fear among those who identified such activity with apostasy. By 1947, 18 districts had organized programs. In that year a committee report was read to the General Council appealing for national recognition.[92] No action was taken, so in 1949 a second appeal was made at the General Council. Finally, in 1951 a resolution authorizing the establishment of a national office to coordinate the various district organizational activities was adopted.[93] The 1953 General Council adopted a constitutional provision for the Women's Missionary Council. By the time the national office was authorized in 1951, 27 districts had already formed their own organizations. By 1955 every district in the fellowship had organized a WMC program. More than any other department created at Assemblies of God headquarters the WMC was a grass roots enterprise. Currently there are 5,500 local units with 70,000 members.[94]

Edith Whipple was chosen to be the first National WMC Secretary. She opened the new office in Springfield in the fall of 1951, remaining as the director until 1959, when Mrs. Mildred Smuland stepped into that role, a position

[90] *The WMC Leader* (Springfield, Missouri: Gospel Publishing House, 1967), pp. 17-18.

[91] *Ibid.*, p. 19.

[92] Interview, Mildred Smuland, September 30, 1967.

[93] General Council minutes, 1951, pp. 32-33.

[94] Interviews, Mildred Smuland, September 30, 1967, and April 15, 1970.

she still maintains. During the course of the years the national office has provided a variety of manuals and aids for local and district leaders, including a standard of excellence designed in 1957.[95] Several periodicals serve the needs of the group, most important of them being the *Slant,* a quarterly leadership journal edited by Mrs. Ann Ahlf, and *Missionettes Memos,* designed for the affiliated girls' group.

The chief function of the WMC program is auxiliary support to other departments, chiefly the Foreign Missions Department, Home Missions Department, CA Department, and the Benevolences Department. More than $24 million has been contributed to these agencies since the beginning of the national WMC office.[96] In addition to service rendered financially, local and district units have furnished a wide range of practical helps and ministries. A significant contribution has been the training program for young women. In 1955 a girls' auxiliary program, known as "Missionettes," was launched.[97] Since 1955, Charlotte Schumitsch has served as Coordinator for this activity. By 1967 the Missionettes had grown to 6,500 local clubs with 75,000 members.[98] A fast-growing new feature is known as "Prims," for seven- and eight-year-old girls. In 1965 a senior girls program, called Young Women's Missionary Council, for unmarried women of ages 16 to 24, was begun. This program is supervised by Mrs. Angeline Tucker, widow of J. W. Tucker, who was martyred in the Congo.

Men's Fellowship

World War II affected the status of laymen in the Assemblies of God. Before that time there were relatively few men with leadership ability or with means in the local churches. Home from the war came a generation of young men, many of whom took advantage of government-sponsored educational opportunities that opened the door to larger horizons. And, at home, many in the fellowship had come into a new prosperity undreamed-of in the days of the

---

[95]*Ibid.*
[96]General Council reports, 1969, p. 125.
[97]Interview, Mildred Smuland, September 30, 1967.
[98]Interview, Mildred Smuland, April 15, 1970.

Great Depression when so many of them had come into the Assemblies of God. The Men's Fellowship came into being to provide opportunity for service for this growing reservoir of abilities and energies that had largely been unharnessed and unrecognized.[99]

The prototype of Men's Fellowship began at Calvary Assembly of God in Inglewood, California, through the inspiration and leadership of Jack Epperson in 1947.[100] The immediate response to this program precipitated an appeal to the General Presbyters in 1948 for the creation of a national men's association to furnish a means for stimulating lay witnessing and to encourage stewardship.[101] A committee was appointed to study the propriety of the laymen's appeal, but its report at the 1949 General Presbyters meeting indicates some reluctance to initiate a program at a national level without a larger grass roots support, such as the Women's Missionary Council had been experiencing.[102] However, in spite of some reluctance on the part of some ministers who feared the creation of a strong laymen's organization, the General Council in 1951 authorized the establishment of a Men's Fellowship Department.[103] Assistant General Superintendent Ralph M. Riggs early in 1952 set up an advisory committee and selected Gospel Publishing House General Manager J. Otis Harrell to serve as the first national secretary of the new organization.[104] Harrell had been the prime mover in the appeal for a national laymen's organization since 1948. Don Mallough and Burton Pierce followed Harrell in the office. In 1966 a businessman from California, Glen Bonds, became the national secretary. The chief publication of the Men's Fellowship Department, the monthly *TEAM,* was introduced in 1954, with Wildon Colbaugh as editor. In 1970 it merged with *The Pentecostal Evangel.*

The Men's Fellowship has not enjoyed the same con-

---

[99]Interview, J. O. Harrell, October 24, 1967.

[100]Interview, Wildon Colbaugh, September 27, 1967.

[101]General Presbytery minutes, 1948, pp. 4, 9.

[102]General Presbytery minutes, 1949, p. 1.

[103]General Council minutes, 1951, p. 24.

[104]Ralph M. Riggs, "The Men's Fellowship of the Assemblies of God" (unpublished report, November, 1952).

sistent growth as the Women's Missionary Council. In the early 1960's there were about 3,000 chapters in existence, but by 1969 this had fallen to 1,334.[105] Only in recent years has a solid program been developed to displace the early image of Men's Fellowship as a "ham and yam" club. Three major programs now constitute a strong focus to which there seems to be considerable response. These are the "Light-for-the-Lost" division, the "Royal Rangers" division, and the "Action Crusades" division.

Two Assemblies of God laymen, Sam Cochran and Everett James, since 1952 had been raising funds for Assemblies of God missions through a corporation in Costa Mesa, California, called the "Missionary Gospel Society." Its primary aim was to supply evangelistic literature to foreign lands. The enterprise became so successful that, at the General Council in San Antonio, the entire enterprise was adopted as a national project for the denomination.[106] That year the Men's Fellowship gave it a new name, "Light-for-the-Lost," and invited Everett James to move to Springfield to continue promotion of the work. In 1962 it was adopted by the Foreign Missions Department as a feature of its urban outreach.[107] It is a significant auxiliary function of the Men's Fellowship Department, serving the interests of world missions. More than $150,000 a year for gospel literature is raised in this fashion.[108]

One of the original reasons for promoting a national men's fellowship was to furnish the framework for development of a specialized training program for boys.[109] In 1955 the General Presbytery authorized Gene Putnam to engage in preliminary work in this direction, utilizing a program he had already developed entitled "Christian Cadets."[110] However, by this time the WMC's had already begun a vigorous program for the training of girls, and this seemed to conflict with Putnam's program which included both girls and

---

[105]Men's Fellowship Department statistics.
[106]*The Pentecostal Evangel*, December 2, 1962, pp. 10-11.
[107]*Ibid.*, p. 11.
[108]Men's Fellowship Department statistics.
[109]Interview, J. O. Harrell, October 24, 1967.
[110]General Presbytery minutes, 1955, p. 4.

boys.[111] Consequently, Johnnie Barnes was brought into the Men's Fellowship Department early in 1962 to create an entirely new program for boys alone. "Royal Rangers" has been the result of Barnes' efforts. In seven years the new program has demonstrated good growth, 5,000 local groups being in operation in 1969, with a total of 95,000 Royal Rangers on record.[112] In 1967 a new feature was added for younger boys 7 and 8 years of age, called the "Buckaroos."

The third major division of the Men's Fellowship Department is known as "Action Crusades," headed by Wildon Colbaugh. This concept also originated in 1962. It is essentially a program of planned witnessing. A Baptist minister, Reverend Gene Edwards, challenged the men of the Assemblies of God to personal evangelism at the General Council in 1959. Pastor Stanton Johnson of Ottumwa, Iowa, applied the principles outlined by Edwards with considerable success. Otis Keener, pastor in Oklahoma City, also found great response from the laymen in his church to a program of planned personal witnessing for Christ. The national secretary of the Men's Fellowship Department at the time, Burton Pierce, encouraged the adoption of a program of planned witnessing as a national emphasis. In 1964 the name "Action Crusades" was given to the effort.[113]

Each of the three major phases of the National Men's Fellowship Department has a laymen's advisory council to outline policy. In spite of the limited growth of the men's groups at the local level, it does represent an important auxiliary function in the Assemblies of God which seeks to provide a significant means for lay participation in the work of the church.

Department of Benevolences

In 1947 the General Council authorized the establishment of a Department of Benevolences to coordinate the growing welfare activities of the denomination.[114] Care for aged ministers, child welfare, and disaster relief were thus brought under the management of a single office.

[111]Interview, Johnnie Barnes, December 15, 1967.
[112]General Council reports, 1969, p. 106.
[113]Interview, Wildon Colbaugh, September 27, 1967.
[114]General Council minutes, 1947, p. 37.

CARE FOR AGED MINISTERS

As early as 1933, the General Council took cognizance of the growing need to provide for pioneers who had sacrificed much and were now growing to retirement years with little of this world's goods accumulated. A committee was appointed to study the problem and report its findings to the next General Council.[115] The 1935 General Council voted to create a fund for needy ministers to be administered by the Executive Presbytery upon recommendation of the district councils. This was entitled "The Ministers' Benevolent Fund."[116] This fund was supplied through earnings from the Gospel Publishing House and from donations. By the end of 1944, a balance of $146,224 had accumulated in the fund. It was at that time that it was reconstituted as "Aged Ministers Assistance," and thereafter semiannual offerings received in the local churches on Memorial Day and Thanksgiving Day have served to replenish the fund.[117] When the Department of Benevolences was created, the administration of this fund was committed to its trust.

In 1945 another important step was taken to make material provision for aging ministers. The General Council in that year arranged for the setting up of a retirement fund to which ministers and churches could contribute.[118] In the first seven months more than 1,000 ministers joined the new retirement program, which was called the "Ministers' Benefit Association."[119] Through the years several changes have been made in the program, the most important being its incorporation as a separate entity apart from all existing General Council structures in 1956.[120] At the end of 1969 there were 1,479 licensed and ordained ministers participating in the retirement program, with 746 churches contributing toward the retirement plan of their pastors.[121]

A committee, chaired by Glen Renick, recommended to

115General Council minutes, 1933, p. 104.
116General Council minutes, 1937, pp. 66-68.
117Interview, Evelyn Dunham, December 15, 1967.
118General Council minutes, 1945, p. 49.
119*Ibid.*
120Interview, Evelyn Dunham, December 15, 1967.
121Statistics from Ministers Benefit Association office.

the General Presbytery in 1946 that the Assemblies of God "proceed with the establishing of Homes for the Aged as soon as possible, thus meeting a real need in our fellowship, not only towards those ministers who have spent their strength and lives in the Gospel ministry and now face their declining years with no place to go or without anyone to care for them, but also for those of the laity who may be in the same position of need."[122] Two years later the old Pinellas Park Hotel, near St. Petersburg, Florida, was purchased for this purpose. It could care for 25 residents only, and eventually became too costly to maintain.[123] In 1959 construction began on the Bethany Retirement Center at Lakeland, Florida. This new facility, with a capacity of 42 persons, was dedicated on May 15, 1960. Five years later an infirmary was added with a 29-bed capacity. The property value of the Center is over half a million dollars.[124] One hundred eleven ministers have made the Bethany Retirement Center their home since it was opened in 1960.[125]

HOMES FOR CHILDREN

Miss Gladys Hinson, a public school teacher, felt a definite calling from the Lord to open a home for deprived children while attending the National Youth Conference in Springfield in 1942.[126] On her own initiative she took steps to establish such a home in Arkansas. In 1944 she entered into a series of negotiations with the Executive Presbyters, securing their endorsement for her project. She opened the home on September 22, 1944, with three children. By year's-end the capacity of the home had been reached, with 17 children under her care.[127] With the creation of the Department of Benevolences, the National Children's Home, as it came to be called, came under its jurisdiction. Through the years new buildings have been added to the property in Hot Springs, so that by 1967 the assets of the home

[122]General Presbytery minutes, 1946, pp. 7-8.
[123]Interview, Stanley Michael, September 22, 1967.
[124]General Council reports, 1967, p. 78.
[125]Benevolences Department statistics, 1970.
[126]*The Pentecostal Evangel*, June 9, 1945, p. 5.
[127]*Ibid.*

amounted to over $367,000.[128] The purpose of the home, which more recently has been renamed the Hillcrest Children's Home, has been for long-term care for children, most of whom are orphaned. More than 500 children have been given a "home" at Hillcrest through the years. Between 60 and 75 live in the home, many of whom the courts or parents will not or cannot release.

A second children's home was opened in August, 1966, in Kansas City, Missouri. A large mansion was donated to the Assemblies of God and was extensively remodeled to provide an adoptive care center, with the purpose being primarily for short-term housing until placement arrangements are made. Within the first year of operation 16 children had been placed in either adoptive or foster homes.[129] About 50 are housed at Highlands at any given time. Highlands Children's Home, as it is known, promises to be a great blessing to a large number of disadvantaged children in the future.

DISASTER RELIEF

As the result of a hurricane striking the Louisiana coast in 1962, causing considerable damage to Assemblies of God churches, steps were taken by the Benevolence Committee of the General Council to set up a fund for providing emergency relief in such situations. By 1964 the Department of Benevolences had established such a fund for the aid of churches, parsonages, and ministers in disaster-stricken areas. Churches suffering from flood damage in Northern California and Oregon in 1965 were the first to benefit from this resource.[130] During the biennium of 1967-68, 23 churches received a total of $10,626 for disaster relief due to floods, fires, and hurricanes.[131]

Additional Service Agencies

In 1954 two agencies were created. Although commonly referred to as "departments," they really operate directly under the supervision of the General Superintendent's Office. These are the Personnel Office and the Public Relations

---

[128]Interview, Stanley Michael, September 22, 1967.
[129]*Ibid.*
[130]*Ibid.*
[131]General Council reports, 1969, p. 76.

Office. Harry Myers established the Public Relations Office in 1954 to attempt to coordinate the various mailings from headquarters which were already beginning to multiply rapidly.[132]

In 1958 the supervision of the military chaplaincy was separated from the Servicemen's Division of the National CA Department. A special Commission on Chaplains was instituted in April, 1967.[133]

In 1954 elementary data processing procedures were introduced into some of the finance office operations.[134] By 1967 the use of such equipment had advanced to the point that a Data Processing Center was established, with Malcolm Campbell being invited to Springfield to direct the work under the supervision of General Treasurer M. B. Netzel.[135]

In a constitutional revision approved in 1947, provision was made for a Department of Finance.[136] Previous to this the offices of General Secretary and General Treasurer had been combined. The new arrangement, necessitated by the increasing volume of General Council business, specified the separation of the offices. Wilfred A. Brown was elected as the first General Treasurer at that Council, J. Roswell Flower retaining his office as General Secretary. This newly created department was the beginning of an evolution in the financial management of the General Council which increasingly brought a coordination and centralization of accounting.

In 1953 a resolution was adopted by the General Council in session to create a Department of Evangelism to serve the needs of evangelists in the fellowship and "to emphasize, encourage and coordinate all phases of evangelism."[137] Ten years later, at the General Council in Memphis, the Department of Evangelism was abolished.[138] At the same Coun-

---

[132]Interview, Harry Myers, November 9, 1967.

[133]General Council reports, 1967, p. 90.

[134]Interview, Evelyn Dunham, September 30, 1967.

[135]General Council reports, 1967, p. 90.

[136]General Council reports, 1947, p. 13.

[137]General Council minutes, 1953, pp. 22-23.

[138]General Council minutes, 1963, pp. 15-19. The 1962 General Presbytery had registered great concern over the need for rekindling evangelistic enthusiasm throughout the fellowship. Consequently, a committee was appointed to give study to the

cil the General Superintendent was given direct oversight over denominational evangelism.[139] A result of this was the appointment by the Executive Presbytery in 1965 of a Spiritual Life–Evangelism Commission to serve under his supervision. D. V. Hurst was named as Coordinator of the commission in 1965, and upon his assuming the presidency of Northwest College in 1966, Charles W. Denton was named in his place. The significance of the Department of Evangelism, its dissolution, and the subsequent creation of the Spiritual Life–Evangelism Commission will be considered in the following chapter.

Summary

In 1941 the Assemblies of God maintained but two departments at its central headquarters in addition to the Gospel Publishing House. Within the next 12 years no fewer than 10 new departments were created, most of which were designed to serve the internal needs of the growing fellowship. This period in the history of the denomination, 1941 to 1953, was the analytical stage of the development in the Assemblies of God. These were the years in which attention shifted to conservation of the fruits of the Pentecostal revival.

---

needs with respect to evangelism in the Assemblies of God. The committee, chaired by Richard Bergstrom, made its report to the 1963 General Presbytery, and upon recommendation of that body, the report was presented a few days later to the General Council in session. The decisions of the 1963 General Council affecting evangelism grew out of that report.

[139] General Council reports, 1965, pp. 8-9.

12

Coordination: The Development of Organizational Structure

Administrative Restructuring–Coordination of Communications–Consolidation of Financial Management–Integrated Planning–Changing Leadership–Summary

With the creation of numerous new departments, agencies, and offices to serve the needs of second- and third-generation Pentecostals, a whole new set of problems confronted the Assemblies of God in the post-World War II years. The supervision of the vast new array of service agencies required an elaboration and reconstitution of the existing executive arrangement. There was a financial problem to be faced. General Councils in the immediate post-war years authorized many new programs, but because of the cooperative fellowship principle, it was not possible to assess local congregations for the support of the new enterprises. There was a communications problem. With the elaboration of national programs an increasing volume of promotional and informational mail descended on the local churches from the Springfield offices which tended to create grass roots suspicion of the "vast bureaucracy at Headquarters." The irony was that much of the demand for such national services had come from the field, and all such programs had been authorized by democratic vote at the denomination's biennial conventions.

As the Assemblies of God refocused attention, in part at least, on multiple internal needs, an awareness began to develop of overlapping of departmental responsibilities, and beyond that, an awareness that with preoccupation with specialized interests, there was danger of losing sight of the central objectives of the denomination. Centralized planning to displace the fragmented planning of the era of proliferation seemed to be a growing mood after the General Council of 1953. Heightening the concern for denominational refocus was the leveling off of the growth rate in membership and new churches in the homeland.

Administrative Restructuring

In 1941 there were three executive officers serving the Assemblies of God, General Superintendent E. S. Williams, Assistant Superintendent Fred Vogler, and General Secretary-Treasurer J. Roswell Flower. Demands upon these good men began to exceed their physical ability during the war years, as a study of their reports indicates.[1] Consequently at the General Council in 1945 a major change was made in the composition of the executive arrangement. A resolution was adopted, in harmony with existing constitutional provisions, for the election without portfolio of four Assistant General Superintendents, "to function in one harmonious group under the direction of the General Superintendent."[2] Following the elections, the General Superintendent was to assign executive portfolios to each, a practice that has been followed ever since. Elected in 1945, in addition to E. S. Williams and J. Roswell Flower who were duly returned to office, were Assistant Superintendents Fred Vogler, Ralph M. Riggs, Gayle F. Lewis, and Wesley R. Steelberg.

Two additional changes were made in following years in the composition of the executive offices. At the General Council in 1947 it was decided that the office of General Secretary-Treasurer had grown to such proportions that its functions should be divided.[3] Wilfred A. Brown, the first full-time General Treasurer, was elected that year, with J. Roswell Flower retaining his post as General Secretary. In 1959, to bring the organizational structure of the Foreign Missions Department into harmony with the pattern of

---

[1]General Council minutes, 1943, pp. 33-34.
[2]General Council minutes, 1945, pp. 7-8.
[3]General Council minutes, 1947, p. 13.

other departments, the office of Foreign Missions Secretary was henceforth to be titled executive director of the Foreign Missions Department, and he was by virtue of his position to be added as a fifth Assistant General Superintendent.[4]

At the 1959 General Council, the Executive Presbytery was enlarged from 12 to 16. With the addition of a fifth Assistant General Superintendent, there were now eight Resident Executive Presbyters. To provide for a wider field representation on the Executive Presbytery, a resolution was adopted arranging for one man to be selected by the General Council from each of eight geographical regions.[5] The duties of this body remained unchanged.

Up to 1945, the General Presbytery was composed of three representatives from each district council in the fellowship, plus the members of the Executive Presbytery who belonged ex officio. At the General Council in that year additional missionary representation was provided for, arranging for not only the Foreign Missions Secretary to participate, but also for the various Field Secretaries.[6] Representative missionaries from the field were added in 1951.[7] In the years that followed, attempts were made to enlarge the General Presbytery on repeated occasions. The appeal for the college presidents to be granted the right to sit on this board came up in 1957 and in 1965 to the General Council, failing on each occasion.[8] An appeal to include representation from Assemblies of God evangelists was likewise denied in 1965.[9]

The role of the General Presbytery was called in question during the General Presbytery meeting in 1955. This came to General Council attention in 1957 and again in 1961. No action was taken, but a study of its definition and task was requested to be made in the interim.[10] At the 1965 General Council the committee charged with studying the matter brought back its findings. It recommended that no

---

[4]General Council minutes, 1959, pp. 24-25.
[5]*Ibid.*, pp. 27-29.
[6]General Council minutes, 1945
[7]General Council minutes, 1957, p. 31.
[8]General Council minutes, 1965, p. 46.
[9]*Ibid.*, p. 47.
[10]General Council minutes, 1961, p. 60.

changes be made in the existing constitutional provision respecting the Executive Presbytery and the General Presbytery, "as it contains provisions for proper relationships and responsibilities, and as it presently appears as a satisfactory and workable arrangement."[11] After 50 years the basic structure of the General Council had proved to be a useful framework, needing only periodic adjustment of representation.

Coordination of Communications

Several communications problems began to emerge as the Assemblies of God headquarters operations grew. The first aspect of this problem to be dealt with was the matter of incoming mail. To facilitate the distribution of mail and interoffice memoranda, a "mail girl" was employed in 1944, carrying such items from office to office.[12] The next year a major step in the direction of centralization of activity was the creation of "Central Mail," a single center for handling all incoming traffic.[13] At first not all were in full sympathy with this move, fearing loss of independence. This seems to demonstrate the evolution of the Assemblies of God headquarters from a rather undifferentiated arrangement toward a more complex, institutionalized operation.

An increasing problem was the proliferation of outgoing mail from headquarters. Increasing sensitivity to the public image of the Assemblies of God, both internally and externally, led Ralph Riggs, newly elected General Superintendent in 1953, to ask for the creation of a Public Relations Office. In June, 1954, Harry Myers was invited to develop such an office.[14] Its functions were to be varied, including attention to means for coordinating mailings. In spite of all efforts, mail from headquarters multiplied, reaching a peak of nearly 4 million pieces of metered mail in 1964.[15] The next year, the first real breakthrough occurred. The magazine for ministers, *Pulpit,* which was begun in 1958 for the

[11]General Council minutes, 1963, pp. 10-11.
[12]Interview, Harry Myers, November 9, 1967.
[13]*Ibid.*
[14]General Council reports, 1955, p. 75.
[15]Statistics supplied by Public Relations Office, December 14, 1967.

personal development of Assemblies of God clergymen, had never reached a large circulation.[16] It was decided by the General Council in 1965 to phase out that publication, and to replace it with one that would contain promotional information for local churches and thus permit a reduction in the number of mass mailings from headquarters.[17] The new magazine, *Advance,* edited by Gwen Jones, has apparently been successful in coordinating much of the information needed for effective communication with the local churches, and has resulted in a significant reduction in the number of mass mailings. The number of mailings to ministers dropped from 56 in 1965 to 23 by the next year![18] This is especially significant in view of the fact that a total of 50 special offering appeals and denominational emphases punctuate the annual church calendar, nearly all of which were promoted through *Advance.*[19]

Consolidation of Financial Management

Prior to 1953 the needs of the several departments were cared for without benefit of consolidated purchasing or accounting.[20] Each office had its own bookkeeping system. There was no budgetary control.[21] However, in spite of the rather elementary financial arrangement that prevailed in those years, there was never any evidence of mismanagement of funds.[22] The mounting problem that had to be faced was that each of the service agencies that had been brought into being was not self-sufficient, but depended on freewill offerings from the field and on subsidization from the earnings of the Gospel Publishing House. Virtually all departments depended on this subsidy, and as new departments were added to the exisiting structure the situation rapidly approached crisis proportions.

The first step toward a consolidated accounting program occurred in 1953 when the Executive Presbytery, acting as a Finance Committee, arranged for the combining of the

[16]General Council reports, 1959, p. 114.
[17]General Council minutes, 1965, p. 46.
[18]Statistics supplied by Public Relations Office.
[19]Statistics supplied by *Advance* office.
[20]Interview, J. O. Harrell, October 24, 1967.
[21]Interview, Evelyn Dunham, September 30, 1967.
[22]Interview, J. O. Harrell, October 24, 1967.

accounting systems of the Gospel Publishing House and the Foreign Missions Department.[23] That same year the General Presbytery appointed a committee to study the problem of proliferation of financial appeals emanating from headquarters.[24] These preliminary steps took on added significance when the General Council at Milwaukee that year authorized a large number of new departments and programs, including provision for incurring an indebtedness of one and a half million dollars to erect a new administration building, authorization for securing of a half-hour network radio broadcast, and approval for the launching of a four-year senior liberal arts college.[25]

In the Ministers' Quarterly Letter, dated March 18, 1954, the Executive Presbytery expressed anxiety to the fellowship over the propensity of the fellowship to vote into being new services, with no thought for the necessary financial support that should accompany them.[26] The General Presbytery Finance Committee in 1954 recommended a denominational budget be established.[27] This committee engaged in serious fieldwork through the course of the year, reporting back to the General Presbytery its recommendations the following autumn. A resolution was adopted at the 1955 General Council as the result of this study which requested that ordained ministers contribute $2 per month to the national headquarters and licensed ministers contribute $1.50 per month.[28] Although this principle had been the common practice for the support of the central offices since 1918, it represented a sizable enlargement.[29]

In the fall of 1955, a professional accounting agency was called in to prescribe solutions for the accounting problems. The first institutional-type audit, accompanied by sweeping recommendations, was submitted on June 30, 1956.[30] A major change suggested was the immediate segregation of all

---

[23]Grace Carroll, "The Evolution of Centralized Accounting" (unpublished manuscript, n.d.).

[24]*Ibid.*

[25]General Council minutes, 1953

[26]"Quarterly Letter," March 18, 1954.

[27]Grace Carroll, *op. cit.*

[28]General Council minutes, 1955, p. 14.

[29]General Council minutes, 1918, p. 7.

[30]Interview, Evelyn Dunham, September 30, 1967.

departmental funds and the institution of a budgetary control system. The years from 1955 to 1957 witnessed a major transition toward the new program recommended for separate funding and central budgetary control.

The low-water mark occurred in 1954. The books that year showed a net earnings for the entire General Council operations of only $20,591, a margin left after subsidies to the various departments, precariously near the bottom of the barrel. Fully 90 percent of the earnings of the Gospel Publishing House were consumed by departmental subsidies. Strict limits were placed on all departments, the hardest hit being the Sunday School Department, which had incurred a deficit of more than $170,000 in 1956.[31] The urgency of fiscal responsibility was a major factor in the shift in mood from expansiveness to consolidation during the middle of the 1950's.

The 1957 General Council made provision for a standing committee on finance which should thereafter serve as a screening agency, furnishing recommendations on the financial feasibility of future projects to the General Council in session.[32] Good management, continued increases in revenues from the field and from the Gospel Publishing House, and more cautious entry into new programs quickly righted the financial ship. Over $37 million had been received in the fiscal biennium ending March 31, 1969, from all offerings and sales of the General Council, representing a 25.8 percent increase over the previous biennium.[33] Payments on the new $3 million administration building were far ahead of schedule, leaving less than $396,000 owing, with the prospect of completing payment far ahead of the original 1975 projected date. The fiscal health of the General Council headquarters is further attested to by the fact that during 1969, while substantial payment was made on the capital indebtedness, an additional $800,000 was expended on new printing equipment that was sorely needed to improve efficiency of operation.[34] Interesting to note is that nearly 60

[31]Interview, M. B. Netzel, September 21, 1967.
[32]General Council minutes, 1959.
[33]General Council reports, 1969.
[34]Interview, Sam Ohler, April 15, 1970.

percent of all General Council revenue and disbursements were in the interest of foreign missions in the latest fiscal year.[35]

Integrated Planning

With the creation of multiple departments at the Assemblies of God headquarters, some overlapping and duplication were inevitable. The first formal recognition of this problem occurred early in 1958. In February of that year the Executive Presbytery asked that a study committee be appointed to consider the various youth-oriented ministries of four departments: Men's Fellowship, Women's Missionary Council, Sunday School, and Christ's Ambassadors.[36] Representatives from each of the departments met, and at the April, 1958, meeting of the Executive Presbytery a recommendation was adopted to set up a permanent committee for the coordination of youth activities.[37] An outgrowth of this study focused attention on the specific problem of duplication of youth camp activities, each of the four departments already having developed extensive camping programs. Consequently, in August, 1958, the Executive Presbytery appointed a permanent Youth Camp Commission, which in the ensuing years has successfully integrated the various camping programs sponsored by the departments at headquarters.[38] The original committee for the coordination of youth activities had an intermittent history, but in 1961 it was revitalized as the Youth Study Committee.[39] By the fall of 1967, some progress had been made in the creation of a full-orbed training program for youth, incorporating resources from each of the relevant departments.[40]

Another evidence of the shift toward integrated planning has been the changing character of denomination-sponsored conventions. The last great Sunday school rally was held in St. Louis in 1954. Not until 1960 was there another such specialized national convention. In May of that year the International Sunday School Convention was held in Min-

[35]General Council reports, 1969, p. 24.
[36]Executive Presbytery minutes, February, 1958, p. 1190.
[37]Executive Presbytery minutes, April, 1958, p. 1240.
[38]Executive Presbytery minutes, August, 1958, p. 1344.
[39]Executive Presbytery minutes, February, 1961, p. 2357.
[40]Interviews, Ralph Harris, January 18, 1968, and April 15, 1970.

neapolis, with an estimated 8,500 workers in attendance, including representatives from 70 nations.[41] Impressive as it was, it somehow seemed anticlimactic after the enormous boom of the early 1950's.

In the years since 1954 the emphasis has moved toward smaller conventions, usually conducted regionally in various parts of the country. More significantly, the trend has been toward a more balanced emphasis on the total program of the church. A good example of these recent trends was the series of five regional conventions, conducted in the spring of 1967, whose purpose was to coordinate all facets of church life with the objective of "taking Christ to the man on the street."[42]

The largest convention since 1954 has been the Fiftieth Anniversary Convention, held in Springfield, Missouri, in April, 1964. More than 10,000 came to that great "all-church" convocation. Because of limited local facilities the evening sessions had to be conducted in three different auditoriums, linked together by closed-circuit televisions.[43] The theme, "Like a River," provided the framework for featuring the multiple facets of the denomination's activities. More than 170 workshop sessions were conducted in 49 separate locations throughout the city during the week.[44]

Perhaps the most important development in the area of centralized planning has been the attempt to redefine the objectives of the Assemblies of God. The first phase of this attempt at redirection seems to have been precipitated by uneasiness over the multiplication of service agencies in the postwar years. At the General Council in 1951 a report was read which called attention to the extensive discussion in the General Presbyters' meeting on the subject of needed emphasis on personal evangelism. A resolution was adopted urging an "all-out effort in Personal Evangelism in the General Council."[45] The significance of this action is that the denomination, at its biennial business session, for the first time faced the reality that it had turned an important

[41]General Council minutes, 1961, p. 17.
[42]*The Pentecostal Evangel*, June 11, 1967, p. 16.
[43]*The Pentecostal Evangel*, June 7, 1964, p. 23.
[44]*Ibid.*
[45]General Council minutes, 1951, p. 34.

corner. No longer was evangelism purely a spontaneous activity; it now demanded planning and nourishing.

The direction taken by the General Council, originally geared to the problem of encouraging individual witnessing throughout the fellowship, shifted to the larger dimensions of evangelism. At the 1953 General Council, responding to a resolution submitted by the Committee on Personal Evangelism, a Department of Evangelism was authorized, "to serve the evangelists and to emphasize, encourage and coordinate all phases of evangelism."[46] Some concrete achievements were forthcoming in the succeeding ten years of the department's existence. A directory of Assemblies of God evangelists was published. An Evangelists' Fellowship was created and several seminars were conducted. A code of ethics governing the relationships of pastors, evangelists, and other ministers was drawn up.[47] However, it became increasingly apparent that the General Council in 1953 had acted with greater enthusiasm than wisdom in creating a Department of Evangelism. Structurally, it was put into the difficult position of being one department among others, but charged with the specific assignment of coordinating the work of the other departments. This it could not accomplish. Ideologically, there was some uncertainty about the meaning of evangelism and how such an activity should be undertaken by the church. Was it primarily the professional task of stated individuals, called evangelists? Was it primarily personal witnessing, a task every member of the church should be engaging in continuously? Was it larger in scope than either of these?

There was a growing awareness that in creating a specific department charged with the promotion of evangelism, the denomination had unwittingly restricted the very enterprise it had been so concerned to emphasize. The urgency of turning the attention of the entire fellowship to outreach seemed to be particularly cogent as the decade of the 1950's came to an end. The statistics of church extension and church membership no longer displayed the characteristic

---

[46]General Council minutes, 1953, pp. 22-23.

[47]*The Pentecostal Evangel*, January 9, 1955, p. 4.

pattern of rapid growth familiar in previous years. Even the Sunday school figures seemed to demonstrate that the great boom was tapering off. In 1959 the Executive Presbytery appointed a Church Membership Committee to study the situation.[48] At the General Council in 1961 this committee reported that the Executive Presbytery had authorized the institution of an annual Church Membership Emphasis Day in an effort to encourage active participants to join local churches.[49] There was some thought that the alarming statistical pattern was occasioned partly by the propensity of Assemblies of God people to disregard church membership, membership figures always being much smaller than active participants, contrary to the pattern of many denominations. The problem of church membership was underscored by the startling announcement that only 3,050 new members had come into the Assemblies of God during the previous biennium.[50] Phinis Lewis, Chairman of the General Council Reports Committee, expressed anxiety over the apparent net gain in new churches during the biennium of only 139, a sharp contrast to the average *yearly* gain of 192 from 1914 to 1961.[51] The General Superintendent, reflecting on the membership gain in the biennium ending in 1963 of less than one percent a year, expressed considerable disappointment.[52] The year 1963 was apparently the low point in the recent history of the Assemblies of God. Since then there has been an encouraging upturn in the number of ordained ministers (11,168 in 1967, a 4 percent increase over 1965; 11,459 in 1969, an additional 2.6 percent increase in the biennium) and in the number of new members (20,066 in 1967, a 3.6 percent increase over the previous biennial experience, with 49,602 additional members reported in 1969, a gain of 8.6 percent.[53] However, there was only a net gain of 64 new churches in the recent biennium, which has continued to be cause of grave concern throughout the fellowship.[54]

[48]General Council minutes, 1961, p. 63.
[49]*Ibid.*
[50]*Ibid.*
[51]*Ibid.*, p. 12; Perkin, *op. cit.*, p. 37.
[52]General Council reports, 1963, pp. 9-10.
[53]General Council reports, 1969, pp. 10-15.
[54]*Ibid.*

Why did the spectacular growth of earlier years, unbroken until about 1957, rapidly taper off at that point? Several reasons have been advanced. The most commonly voiced observation is concern over the decreased spiritual vitality in the fellowship, being reflected in less personal initiative and less individual concern. Related to this is the opinion that the affluence of many in the denomination achieved during and after World War II has resulted in a degree of complacency. During the 1950's the advent of television seemed to be a factor in the decline in attendance at the traditional Sunday night evangelistic services. The resurgence of interest in religion in the 1950's, symbolized by the Billy Graham crusades, furnished a new kind of challenge to the Assemblies of God. Although there were remarkably few defections from the Assemblies of God clergy, apparently many unchurched who were won by the Assemblies of God passed on to other denominations. This phenomenon has been partly cultural, but partly due to inadequate training in the local churches.[55] Accessions of independent congregations, which had been numerous before World War II, no longer swelled the growth figures, which has been no insignificant factor.

In an effort to meet the mounting problem of domestic growth, the General Council of 1963 at Memphis enacted sweeping changes. Three important decisions were made. The Department of Evangelism, which had languished for 10 years, was abolished.[56] A bylaw revision was approved in which each department of the General Council was to have as its stated purpose for existence the advancement of evangelism.[57] And, the work of evangelism was to be correlated and centered in the office of the General Superintendent.[58] Ninety percent of the work of that historic convocation was related to the task of evangelism.[59]

To implement the newly defined task of the General Superintendent, a Spiritual Life–Evangelism Commission

---

[55]Interview, J. Roswell Flower, June 26, 1967.
[56]General Council minutes, 1963, pp. 18-19.
[57]*Ibid.*, pp. 16-18.
[58]*Ibid.*
[59]Interview, D. V. Hurst, June 26, 1967.

was established in 1965. It was accorded four functions: (1) the coordination of evangelism in all of the headquarters departments and the spotlighting of denomination-wide goals, (2) the providing of a placement service to assist laymen in locating in new areas to aid in the establishment of pioneer churches, (3) the planning and promoting of various spiritual emphases throughout the denomination, and (4) the serving of the Fellowship of Evangelists.[60] Two existing committees were named to furnish counsel for this enterprise, the General Council Spiritual Life Committee and The Standing Committee on Evangelism. D. V. Hurst was asked to assume the responsibility of setting up the new office. He remained as Coordinator of the Commission until 1966, when he left to accept the presidency of Northwest College. Since that time Charles W. Denton has occupied that strategic post. In 1967, Norman Correll joined Charles Denton as a field representative. In 1968, John Ohlin succeeded Correll, who accepted the post of National Secretary of the Christ's Ambassadors Department. His responsibilities are chiefly to develop the commission's Mobilization and Placement Service.

The next step, and perhaps the most important, in the attempt to rearticulate denominational purposes, was the decision of the Executive Presbytery in March, 1967, to launch an exhaustive diagnostic self-study of the Assemblies of God.[61] Without question the basic issue underlying this investigation was the need to search out reasons for the slowdown in the denominational growth and to seek corrective solutions.[62] By June, 1967, the Executive Presbyters had appointed a committee of fifteen representative men from various facets of church life—executives, editors, schoolmen, pastors, and one layman—to undertake what was expected to be a yearlong study.[63] It was anticipated that a Five-Year Plan of Advance would be the outcome of this

[60]*The Pentecostal Evangel*, February 12, 1967, p. 28.

[61]Executive Presbytery minutes, March, 1967, p. 13.

[62]Interview, Charles Denton, September 8, 1967.

[63]Members of this committee were: Thomas F. Zimmerman, chairman, Dr. Gene Scott, research director, Lowell Ashbrook, G. Raymond Carlson, Charles Denton, Theodore Gannon, James Hamill, Ralph Harris, Philip Hogan, Cyril Homer, D. V. Hurst, Donald Johns, Harry Myers, Andrew Nelli, and William Vickery.

first year's work, with the first implementation of the fruits of the study being a denominational convention to be held in St. Louis in August, 1968, at which the new foci and goals would be enunciated.

The most significant result of the committee's work in its opening phase, before the end of 1967, was the redefinition of the task of the church, in which evangelism was given an important role in the church, but not the exclusive role. This had the effect of giving greater precision to the meaning of evangelism as "winning the lost to Christ," so that it no longer carried the broader, more vague connotation of being the total work of the church, an implication left by the action of the Memphis General Council in 1963. A preliminary statement of purpose, drawn up by the Committee on Advance, was approved in principle by the Executive Presbytery on November 30, 1967.[64] This statement was incorporated, in principle, into the Statement of Fundamental Truths at the 1969 General Council in Dallas, Texas.[65] It has clarified the objectives of the Assemblies of God and has given each facet of the organization a useful instrument for measuring the degree to which it corresponds with the primary purposes for which the fellowship exists. It appears that this attempt at self-analysis of purposes and functions in the Assemblies of God has resulted in the articulation of a statement which the grass roots of the fellowship has received with enthusiasm. This statement, which received such overwhelming public response, was given expression at the Council on Evangelism, held in St. Louis, August 26-29, 1968.[66]

The great Council on Evangelism was a direct outgrowth of the Study Committee on Advance. It was intended to be an opportunity for the entire fellowship to come together, not to conduct business, but to pray together, to worship together, and to think deeply together about the mission of the Assemblies of God in the last part of the 20th century. A total of 7,072 persons registered for this great convention, a number exceeding registration at the 32nd biennial Gen-

---

[64]Executive Presbytery minutes, November 30, 1967, p. 19.

[65]General Council minutes, 1969, p. 60.

[66]The full text of the "St. Louis Declaration" is supplied in Appendix B.

eral Council at Long Beach, California, a year earlier. Evening sessions, attended by as many as 7,000 in Kiel Auditorium, featured the Church—its mission, its mandate, its message, and its motivation. Morning sessions at local hotels provided opportunity for Biblical expositions. Mass meetings held in Kiel Auditorium each afternoon gave opportunity for representatives of the Study Committee on Advance to articulate definitions of various aspects of the mission of the Assemblies of God to contemporary society, to minister to the Lord, to the saints, and to the world. The afternoon sessions also furnished opportunity for supplying guidelines for the first major thrust encouraged by the Study Committee on Advance, calling for the year 1969 to be a Year of Revival. An especially interesting feature of the unique St. Louis convention was the large number of seminars conducted each morning following the Biblical expositions. Twenty-four seminars were conducted in each of the two convention hotels. Papers and panelists found excited and enthusiastic participation from the delegates who thronged the sessions. Just prior to the evening services an additional 11 seminars were held, again with large attendance. Official recorders indicated that at session after session there was standing room only![67]

Robert Cunningham, in an editorial printed in *The Pentecostal Evangel* shortly after the Council, describes the mood of that historic meeting:

> Spiritually speaking, last month's Council on Evangelism was a "council of war." The delegates gathered around "council fires" kindled by the Holy Ghost and plotted new advances for Christ.
>
> They determined that the mission of the Assemblies of God is to be an agency of God for evangelizing the world; a corporate body in which man may worship God; a channel of God's purpose to build a body of saints being perfected in the image of His Son. This threefold purpose was set forth with great force and clarity. From Brother Zimmerman's keynote message to the commitment service which climaxed the four-day Council, our mission in today's world was impressed upon all—illuminated by the Word of God and confirmed by the moving of the Holy Spirit.

---

[67]See Richard Champion, E. S. Caldwell, Gary Leggett, eds., *Our Mission in Today's World* (Springfield, Missouri: Gospel Publishing House, 1968) for a complete report of the messages given at the Council on Evangelism.

In physical dimensions, the scenes at Kiel Auditorium in St. Louis were like those of a biennial General Council. The 7,072 registered delegates represented all parts of the country and included both ministers and laymen, the young as well as the old. In spiritual dimensions the Council surpassed any meeting in recent history, in the opinion of many. One feature that made it different was the every-member participation. In several services delegates seized the opportunity to offer comments and to ask questions which often evoked frank answers. Fellowship ties were strengthened by the common desire to let the Lord search our hearts and make us more effective soldiers of the Cross.[68]

Following the great St. Louis Council on Evangelism, the Study Committee on Advance continued to meet for some months, laying long-range strategy for presentation as the Five-Year Plan of Advance. Three fundamental products came out of this continuing study. (1) Recommendations to the 1969 General Council for revisions in the Constitution to embody the new definition of denominational purpose. (2) Recommendations for further studies in special areas needing in-depth, long-range thought.[69] (3) Spelling out of specific emphases for the Five-Year Plan of Advance.

The Five-Year Plan of Advance came to envisage the following priorities: "1969-Year of Revival"; "Impact '70: Go and Tell," featuring evangelism; "Impact '71: Take the Word," an emphasis on the Scriptures; "Impact '72: Be Filled with the Spirit," giving attention to the Pentecostal distinctive; "Impact '73: Go Forward," with emphasis on the total mobilization of the fellowship to fulfill its threefold mission, as the denomination stands on the threshold of its sixtieth anniversary.[70]

---

[68]Robert C. Cunningham, "Council Fires in St. Louis," *The Pentecostal Evangel*, September 22, 1968, p. 4.

[69]The 1969 General Council called for a special committee on organizational structure to be created by the Executive Presbytery to study the entire headquarters arrangement, with a view to recommending changes to a subsequent General Council (General Council minutes, 1969, pp. 52-53). This committee was appointed late in 1969, and is at this writing engaged in its task.

One further outgrowth of the Study Committee on Advance (the original Committee was disbanded in 1969), was the recommendation that the Executive Presbytery appoint a special task force to study the entire educational program of the Assemblies of God, and to supply recommendations to the General Council in 1971. This action was carried out in March, 1970.

[70]Thomas F. Zimmerman, "Facing a Decade of Destiny," *Advance*, January, 1970, pp. 4-5.

Changing Leadership

Three personalities who have served as General Superintendent during the period under consideration, 1941-1967, epitomize the changing ethos of the Assemblies of God. Ernest S. Williams had already long been in office when the United States entered World War II. Beloved for his kindliness and humility, Ernest S. Williams was an outstanding example of godliness and spirituality. It was his fortune to preside over the Assemblies of God during days of enormous growth and relative tranquility. It was only in the closing years of his administration that the problems of an increasingly complex organization began to crowd in. After 20 years of service as General Superintendent, Ernest S. Williams stepped down in 1949, retiring with the esteem of the entire fellowship. His retirement symbolizes the end of the era of simplistic, undifferentiated development, for already, as we have seen, many new programs were being instituted. An ebullient, progressive mood was in the air.

Succeeding E. S. Williams in 1949 was Wesley R. Steelberg. Steelberg, like Williams, was a charismatic leader. He was highly regarded by his colleagues for his spirituality. Unfortunately, while on a speaking tour of Europe, he was stricken with a fatal heart attack. He died at Cardiff, Wales, on July 8, 1952.[71] His passing was mourned greatly by the fellowship which had come to appreciate his depth of spiritual life. Chosen to fill the unexpired term was Assistant General Superintendent Gayle F. Lewis. He, like his immediate predecessors, was an advocate of moderation and balance. The mood of the famous 1953 General Council was ultraprogressive. It was Ralph M. Riggs who was elected as the man of the hour.[72] Consequently, neither Steelberg nor Lewis was in office a sufficient length of time to make a profound impact on the denomination.

Following the Williams era, the next significant influence on the Assemblies of God fellowship was Ralph M. Riggs. Already before his election he had demonstrated a degree of creative and farsighted leadership. His primary concern

---

[71]*The Pentecostal Evangel*, July 27, 1952, p. 5.

[72]General Council minutes, 1953, p. 4.

had been the upgrading of Assemblies of God education.[73] It seemed that a culmination of his efforts was the decision at the General Council at Milwaukee in 1953 to launch a four-year senior liberal arts college. The next six years Riggs faced the problems that the 1953 General Council had inadvertently brought on—the need for financial stabilization and organizational restructuring to handle the new programs that had been voted into existence. This demanded a new image for the office of the General Superintendent, an image of executive leadership rather than charismatic leadership. Riggs ably supplied the leadership demanded in the critical period of adjustment that his administration spanned. However, at the General Council in San Antonio in 1959, the prevailing mood was disenchantment with the progressivism of the Riggs era, particularly the educational emphasis that he had so strongly supported. He was not returned to office. It appears that his defeat was the price he paid for advocating innovations, especially in the realm of education, which were ahead of their time in the Assemblies of God.[74]

The transition from charismatic leadership to a charismatic-statesmanship type is exemplified in the administration of Thomas F. Zimmerman, elected General Superintendent in 1959. He has successfully combined a deep concern for the spiritual interests of the fellowship with a high degree of business acumen. His skill in leadership has brought him into administrative roles in the councils of evangelicalism, as well as in the Pentecostal world, commanding the respect and appreciation of the evangelical world.[75] As it fell to the lot of Riggs to cope with the problem of absorbing the proliferation of organization which his era symbolized, so it fell to the administration of Zimmerman to undertake the task of consolidating the gains made, redefining the goals that must be pursued for the future.

Thomas F. Zimmerman was born in Indianapolis, Indiana, March 26, 1912. The parents were well along in years when Thomas joined the family. His godly mother

---

[73]Interview, Ralph M. Riggs, August 24, 1967.
[74]Interview, Ralph M. Riggs, August 24, 1967.
[75]Interview, Arthur Climenhaga, June 21, 1967.

considered him to be a child of promise, for the two previous children born to them did not survive. She prayed earnestly for this child, promising him to the Lord for full-time service if the Lord would bless her with a child that would live.

Brother Zimmerman recalls a degree of austerity in his boyhood home. His father was engaged in the restaurant and bakery business, but did not enjoy much financial success. Thomas won a scholarship to the University of Indiana during his high school days, but found it necessary to return to his home after but one year of college to aid in the support of his family, for business reverses had seriously depleted his aged parents' financial resources. God evidently had other avenues for training necessary for equipping this young man for future service.

The Zimmerman family were faithful and active in the Methodist Protestant Church. It was at an old-fashioned Methodist altar that Thomas gave his heart to the Lord in response to a gospel invitation at the close of a service. He was five years of age.

About the time that young Tom found the Lord, his mother became acutely ill with tuberculosis. Her condition deteriorated. The doctor at last gave her but three months to live. It was during this severe test, that she attended a local Pentecostal meeting for the first time. Her second cousin, Alice Reynolds (later Mrs. J. Roswell Flower), took her to the Indianapolis Gospel Tabernacle. Brother Zimmerman recalls, "Mother became frightened and left the meeting. The emotional behavior of the people was foreign to her." However, a recollection of the fervor of the people, and the awareness that they prayed for the sick led the Zimmermans to call upon the pastor of this group for help when it looked as though she were going to die. In response to their appeal, a Baptist minister who had received the Pentecostal experience and two of his parishoners came to the home, anointed Mrs. Zimmerman and offered a simple prayer for her recovery. There was no apparent change in her condition. That evening she asked her husband to get her clothes so she could get dressed, but this alarmed him, for he felt this was but a last rally before her expiration that the doctor had warned him would occur. However, the next morning, as the father and son were eating their breakfast, Mrs. Zimmerman appeared at the kitchen door, obviously not in her death agony! After two weeks a medical examination disclosed a complete deliverance from the disease!

This notable miracle, together with the increase in hunger among many in the Methodist Church, precipitated a crisis. It was the custom in those days for those who had Pentecostal leanings to attend their own church services on Sunday morning, and to attend a "conventicle," or Sunday afternoon prayer meeting, which stretched across all kinds of denominational lines. When the minister of their church asked Mr. Zimmerman to restrain his wife from giving her testimony, this occasioned the final separation of the family from that connection. Henceforth they threw all their energies into the young Pentecostal group. The Sunday afternoon nucleus in Indianapolis eventually became the Parkway Assembly of God. This occurred about 1919, when Tom was seven years of age.

On October 23, 1923, when Tom was 11, he entered into the Pentecostal experience at the Pentecostal church in Indianapolis. At that time it was still called The Apostolic Church, prior to its affiliation with the Assemblies of God. He had been seeking the baptism in the Holy Spirit for two years. One night, when he was about 10 years of age, during the course of his seeking God for His fullness, he experienced the only vision he has ever had. "I saw the Lord. He stood before me beckoning," he recalls. Brother Zimmerman feels that this unique experience was a definite call to service.

Brother Zimmerman began to preach while he was still in high school. When he was about 16, he was very active in the youth group of the Pentecostal church. This vibrant band started regular street services in the nearby town of Franklin, Indiana, at which Tom frequently preached. This was the beginning of the Assemblies of God church in that community. He preached frequently in his home church, too.

Pastor Price, who served the congregation for a total of 33 years, invited this promising young man to join him as his assistant. For several years Brother Zimmerman had been working as a foreman in the Bemis Brothers Bag Company, supporting his family and continuing his lay ministry.

In 1933, in the depths of the depression, Brother Zimmerman took unto himself a wife, Elizabeth, eldest daughter of Pastor John L. Price. For some time he had been commuting to nearby communities to aid in the opening of new works. He engaged in this extension ministry at Marion and Kokomo. In 1934 a call came from Harrodsburg, Indiana. After a time, this dedicated young couple decided to move to Harrodsburg. Brother Zimmerman gave up a salaried position with a promising future in the business world to take a new wife into a pioneer church situation where 90 percent of the people were on relief and the offerings averaged less than three dollars per week! But the Lord honored their faith and vision! Their table was never bare!

This first full-time venture in Harrodsburg was followed by a succession of pastorates. He served in South Bend, Indiana; Granite City, Illinois; Central Assembly in Springfield, Missouri; and finally, Cleveland, Ohio. Meanwhile, in addition to pastoral responsibilities, Brother Zimmerman filled several administrative posts. He served as assistant district superintendent of both the Illinois and Southern Missouri District Councils. From 1945 to 1949 he was the first director of the initial national broadcast of the Assemblies of God. He was serving as Secretary-treasurer of the Southern Missouri District Council in 1951 when the fellowship called him to higher service, choosing him to fill a post as Assistant General Superintendent. For eight years Brother Zimmerman occupied that position, and then, in 1959, at the San Antonio General Council, he was elected to the office of General Superintendent.[76]

Whom have the people of the Assemblies of God chosen to work with the General Superintendent? The answer to this may be a productive way to illustrate the kind of men

[76]Interview, Thomas F. Zimmerman, July 24, 1970.

highly esteemed in the fellowship in recent years, men who represent the finest quality of ministerial leadership within the denomination. Brief biographical sketches of all the resident Executive Presbyters have been supplied in Part One. Below are glimpses into the lives of the nonresident Executive Presbyters who were serving in 1970.

George W. Hardcastle, presbyter of the Gulf States region since 1953, was born in the southern foothills of the Ozark Mountains in the village of Scottsville, Arkansas. At 18 he became a rural schoolteacher, a profession which he followed for 12 years. When he was 25 years of age, he was wonderfully converted during a district council session of the Assemblies of God which was convening at Russellville, Arkansas. He felt a call to the ministry soon after his conversion, and began to preach in a brush arbor in a nearby community. During a six-weeks' campaign he and another youthful preacher conducted there, 25 people were saved, 18 of whom received the Pentecostal experience. Following a preaching tour of the Pacific Northwest, Hardcastle was ordained in Arkansas in 1925 by the Assemblies of God. He continued to hold meetings in schoolhouses and brush arbors until the church in Van Buren, Arkansas, invited him to become full-time pastor. Over the years, Brother Hardcastle has pastored, not only in Arkansas, but in California, Oklahoma, and Texas. He has been superintendent of two districts, Oklahoma and Arkansas. A favorite camp and convention speaker, Brother Hardcastle has ministered widely in the fellowship. He truly represents the Pentecostal pioneer who has endured persecution and privation to bring the Full Gospel message to his generation.[77]

Dwight H. McLaughlin, Presbyter from the Southwest Region, currently pastors in Ventura, California. Tall and rugged, Brother McLaughlin has long exercised leadership in the Assemblies of God. He was born in North Carolina in 1905. At the age of 25 he was ordained into the ministry of the Assemblies of God, in the Pacific Northwest. His ministry began at Klamath Falls, Oregon, in 1929, where he served as assistant pastor. Following this initial venture, a

[77]Letter from G. W. Hardcastle, June 3, 1970.

series of lengthy pastorates ensued, 11 years at Walla Walla, Washington, eight years at Tacoma, and seven more years at Bakersfield, California, prior to his accepting his present pastorate in Ventura, California. Sandwiched between his Washington and California ministry was a period in the early 1950's during which he traveled extensively as an evangelist. For seven years, from 1952 to 1958 he served as superintendent of the Northwest District Council. During that period the General Council of the Assemblies of God elected him to serve as nonresident Executive Presbyter. His subsequent move to California made it necessary for him to relinquish that honor, but at the very next General Council the fellowship elected him to fill a similar position for the Southwest Region, a position he has continued to fill since 1953. Brother McLaughlin is perhaps best described as typifying one with a genuine pastor's heart.

Roy Wead was born in Fort Rice, North Dakota, in 1916. During his high school days, he was an outstanding athlete and graduated as valedictorian of his class. During these teen-years, he determined to quit smoking and drinking in order to live a more disciplined life, but found that he did not have the ability on his own to do this. He turned to God, and was wonderfully converted. Roy dedicated himself totally to God and to His service. Upon high school graduation he enrolled at Central Bible Institute, graduating in the Class of 1936.

Brother Wead launched into full-time ministry at Cambridge, Ohio. He was married while in this first pastorate, and also received ordination from the Assemblies of God. Three years of fruitful ministry from 1940 to 1943 were spent at Cuyahoga Falls, Ohio, and three more at Muncie, Indiana. In 1947 he became the first district superintendent of the newly formed Indiana District Council. At the time he was only 29, the youngest district superintendent in the fellowship. During the 14 years he served the Indiana District Council, more than 120 new churches were opened. When Brother Wead resigned his office as superintendent in 1959 he moved to South Bend to assume the pastorate of

Calvary Temple, one of the largest churches in the denomination. In 1968 he accepted an invitation to become president of Trinity Bible Institute in Jamestown, North Dakota. Since 1957 Roy Wead has served as an Executive Presbyter of the Assemblies of God.[78]

N. D. Davidson was converted in 1925 in a tent meeting conducted by a group of young people who had been sent out from Angelus Temple in Los Angeles to the town of Santa Paula, located in southern California. Brother Davidson at once became very active in the youth program of the newly formed Foursquare congregation in Santa Paula. Two years later he was ordained by the Foursquare people. He pioneered a church in the area of his home, all the while continuing to support himself by secular employment. In 1934 the El Centro Assembly of God called him to be their full-time pastor. The Assemblies of God ordained him the following year. In 1939 Brother Davidson went to pastor what is now known as First Assembly of God in Phoenix, Arizona. He was subsequently elected to serve as the first district superintendent of the Arizona District Council, when that state separated from the Southern California District. In 1947 he accepted a call to what is now First Assembly of God in Portland, Oregon. During his long pastorate there the church experienced unusual growth. For nearly 30 years Brother Davidson has served as either a General Presbyter or an Executive Presbyter of the Assemblies of God, the latter position having been bestowed on him in August, 1958. Without question the familiar figure of N. D. Davidson is recognized by a host of ministers and laymen in the fast-growing Pacific Northwest as one of the outstanding leaders in that part of the nation.[79]

A fiery preacher from the Southland is Edgar W. Bethany. A native of Mississippi, he began his ministry there in 1925. Two years later the Mississippi District Council ordained Brother Bethany. During these years he traveled with the D. P. Holloway Evangelistic Party, all told spending four years on the field. In 1929 the Kingston Assembly in Laurel,

---

[78]Roy Wead, unpublished manuscript, July, 1970.

[79]Letter from N. D. Davidson, June 30, 1970.

Mississippi, invited him to be their pastor. After two years he was asked to serve South-Eastern Bible Institute as principal, a position he filled until 1935. Pastorates in Spartanburg, South Carolina, and Columbus, Georgia, were punctuated with a brief stint as principal of South-Eastern Bible Institute again. He has held the position of district secretary of three districts: Mississippi, Alabama, and South Carolina, and has been a General Presbyter intermittently since 1935. In 1961 the General Council chose him to represent the Southeast Region of the United States as a nonresident Executive Presbyter.[80]

In 1965 the General Council elected Joseph R. Flower to serve as nonresident Executive Presbyter for the Northeast Region. Joseph was born to J. Roswell and Alice Reynolds Flower in 1913, in the year that the initial call was sent out to form the General Council. Joseph recalls frequent moves in his early years, as his busy parents engaged in varied ministries in the young denomination. Important in the shaping of his life was the influence of that godly home. "The family altar in our home through the childhood years was a major factor in setting us on the right course," Joseph recalls. It was in 1926, while his father was serving as Missionary Secretary in Springfield, that young Joseph, a lad of 13, received the Pentecostal experience. This occurred during a revival campaign conducted by William Booth-Clibborn. Joseph, upon graduation from high school, enrolled at Franklin and Marshall College in Lancaster, Pennsylvania. A profound spiritual experience at Ebenezer Camp near Buffalo, New York, in 1932, under the ministry of Charles S. Price, led Joseph to transfer to Central Bible Institute to prepare for ministry. Even before graduation in 1934, Joseph was busy in ministerial work during summers, helping to establish a church at Hudson Falls, New York. The next 20 years were spent in fruitful ministry, as pastor and evangelist throughout the Northeast, from Pennsylvania to Massachusetts. In 1954, when the New York and New Jersey Districts divided to form separate structures, Joseph R. Flower was elected to serve the New York Dis-

---

[80]Letter from Edgar W. Bethany, July 30, 1970.

trict Council as its first superintendent. He has held that position ever since. In many ways, even in appearance, Joseph calls to mind his esteemed father. In his own right he has earned the respect and admiration of the fellowship as a spiritual leader within the Assemblies of God.[81]

At the 1969 General Council in Dallas, E. M. Clark, Superintendent of the Illinois District, was elected to the post of nonresident Executive Presbyter for the Great Lakes Region. Brother Clark was born in Darbyville, Iowa, in 1911. His maternal grandmother held the infant in her arms and claimed him for the Christian ministry, but the lad grew up almost entirely without religious influence. While he was growing up, his parents and older sisters were converted in a Methodist revival at Springview, Nebraska, but Brother Clark, although uncomfortable for a time because of conviction, did not accept Christ. When he was 20 years of age, a Pentecostal meeting held at Burton, Nebraska, in a city park arrested his attention. Later that afternoon he attended a bapismal service at a nearby lake. "A woman came up out of the water shouting and speaking in other tongues. This almost held me transfixed. Others around me laughed about it, but to me it was a very serious thing." The next year E. M. Clark attended a revival meeting in Bassett, Nebraska, and it was there, in 1932, that he found Christ as Saviour. A year later he received the Pentecostal Baptism and felt a call to preach. Ministry in South Dakota and Michigan was followed by extensive evangelistic and pastoral ministry in Nebraska. In 1951, in part because of his reputation for gospel broadcasting on the Yankton, South Dakota, Radio Station WNAX, he was invited to become National Secretary of Radio in Springfield, Missouri. In 1958 the Clarks accepted an invitation to pastor in Quincy, Illinois. Two years later he was elected district superintendent. Brother Clark, at present President of North Central Bible College, recalls a notable episode in his ministry that occurred the year he was married, 1938. He conducted a tent meeting near Anselmo, Nebraska, for 13 weeks. "Meetings lasted until well after midnight every night, people

[81]Letter from Joseph R. Flower, June 20, 1970.

being saved and filled with the Holy Spirit every evening. This was one of the greatest outpourings of the Spirit I have ever been in."[82]

Paul E. Lowenberg, district superintendent of the Kansas District, was elected to serve as a nonresident Executive Presbyter at the 1969 General Council. Brother Lowenberg was born in Saskatchewan in 1914. He recalls the dust storms and the difficulties of the Great Depression which were vivid parts of his adolescent years. The Lowenberg family were loyal members of the Reformed Church, and were considered to be "fairly religious" people. However, Paul was not a born-again believer, in spite of the religious activities of the family. In 1931 a young man who had grown up in the community and had become quite a celebrity as a hockey and baseball player returned for a two-week revival campaign. He rented a local theater to conduct his Pentecostal services. Paul was saved in that meeting, and shortly afterward received the baptism in the Holy Spirit. About a year later, in a cottage prayer meeting, he felt a definite call to the ministry. In 1933, in company with two older brothers and a sister, Paul went to Lemsford, a small town not far distant, to hold a meeting at the request of relatives. "I went along for the ride—to play the guitar and sing. Through a strange chain of events, my two older brothers had to return to their homes, my sister took violently ill and was ordered home by the doctor, and I was left with a fledgling church. So I became a pastor without planning it." The next 10 years Brother Lowenberg spent in tent meetings, brush arbors, schoolhouses, hay barns, and even in a pool room. A small independent organization conferred credentials on him in 1935. In 1952, he was ordained by the Assemblies of God. Twelve years later the Kansas District chose him to be their superintendent. Brother Lowenberg has had a wide preaching ministry, and is recognized as one of the great pulpiteers of the fellowship.[83]

Summary

To cope with problems arising from the rapid multipli-

---

[82]Letter from E. M. Clark, June 22, 1970.

[83]Letter from Paul E. Lowenberg, June 24, 1970.

cation of new service agencies in the years from 1941 to 1953, the Assemblies of God had to make numerous adjustments. There was an enlargement of executive personnel to provide the necessary guidance for the proliferated activities. Various means were employed to coordinate communications, most notable being the creation of a Public Relations Office and a new church periodical, *Advance*. Increasing complexity of organizational structure precipitated a more businesslike mode of caring for financial matters. To coordinate the efforts of the denomination in an era when outreach was no longer strictly a spontaneous activity, a succession of trial-and-error attempts were undertaken, beginning with the creation of a Department of Evangelism in 1953 and culminating in the highly sophisticated Study on Advance in 1967. Hopefully there will be a continuing large response from the grass roots to match the earnest endeavors of the committee of fifteen. A significant rearticulation of purpose was enunciated at the Council on Evangelism in 1968, giving promise for meaningful guidelines for fresh growth in the Assemblies of God. The Five-Year Plan of Advance represents a vigorous, bold attempt to face the changing needs of contemporary society.

13

Controversy: The Voices of Dissent

Theological Issues—Practical Issues—Summary

The Assemblies of God fellowship has been remarkably free of serious discord since the resolution of the "New Issue" problem in the earliest years of the denomination's history. What issues there have been may be considered under two headings, theological and practical.

Theological Issues

The extent of the harmony within the Assemblies of God is demonstrated by the fact that defections from the ordained ministry for theological reasons have been surprisingly few.[1] The flow into the Assemblies of God ministry from other groups has been consistently higher than the flow outward in the years since the "New Issue" crisis.[2]

Following the drafting of the original Statement of Fundamental Truths in 1916, no changes whatsoever were made until the General Council in 1961, and then the modifications were only in the nature of minor rewording to supply greater clarity. The most significant change occurred in the section respecting Sanctification. Some changes have been made in the bylaw article governing "Doctrines and Practices Disapproved." There has also been important revision in the article on "Military Service." In addition, some issues have occurred that have not required changes or clarification in the legal documents governing the fellowship.

Although there have been surprisingly few defections

[1]Interview, Bartlett Peterson, April 16, 1970.
[2]*Ibid.*

from the Assemblies of God ministerial ranks for doctrinal reasons, there has been a concern for the preservation of doctrinal integrity within the denomination. The clearest exemplification of this was the adoption of a resolution at the 1959 General Council calling for an annual doctrinal questionnaire to be prepared by the Executive Presbytery and submitted to all ordained ministers as part of the credentials renewal arrangement.[3] This procedure has not resulted in any significant increase in the number of defections.[4]

OLDER ISSUES

Sanctification. At the time of the forming of the General Council of the Assemblies of God, the "Finished Work" teaching of Pastor Durham from Chicago and the Wesleyan teaching of the Holiness groups were live options. However, the Reformed view of Durham was adopted, as the Statement of Fundamental Truths of 1916 clearly indicates. Apparently to mollify advocates of a stronger Wesleyan position, the language of "entire sanctification" was employed. This continued to create ambiguity in the fellowship, requiring redefinition through the years.[5] The clarification of 1961 specified the belief that the imputed righteousness accorded the believer at his justification was to be exhibited in a life of holiness, but the ambiguous term "entire sanctification" was omitted.[6]

The "New Issue." A series of "Jesus Only" or "Oneness" denominations developed, with greatest strength in the Midwest and South Central United States, following the decision of the Assemblies of God in 1916 forcing the exponents of this teaching out of the fellowship. No basis of fellowship has been found with these groups. It is significant that the Pentecostal Fellowship of North America has not accorded them membership, an orthodox belief in the Trinity being

---

[3]General Council minutes, 1959, p. 49.

[4]Interview, Bartlett Peterson, April 16, 1970.

[5]*The Pentecostal Evangel*, July 6, 1946, pp. 2-3. This article distinguishes clearly between the positional righteousness imputed to the believer and the experience subsequent to justification of enduement with power, called the baptism in the Holy Spirit. This view is clearly enunciated by Myer Pearlman in the standard doctrine book of the denomination, *Knowing the Doctrines of the Bible* (Springfield, Missouri: Gospel Publishing House, 1937), pp. 249-66.

[6]General Council minutes, 1961, p. 92.

an irreducible minimum necessary for cooperative fellowship.[7] A resolution adopted at the 1947 General Council, acknowledging the increased mobility of the population, encouraged pastors to follow their parishioners with sufficient communication so that they could be happily relocated in another Assembly, and not be unwittingly lured into association with a Pentecostal church which might be "Jesus Only."[8] Although sporadic episodes of local friction have occurred, for all practical purposes the "New Issue" is no longer a live problem.[9]

Eternal Security. The Assemblies of God has sought to take a mediating position between extreme Arminian and extreme Calvinistic teaching with respect to the perseverance of the believer. By 1945, articles began to appear in *The Pentecostal Evangel* articulating this posture.[10] In 1946, F.M. Bellsmith enunciated the position quite clearly by employing the expression, "We are secure if we follow Him."[11] At the 1967 General Council a revision of the article on "Doctrines Disapproved" was aimed specifically at clarifying the previous language, adopted in 1927, which had been used to refer to the eternal security teaching. The use of the term "extreme eternal security teaching" had resulted in ambiguity. Accepted in lieu of the older statement was the following clarification:

> In view of the Biblical teaching that the security of the believer depends on a living relationship with Christ, and in view of the Bible's call to a life of holiness, the General Council disapproves of the unconditional eternal security position which holds "once saved always saved."[12]

The Initial Evidence. The incident in which F. F. Bosworth played a leading role seemed to terminate serious disagreement regarding the teaching that speaking with tongues is to be regarded as "the initial physical evidence"

---

[7]Fischer, *op. cit.*, p. 53.

[8]General Council minutes, 1947, p. 44.

[9]Interview, J. Roswell Flower, June 26, 1967.

[10]Donald Gee, "Extreme Eternal Security Teaching," *The Pentecostal Evangel*, March 3, 1945, pp. 2-3.

[11]F. M. Bellsmith, "Security, True and False," *The Pentecostal Evangel*, July 27, 1946, p. 7.

[12]General Council minutes, 1967, p. 40. The Executive Presbytery appointed a committee to restudy Article XXIII, "Doctrines and Practices Disapproved," in its

of the Spirit's baptism of believers. By a firm resolution, the 1918 General Council underscored the traditional Pentecostal teaching.[13] Bosworth left the fellowship, taking very few with him, making no important subsequent impact.[14]

In the post-World War II era the question began to appear again sporadically. The ministerial "Quarterly Letter" of June, 1959, carried a brief notice indicating that in one district "a few of its preachers have confessed doubt in their attitude toward our doctrine of tongues as the initial physical evidence of the Baptism of the Holy Spirit."[15] This issue never seemed to gain great momentum, always occurring in isolated situations.[16] One important reason for this issue apparently failing to pose a major threat within the denomination has been the rise of Neo-Pentecostalism coincident with the eruption of such questioning in recent years. The fact that across a wide spectrum of theological positions there has been a fresh appreciation of the values that Pentecostalism has held dear seemed to furnish a rather strong argument in favor of the traditional theology of the Assemblies of God for many would-be dissenters.

In a position paper written by the General Superintendent, a strong reaffirmation of the historic position on evidential tongues was given: "Time has brought changes, but no modification in the emphasis, teaching, and experience of the baptism of the Spirit."[17] The General Secretary, writing in the ministerial "Quarterly Letter," in September, 1966, said, "Our position is unchanged with regard to the Baptism of the Holy Spirit and speaking in other tongues."[18]

---

entirety in 1968. Out of this came a rather thorough revision of the article, including a slight editing of the content of the section on eternal security, which had been adopted at the 1967 General Council. The changes in that section consisted almost entirely in the addition of appropriate Scriptures. At the 1969 General Council, the entire content of Article XXIII was relocated as Article VIII, when the Constitution was rather thoroughly restructured to conform to the recommendations growing out of the Study Committee on Advance. (See pages 116-21 of the 1969 General Council minutes.)

[13]General Council minutes, 1918, pp. 8-10.

[14]Interview, E. S. Williams, June 27, 1967.

[15]"Quarterly Letter," June 12, 1959.

[16]Interview, Bartlett Peterson, April 16, 1970.

[17]T. F. Zimmerman, "The Pentecostal Position," *The Pentecostal Evangel*, February 10, 1963, pp. 2, 3, 7.

[18]"Quarterly Letter," September 23, 1966.

The Divorce Problem. When the Assemblies of God was formed in 1914, one of the first issues was whether or not to grant fellowship to ministers who had been divorced and remarried. By 1921 a resolution was adopted discouraging any minister from performing a marriage ceremony between any believer and a divorced person whose former companion was still living, on penalty of having his credentials jeopardized.[19] This resolution was reworded even more strongly in 1933.[20] Few issues have come into contention with greater frequency throughout the history of the denomination than this. At the General Council in Atlanta in 1951 an appeal was made for a restudy of the problem to be undertaken, growing out of an extensive debate on the floor of the Council.[21] At the following General Council in 1953, the committee report was read by Chairman J. D. Menzie, recommending a reaffirmation of the existing position. With slight rewording, the original bylaw was accepted.[22]

This decision did not quell all dissent, however. Four years later, General Superintendent Ralph M. Riggs found it necessary to write a fresh Biblical exposition on the subject in an effort to resolve continuing contention over the issue.[23] Occasional rumblings are still heard on the subject. At the 1969 General Council the committee which presented a proposal for revision of the article governing "Doctrines and Practices Disapproved" passed on to the General Council the section of that article governing divorce and remarriage intact as it had existed for years. However, discussion on the floor led to the adoption of a motion requesting that the committee restudy that section with a view to presenting fresh thinking on the subject for the 1971 General Council.[24] This would indicate the issue is still not closed.

THE "NEW ORDER OF THE LATTER RAIN"

The most dramatic controversy to affect the Pentecostal

[19]General Council minutes, 1921, pp. 58-59.
[20]General Council minutes, 1933, p. 97.
[21]General Council minutes, 1951, pp. 27-28.
[22]General Council minutes, 1953, pp. 9-12.
[23]Ralph M. Riggs, "Divorce and Remarriage," *The Pentecostal Evangel*, March 3, 1957, pp. 4-5.
[24]General Council minutes, 1969, p. 23.

Movement since World War II has been the "New Order of the Latter Rain," a meteoric movement appealing to the sensational. It succeeded in generating widespread hysteria throughout the Pentecostal denominations in the late 1940's, but by the early 1950's it had subsided to a minor ripple.

Although similar episodes had occurred in the 1920's, and especially in eastern Pennyslvania in the early 1930's, these were but flurries compared to the storm that had its origins in the prairies of Western Canada in the fall of 1948.[25]

In 1947, George Hawtin and Percy Hunt launched an independent Bible school in North Battleford, Saskatchewan. Mr. Hawtin had formerly been the principal of a Bible school operated by the Pentecostal Assemblies of Canada at Saskatoon, Saskatchewan, but he had withdrawn for personal reasons and turned in his credentials. They evolved a teaching that emphasized extreme congregationalism with local authority committed to a restored order of apostles, who, through receiving a special dispensation derived from the laying on of hands, could in turn dispense a variety of spiritual gifts. Their extravagant claims and their belligerent attack on existing Pentecostal groups brought open conflict. Many sincere Christians followed the new group, which boasted of being a fresh revival displacing the "apostasized" Pentecostals.[26]

The new teaching spread rapidly. The radio was an effective instrument, as was the printed page. A monthly periodical, the *Sharon Star,* published by Hawtin in North Battleford, was their chief voice.[27] Little attention was paid the "Sharon group," until it made a major penetration into the Assemblies of God in the United States.

Mrs. Myrtle Beall, an ordained minister of the Assemblies of God, had established a strong church on the east side of Detroit, Bethesda Tabernacle. She was a sincere woman, but inclined to be visionary.[28] In the fall of 1948 she invited

---

[25]Interview, E. S. Williams, June 27, 1967.

[26]Atter, *op. cit.*, p. 142.

[27]*Ibid.*, p. 142.

[28]Interview, C. W. H. Scott, September 19, 1967.

some of the people from the "Sharon group" to hold a series of meetings in her church. These workers had come to Detroit and had spent several months there, finally convincing Mrs. Beall that they were the envoys of a fresh revival. Bethesda Tabernacle was destined to become the chief center for propagating the message after 1948, for people came to the "revival" from all parts of the country. The Wings of Healing Temple, Portland, Oregon, pastored by Dr. Thomas Wyatt, was a key center for the new movement for a time.[29] Groups sprang up in New York, Tennessee, Missouri, Texas, Illinois, and on the West Coast, as well as in Canada. Pastors and congregations of several Pentecostal denominations were affected.

Illustrative of the way various leaders dealt with the problem throughout the country is the Michigan story. Charles Scott, district superintendent of Michigan, had some conferences with Mrs. Beall and the leading "Latter Rain" exponent from Canada, Evangelist Elmer Frink. Just at this time, the editor of *The Pentecostal Evangel,* Stanley Frodsham, arrived on the scene as the result of an invitation from Mrs. Beall. He was swept away by the revival taking place in Detroit, announcing in sincerity to Superintendent Scott that "this is God."[30] He was moved deeply by scenes of people under great conviction of sin, making confession and finding peace.[31] This was in January, 1949. By the time of the annual Michigan Ministers' Institute, scheduled for February at the Dearborn Gospel Tabernacle, Frodsham's influence had threatened to cause a serious number of defections from the Assemblies of God in Michigan.

At the Ministers' Institute, Scott outlined the history and the errors of the new teaching. He emphasized in particcular the misplaced emphasis on the gift of prophecy, the impartation of gifts of the Spirit by the laying on of hands by self-styled apostles and prophets, and the fact that the revival was not, after all, new at all, but rather the reappearance of enthusiastic mysticism common in church his-

[29]E. L. Moore, "Handbook of Pentecostal Denominations in the United States" (unpublished M.A. thesis, Pasadena College, 1954), p. 319.

[30]Interview, C. W. H. Scott, September 19, 1967.

[31]Interview, Stanley Frodsham, September 22, 1967.

tory.[32] No individuals were attacked. Nothing more was said of the matter thereafter. Silence was maintained for an entire year.

At the District Council session in May, 1950, now that time for reflection had been given, decisive action was taken. Out of 200 ministers, only two left. One, a Canadian, resigned and left the country. The other took his church with him out of the Assemblies of God. That ended the issue in Michigan.[33] Bethesda Tabernacle remained the single center of influence.

On the national level, the first evidence of concern came in the "Quarterly Letter" of February, 1949. A brief, quite general, statement entitled "Bestowing Gifts" was supplied by the General Superintendent, Ernest S. Williams, obviously to point up acceptable teaching on the subject, without overtly referring to the "Latter Rain" problem.[34] A special edition of the "Quarterly Letter," dated April 20, 1949, aired the problem quite thoroughly, enunciating its history and the errors which the Assemblies of God Executive Presbytery felt it contained.[35] In this letter it was confirmed that the editor of *The Pentecostal Evangel* had participated in the revival.

At the annual General Presbyters' meeting, just prior to the General Council in Seattle that fall, General Superintendent E. S. Williams gave a brief résumé of the teachings of the new movement, and then referred to the vigorous defense R. E. McAlister of Canada had been making through a periodical known as the *Truth Advocate.* He recommended that this material be edited, with the permission of Mr. McAlister, and reprinted as a series in *The Pentecostal Evangel.*[36] This was agreeable to the assembled body, the series subsequently appearing in November and December, 1949, under the title, "Spiritual Gifts," edited by Frank M. Boyd. He did not actually refer to the "Latter Rain" move-

[32]Charles Scott, "What Is Latter Rain?" (unpublished sermon notes, February 14, 1949).

[33]Interview, C. W. H. Scott, September 19, 1967.

[34]"Quarterly Letter," February 24, 1949.

[35]"Quarterly Letter," April 20, 1949.

[36]General Presbytery minutes, 1949, p. 5.

ment, but by positive teaching on Biblical principles he sought to counter the errors of the group.

At the General Council that year, a resolution was adopted disapproving of the practices of the "Latter Rain." Six errors were specified:

1. The overemphasis relative to imparting, identifying, bestowing or confirming of gifts by the laying on of hands and prophecy.

2. The erroneous teaching that the Church is built on the foundation of present-day apostles and prophets.

3. The extreme teaching as advocated by the "New Order" regarding the confession of sin to man and deliverance as practiced, which claims prerogatives to human agency which belong only to Christ.

4. The erroneous teaching concerning the impartation of the gift of languages as special equipment for missionary service.

5. The extreme and unscriptural practice of imparting or imposing personal leadings by the means of gifts of utterance.

6. Such other wrestings and distortions of Scripture interpretations which are in opposition to teachings and practices generally accepted among us.[37]

The last issue of the "Quarterly Letter" that mentioned the problem at all was that of June, 1950.[38] A year later, at the General Council, J. Roswell Flower reported that very few churches had withdrawn from the Assemblies of God, and only a small number of ministers, in the preceding year, due to the "Latter Rain" issue.[39] Some of those who had defected later were reinstated, the net loss being very small. The issue, for all practical purposes, was at an end.

The lone center that has maintained vigor is the Detroit church, now renamed Bethesda Missionary Temple. Mrs. Beall's son, James, is the pastor, but Mrs. Beall continues to exercise a kind of charismatic leadership.[40] Her daughter-in-law, Mrs. Patricia D. Gruits, seems to have assumed a position as official theologian of the group. Her book, *Understanding God,* apparently passes as the standard of doctrine among them.[41]

---

[37]General Council minutes, 1949, pp. 26-27.

[38]"Quarterly Letter," June 1, 1950.

[39]General Council reports, 1951, pp. 8-9.

[40]Letter from Richard Dobbins, January 3, 1968.

[41]Patricia D. Gruits, *Understanding God* (Detroit, Michigan: The Evangel Press, 1962).

MILITARY SERVICE

The infant Assemblies of God had not fully recovered from the New Issue crisis when the United States was plunged into World War I. The Assemblies of God had made no statement respecting its stand on military service when it was founded in 1914, but with the entry of the United States into war, with conscription imminent, the leaders found it necessary to draw up a statement. A paper, approved by both the Executive and General Presbyteries, established the official position of the Assemblies of God as pacifist.[42] A copy of this document was forwarded to President Wilson on April 28, 1917. A letter was received from D. L. Roscoe, Captain of Cavalry, U.S.A., on May 4, in response, advising that the House had before it a bill respecting exemptions. News releases carried in the press on July 1, 1917, outlined the exemptions from military service that the Congress had granted. Among them was the provision exempting ordained ministers.[43] The government also made provision for conscientious objectors to serve in special camps during the war, some Assemblies of God laymen evidently choosing this path, although there is no record of the number involved.

The General Council in 1927, at the time of the formulation of the Constitution, adopted as an article in the bylaws a statement on military service articulating the pacifist position adopted 10 years earler.[44] This posture seemed to remain fairly consistent up to the dramatic events of December 7, 1941. The 1939 General Council passed a resolution directing the General Superintendent and General Secretary to draft a telegram to be dispatched to the President of the United States expressing appreciation of his earnest efforts in maintaining American neutrality.[45] A statement appearing in the October 12, 1940, issue of *The Pentecostal Evangel,* immediately following the announcement of national conscription, reaffirmed the pacifist

[42]Harrison, *op. cit.*, p. 155.
[43]*Ibid.*
[44]General Council minutes, 1927, pp. 28-29.
[45]General Council minutes, 1939, p. 57.

position of the Assemblies of God, harking back to the 1917 decision.[46]

A radical change occurred in the attitude of Assemblies of God people respecting military service sometime in the interval between World War I and World War II, in spite of official pronouncements. The attack on Pearl Harbor apparently was the catalyst that brought the changed attitude into sharp relief. By the fall of 1942 *The Pentecostal Evangel* published a feature story on the first Assemblies of God minister to serve as a military chaplain, First Lieutenant Clarence P. Smales, of the United States Army.[47] This would appear to be the first public acknowledgement of the role that Assemblies of God personnel could play in the military.

The next spring General Secretary J. Roswell Flower pointed out that not more than 20 Assemblies of God men had taken advantage of the conscientious objector provision allowable because of the official denominational stand, but that "quite a number" had appealed for, and obtained, classification as noncombatants. He concluded, regarding the majority, "Some of those who have been inducted into the armed forces have weighed the problem in the light of personal responsibility versus responsibility to the State, and have reached the conclusion that upon induction into the armed forces personal responsibility ceases."[48] By 1944 more than 50,000 Assemblies of God men were serving in the armed services.[49]

In the General Presbytery meeting of 1943 a discussion arose regarding the need to reconsider the bylaw statement governing military service. No action was taken, but a committee was appointed to consider the matter.[50] Apparently the end of the war intervened before the matter was considered further.

The 1945 General Council heard a report indicating that the denomination had spent more than $13,000 for the sup-

---

[46]*The Pentecostal Evangel*, October 12, 1940, p. 13.
[47]*The Pentecostal Evangel*, October 17, 1942, p. 3.
[48]*The Pentecostal Evangel*, June 12, 1943, p. 6.
[49]*The Pentecostal Evangel*, March 18, 1944, p. 12.
[50]General Presbytery minutes, 1943, p. 10.

port of families of Assemblies of God men who had been sent to C.P.S. camps for conscience' sake.[51] Only 35 actually served in such camps during World War II.[52]

When the Korean War erupted, the General Secretary presented to the ministers the procedure to follow to secure conscientious objector status for any men in the local churches desiring such consideration. However, there was little need for this by that time.[53] Still, the bylaw statement maintained the pacifist position as the official Assemblies of God stand.

It was not until the Vietnam War that definite action was taken to revise the denominational statement so that it would reflect more realistically the general viewpoint. At the 1965 General Council in Des Moines, a resolution was adopted arranging for a committee to be appointed which should study the matter and bring its report to the subsequent General Council.[54] At the Long Beach Council in 1967, the committee report led to the adoption of a resolution altering the Military Service bylaw article to read:

> As a movement we affirm our loyalty to the government of the United States in war or peace.
> We shall continue to insist, as we have historically, on the right of each member to choose for himself whether to declare his position as a combatant, a noncombatant, or a conscientious objector.[55]

The denomination no longer officially affirmed a pacifist position.

ESCHATOLOGY

Millennial expectations formed an important part of the message of the early Pentecostalists. Imbued with a sense of the nearness of the end of the age, and that the Pentecostal revival was the harbinger of the cataclysm, the cry was heralded abroad "Jesus is coming soon." Coincident with the rise of the Pentecostal Movement was the flowering of the dispensationalist brand of Fundamentalism.[56] It was an

[51] General Council minutes, 1945, p. 45.
[52] "Quarterly Letter," March 24, 1951.
[53] *Ibid.*
[54] General Council minutes, 1965, p. 61.
[55] General Council minutes, 1967, p. 35.
[56] For a detailed description of dispensational Fundamentalism, see Chapters 1 and 9.

easy exercise to adapt the teaching and literature of Scofieldian dispensationalism to the Pentecostal emphasis. The fact that dispensational teaching of the Fundamentalist type denied the possibility of a modern Pentecostal experience was lightly glossed over by those who saw the dispensational motif, given a proper Pentecostal baptism, as a helpful aid in underscoring the importance of the doctrine of the second coming of Christ.[57]

It is interesting to observe that four of the 16 items in the Statement of Fundamental Truths adopted in 1916 were eschatological in substance, indicating the relative importance in the Pentecostal message from early years of the coming end of the age. However, these statements commit the Assemblies of God to premillennialism, but not necessarily to dispensationalism. In most recent years, there has been a tendency to emphasize the second coming of Christ, and the cataclysmic judgment of the present order, but without depending so heavily on the dispensational categories. The best example of this is the latest book on eschatology published by the Assemblies of God in which the term "dispensation" does not even occur, although it is clearly premillennial.[58]

There has been an unevenness in eschatological emphasis through the years in the Assemblies of God. In the late 1930's, as the ominous clouds of war gathered over Europe, Pentecostal preachers rang the changes on prophecy with regularity. The tempo increased as the terrible events of 1939 and 1940 came to pass. The preoccupation of Pentecostal people with the concerns of Biblical prophecy reached a crescendo in 1941. In the first three months of that fateful year, 31 out of the 90 major articles in *The Pentecostal Evangel* were directly related to the war in Europe and Biblical prophecy. During these years it was not uncommon to identify one or more of the dictators with Antichrist, or at least to see the current world powers as

---

[57]A classic example of Pentecostal adaptation of the dispensational motif is Frank M. Boyd's *Ages and Dispensations*, published in 1949 by the Gospel Publishing House.

[58]Stanley Horton, *The Promise of His Coming* (Springfield, Missouri: Gospel Publishing House, 1967).

direct expressions of forces spoken of in the Book of Revelation.[59]

With the termination of World War II, the emphasis on prophecy declined. A good many sermons that had been popular were no longer serviceable after the death of Mussolini and Hitler. In more recent years, with the rise of the Ecumenical Movement, the target of prophetic concern has shifted in that direction. The General Council resolution disapproving of the Ecumenical Movement, adopted in 1963, specified as a major reason for such reaction the belief that the movement is "a sign of the times," and that "the combination of many denominations into a World Super Church will probably culminate in the Scarlet Woman or Religious Babylon of Revelation."[60]

Practical Issues

Several problems affecting the Assemblies of God that have not been primarily theological are sufficiently important to merit consideration.

THE "SALVATION-HEALING" MOVEMENT

In the years following World War II there were two phenomena that appeared in the Pentecostal world that seem to have common characteristics, although one was primarily a theological issue and the other a practical concern. The "New Order of the Latter Rain" and the "Salvation-Healing" movements both appeared in the late 1940's, the former reaching its zenith and fading quite rapidly, the latter cresting in the late 1950's. Both seemed to strike a sympathetic chord in many Pentecostals, and gained some support until some errors began to become apparent. Quite possibly the tendency in groups like the Assemblies of God to curb the sensational, to place supernatural manifestations in an orderly context, did not satisfy all comers, especially in the restive years immediately after the war. Perhaps the restrictions imposed by the war years built up an appetite for the sensational in a sizable proportion of the Pentecostal following. An example of this may be seen in the General

---

[59]D. P. Holloway, "The Present World Crisis in the Light of Prophecy," *The Pentecostal Evangel*, October 25, 1941, p. 8. This was a sermon preached at the General Council that year.

[60]General Council minutes, 1963, pp. 52-53.

Council of 1947 which convened at Grand Rapids. Retired General Superintendent E. S. Williams recalls that meeting as being a low-water mark for its extravagant outbursts, for its bombastic preaching.[61] More conservative spirits were bewildered, almost numbed, by the pyrotechnics that characterized that convention.

The Assemblies of God had always believed and practiced divine healing. There was no quarrel with the message that God can heal the sick in response to believing prayer. The real issue was the awareness that some of the evangelists who traveled about featuring prayer for the sick appeared to be exploiting the pulpit for the sake of personal gain, employing practices that brought discredit, not only to the evangelists themselves, but also to the entire Pentecostal Movement. What made the situation especially painful was the fact that many reputable evangelists, both inside and outside the Assemblies of God, who felt called to such a ministry but deplored the actions of the few, suffered considerable opprobrium nonetheless by virtue of their associations. This was a situation quite unlike the pre-World War II era in which evangelists such as Dr. Charles S. Price had brought a degree of respect to large meetings featuring prayer for the sick.[62]

The most famous of the great "Salvation-Healing" evangelists has been Oral Roberts. A Pentecostal Holiness preacher, Oral Roberts first came to public prominence as the result of a crusade in Tulsa, Oklahoma, in 1947.[63] His subsequent campaigns were so successful that several ancillary enterprises were added to multiply the outreach of his ministry, the most notable being the establishment of a multimillion dollar university in 1965 in Tulsa.[64] He avoided identification with associations of healing evangelists choosing to remain apart. Most of the others have come

---

[61]Interview, Ernest S. Williams, June 27, 1967.

[62]Charles S. Price, *The Story of My Life* (Pasadena, California: Charles S. Price Publishing Company, 1947).

[63]Oral Roberts, *My Story* (Tulsa, Oklahoma: Summit Book Company, 1961), p. 141.

[64]Raymond O. Corvin, "Religious and Educational Backgrounds in the Founding of Oral Roberts University" (unpublished Ph.D. dissertation, The University of Oklahoma, 1967), p. 160.

and gone, but long after the heyday of the healing evangelist, Roberts has managed to survive. His joining the Methodist Church in 1969 jarred many of his Pentecostal friends.

Among the several organizations that arose during this period was the association formed by Gordon Lindsay in 1949. Two years before, Lindsay had become acquainted with William Branham who was just then beginning a healing type of ministry.[65] Lindsay began publication of a magazine originally designed to promote the ministry of Branham. The magazine was entitled *The Voice of Healing.* Branham encouraged Lindsay to broaden the scope of the paper so as to include news of other evangelists as well. Within a short time a sizable group of evangelists, many of them holding Assemblies of God credentials, were being featured in the pages of *The Voice of Healing.* By 1950 its circulation was approaching 100,000.[66]

In December, 1949, a convention of healing evangelists was suggested to Lindsay.[67] With but the briefest preparation, a convention was conducted in connection with a crusade being held in Dallas, Texas. This was the beginning of the association known as "The Voice of Healing." It never was formally organized and had no documents to govern its operation. It was rather an informal fellowship arrangement that looked to the editor of *The Voice of Healing* for coordination. Lindsay referred to the evangelists he featured in his publication as "associate evangelists."[68] By the end of 1952, 49 evangelists were so listed in the magazine.[69] Of these a fair proportion were Assemblies of God ministers. However, Lindsay was unable to verify all the reports that were submitted to him for publication, nor was he able to check the character of the men whom he served. He was sincere in his efforts, but the undisciplined nature of the association led to its dissolution. Some evangelists who had begun well, and who evidently were sincere, began to com-

[65]Gordon Lindsay, *The Gordon Lindsay Story* (Dallas, Texas: The Voice of Healing Publishing Company, n.d.), p. 157.

[66]*Ibid.*, p. 164.

[67]*Ibid.*, pp. 164-65.

[68]*The Voice of Healing*, December, 1952, p. 4.

[69]*Ibid.*

mercialize their ministry, some eventually dropping out of the association to form little empires of their own, complete with colorful magazines and extensive mailing lists.[70] Other men who had earlier associated with the group, seeing the unfortunate turn that many were taking, withdrew from all connection with the movement. By 1956 the number of "associate evangelists" in *The Voice of Healing* had begun to dwindle noticeably, and by 1960 fewer than a dozen were being promoted regularly in the magazine.[71] By 1967 the association was virtually dead. In that year Lindsay changed the name of the magazine to *Christ for the Nations,* apparently hoping to generate a new image for the paper.[72]

With the healing evangelists' association falling into decay, Lindsay invited ministers of independent Pentecostal churches to an exploratory meeting in Dallas, Texas, in 1962. Lindsay, from sad experience, saw the necessity of some means for screening out the unsavory elements that had occasioned the destruction of his earlier association. The new association became known as "The Full Gospel Fellowship of Christian Churches and Ministers, International." During the first years of its operation the pages of *The Voice of Healing* were used to promote its conventions and activities, but in 1967 a separate organ was created for this purpose. By 1967 the association boasted 1,500 ministers and 500 churches.[73] What future directions this body will take are uncertain.

In the early 1950's some of the great international crusades conducted by the healing evangelists proved highly beneficial to the cause of missions, including the Assemblies of God missionary enterprise.[74] However, by the mid-1950's, a new problem arose that compounded the anxiety of Assemblies of God leaders. Assemblies of God missionaries were grateful for the interest created in the Pentecostal message generated by these great crusades, but when some

---

[70]Interview, H. C. Noah, November 2, 1967.

[71]These statistics derived from perusal of the magazine.

[72]Interview, Gordon Lindsay, June 29, 1967.

[73]Interview, Gordon Lindsay, June 29, 1967.

[74]Leonard Steiner, *Mit Folgenden Zeichen* (Basel: Verlag Mission fur das volle Evangelium, 1954), pp. 114-19.

of these evangelists began to promote their work by featuring the support of national evangelists, a reaction set in. What happened apparently was that some of these men found that a spark of fresh interest in their ministry was being created by appealing for funds that were promised to nationals. By the late 1950's large sums were being collected from American donors, processed through the offices of the healing evangelists, and given to the missionary agencies of Pentecostal denominations for redistribution to "native evangelism." Ostensibly, it appeared to be a worthy enterprise, but on the field the missionaries who had to live with it discovered that the program was producing a new wave of "rice Christians," and was effectively contravening the carefully developed philosophy of indigenous church planting.[75] Although sizable sums were thus passed on to established Pentecostal denominations, there was also the question of how much of the donations was being kept for operational expenses, since the independent evangelists were answerable to no one.

How then did the Assemblies of God react to this "Salvation-Healing" ministry? To be sure, there was widespread grass roots support for such ministry, for not all such evangelists were inspired by dubious motives, and many of the people in local congregations failed to see some of the questionable dimensions of the others. On an official level, several actions were taken.

In 1949, at the General Presbytery meeting, the question was raised about the policy of *The Pentecostal Evangel* not to print reports of these great campaigns, which already by then were gaining popular support. General Superintendent E. S. Williams responded by stating that inasmuch as it was difficult to verify many of the testimonies associated with such mass meetings, it was not considered advisable by the Executive Presbytery to print them. With this explanation, the action of the Executive Presbytery was sustained by the General Presbyters.[76] However, the traditional practice of *The Pentecostal Evangel* to carry testimonies of individual healings endorsed by the

[75]Interview, David Womack, January 11, 1967.
[76]General Presbytery minutes, 1949, p. 5.

Movement's pastors was maintained without interruption.

At the General Presbytery meeting of 1952 an extensive discussion took place that resulted in a series of resolutions pertaining to the "Salvation-Healing" movement, including a reaffirmation of the denominational belief in the doctrine of divine healing and a repudiation of questionable practices reported of some evangelists.[77] Again, in 1956, the General Presbyters considered the alleged "unscriptural, unethical, and extravagant practices" of some of the evangelists in the movement, with the result that a committee was appointed to study the matter further.[78] That same year, General Superintendent Ralph Riggs wrote an open letter to the fellowship entitled "The Doctrine of Divine Healing Is Being Wounded in the House of Its Friends."[79]

Following the increasing disenchantment with the exploitation of divine healing in the mid-1950's, the Assemblies of God leadership moved toward the adoption of some means for discouraging the ministers in the denomination from participating in undisciplined associations that were beyond the control of the denomination. It was the "Salvation-Healing" movement, among others, that precipitated the eventual adoption of the "Criteria for Independent Corporations," a policy adopted at the General Council of 1965.

THE ROLE OF LAYMEN

During the earlier years of the Assemblies of God, the lay preacher invaded community after community, erecting a simple structure and gathering a congregation. Before World War II there were few churches with more than two or three hundred members, the vast majority being quite small, composed of converts who as yet had not developed leadership skills. The preacher in those days had, of necessity, a disproportionate responsibility for the conducting of church affairs, both in the local church and in district and national councils. After World War II, this began to change. Servicemen returning from the war went to colleges in large numbers, children of the second and

---

[77]General Presbytery minutes, 1952, pp. 14-15.

[78]General Presbytery minutes, 1956, p. 20.

[79]*The Pentecostal Evangel*, November 4, 1956, p. 6.

third generation were encouraged for the first time to obtain advanced secular education, and a consequent wave of informed, skilled lay leaders appeared in Assemblies of God churches. In the meantime, the preacher had grown accustomed to his role as leader, and he did not always make sufficient room for the emerging talents of the layman. By the late 1950's this tension was felt in the General Councils, but in the years since then, increased recognition of the role of the layman has tended to dispel anxiety regarding the problem. In fact, in 1965 there was a renewed appeal for youth to consider "full-time service," because the denomination appeared to be facing a shortage of ministers for the first time in its history.[80]

In the constitutional provisions of the Assemblies of God, ordained ministers and missionaries are members of the General Council, and also one lay delegate from each local assembly is accorded a vote as well.[81] Through the pre-World War II years, there were very few lay delegates at the Councils, and frequently, for convenience' sake, a church would send the pastor's wife with him, designating her as their representative. In 1941 only 136 lay delegates were reported out of a voting registration of 1,157, or just 11.7 percent. This reached an all-time high of 22.7 percent at the 1959 General Council, nearly a 100 percent increase in the postwar years. It has remained close to 20 percent ever since.[82]

The 1957 General Council was something of a turning point with regard to lay influence in the Assemblies of God. Some laymen expressed the opinion that the Assemblies of God was a "preachers' denomination."[83] There were verbal exchanges on both sides of the issue, but it would be pressing the point to call it a "revolt."[84] That General Council did authorize a "Foreign Missions Advisory

[80]Although the reports of the General Secretary had been pointing to a possible ministerial shortage since 1961, it was not until 1965 that this was sounded as a public alarm by the General Superintendent in his keynote address. See "Where the Spirit Leads," *The Pentecostal Evangel*, October 10, 1965, pp. 8-9.

[81]General Council minutes, 1967, p. 67.

[82]These figures derived from General Council reports.

[83]Interview, Howard S. Bush, September 13, 1967.

[84]Interview, Thomas F. Zimmerman, December 8, 1967.

Committee," to be composed of six laymen who should work in cooperation with the Foreign Missions Board.[85]

At the General Council in San Antonio in 1959, a leading layman in the denomination felt impressed to make a public statement from the floor on the issue that had been smoldering since the previous General Council in Cleveland. This seemed to be instrumental in healing the wounds opened at the previous convention.[86] The result was the adoption of an irenic resolution that served to mollify the ruffled feelings of both ministers and laymen, although some discontent still exists.

> Resolved, That since we are predominantly ministers, and that it has been stated that we are a movement of ministers, that we go on record at this Council that we are a group of laymen, ministers and missionaries, united together to go forward declaring our common bond of Christian fellowship and objectives.[87]

At the following General Council retired General Secretary J. Roswell Flower, who had been asked to serve as chairman of a committee on Definition of General Council Terminology, included in his report the observation "that a layman can serve in any capacity, unless the Constitution and bylaws state otherwise."[88]

One of the catalytic agents in the raising of the question regarding the role of the layman was the emergence of the "Full Gospel Business Men's Fellowship, International." Demos Shakarian, a prominent West Coast dairy executive, had become interested in the possibility of united Pentecostal efforts as early as 1948. Encouraged by Oral Roberts and others, he invited several businessmen to a meeting in Los Angeles in 1951. About 200 came to the meeting, which featured Oral Roberts as the main speaker. Shortly after this exploratory session, a second such meeting was held in Fresno, at which the FGBMFI was formally organized, Demos Shakarian being selected as chairman. The next year the organization was legally incorporated, and Thomas R. Nickel was selected to serve as editor and publisher of an official organ, *The Full Gospel Men's Voice.*

---

[85]General Council minutes, 1957, p. 51.
[86]Interview, Andrew Nelli, November 9, 1967.
[87]General Council minutes, 1959, pp. 19-20.
[88]General Council minutes, 1961, p. 30.

Oral Roberts and Gordon Lindsay promoted the new organization in its formative stages.[89]

Originally designed as a means for stimulating fellowship among Pentecostal laymen, cutting across Pentecostal denominational lines, it began to change character by the late 1950's.[90] When non-Pentecostal people began to receive the experience the FGBMFI became a major promotional agency of Neo-Pentecostalism. The glamour and excitement of the conventions, around which the entire operation rotates, appealed to many Assemblies of God laymen for whom the more prosaic programs of local church activity seemed somewhat less attractive.[91] By the end of the decade it was clear that the FGBMFI was posing serious competition to the denominational Men's Fellowship enterprise.

Attempts were made to harmonize the efforts of the FGBMFI with Assemblies of God programs in 1957, but after an additional decade, no formal agreement had yet been reached.[92] Participation by Assemblies of God personnel has been mixed. The executive board of FGBMFI has more than 50 percent membership from the ranks of the Assemblies of God.[93] In various localities, there is strong support for the local organization by pastor and layman alike. In other places, the unfortunate image of the FGBMFI as a "lay church," pictured as arrogantly repudiating any counsel or support by established Pentecostal churches or ministers, has created severely strained relationships. Officially this latter image has been rejected by the leadership of the FGBMFI.[94]

The group has shown signs of vigorous growth. The principal mouthpiece of the organization, *Voice*, reached a circulation of 225,000 in 1969. More than 425 chapters exist locally. The Los Angeles headquarters staff consists of 37 persons.[95] In spite of this apparent growth, at least one well-

---

[89]Demos Shakarian, "How Our Fellowship Came Into Being," *Voice*, February, 1953, pp. 3-4.

[90]Interview, Anthony Calvanico, August 21, 1967.

[91]Hollenweger, *Handbuch*, Vol. VI, p. 642.

[92]General Council minutes, 1957, p. 49.

[93]Interview, Anthony Calvanico, August 21, 1967, and "EPA Membership Directory," 1969.

[94]*Ibid.*

[95]*Ibid.*

traveled observer has expressed the opinion that the movement crested in 1966. Since then he sees evidences that the initial enthusiasm, predicated on an extrachurch emphasis, has been losing its punch.[96]

CRITERIA FOR INDEPENDENT CORPORATIONS

A phenomenon of the post-World War II era was the establishment of a wide variety of independent corporations in which Assemblies of God ministers participated. Some of these organizations had missionary activity as their focus, some evangelism, but none came under the disciplines of the denomination. Although some of these corporations were managed well, others gained a reputation for mismanagement of funds, and some tended to compete with denominational programs.

Perhaps the event that moved the leadership of the Assemblies of God to action was receipt of a lengthy letter addressed to General Superintendent Ralph Riggs, written by District Superintendent W. T. Gaston of the Northern California-Nevada District, dated March 29, 1956. Its seven pages list the "unbearable abuses by full gospel evangelists" who seemed to be flourishing without restraint.[97] Included in the list of extravagant and unscrupulous methods employed by some of these religious hucksters was the drain of missionary offerings away from responsible groups. "Our missionaries have to beat the bushes to get back to the field and they must render a strict account for every thin dime, while we allow our churches to be 'cleaned out' periodically by men who are accountable to no one on earth or in heaven. All this, to my way of thinking, is unreasonable and immoral."[98] Because of this ringing challenge in part at least, the General Presbytery that year adopted a statement on ethical practices.[99] In 1960 this same body elaborated the position on fundraising articulated two years earlier.[100] The Executive Presbytery in 1961 urged the various districts to take disciplinary action against Assemblies of God ministers

---

[96]Interview, Andrew Nelli, November 9, 1967.
[97]Letter from W. T. Gaston to Ralph M. Riggs, March 29, 1956.
[98]Gaston letter to Riggs, March 29, 1956.
[99]General Presbytery minutes, 1956, p. 34.
[100]General Presbytery minutes, 1960, p. 39.

violating the standards spelled out by the General Presbytery, and appointed a committee to study the standards or criteria for judging the worthiness of independent corporations. The General Council later in the same year adopted a resolution favoring greater supervision of missionary projects being promoted by individual missionaries.[101]

The culmination of decisions by Executive and General Presbyteries and the General Council in session was the adoption of a document at Des Moines at the 1965 General Council. This was the revised "Statement of Criteria."[102] With this action, the Assemblies of God had taken a strong position on self-discipline. It did not, however, come without reverberations of dissent. Some felt that this was but a further step in the direction of centralized authority, with consequent loss of individual freedom. Nearly all felt, however, that the time for some controls over participation in independent operations was long overdue.

BEHAVIORAL STANDARDS

In the beginning of the Pentecostal Movement, a significant number of people either came from, or were strongly influenced by, the Holiness tradition. Moral rigorism was a pervasive characteristic of most Pentecostal groups. This was manifested in some localities by a rather rigid and extensive code of legalistic prohibitions.[103] But, everywhere, there was a marked degree of "separation from the world."

In more recent years the accessions to the Assemblies of God have been largely from beyond the Holiness sphere, with the result that the earlier homogeneity of outlook on "standards of holiness" began to be fragmented.[104] There was also an economic factor. With more money for fashionable clothing and participation in leisure-time recreation in the years after World War II, Assemblies of God people tended to lose their image of separateness from the prevailing norms of society.[105] Retired General Superintendent Ernest S. Wil-

---

[101]General Council minutes, 1961, pp. 54-55.

[102]General Council minutes, 1965, pp. 9, 15, 57-58.

[103]Eugene N. Hastie, *History of the West Central District Council of the Assemblies of God* (Fort Dodge, Iowa: Walterick Publishing Company, 1948), p. 74.

[104]Interview, J. Roswell Flower, June 26, 1967.

[105]Interview, Stanley Horton, June 22, 1967.

liams noted sadly that, as in similar revival movements, some have tended to emphasize the more superficial aspects of religion, giving priority to manifestations of exuberance rather than attention to the more internal matters of commitment and character, which has resulted in some Assemblies of God people developing an unstable pattern of behavior.[106] It is also quite likely that some have tended to overreact against all behavioral codes, considering them to be but legalistic, culturally-derived, and nonessential.

There does not seem to be any discernible regional pattern in the prevailing standards of conduct in the various districts. Gross has compiled extensive data from 36 of the 44 districts on the question of standards, and has concluded that there is no regional pattern.[107] However, he did note that the guidelines spelled out on the General Council level tended to be nonspecific and comprehensive, whereas the pronouncements of the District Councils tended to be more precise and, in half of the districts studied, more elaborate than the norms of the General Council.[108] The changes that have occurred in behavioral standards appear to be more a function of urbanization than of geographical distribution. Throughout the country, regardless of district, the larger metropolitan churches have adopted a much broader outlook on matters that to the smaller, rural, neighboring churches are still issues.

What has been the official reaction to this developing ambiguity on acceptable behavior in the denomination? As early as 1942 the General Presbytery took notice of the loosening of standards in the fellowship. In the "Quarterly Letter" of September, 1942, excerpts from the Presbyters' meeting were reported. There was included an exhortation for pastors to discourage the showing of moving pictures in the churches, to refrain from organizing church-league ball teams, to discourage mixed swimming.[109]

The problem of erosion of standards had become a suf-

---

[106]Interview, Ernest S. Williams, June 27, 1967.

[107]George Gross, "A Study of Norms of Conduct in the Assemblies of God" (unpublished M.A. thesis, Central Bible Institute, 1961), p. 60.

[108]*Ibid.*, pp. 53-55.

[109]"Quarterly Letter," September 21, 1942.

ficiently serious matter that in 1956 the District Superintendents gathered in Springfield for their annual seminar with this issue as the major item on their agenda. From this meeting came a declaration that was entitled, "A Call to Holiness," a statement endorsed by the entire body of superintendents. It included this significant paragraph:

> It has been our sad part to take note of a trend to worldliness and a declension from early spiritual principles in some quarters. We have been shocked and grieved by cases of immorality and sin in the lives of some. There is an ever-increasing problem of discipline in the churches and districts, and a rising tide of indifference to any standard of Christian living which may depart from the personal opinion or desire of the individual.[110]

As a direct result of this manifesto by the District Superintendents, the General Council the next year by resolution reaffirmed the denominational position on Worldliness, a bylaw statement couched in general language.[111]

As a symbolic action to establish a national example, a standard of behavior for employees at General Council headquarters was promulgated in 1959. It appealed to the workers to avoid questionable places of amusement, to pay their debts, to avoid careless living, not to indulge in gossip nor rumor-spreading, and specified standards of appropriate personal appearance.[112] Since that time there does not appear to have been any further attempts at particularizing and defining specific standards of acceptable conduct, appearance, and attitude on a national level.

Summary

The Assemblies of God has been remarkably free of theological dispute throughout its history. Most of the problems of a theological nature that the Assemblies of God has encountered in the years since World War II have been alien importations that have threatened the internal tranquility of the group. The most serious of these issues, the so-called "New Order of the Latter Rain," was but a fleeting episode.

---

[110] *The Pentecostal Evangel*, December 16, 1956, p. 2.
[111] General Council minutes, 1957, p. 53.
[112] "Quarterly Letter," June 12, 1959.

More complex have been the practical issues in the recent history of the Assemblies of God. The emergence of indepen-ent, somewhat predatory, movements has forced the denomination to risk a degree of centralization of authority in an effort to shore up its discipline around the fringes. Interwoven in this has been the question of the role of the laity in the fellowship. Standards of holiness have been a vexing problem to some, but in the larger urban centers this has apparently ceased to be a major contention.

14

Culture: The Church and Social Change

Changes in Worship Practices—Developments in Education—Social Concern—Summary

Interaction with contemporary American society and maturation within the denomination have produced several significant changes in certain aspects of the character of the Assemblies of God. Much of this development has occurred since the entry of the United States into World War II. Three features of church life bear examination as evidences of changing social outlook. Worship, education, and concern with social issues will serve to illustrate the nature of cultural change occurring in the denomination since 1941.

Changes in Worship Practices

Prior to World War II, Assemblies of God church services could be readily identified in almost any locale. There were certain distinguishing characteristics of Pentecostal worship that seemed to be a fairly uniform pattern until 1940.[1] Since then, the basic pattern has been perpetuated, but wide variations from the previous norm have tended to destroy the possibility of creating a stereotyped image. This is true of the form and frequency of services, of the music and architecture.

Participation was a key word in Pentecostal worship from earliest days. Services were informal. The lack of structure intended to permit maximum participation of the congregation through testimony, song, exhortation, or manifesta-

[1]Kelsey, *op. cit.*, p. 82.

tions of the Spirit. The congregations were seldom large, and each attendant was made to feel a part of the service. Prayer was a collective activity, with combined voices rising in a chorus. Not only were individual worship services arranged for maximum involvement, but the schedule of services through the week suggested that for many the church was the center of social life. Meetings were scheduled morning and evening on Sunday, with the morning service preceded by a Sunday school hour for young and old alike. Frequently the hour prior to the evening service was employed for a youth service. During the week at least one service was scheduled, and often two—one for Bible study, the other for prayer. And, it was common custom for various evangelistic enterprises to be scheduled either on Sunday afternoon or on nonchurch nights through the week, such as street meetings, jail services, and house-to-house visitation. In later years the addition of special-interest groups, particularly the Women's Missionary Council, provided an increased means of furnishing church-related activity for the entire family. Gradually diminishing in appeal, but a vital force in the earlier years, was the opportunity for sectional rallies and fellowship meetings where saints from various nearby communities joined together in enthusiastic worship. Keene observed one church in the 1930's that had 28 public meetings scheduled each week.[2] Summer camp meetings were an important annual family event.

Enthusiasm was another important characteristic of earlier Pentecostal worship. Emotion was relatively more important than liturgy. Little emphasis was laid on the sacramental elements of religion. Church membership was stressed far less than the urgency of up-to-date vital and personal experience. The rites of believer's baptism and the Lord's Supper, called ordinances rather than sacraments, were practiced with regularity. These were stressed as memorials, in the Zwinglian tradition. A usual custom was monthly or quarterly observance of the Lord's Supper. The emotional content of the Pentecostal worship resulted in adverse pub-

[2]Gertrude B. Keene, "Distinctive Social Values of the Pentecostal Churches: A Sociological Field Study" (unpublished M.A. thesis, University of Southern California, 1938), p. 32.

lic relations, producing the pejorative reputation as "holy rollers," but was nontheless a genuine expression of an inner reality for many. Spiritual dynamic inspired evangelistic zeal uncommon for the churches in the era of the Great Depression.

This enthusiastic spirit found expression in generosity, as well. Keene observed of several Los Angeles congregations, some of them Assemblies of God, "The congregations visited usually appear to be composed of persons who do not receive incomes beyond two thousand annually, because most of the people wear inexpensive but presentable clothing, and use inexpensive cars. Even so, the collection looks much better than any loose collection in other churches."[3]

There was a strong emphasis on the supernatural in Pentecostal churches from the beginning. Faith was preached vigorously, faith for daily needs, physical healing, and for spiritual welfare. Jesus was preached as the living, resurrected Christ, and heaven and hell were real. No question was raised about the inspiration of the Bible; too many had experienced the reality of its message. The Pentecostals were incurable optimists, for they believed that the Holy Spirit had been given them to minister with effectiveness to a world they considered to be desperately in need. They had found the solution to this world's ills.

Variations from this typical "old-time Pentecost" theme gradually crept into the picture, but with acceleration after our entry into the war. As late as 1952 the following report was still somewhat typical. Howard submitted a questionnaire to members of a Midwestern Assemblies of God congregation, receiving 52 responses.

> They were unanimous in saying that they had been converted. Everyone said that they prayed daily, almost twenty-five percent praying more than thirty minutes a day. All claimed that prayer changes things. About seventy percent read the Bible daily. Forty-four out of fifty-two tithe or give ten percent of their income to gospel and charitable purposes. The attendance record was astonishing. The total group that answered averaged approximately forty-six Sundays out of the year at Sunday school and Sunday morning

---

[3]Keene, *op. cit.*, p. 30.

church service, about forty-five Sunday evening services during the year, and thirty-seven midweek prayer meetings.[4]

A most significant change that has altered the worship picture quite generally is the decline of the Sunday night evangelistic service. An inversion in the character of the Sunday night and Sunday morning services began to occur. No longer were there more sinners at the Sunday night service who were candidates for evangelistic appeals—they came on Sunday morning, if at all. This fact, together with the need to schedule meetings around the farm chore routines being no longer necessary for the urbanized congregations of recent years, led to a shift in the time of the evening service to an earlier hour. The result has been, in effect, an evening vesper hour for the saints, complete with extended time of prayer following the service around the altar, but with fewer sinners being converted during the traditional Sunday night hour.

Another shift that has been evident has been the limiting of the activities in the church to fewer nights during the week. Common in recent years has been the Wednesday "family night," when activities for various age-levels are offered at the same hour, with the traditional midweek prayer meeting being the adult age-level activity for the evening.

The fellowship meetings and sectional rallies that had meant so much to isolated churches in earlier years have steadily lost their appeal to the urban churchgoers who look increasingly elsewhere for social concourse.[5] The traditional "revival meeting," or protracted evangelistic services, previously lasted at least two weeks, with services scheduled every night. The two-week meetings are still a semiannual event in most church calendars, but it is more and more frequent for one or more week-nights being stricken for families to stay home. Attendance at week-night events has continued to decline, so much so that some churches have resorted to scheduling evangelistic meetings

---

[4]Ivan Howard, "A Review of the Assemblies of God" (unpublished manuscript, 1952), p. 24.

[5]Interview, J. Roswell Flower, June 26, 1967.

over a long weekend, eliminating the midweek services from such special gatherings altogether.

The spontaneity of worship is not as obvious in many congregations as it once was. As the churches have become larger and more urbane, there has been increased demand for a professional clergy, a robed choir, and sophistication in the sanctuary. This trend toward formalism has had a mixed response. Some view with anxiety the apparent loss of fervor; others are relieved to see reverence and content displace noise and unintelligibility. Still others see values in both the "old-time Pentecost" and in the increased refinement in expression of corporate worship, preferring a "middle-of-the-road" journey.[6] It appears that at least three general categories of Assemblies of God worship are to be found in most parts of the country in recent years: one attempting to perpetuate the image of unrestrained, exuberant worship; one reacting violently with a resultant formalism that has little typically Pentecostal remaining; and the bulk of the churches lying somewhere in between, attempting to maintain a balance between freedom and discipline in worship.

Giving has continued to be relatively generous, although the large increases in missionary giving, for example, may be partially offset by the increased ability of the people to give. It may be that giving is a way of vicarious participation appealing to many, for it does not seem to be matched by the same degree of personal involvement. There is far less spontaneous participation in extrachurch evangelism such as personal witnessing and conducting of informal street services or jail services. Such activities have moved from a spontaneous level to a programmed level, and even then many congregations have largely reduced their religious activity to attendance at services and activities within the church building.[7] The paid clergy engage in much of the outreach that is accomplished in such churches. Increased respectability in the community has not always been matched by increased vitality and growth.

---

[6]Interview, James Hamill, November 10, 1967.

[7]Interview, Melvin Hodges, September 17, 1967.

An awareness of the unfavorable image that had been generated regarding much Assemblies of God worship appears in an article in *The Pentecostal Evangel* in 1945. "The Pentecostal movement is often criticized for displaying too much of the emotional. There is a sense in which there is some fairness in this criticism," Briggs said.[8] He appealed for a restraint on emotional worship so that it would reflect genuine spirituality and not mere human enthusiasm. Occasionally thereafter this type of appeal for correction in worship appears.[9] Sometime during the postwar period the emphasis in many churches shifted from devices to stir the emotions to employment of means to cause the people to consider, to reflect.[10]

In spite of the appearance of more formal patterns in the worship service in many of the churches, and an obvious decline in the general level of congregational participation and fervor, "it is safe to say that the leadership of the Holy Spirit is assumed as an a priori fact in the act of worship of the Assemblies of God Church."[11] Although the biennial denominational conventions appear to have become more and more promotional in character and opportunities for social interaction rather than occasions for spiritual enrichment, as late as 1965 this significant notice appeared in the General Secretary's minutes: "A great altar service followed the preaching of the Word. About 75 persons sought Christ for salvation and a number were filled with the Holy Spirit."[12]

There seems to be evidence that following the spectacular success in gathering converts during the Great Depression, there was a tendency to displace the spontaneity, the inner reality, that dominated the 1930's with "techniques," with gimmicks.[13] After a generation has passed, a period in which proliferation of special programs has replaced the earlier simplicity, there seems to be a growing quest for spiritual

[8]Dingman Briggs, *The Pentecostal Evangel,* December 1, 1945, pp. 2-3.

[9]Lloyd Christiansen, "A Plea for Reverence," *The Pentecostal Evangel,* November 30, 1952, pp. 3, 21.

[10]Kelsey, *op. cit.*, pp. 93-94.

[11]Masserano, *op. cit.*, p. 74.

[12]General Council minutes, 1965, p. 53.

[13]Interview, J. R. Ashcroft, September 20, 1967.

renewal on all levels of the fellowship. The collective denominational soul-searching expressed by the Committee on Advance does seem to have a grass roots counterpart. Pastors, youth leaders, individuals in various parts of the land are thirsting for the springs to flow again.[14]

MUSIC

The earliest musical expressions in Pentecostalism were quite unusual. Congregational singing was not directed by a specially designated person. Anyone might start a song, with others joining in. Frequently there was no piano or organ. Special songs might be sung by whoever wished, but there was little rehearsal. The emphasis was on spontaneity, on following the momentary leading of the Holy Spirit.[15]

Quite early, however, a more formalized pattern developed. Songbooks of an inexpensive, paperback sort were produced even before the organization of the Assemblies of God by R. E. Winsett, possibly the first Pentecostal music publisher.[16] Much of the music from the earliest days was startling to the religious public. The distinctions between the sacred and the worldly had been fairly well-defined popularly. As an expression of their newfound joy, the Pentecostals were among the first to engage "worldly" rhythm as a medium in religious music. "The fast singing style was really another of God's safety valves in our work, as well as a chance to shout His praises."[17]

In 1930 the Assemblies of God published its first songbook, *Spiritual Songs*. Compiled by Arthur Graves, it brought into one paperback volume the fruit of the early years of the Pentecostal revival, featuring testimonies of salvation and deliverance, healing, the Pentecostal experience, and a joyful expectation of the soon return of Jesus.[18] Notably missing from this collection were the familiar Protestant hymns. A second book in the series, this time offered in a hardback edition, was *Songs of Praise*, published in 1935.

---

[14]Interview, Russell Cox, September 27, 1967.

[15]Kendrick, *op. cit.*, p. 71.

[16]Goss, *op cit.*, p. 129.

[17]*Ibid.*

[18]Edwin Anderson, "Music in the Assemblies of God Tradition," *Church Music in Dimension*, II (Second issue, 1966), p. 4.

Much like the earlier book, but somewhat larger, it served as the basic tool for congregational singing for some years. An interesting feature of these books was the use of many Holiness songs that had originally been written to describe the experience of sanctification. In spite of the theological problems this raised, few bothered to consider the implications of the lyrics, content to sing joyfully of the working of the Holy Spirit, however it was defined.

In 1948 another in the original series was produced, this one called *Assembly Songs.* There was really not much difference in the content of the newer book. More than a quarter-million copies of this volume were sold before a major revision was made in 1957.[19] In that year, the newly created Music Division, headed by Edwin Anderson, came out with a songbook entitled *Melodies of Praise.* This new book had essentially the same gospel song content, plus an extensive section of selections suitable for vocal solos and ensembles.[20] An additional feature was the availability of an orchestration manual for many of the songs in the book. This was a valuable aid, for many churches from early years had small bands or orchestras to assist in the worship services.[21]

The most recent development has been the preparation of *Hymns of Glorious Praise,* the first true hymnal to be published by the denomination. While the earlier books, going back to those in use in 1941, had about 310 songs, the new one contains more than 500 hymns. Its chief difference from previous books is the addition of a number of traditional Protestant hymns, and the deletion of many of the "special" songs which are not suited to congregational singing.[22]

There are apparently three strands of musical programming evident in the Assemblies of God today. The central

[19]Statistics supplied by the Merchandising Division, Gospel Publishing House.

[20]Interview, Cyril McLellan, April 8, 1968.

[21]Masserano, *op. cit.,* pp. 66-67. The results of his survey based on 100 questionnaires returned from Assemblies of God pastors, chiefly in the eastern states, revealed that 74 percent regularly use a choir; 93 percent, an organ; 100, a piano; 18, guitar; 35, accordion; 41, brass; 30 percent, woodwinds; and 34 percent regularly use strings.

[22]Interview, Cyril McLellan, April 8, 1968.

strand perpetuates the gospel song emphasis prominent since earlier days. "Revivaltime," the national denominational radio broadcast, reflects this posture, but because of its exclusively evangelistic purpose does not make use of any hymns, while most of the churches include some. To one side of this pattern is the more marked adaptation of "jazzy" type music, with little to distinguish it from its secular counterpart but some of the lyrics. On the other side of the central mean is the attempt at sophistication in music, complete with formally robed choirs and anthems.[23] In effect there is a much wider cultural stream represented by Assemblies of God music than there was at the outset of World War II.

Of the strands enumerated, there has been self-consciousness about the "jazzy" type. An article appearing in 1956 in *The Pentecostal Evangel* seems to reflect the feeling of many in the denomination. It said, "Many are concerned about a trend which has been noticed in some of our Pentecostal churches: a lightness and irreverence in our music which I feel is very unbecoming to deep spirituality. . . ."[24] Most of the larger churches are moving rapidly in the direction of greater sophistication in their music. The appearance of a hymnal for the first time seems to be in harmony with this trend.

ARCHITECTURE

The architecture in the Assemblies of God reflects its history and culture. The houses of worship in earliest years were often quite temporary, since permanence was not paramount with many of the pioneer evangelists. Little property at all was actually owned; halls were rented or tents were pitched.[25] The construction of the 1920's was chiefly of a simple frame tabernacle type. It was quite common then, and later, during the Great Depression, to purchase abandoned church buildings left by the older denominations.[26] During the 1930's and into the 1940's there was an evolution in building, with more contemporary architecture—but not

[23] *Ibid.*
[24] R. A. Brown, "Jazz at Church," *The Pentecostal Evangel,* March 4, 1956, p. 29.
[25] Hastie, *op. cit.,* pp. 123-24.
[26] Interview, E. E. Krogstad, October 11, 1967.

churchly—beginning to displace the rudest boxlike structures.

The real change in architecture came in the postwar years. This was the real watershed.[27] It was a period in which the denomination seemed to become enamored with concreteness, with structure and statistics, rather than ideology. A striking evidence of this is symbolized by the cover photographs of *The Pentecostal Evangel.* On February 4, 1950, the first photograph to feature a new church building appeared. It was of block construction. In 1964 this cover-photo feature emphasizing new buildings faded out. To be sure, there continued to be photograph-stories of new edifices on the inside pages, but the emphasis had obviously subsided by then.

An interesting development in church construction in the Assemblies of God has been the erection of special-purpose buildings to supplement the worship hall. The first such evidence in *The Pentecostal Evangel* of this trend came in 1955, although it is certain that such educational units were being built earlier.[28] It does seem to coincide with the era of proliferation of services charactering the denomination in the early 1950's.

What has motivated the changes in style in the denomination? Why is there currently a decided trend toward churchly buildings? "I would conclude that the changes in Assembly of God architecture are more sociological than theological with the plan, function and structure being based more on the program of the church operation rather than the theology involved," says the chairman of the Home Missions Church Building Committee who has served for many years.[29]

Where have the new buildings been located? In earlier years the urban churches were situated in low-income districts for the most part. In the middle 1940's Oliver noted that 11 out of 18 Assemblies of God congregations in the Detroit metropolitan area were located in the two lowest ecological districts.[30] This picture has been altered quite

[27]Letter from Joseph Colombo, A.I.A., October 5, 1967.

[28]*The Pentecostal Evangel,* July 17, 1955, p. 13.

[29]Letter from Joseph Colombo, A.I.A., October 5, 1967.

[30]Oliver, *op. cit.,* p. 248.

dramatically. The Assemblies of God congregations have been engaged in a persistent effort to relocate in suburbia since World War II.

Developments in Education

No issue has more clearly reflected the sociological changes within the Assemblies of God than the evolution in the training of the denomination's youth. The changing character of the Bible institutes, the development of general educational institutions, and the laying of groundwork in anticipation of a school of graduate theological training furnish important foci for discussion.

THE BIBLE SCHOOLS

At the first General Council in April, 1914, the assembled brethren acknowledged the existence of two privately owned, rather informal, schools, one a children's day school, the other a school for the training of gospel workers.[31] Concern for the preparation of Pentecostal ministers was evident from the beginning, although the General Council did not take steps to establish its own institution until 1920.[32] The ill-fated Midwest Bible School in Auburn, Nebraska, which lasted but a single year, was superseded by a more enduring effort in 1922, Central Bible Institute of Springfield, Missouri.[33] D. W. Kerr, who had been instrumental in establishing two West Coast schools, was invited to Springfield to become the first principal of Central Bible Institute.[34] To achieve the goal of producing graduates who would have the ability to pioneer new churches and who would have a passionate zeal, the three-year Bible institute pattern already successfully developed by D. L. Moody and A. B. Simpson was readily adopted. The school established a three-year program featuring Bible content as the heart of the curriculum, with a strong extracurricular emphasis on practical field work. The ethos of the school was designed to be an intense spiritual atmosphere, an atmosphere created by scheduling numerous prayer meetings and worship services throughout the week. The center of gravity was spir-

[31] General Council minutes, 1914, p. 7.
[32] General Council minutes, 1920, p. 43.
[33] Harrison, *op. cit.*, p. 173.
[34] *Ibid.*

itual development rather than academic excellence. Few of the teachers, even as late as World War II, were college graduates themselves.[35] The average post-high school education of the faculty in the 1943-44 school year was 3.9 years.[36]

Numerous schools, usually started by a local church, came and went in the years before World War II, all of them designed for the training of Christian workers. Collins has traced the history of 15 Bible schools which ceased to exist or merged with other schools before 1941.[37] Another seven that were in existence in 1941 have closed down or have merged.[38] Three schools that were launched after 1941 have not survived. Only one school attempted since 1941, Evangel College, still exists. Eight Bible schools in existence in 1941 have survived. Of the 12 schools operating in 1941, all were three-year Bible institutes with the exception of one. Southern California Bible College in 1949 had become the first Assemblies of God school to offer a four-year degree, a B.A. in Bible.[39]

The value of the Bible institutes to the Assemblies of God has been impressive. A report prepared by Ralph M. Riggs disclosed that by 1949, 36 percent of all ordained ministers and 74 percent of all missionaries in the Assemblies of God had been trained in the Bible schools, and during the following four-year period, the percentages had leaped to 60 percent for ordained ministers and 93 percent for missionaries.[40] In 1966, Masserano's survey of Assemblies of God ministers in the East tended to support this marked influence of the Bible institute movement on the denomination. His study showed that 49 percent were Bible school graduates, with another 21 percent obtaining college or seminary degrees.[41] Presumably a large proportion of the latter were also graduates of a Bible school.

Several important trends have developed within the

---

[35]"Central Bible Institute Catalog," 1940, 1941.

[36]Thomas Henstock, "A History and Interpretation of the Curriculum of Central Bible Institute" (unpublished M.A. thesis, Central Bible Institute, 1963), p. 21.

[37]Collins, *op. cit.*, pp. 31-36.

[38]*Ibid.*

[39]Harrison, *op. cit.*, p. 197.

[40]General Council reports, 1953, p. 34.

[41]Masserano, *op. cit.*, p. 83.

Bible institute program in the Assemblies of God. Even before World War II the denomination was putting pressure on the privately owned schools to relinquish control to district councils. This was only gradually achieved. The creation of a Department of Home Missions and Education in 1937 provided opportunity to establish standards for endorsement. One feature of such denominational endorsement that was insisted on was surrender of private ownership. In 1940, Southern California Bible College was made a district school.[42] That same year Southwestern Bible Institute was accorded district control.[43] The last school (of those surviving to the present) to pass from private ownership was Glad Tidings Bible Institute. In 1947, GTBI (now known as Bethany Bible College) became an operation of the Northern California-Nevada District Council.[44]

Another important trend has been the regionalization of the schools. Competition and soaring costs forced the weaker schools to close their doors. Only Central Bible College and Evangel College, both located in Springfield, Missouri, have been nationally sponsored schools. The other schools either started as district enterprises or passed into the control of various district councils. Economic pressures forced the schools to seek a wider base of support during World War II. In 1942 the school now known as South-Eastern Bible College became the responsibility of several districts in the southeastern part of the country, a successful venture followed by other schools in the following years.[45] In 1951 the school located in the state of Washington was adopted by the Montana District, in addition to the mother district, the Northwest District. In 1957, the Southern Idaho District Council joined in the support of that school, now located at Kirkland, Washington, and known as Northwest College of the Assemblies of God.[46] In the state of Texas, Southwestern Bible Institute gained the support of seven districts in the south central region of the country.[47] In 1962

[42]"Southern California College Catalog, 1967-1968," p. 3.
[43]Collins, *op. cit.*, p. 129.
[44]"Bethany Bible College Bulletin, 1967-1968," p. 7.
[45]Collins, *op. cit.*, p. 124.
[46]"Northwest College of the Assemblies of God, 1966-1968 Catalog," p. 3.
[47]"Southwestern Assemblies of God College, Bulletin 1967-1968," p. 14.

both North Central Bible College and Northeast Bible Institute became regionally controlled schools. Only Bethany Bible College in Santa Cruz, California, and Southern California College in Costa Mesa remain as district-sponsored schools.

The national map now discloses three schools on the West Coast: Northwest Assemblies of God college featuring a junior college program, Bethany Bible College maintaining the traditional emphasis of the Bible institute, and Southern California College with a standard four-year liberal arts offering. The central part of the country has four schools. In the upper-Midwest region is North Central Bible College at Minneapolis. Farther south, in Springfield, Missouri, are the two schools, Central Bible College and Evangel College, the former maintaining the traditional Bible institute emphasis, the latter featuring liberal arts. Farther to the south is Southwestern Assemblies of God College at Waxahachie, Texas, combining two programs under one roof, a junior college and a traditional Bible college program. In the East are two schools. In Green Lane, Pennsylvania, is Northeast Bible Institute, and at Lakeland, Florida, is South-Eastern Bible College.

Competition among the schools has generally been resolved along regional boundary lines, in harmony with guidelines established in 1958 by the Committee on Education.[48] The two nationally sponsored schools, Central Bible College and Evangel College have no regional limitations, but neither have they regional support. An unresolved issue lingering yet is the relationship of the denominationally sponsored schools to the regionally and district sponsored schools.

World War II disclosed the need for accreditation of Bible institutes in the evangelical world, for it was apparent that ministry in the chaplaincy was denied many for this reason. The result was the establishment in 1947 of the Accrediting Association of Bible Institutes and Bible Colleges (now known as AABC).[49] Immediately following this

---

[48]Committee of Education minutes, October 28-29, 1958.
[49]See Chapter 9 for the origins of AABC.

development, the various Assemblies of God schools were confronted with a decision: to seek accreditation or not to seek accreditation. Central Bible Institute, the lone General Council-sponsored school, became the focal point of contention over this issue. In the General Presbytery meeting of 1948, a letter from one of the district councils in the East was read, protesting the entry of CBI into the AABC. Intense debate followed, but no action was taken.[50] The General Council in 1949 was likewise marked by sharp contention, for some felt that to submit CBI to the scrutiny and judgment of non-Pentecostals would jeopardize the Pentecostal freedom that had been a special heritage of the movement. However, the resolution was adopted, and CBI, along with other schools in the fellowship, immediately applied for accreditation.[51] By 1951 all the schools were accredited on either the collegiate or institute level, fully or provisionally.[52]

An immediate result of the application of the schools for recognition in the AABC was a rapid elevation of the academic standards of the schools. By 1969 the average number of post-high school years of education for the faculties of the nine colleges had climbed to 6.63, a far cry from the World War II days when few of the teachers had college degrees.[53]

The demand for improved training in the schools was accelerated by the flood of returning servicemen at the end of World War II. Thirty-three percent of the entire Assemblies of God student enrollment in the 1948-49 school year were GI's. Since all the schools were geared directly toward the preparation of church workers, the Assemblies of God was training 7.5 percent of all United States veterans receiving theological training, but its denominational membership was only one-third of 1 percent of the national total.[54]

Southern California Bible College had been offering

[50]General Presbytery minutes, 1948, p. 3.
[51]"Quarterly Letter," October 1, 1949.
[52]Kendrick, *op. cit.*, p. 135.
[53]"Annual Report: Assemblies of God Department of Education, October, 1969."
[54]General Council reports, 1949, p. 19.

baccalaureate degrees in Bible since 1939, but after the war, several other schools took steps to increase their programs from three to four years, as well. In 1946, Southwestern Bible Institute added a fourth year.[55] The next year Northwest Bible Institute (now Northwest College of the Assemblies of God) offered a four-year baccalaureate degree in Bible.[56] In 1947 the General Council authorized Central Bible Institute to add a fourth year, and a fifth, if desired.[57] By 1967 all nine colleges in the Assemblies of God were offering baccalaureate degrees. It is significant that whereas in 1941 only one school was titled "college," in 1970 only one school still retained the title "institute."

The addition of a fourth year to the traditional three-year program of the Bible institute was the first major step in the introduction of general education into the curricula of Assemblies of God education. To meet requirements for issuing baccalaureate degrees the Bible courses were augmented by additional courses in the humanities and sciences. A further step toward furnishing general education to the youth of the denomination was the introduction of junior college programs. In 1944, Southwestern Bible Institute in Texas initiated the first such two-year general education program as an option available to students at the Bible institute.[58] In 1955, Northwest Bible Institute (Northwest College of the Assemblies of God) offered a similar program.[59]

In addition to the two schools that offer junior college work in the Bible college environment, several other Bible colleges have engaged in modifications of their traditional programs to accommodate to the growing pressures of contemporary culture. Southern California Bible College evolved into a liberal arts college over a period of several years. In 1950 the school's offerings were divided into two divisions, the division of arts and sciences being separated from the college of Bible. President Harrison explained the

---

[55]Harrison, *op. cit.*, p. 199.

[56]*Ibid.*, p. 198.

[57]General Council minutes, 1947, p. 24.

[58]Harrison, *op. cit.*, p. 199.

[59]"Northwest College of the Assemblies of God, 1966-1968 Catalog," p. 3.

reason for the change by pointing out that half of the students in Assemblies of God schools were not preparing for the ministry and needed practical equipment for secular vocations.[60] With this move, SCBC became the first four-year liberal arts school in the denomination. On March 5, 1959, the Southern California District Council in session at Wilmington voted to drop "Bible" from the name of the school, symbolizing the evolution of the college from its Bible institute origins to its status as a senior liberal arts college.[61] It gradually dropped out of contact with the AABC and in 1964 became the first school in the Assemblies of God to gain full regional accreditation.[62]

Bethany Bible College has sought to broaden its scope of offerings. It has enjoyed AABC accreditation for years, but in 1966 it received a special accreditation with the Western Regional Accrediting Association on the basis of its general education content, as a private professional school.[63] It is a good example of the Bible college under great economic and social pressure from parents and students to furnish more general education, but within a Bible-oriented context. The need to furnish the kind of functional training that would allow graduates to enter business or public school teaching has been building since World War II.[64] The latest accommodation to the pressure for functional training has occurred at South-Eastern Bible College. In the fall of 1967 an education major was introduced into the curriculum, complete with public school student-teaching internship, and state board certification. About 40 percent of the enrollment of the college is in the education program.[65]

One trend that appears to have reached a plateau is the ratio of students enrolled in liberal arts programs compared with those enrolled in theological programs in As-

---

[60]*The Pentecostal Evangel*, May 6, 1950, p. 7.

[61]*Educator*, May-June, 1959, p. 3.

[62]"Southern California College Catalog, 1967-1968," p. 3.

[63]*The Pentecostal Evangel*, March 13, 1966, p. 23.

[64]Richard D. Strahan, "A Study to Introduce Curriculum Approaches and Student Personnel Services for Evangel College" (unpublished Ed.D. dissertation, University of Houston, 1955), pp. 87-88.

[65]Letter from Arthur H. Graves, December 22, 1967.

semblies of God schools. The first year that the Department of Education prepared such statistics, 1956, the ratio was 13.9 percent in liberal arts compared with 86.1 percent in theology. A fairly steady shift developed in the succeeding decade, reaching an extremity in 1965. In that year the liberal arts students accounted for 40.8 percent of the total; theology students only 59.2 percent. But in 1966 the trend began to reverse, with theology students accounting for 61.8 percent, in 1967, 63.0 percent, and in 1968, 63.1 percent.[66] It is interesting that this coincides with the first general public sounding of alarm at the threat of a ministerial shortage, articulated by General Superintendent Zimmerman at the 1965 Des Moines General Council.[67]

Since 1941 the number of institutions has declined from 12 to 9, but the combined enrollment has increased greatly. In 1941 there were 1,754 students enrolled at the schools; all were studying for church vocations.[68] In the fall of 1969, there were 5,288 enrolled in both liberal arts and theology.[69] The decline in number of institutions and the accommodations to general education are indices of economic and social pressure within the denomination.

The appreciation of a better quality of training, both in the theological and general education areas, seems to stem largely from the growing affluence and social consciousness of the rank and file within the denomination. The desire of parents, themselves largely without much formal academic preparation, for something better for their children seems to be reflected in Strahan's inventory of 511 Bible school freshmen in the school year of 1954-1955. The typical student he described as coming from the "upper-lower" class of American society. His father was a skilled workman, a farmer, or was engaged in a service-type occupation, with an income annually of about $4,000 per year. Both his father and mother failed to finish high school. Of the students 72.2 percent indicated that they had already chosen

[66]"Annual Report: Assemblies of God Department of Education, October, 1969."

[67]Thomas F. Zimmerman, "Where the Spirit Leads," *The Pentecostal Evangel*, October 10, 1965, pp. 8-9.

[68]General Council minutes, 1941, p. 74.

[69]"Annual Report: Assemblies of God Department of Education, October, 1969."

a church-related profession, but Strahan concluded that one-third of the students he checked were educational misfits as far as vocational plans were concerned.[70]

Although there has been a strong shift in popular attitude toward type and quality of education desired for their children since World War II, the parents do not seem to be matching such concern with financial investment. For whatever reasons, the general distribution of gifts to the denomination has remained fairly constant for a number of years, gifts to educational enterprises constituting but a very small portion of the total receipts recorded.[71] In just the last year, however, there was a sizable jump in giving to education in the Assemblies of God, with an increase of 76.8 percent reported for 1969, according to Raymond Hudson, secretary of the denomination's stewardship division.[72] The denomination reported about $15 million received for its various enterprises, with more than 50 percent of this going directly to world missions. The nine schools reported total gifts of $784,181 for the 1966-67 school year.[73] The main theological training institution, Central Bible College, although sponsored by the denomination, is expected to live within its income, and receives no regular subsidy. In the 1968-69 school year, CBC operated on a budget that depended on student fees and auxiliaries for 98.3 percent of the total; only 1.7 percent coming from endowments and gifts.[74]

EVANGEL COLLEGE

While the district and regional schools were grappling with the problems of education in the post-World War II era, the denomination as a whole was confronted with the challenge, as well. Should the Assemblies of God enter the field of general education on a national scale? Few issues have been as controversial and persistent as this.

As early as 1929 the General Council Committee on Bible Schools recommended exploration of the feasibility

---

[70]Strahan, *op. cit.*, pp. 91-92, 131.

[71]Interview, M. B. Netzel, September 21, 1967.

[72]Public Relations Office news release, April 10, 1970.

[73]"Annual Report: Assemblies of God Department of Education, October, 1967."

[74]"The President's Report," 1969.

of establishing "academic schools of our faith in different parts of our country to provide education without contamination of worldy and antichristian influences."[75] Without question the principal motivation behind the desire for the creation of such a school has been the conservation of the youth of the denomination, and directly related to this, the concern for the preservaton of the Assemblies of God as an institution.[76]

At the 1935 General Council a report of the Educational Committee was adopted, which endorsed a thorough survey of the schools already in existence, and an appraisal of the future needs of the fellowship, including a study of the need for a "literary institution."[77] The committee reported back to the 1937 General Council, and out of that report the recommendation for the establishment of a Department of Education was implemented.[78] The war intervened before further significant action could be taken.

During World War II the shift in denominational attitude toward military service resulted in large numbers of Assemblies of God men participating in the war, some of whom aspired to service as military chaplains. Many found to their dismay that their unaccredited diplomas from Assemblies of God Bible schools denied them this avenue of ministry. Executives in Springfield felt growing pressure from servicemen who were disappointed by the educational deficiencies of the schools.[79]

Ralph M. Riggs, Secretary of Education, called together representatives from the various schools at Columbus, Ohio, in April, 1944, in connection with the annual meeting of the National Association of Evangelicals. These men expressed themselves as being in favor of the establishment of a denominationally sponsored liberal arts college.[80] During the following Christmas holidays representatives from the Bible schools met with the Executive Presbytery, and out

[75]General Council minutes, 1929, p. 83.

[76]Donald F. Johns, "A Philosophy of Religious Education for the Assemblies of God" (unpublished Ph.D. dissertation, New York University, 1962), p. 59.

[77]General Council minutes, 1935, pp. 9-11.

[78]General Council minutes, 1937, pp. 97-98.

[79]"Quarterly Letter," January 24, 1944.

[80]General Presbytery minutes, 1944, p. 8.

of that meeting came a favorable statement respecting a liberal arts college. In the summer of 1945 the General Council Presbytery added its assent to the proposal, and a positive report was presented to the General Council that year.[81] No action was taken.

It was not until 1947 that a formal resolution calling for the creation of a liberal arts college was presented to the General Council. That was the Council memorable for its reactionary spirit. The appeal was decisively defeated. The mood in 1953 was ultraprogressive. When the proposal came to the floor that year, it was adopted at last.[82] Already there were vigorous general education programs advancing in several of the regional and district schools. The reluctance of the constituency of the General Council sessions to adopt such a program quickly reveals something of the anxiety about what long-range impact such a move might produce in the fellowship. Let it be remembered that few of the ministers had themselves experienced liberal arts education.

A committee of 35 began immediate plans for bringing the college into being. A board of directors, consisting of 15 ordained ministers and nine laymen, was selected, a constitution was adopted, and a president named.[83] Charles Scott was selected to serve as chairman of the board, and Klaude Kendrick was invited to be the president. By September, 1955, Evangel College opened its doors for its first term.

In the early stages of development two decisions were made that were to have an important bearing on the subsequent history of the school. To avoid competition with the existing Bible schools, the liberal arts college was not to offer a major in Bible or religion. Southern California Bible College offered its campus as a possible location for the proposed national liberal arts school, but negotiations broke down when it became apparent that the site would be acceptable only if the college agreed to drop its Bible major. The anomaly of an Assemblies of God school not having a

[81]General Council minutes, 1945, p. 76.
[82]General Council minutes, 1953, pp. 30-31.
[83]*The Pentecostal Evangel*, June 27, 1954, p. 10.

strong Biblical program continued to be a source of perplexity within the fellowship for years, but was happily resolved in 1969 with the strengthening of Bible offerings in the curriculum.

Another decision of considerable importance was the locating of the school in Springfield. The million-dollar facilities of O'Reilly General Hospital, a wartime institution no longer needed by the government, were made available to the Assemblies of God for one dollar. Sixty-eight buildings on 59 acres looked like an answer to prayer.[84] However, this put into close proximity two schools, for Central Bible Institute was situated in the same city. Although there has been a high degree of harmony between the two schools through the years, their close situation has tended to create an artificial polarization, each school feeling the need to justify its distinctive character. In some respects it has created the impression of a dual system of values, one for the laity, one for the clergy. In 1958, J. Robert Ashcroft, then Secretary of Education, was invited to become president of both schools.[85] The merging of some features of administrative operation was designed to prevent unnecessary duplication of effort and to prevent petty antagonisms between the two institutions from developing. After five years of joint administration, the union was dissolved. It appeared that the operation of the two campuses had become too large for one administration to handle effectively. Ashcroft stayed on to assume the presidency of Evangel College, and Philip Crouch, a Central Bible Institute faculty member, was chosen to assume the presidency of that school.[86] Both Evangel College and Central Bible College have displayed growth.[87] Although each school continues to operate within its own province, the separate campuses seem to be a rather vivid reminder of the lack of a clearly articulated philosophy of education for the entire denomina-

---

[84]Collins, *op. cit.*, p. 110.

[85]*The Pentecostal Evangel*, March 16, 1958, p. 11.

[86]*The Pentecostal Evangel*, January 13, 1963, p. 28.

[87]In the fall of 1969 there were 749 students enrolled at Central Bible College; 977 at Evangel College. "Annual Report: Assemblies of God Department of Education, October, 1969."

tion, a lack discussed in the Board of Education since 1961, but without action taken to date.[88]

Evangel College received full endorsement by the North Central Association of Colleges and Secondary Schools in 1965, just 10 years after the school opened.[89] The college has become well established as a flourishing institution, but continuing ambiguity regarding the role of liberal arts education in the denomination persists.[90] Part of the uneasiness may be attributed to the rather more expensive operation required for first-rate liberal arts education compared with the traditional financial patterns experienced in the operation of the Bible schools. Hopefully the special committee appointed by the Executive Presbytery in March, 1970, to give in-depth study to the educational needs of the Assemblies of God will help the denomination to articulate an overarching philosophy of education. Perhaps this guidance will enable the evolving educational enterprises in the denomination to fulfill an even more meaningful role in days to come.

GRADUATE THEOLOGICAL TRAINING

A parallel issue to the problem of undergraduate general education has been the question of denominationally sponsored graduate theological training. Both Central Bible College and Northwest College of the Assemblies of God had engaged in experimentation with programs leading to master's degrees, but neither could afford to continue such activity. The real issue has been the willingness of the denomination as a whole to support a seminary.

The 1949 General Council had agreed to ratify the arrangement of Central Bible Institute with the AABC for accreditation, but this had precipitated a heated discussion about the possible future requirement of academic degrees for ordination which some feared would eventually follow. C. C. Burnett, an ardent advocate of accredited training, presented a resolution to the Council after the accreditation issue had narrowly passed (by a vote of 369 to 313). His

[88]Board of Education minutes, June 1-2, 1961.

[89]*The Pentecostal Evangel*, May 9, 1965, pp. 24-25.

[90]The General Presbytery was engaged in a review of the philosophy of Evangel College as late as 1965. General Presbytery minutes, 1965.

proposal was that the General Council go on record as opposed to academic degrees ever being a requirement for Assemblies of God ordination. This resolution was adopted, and served to mollify ruffled feelings.[91] The next General Council voted this provision into the bylaws.[92] This unrest over academic qualifications for the minstry has been an important factor in the history of the debate over a seminary program.

Following the 1953 approval for the establishment of a denominationally sponsored liberal arts college, a kind of reaction began to set in. At the following Council, in 1955, a revision of the bylaws was agreed upon, taking the provision for the establishment of a seminary out of the hands of the Education Department (it had been granted such authorization in 1947[93]) and placing it solely in the hands of the General Council in session.[94]

Persistent arguments continued to be presented to the denomination as reasons for a graduate theological school being urgently needed. One was the loss of capable young men who were studying in the seminaries of other denominations. Many of these did not return to serve the Assemblies of God. In 1955 there were 150 Assemblies of God youth in graduate schools and seminaries outside the Assemblies of God.[95] The rising social mobility of the constituency may have motivated a desire for a better-trained ministry.[96] Then, too, such a program was necessary for the Assemblies of God to be able to train its own military chaplains.[97] These were the arguments. Gradually the exponents of seminary training won the day. The 1961 General Council granted authorization for the Board of Education, in consultation with the Executive Presbytery, to establish a suitable seminary "at such a time and place as they deem necessary."[98]

---

[91]General Council minutes, 1949, p. 30.

[92]General Council minutes, 1951, p. 9.

[93]General Council minutes, 1947, p. 77.

[94]General Council minutes, 1955, p. 43.

[95]*Ibid.*, p. 39.

[96]Board of Education minutes, August 28, 1957.

[97]General Council reports, 1959, p. 86.

[98]General Council minutes, 1961, p. 38.

The interesting postscript to this action has been the deliberate and cautious planning for the proposed seminary. This seems to be in striking contrast to the rapid implementation of the 1953 decision to create a liberal arts college. In 1964, Dr. Merrill C. Tenney, dean of the graduate school at Wheaton College, was invited to Springfield as a consultant on the project.[99] From his recommendations there issued a spirit of reassessment of just how real the need was for a seminary for the Assemblies of God.[100] The General Council report by the Board of Education in 1965 reflected a target date no earlier than 1967 for the opening of such a school.[101] The 1966 General Presbyters were informed that the target date was projected for September, 1968.[102] The Board of Education in August, 1967, proposed a new target date of 1970.[103] Included in that proposal was the concern that more time should be taken for exploration of the variety of new programs currently being undertaken by several graduate schools so that curriculum, nomenclature, and objectives most helpful to the denomination be selected. On February 17, 1970, the Executive Committee of the Board of Education adopted a resolution recommending the temporary suspension of plans to implement a graduate school of theology until the special education committee appointed by the Executive Presbytery could draw up a comprehensive philosophy of education for the denomination. This recommendation was adopted by the Executive Presbytery on March 19, 1970.[104] There has been a mood of calm discussion regarding this entire issue, and it is hopeful that a school tailored to meet the needs of the Assemblies of God will be forthcoming, and that it will come to pass without undue emotional turbulence.

CHRISTIAN DAY SCHOOLS

Operated entirely on a local or district basis, a number of high schools, elementary schools, and nursery schools have burgeoned in the Assemblies of God. At least two

---

[99]General Presbytery minutes, 1964, pp. 29-30.
[100]Board of Education minutes, August 25, 1965.
[101]General Council minutes, 1965, pp. 68-69.
[102]General Presbytery minutes, 1966, pp. 35-38.
[103]Board of Education minutes, August 24, 1967.
[104]Executive Presbytery minutes, March 19, 1970, pp. 19-20.

high schools were in operation before World War II, one in Oregon and one in Texas.[105] In 1946 the Assembly in Wilmington, California, became the first church to sponsor a parochial elementary school.[106] Others followed in quick succession, for the erection of elaborate educational units in the postwar years furnished numerous churches with adequate facilities for such ventures. At the 1955 General Council, the report of the Department of Education encouraging the employment of local church facilities for school activity was received, and the department was encouraged to establish standards for the operation of such schools.[107] In 1967 the Board of Education adopted a set of criteria for Christian day schools.[108] In the fall of 1969 there were 36 day schools being operated with a total enrollment of 5,123 students. These were situated mostly on the West Coast and in the Southwest. Of this number, three had secondary programs.[109]

Social Concern

Evangelism has always overshadowed social concern in the Assemblies of God. However, concern for human need has been a spontaneous feature of local church life, nonetheless.[110] The significant change has been the growing consciousness of social issues and the development of programs to deal with such problems. Most noteworthy has been the provision within the fellowship for care of the elderly and of disadvantaged children, programs carried on under the supervision of the Department of Benevolences.[111]

The race issue represents more vividly than any other the development of social concern regarding matters beyond the welfare of members within the Assemblies of God itself. It was during World War II that the needs of the black people within the United States first came to the attention

---

[105]*The Pentecostal Evangel*, August 28, 1948, p. 11. Collins, *op. cit.*, pp. 64-65.

[106]Eleanor R. Guynes, "Development of the Educational Program of the Assemblies of God from the School Year 1948-49 up to the Present Time" (unpublished M.A. thesis, Southern Methodist University, 1966), pp. 24-25.

[107]General Council minutes, 1955, pp. 38-39.

[108]Board of Education minutes, August 24, 1967.

[109]Statistics supplied by the Department of Education.

[110]Harrison, *op. cit.*, pp. 291-92.

[111]See Chapter 11 for a discussion of the history of the Department of Benevolences.

of the General Council in session. In 1943 a resolution was presented urging "that provision be made through our Missions Department in cooperation with our various District Councils to promote missionary activity among our American black people."[112] The resolution was not adopted, and the matter was referred to the Executive Presbytery, principally because of fear that such action might be "working in competition with the Church of God in Christ (black) if such work were undertaken."[113] The Church of God in Christ was one of the southern Holiness bodies that were swept wholesale into the Pentecostal camp during the first flush of revival at Azusa Street. Ten years after the founding of the denomination by Bishop C. H. Mason in 1897, this Negro Holiness body joined the ranks of the Pentecostals.[114] An unwritten policy gradually developed in which this group, although its doctrine was Wesleyan, was considered to be the Negro counterpart of the Assemblies of God.

At the next General Council a motion was adopted "that we encourage the establishment of Assembly of God churches for the colored race and that when such churches are established they be authorized to display the name, 'Assembly of God–Colored Branch.' "[115] This arrangement was discussed, leading to the recommendation that such a black branch be handled on the same basis as the foreign language branches that were supervised by the Department of Home Missions.[116] However, the resolution adopted in 1945 was merely an expression of sentiment. No action was immediately forthcoming.

In the General Presbytery session of 1946 a motion was adopted which asked for the formation of a completely separate Pentecostal church body for blacks, but that every assistance and encouragement be provided for them by the Assemblies of God.[117] That there was not general agreement on this proposal seems clear from the action taken at the

[112]General Council minutes, 1943, p. 13.
[113]*Ibid.*
[114]Atter, *op. cit.*, p. 61.
[115]General Council minutes, 1945, p. 31.
[116]*Ibid.*, p. 36.
[117]General Presbytery minutes, 1946, p. 12.

General Council a year later. At Grand Rapids in 1947 the Chairman of the Resolutions Committee introduced an appeal for the creation of a black branch of the Assemblies of God, much like the proposal of 1945.[118] This evoked considerable discussion, with the result that it was agreed that a committee of "representative brethren from the North and the South" be appointed by the General Superintendent to study the matter and return to the next Council with a recommendation.[119]

The recommendation was never made. As a result of the committee's visit to Memphis, the headquarters of the Church of God in Christ, it was agreed that no special purpose would be served by arranging for a black branch of the Assemblies of God, since the committee seemed favorably impressed with the operation of the Church of God in Christ denomination, a body claiming 485,000 members, twice that of the Assemblies of God.[120]

The Assemblies of God had moved some distance from the issues of the 1940's and 1950's, which had circulated about whether or not to set up a segregated black fellowship. At the 1965 General Council a strong resolution favoring civil rights and deploring any practice of discrimination was adopted by recommendation of the Executive Presbytery.[121]

As evidence of this new posture, an associate evangelist of the Billy Graham Evangelistic Association, Robert Harrison, a Negro who had been graduated from Bethany Bible College, was approved for service under missionary appointment by the Assemblies of God Foreign Missions Department in 1964.[122] About the same time, Thurman Faison, a graduate of a Canadian Bible school, began a pilot project in Harlem, sponsored by the Home Missions Department, to minister to the blacks of that community.[123] There are only limited statistics available, but schools and churches in

---

[118]General Council minutes, 1947, p. 43.

[119]*Ibid.*

[120]"Quarterly Letter," March 24, 1948. Accurate figures are difficult to document for this group, however.

[121]General Council minutes, 1965, pp. 60-61.

[122]*Educator*, March-April, 1964, p. 3.

[123]*The Pentecostal Evangel*, May 14, 1967, p. 10.

the Assemblies of God, at least in some regions, seem to be quietly, howbeit slowly, integrating the races. These are encouraging developments, but General Superintendent Zimmerman is dissatisfied with the lack of aggressive facing up to the race question in the denomination. He feels that out of a desire to maintain a spirit of unity in the fellowship when it appeared that sectional and racist feelings were being exerted, the majority looked the other way.[124]

A recent encouraging encounter took place in January, 1970. A significant and helpful meeting was arranged in Springfield, presided over by General Superintendent Zimmerman, to which were invited two black Assemblies of God leaders, Evangelist Robert Harrison and Pastor Thurman Faison. Executive Director of Home Missions C. W. H. Scott also participated in this historic conference. Earnest discussion took place to determine how the Assemblies of God could better meet the needs of black Americans. In the course of the conference it was reported that there were at the beginning of 1970 25 ordained black Assemblies of God clergymen. The Negro representatives expressed special commendation to the Illinois District Council for the farsighted labors of the men in that district in their aiding of black evangelistic enterprises.[125]

The most important official statement ever made by the Assemblies of God on matters of social concern came about in 1968. A statement on social responsibility was formulated by the Executive Presbytery and submitted with a recommendation for adoption to the General Presbytery. On August 21, 1968, the General Presbytery unanimously adopted the statement.[126]

Summary

Upward social mobility occasioned by higher income during and following World War II, an increasingly suburban clientele, and the maturation of the Pentecostal Movement have all been factors in the changing worship pat-

---

[124]Interview, Thomas F. Zimmerman, December 8, 1967.

[125]"How Can We Reach Black Americans for Christ?" *The Pentecostal Evangel*, April 26, 1970, pp. 6-8, 20.

[126]General Presbytery minutes, November 1968, pp. 24-26. The full text of the Statement on Social Concern is reproduced in Appendix C.

terns, educational outlook, and social consciousness of Assemblies of God people. Traditional Pentecostal worship has been perpetuated, but accompanying these patterns have been more sophisticated forms, as well, in the years since World War II. The general fervor, characteristic of earlier years, seems to have waned, although such activities which do not involve immediate, personal responsibility, like giving to foreign missions, have shown continuing vigor.

The pattern of educational institutions operated by the denomination has displayed considerable change since World War II. Prior to that time, all the schools furnishing post-high school education were geared directly to the training of ministers and missionaries. They were nonaccredited, three-year programs with little general education, with one exception. Since 1941, all the schools have moved to a four-year accredited degree-granting level, and some have sought dual accreditation so that the general education content in the curricula would have functional, transfer value. One Bible school has evolved into a liberal arts college, and the denomination for the first time established its own senior liberal arts college. The changes seem to have been occasioned largely by economic and social pressures, not matched by an overarching philosophy of education. The result of unassimilated changes has produced a degree of uncertainty and competition on the undergraduate level. Graduate theological training is still in the planning stage. The caution disclosed in this venture seems to be a reflection of unresolved issues on the undergraduate scene. Christian day schools seem to be flourishing, a development occasioned by the great building boom of the 1950's in which elaborate educational units were constructed by many congregations.

A developing social concern, howbeit limited, is illustrated by the discussions and action in the post-World War II years in the Assemblies of God with respect to racial relations. Internally, the care of the aged and of children by the Department of Benevolences serves as testimony of awareness of needs within the fellowship itself.

15
Conclusion

A Summary of Denominational Development—The Denominational Life Cycle—Concluding Remarks

The Assemblies of God arose in the early part of the current century out of an awareness that the modern American Pentecostal Movement needed at least a modicum of structure to conserve the fruits of revival. It was nourished in the context of the American free-church tradition, gradually evolving its own patterns without external political coercion or restriction. It did not develop in a vacuum, however, for its founders drew heavily, not only on New Testament ideals, but also on Evangelical and Holiness traditions rooted deep in the nineteenth century. Nor did it grow in total isolation from the changing contemporary society. Now then, after more than 50 years of history upon which to reflect, one may ask several searching questions regarding the course that has been traced by the Assemblies of God. Since the Assemblies of God serves as a model, as a sample, of the modern American Pentecostal Movement, such an evaluation may serve far more than parochial interest. What have been the dynamic characteristics of the Assemblies of God? What evidence is there that the denomination has been following a life cycle pattern of similar groups? What dangers and opportunities confront the Assemblies of God?

A Summary of Denominational Development

1. *Structural Stages.* There appear to be three general stages of structural development in the denomination. The

period from 1914 to 1941 was an era of undifferentiated growth, characterized by spontaneous outreach, local initiative, and simple organization. The years 1941 to 1953 were years of analytical development. Numerous new departments and service agencies were created at the national and district levels, designed to conserve the fruits of the expansion already enjoyed, and to channel the energies of emerging subgroups within the fellowship. Since 1953 there has been a changing mood, shifting from analysis to synthesis. The theme of recent years has been the coordination of effort, characterized by central planning and efforts to redefine denominational objectives. Most significant of all has been the launching of the Study on Advance in 1967, which has as its purpose the evaluation of the denomination's strengths and weaknesses and the articulation of fresh goals. It may signal the end of an era and the beginning of a new phase of development as yet undetermined.

2. *Changing Leadership.* The leaders in the Assemblies of God from early days until 1953 could be described as "charismatic." Since then the leadership has had to concern itself with the demands of an increasingly complex institutional apparatus. The double responsibility of spiritual oversight and expanded administrative concerns has brought to the fore types of men who may be described as "charismatic-statesmen." In spite of the burden of organization, there continues to be evidence of vital spiritual leadership.

3. *Growth Patterns.* Domestic growth has been uneven. Prior to 1941 the Assemblies of God grew at a prodigious rate, drawing chiefly from the distressed classes of society. This growth manifested itself in the creation of numerous congregations. Since 1941 the spectacular growth has been in the new, creative avenues of special outreach, such as the ministry to the deaf and Teen Challenge. New churches were added at a rapid rate until 1957, but the last decade has disclosed a sharp contrast in growth rate to the earlier history of the denomination. Signs of fresh growth, however, are once again appearing at the dawn of the 1970's.

Since World War II the urban congregations have been engaged in a steady exodus to the suburbs. The clientele of the churches can no longer be easily stereotyped, for in addition to the lower social classes there has been an accession of middle-class people to the fellowship. There are marked indications of upward social mobility, strongly linked to the economic effects of World War II among the working classes, and the enlarged horizons of the men who returned from the military service.

Foreign missionary activity has continued to grow at a fast pace. Financial support at home and a continuing supply of candidates for foreign service demonstrate continued enthusiasm for foreign outreach.

4. *Conformity.* The denomination has been surprisingly free of theological controversy, possibly owing to the relative unconcern in the fellowship with niceties of doctrinal distinctions, in part at least. The traditional emphasis has been experiential and practical, not ideological. Absolute trust in the Bible and general agreement on fundamentals of the faith have served to furnish a fairly tolerant basis of fellowship. The requirement for credentials renewal for ordained ministers of an annual statement of faith, inaugurated in 1959, may indicate an increased concern for theological conformity. There is no evidence of any pattern of significant defection from the ministry for theological reasons.

The appearance of a variety of independent Pentecostal organizations in the post-World War II era that seemed to depend on support from established denominations, but that were responsible to none, led to the adoption of a disciplinary policy in 1965 in the Assemblies of God. The "Criteria for Independent Corporations" was the result of a general agreement within the fellowship that some kind of safeguard against religious huckstering was quite necessary. Some have concluded that this action is evidence of an increasingly centralized mode of denominational operation.

5. *Vitality.* The data reveal a mixed situation. Worship patterns have tended to reflect a gravitation toward more reserved, sophisticated forms, but there is still a broad base of traditional enthusiastic Pentecostal worship. With respect to outreach, personal involvement seems to be more

and more displaced by vicarious participation, such as generous giving to missions. This has occurred in spite of the appearance of creative, specialized agencies designed to serve the needs of a variety of subgroups within the congregation. That there continues to be an abundant reservoir of missions candidates suggests that part of the reason for the introversion of the churches may be in failure of the clergy to furnish adequate challenge and opportunity for service to the laymen in the congregation. Quite likely there is still a high degree of vitality within the fellowship, but it has not been given full expression.

6. *Acculturation.* Standards of separation from the prevailing norms of contemporary society were an important heritage from the Holiness roots of the Assemblies of God. Prior to 1941 there was a fair degree of uniformity throughout the fellowship, with some notable regional exceptions. The degree of agreement on behavioral standards since World War II has diminished markedly. Some feel this to be an indicator of denominational spiritual entropy; some feel that this is simply a cultural issue. The degree of accommodation to prevailing social norms seems to be correlated with the size of congregation and community. No regional pattern is discernible in recent years.

7. *Education.* Significant changes have occurred in the character of the educational institutions operated by the Assemblies of God, both at the national and the regional levels. The total number of schools has declined since 1941, but the total enrollment has increased, indicating the economic need for consolidation of resources. The traditional three-year Bible school diploma program that was standard in 1941 has rapidly given way to accredited four-year degree programs. In 1941 all students were enrolled in theological programs; by 1970 this had changed so that nearly 40 percent of the students were studying in liberal arts programs. In most cases the Bible schools have been evolving toward liberal arts programs; in no case has there not been some degree of accommodation to general education. Competition among the schools and pressure from pastors, parents, and students have been significant factors in this evolution.

Considerable debate circulated about the propriety of establishing a national liberal arts college. Lack of a comprehensive philosophy of education for the denomination continues to be a source of ambiguity for undergraduate training. This seems, in part at least, to be a reflection of uncertainty about the roles of laity and clergy in the denomination.

The need for a denominational graduate school of theology has been an issue of most recent concern. The deliberation with which plans are being formulated for this enterprise indicates a much less emotionalized atmosphere surrounding this matter than that which colored the issue of liberal arts training in the early 1950's.

Although there has been a striking shift in the attitude of the general membership since 1941 over the importance of formal education, this has not been reflected in the support to educational institutions.

8. *Social Concern.* Preoccupation with direct evangelism and reaction to the "social gospel" may account for the lack of organized denominational action with respect to social evils prior to 1941. There was, to be sure, a growing concern over the welfare of the aged within the fellowship. And, practical help to those in physical need has always been a concern of the local churches from earliest days. In more recent years, in addition to services internally to those within the fellowship, such as are supervised by the Department of Benevolences, formal denominational action has been begun in at least one area. Although embryonic in nature, the actions of the General Councils since 1941 in the matter of race relations do indicate an awakening denominational social consciousness.

9. *Interaction.* The Assemblies of God grew up in virtual isolation from the rest of the church world until the advent of World War II. This isolation was not by choice but by necessity, since Fundamentalists, Holiness people, and those from the larger church world either ignored or openly repudiated the Pentecostals. Beginning in 1942, the evangelical world has gradually made room for the Pentecostals. Holiness attitudes have softened, but the militant Funda-

mentalists have not changed noticeably. Owing in large measure to the advent of Neo-Pentecostalism, some representatives from the larger church world have taken fresh notice of the traditional Pentecostal Movement.

The Assemblies of God has developed a strong attraction to the moderate wing of Evangelicalism. From this quarter the denomination has received considerable assistance, notably in the improving of the standards of its schools and publications, and in securing a united voice in diplomatic matters. Some have felt that this strong identification has unnecessarily restricted dialogue with the larger church world. Some have wondered, as well, if such association has not cost the denomination some of its individuality. Nearly all within the Assemblies of God have welcomed the opportunity for interaction with others of evangelical faith.

A direct outgrowth of association with others in the evangelical world has been American Pentecostal fellowship across denominational lines. The bringing together of American Pentecostal denominations is a product of the post-World War II era. The traditional Pentecostal denominations, including the Assemblies of God, have been somewhat uncertain about the significance of Neo-Pentecostalism, and how to relate to this relatively recent phenomenon.

The Denominational Life Cycle

Does a revival movement tend to follow a typical pattern of development? If so, what implications does the history of the Assemblies of God have for the modern American Pentecostal Movement?

Ernst Troeltsch may be credited with the erection of the "church-sect" typology which has served as the basic frame of reference for interpreters of the life cycle continuum of Christian movements.[1] The terminology has not seemed to be entirely satisfactory, for the implication is left that the "sect" is somehow inferior to "church." Littell has suggested that a more Biblical approach might be to call the revival movement in its initial phase "church," since it at

[1]Ernst Troeltsch, *The Social Teaching of the Christian Churches*, trans. Olive Wyon (London: George Allen and Unwin, 1931), II, p. 993. Richard Niebuhr, Liston Pope, Joachim Wach and others follow in this tradition.

that point tends to correspond with the ideals of the New Testament apostolic community. As it gradually loses its apostolic distinctives and assimilates the characteristics of prevailing society, he would describe such accommodation as "culture religion."[2] This, too, carries a pejorative connotation, tending to judge all change as degenerative. However, regardless of terminology, that there is a kind of "natural history" of revival movements seems to be a common judgment.

Does the story of the Assemblies of God fit any particular pattern? That changes have occurred is manifest, but are they upward or downward? Moberg has established a theory of institutional life cycles that seems to acknowledge some changes as salutary and some as evidence of decay, a view that appears to correspond rather well with the experience of the Assemblies of God.[3]

He describes five stages of development in a typical religious institution. The initial phase he calls "incipient organization." This is the revolutionary period of dissatisfaction with existing churches, a period of "collective excitement," in which no founder may be identifiable.[4]

The second stage he describes as that of "formal organization," in which formal leadership arises, goals are formulated, a creed is developed, and specialized behavior is developed.[5]

The third stage he calls "maximum efficiency." Thirteen characteristics may be listed. The correspondence of this list with the summary of recent characteristics in the Assemblies of God appears to be striking.

1. Leadership is less emotional and more statesmanlike.
2. Rational organization displaces charismatic leadership.
3. Historians and apologists emerge.
4. Propaganda becomes prominent; mass media are employed to publicize the aims and activities of the group.

---

[2]Franklin H. Littell, "The Historical Free Church Tradition Defined" (a privately circulated manuscript).

[3]David O. Moberg, *The Church as a Social Institution* (Englewood Cliffs, New Jersey: Prentice-Hall, 1962), pp. 119-23.

[4]*Ibid.*, p. 119.

[5]*Ibid.*, p. 120.

5. Programs of action are formulated by rational consideration of relevant information.

6. Intellectuals repelled previously by display of emotion begin to give approval and transfer their allegiances accordingly.

7. Psychologically, the group has moved from the position of a despised sect to near-equality with previously recognized denominations.

8. Hostility toward others diminishes; fanatical resolution to maintain sharply different ways becomes relaxed. Most of the first generation of converts have passed from the scene.

9. A formal structure grows rapidly, with new committees, boards, and executives being appointed to meet the needs of a growing organization.

10. Official leaders perform their duties enthusiastically and efficiently.

11. Rituals and procedures in worship and administration are still viewed as means rather than as ends in themselves.

12. The institution is at its stage of maximum vitality or "youthful vigor." Growth may be very rapid.

13. Growth is likely to be episodic, with periods of growth being followed by a period of absorption and assimilation. At this stage, if integration of new growth is not effected, internal dissensions or splinter groups may emerge.[6]

The fourth stage Moberg calls the "institutional stage." Formalism saps the vitality of the group. The leadership becomes more preoccupied with the establishment of a bureaucracy than maintaining the distinctives that brought the group into existence originally. Mechanisms become an end in themselves. Creeds become venerated relics. Ritual and symbol displace vital worship. Conflict with the outside world has been displaced entirely by complete toleration of societal folkways and mores.[7]

The last phase of the life cycle Moberg titles "disintegration." The diseases of formalism, indifferentism, obsolescence, absolutism, red tape, patronage, and corruption are

---

[6]*Ibid.*, pp. 120-21.
[7]*Ibid.*, p. 121.

the common symptoms of the dissolution of a once vital institution.[8]

That such a sequence of ultimate deterioration, once the period of "maximum efficiency" has been reached, is inevitable, Moberg denies.[9] Internal reform may reverse the process. Nida, in discussing the problem of the "cooling off" of revival movements, concurs with this possibility of renewal.[10]

In any event, employing this sample of a life cycle system as a gauge, one may conclude that the Assemblies of God is somewhere near the optimum in the delicate balance between spiritual vitality and efficient organization.

Concluding Remarks

The Assemblies of God is now three generations old. The story of its development is indeed a fascinating description of what God can do through men and women set on fire by the anointing of the Holy Spirit. Unnumbered thousands have been led to the Saviour by heroes of the Cross who caught the vision of God's love in places both far and near. Courageous pioneers dared to believe the Word of God, claiming the pattern of the New Testament church for the twentieth century. The faith such farsighted stalwarts exercised brought the presence of God in a new dimension into today's world. They became instruments of a supernatural revival, characterized by the fruits and gifts of the Spirit poured out in glorious profusion on responsive worshipers. The church world at large has been challenged to consider afresh the person and work of the Third Person of the Trinity through the display of God's power evidenced in such groups as the Assemblies of God. It has been a thrilling time, a season of refreshing in the history of the Church.

Now, what of the future? The appointment of the Committee on Advance by the Executive Presbytery early in 1967 symbolizes the self-awareness within the leadership

---

[8] *Ibid.*, p. 122.
[9] *Ibid.*, p. 123.
[10] Eugene Nida, *Message and Mission* (New York: Harper and Brothers, 1960), pp. 155-57.

of the fellowship that the continued vitality and growth of the Assemblies of God will require thoughtful, prayerful reassessment of denominational structures and objectives. Should the yearning at the grass roots for spiritual renewal match in intensity and desire the burden of the denominational leadership, the Five-Year Plan of Advance may well prove to be a most significant rallying point for a great general refreshing within the fellowship, the harbinger of great days ahead. Perhaps God will use this time of soul-searching as a mighty occasion for calling the Assemblies of God to a new level of usefulness in the kingdom of God, far beyond even the dreams and visions of saints of yesteryear.

Could it be that the Pentecostal Movement, exemplified by the Assemblies of God, is poised at the beginning of a whole new era? Future historians alone will be able to weigh the wisdom and courage of the decisions and commitments made in these crucial, pivotal years. The future alone will disclose whether or not this remarkable revival movement, having reached a plateau of consolidation in the decade of the 1960's, will move into the decade of the 1970's with a fresh glow from God to grace the closing years of this century by continuing to toil upwards toward the heights, or whether the people called Pentecostal will be content to rest in an upland meadow while others pass them by in their journey to do God's bidding in this world.

Standing, then, as we are between the achievements of the past and the awesome potential of the uncharted future, let the people of God listen afresh to the watchword by which this movement has marched through the years: "Not by might, nor by power, but by my Spirit, saith the Lord of hosts!"

APPENDIXES

Appendix A

CONSTITUTIONAL DECLARATION AND STATEMENT OF FUNDAMENTAL TRUTHS[1]

CONSTITUTIONAL DECLARATION

WE BELIEVE:

That God's purpose concerning man is 1) to seek and to save that which is lost, 2) to be worshiped by man, and 3) to build a body of believers in the image of His Son.

That these believers saved and called out of the world constitute the body or church of Jesus Christ built and established upon the foundation of the apostles and prophets, Jesus Christ Himself being the chief cornerstone.

That the members of the body, the church (ecclesia) of Jesus Christ, are enjoined to assemble themselves for worship, fellowship, counsel, and instruction in the Word of God, the work of the ministry and for the exercise of those spiritual gifts and offices provided for New Testament church order.

That it is evident the early apostolic churches came together in fellowship as a representative body of saved, Spirit-filled believers, who ordained and sent out evangelists and missionaries, and under the supervision of the Holy Spirit set over the church, pastors and teachers.

That the priority reason-for-being of the Assemblies of God is to be an agency of God for evangelizing the world, to be a corporate body in which man may worship God, and to be a channel of God's purpose to build a body of saints being perfected in the image of His Son.

That the Assemblies of God exists expressly to give continuing emphasis to this reason-for-being in the New Testament apostolic pattern by teaching and encouraging believers to be baptized in the Holy Spirit which enables them to evangelize in the power of the Spirit with accompanying supernatural signs, adding a necessary dimension to worshipful relationship with God, and enabling them to respond to the full working of the Holy Spirit in expression of fruit and gifts and ministries as in New Testament times for the edifying of the body of Christ.

[1]Minutes of the Thirty-third General Council of the Assemblies of God, Convened at Dallas, Texas, August 21-26, 1969, pp. 93-100.

That we are a cooperative fellowship of Pentecostal, Spirit-baptized saints from local Pentecostal Assemblies of like precious faith throughout the United States and foreign lands to be known as The General Council of the Assemblies of God whose purpose is neither to usurp authority over the various local assemblies, nor to deprive them of their scriptural and local rights and privileges; but to recognize and promote scriptural methods and order for worship, unity, fellowship, work, and business for God; and to disapprove unscriptural methods, doctrines and conduct, endeavoring to keep the unity of the Spirit in the bond of peace, "till we all come in the unity of the faith, and of the knowledge of the Son of God, unto a perfect man, unto the measure of the stature of the fullness of Christ." (Ephesians 4:13)

STATEMENT OF FUNDAMENTAL TRUTHS

The Bible is our all-sufficient rule for faith and practice. This Statement of Fundamental Truths is intended simply as a basis of fellowship among us (i.e., that we all speak the same thing, 1 Cor. 1:10; Acts 2:42). The phraseology employed in this Statement is not inspired or contended for, but the truth set forth is held to be essential to a Full Gospel ministry. No claim is made that it contains all Biblical truth, only that it covers our need as to these fundamental doctrines.

1. The Scriptures Inspired

The Scriptures, both the Old and New Testaments, are verbally inspired of God and are the revelation of God to man, the infallible, authoritative rule of faith and conduct (2 Tim. 3:15-17; 1 Thess. 2:13; 2 Peter 1:21).

2. The One True God

The one true God has revealed Himself as the eternally self-existent "I AM," the Creator of heaven and earth and the Redeemer of mankind. He has further revealed Himself as embodying the principles of relationship and association as Father, Son, and Holy Ghost (Deut. 6:4; Isaiah 43:10, 11; Matthew 28:19; Luke 3:22).

THE ADORABLE GODHEAD

(a) terms defined

The terms "Trinity" and "persons," as related to the Godhead, while not found in the Scriptures, are words in harmony with Scripture, whereby we may convey to others our immediate understanding of the doctrine of Christ respecting the Being of God, as distinguished from "gods many and lords many." We therefore may speak with propriety of the Lord our God, who is One Lord, as a trinity or as one Being of three persons, and still be absolutely Scriptural (examples, Matt. 28:19; 2 Cor. 13:14; John 14:16, 17).

(b) distinction and relationship in the godhead

Christ taught a distinction of Persons in the Godhead which He expressed in specific terms of relationship, as Father, Son, and Holy Ghost, but that this distinction and relationship, as to its mode is inscrutable and incomprehensible, because unexplained. Luke 1:35; 1 Cor. 1:24; Matt. 11:25-27; 28:19; 2 Cor. 13:14; 1 John 1:3, 4.

(c) UNITY OF THE ONE BEING OF FATHER, SON, AND HOLY GHOST

Accordingly, therefore, there is *that* in the Son which constitutes Him *the* Son and not the Father; and there is *that* in the Holy Ghost which constitutes Him *the Holy Ghost* and not either the Father or the Son. Wherefore the Father is the Begetter, the Son is the Begotten; and the Holy Ghost is the one proceeding from the Father and the Son. Therefore, because these three persons in the Godhead are in a state of unity, there is but one Lord God Almighty and His name one. John 1:18; 15:26; 17:11, 21; Zech. 14:9.

(D) IDENTITY AND COOPERATION IN THE GODHEAD

The Father, the Son, and the Holy Ghost are never *identical* as to *Person;* nor *confused* as to *relation;* nor *divided* in respect to the Godhead; nor *opposed* as to *cooperation.* The Son is *in* the Father and the Father is *in* the Son as to relationship. The Son is *with* the Father and the Father is *with* the Son, as to fellowship. The Father is not *from* the Son, but the Son is *from* the Father, as to authority. The Holy Ghost is *from* the Father and Son proceeding, as to nature, relationship, cooperation and authority. Hence, neither Person in the Godhead either exists or works separately or independently of the others. John 5:17-30, 32, 37; John 8:17, 18.

(E) THE TITLE, LORD JESUS CHRIST

The appellation, "Lord Jesus Christ," is a proper name. It is never applied, in the New Testament, either to the Father or to the Holy Ghost. It therefore belongs exclusively to the *Son of God.* Rom. 1:1-3, 7; 2 John 3.

(F) THE LORD JESUS CHRIST, GOD WITH US

The Lord Jesus Christ, as to His divine and eternal nature, is the proper and only Begotten of the Father, but as to His human nature, He is the proper Son of Man. He is, therefore, acknowledged to be both God and man; who because He is God and man, is "Immanuel," God with us. Matt. 1:23; 1 John 4:2, 10, 14; Rev. 1:13, 17.

(G) THE TITLE, SON OF GOD

Since the name "Immanuel" embraces both God and man in the one Person, our Lord Jesus Christ, it follows that the title, Son of God, describes His proper diety, and the title Son of Man, His proper humanity. Therefore, the title, Son of God, belongs to the *order of eternity,* and the title, Son of Man to the order of *time.* Matt. 1:21-23; 2 John 3; 1 John 3:8; Heb. 7:3; 1:1-13.

(H) TRANSGRESSION OF THE DOCTRINE OF CHRIST

Wherefore, it is a transgression of the Doctrine of Christ to say that Jesus Christ derived the title, Son of God, solely from the fact of the incarnation, or because of His relation to the economy of redemption. Therefore, to deny that the Father is a real and eternal Father, and that the Son is a real and eternal Son, is a denial of the distinction and relationship in the Being of God; a denial of the Father and the Son; and a displacement of the truth that Jesus Christ is come in the flesh. 2 John 9; John 1:1, 2, 14, 18, 29, 49; 1 John 2:22, 23; 4:1-5; Heb. 12:2.

(I) EXALTATION OF JESUS CHRIST AS LORD

The Son of God, our Lord Jesus Christ, having by Himself purged our sins, sat down on the right hand of the Majesty on high; angels and principalities and powers having been made subject unto Him. And having been made both Lord and Christ, He sent the Holy Ghost that we, in the name of Jesus, might bow our knees and confess that Jesus Christ is Lord to the glory of God the Father until the end, when the Son shall become subject to the Father that God may be all in all. Heb. 1:3; 1 Peter 3:22; Acts 2:32-36; Rom. 14:11; 1 Cor. 15:24-28.

(J) EQUAL HONOR TO THE FATHER AND TO THE SON

Wherefore, since the Father has delivered all judgment unto the Son, it is not only the *express duty* of all in heaven and on earth to bow the knee, but it is an *unspeakable* joy in the Holy Ghost to ascribe unto the Son all the attributes of Deity, and to give Him all the honor and the glory contained in all the names and titles of the Godhead (except those which express relationship. See paragraphs b, c, and d), and thus honor the Son even as we honor the Father. John 5:22, 23; 1 Peter 1:8; Rev. 5:6-14; Phil. 2:8, 9; Rev. 7:9, 10; 4:8-11.

3. The Deity of the Lord Jesus Christ

The Lord Jesus Christ is the eternal Son of God. The Scriptures declare:

(a) His virgin birth (Matthew 1:23; Luke 1:31, 35).
(b) His sinless life (Hebrews 7:26; 1 Peter 2:22).
(c) His miracles (Acts 2:22; 10:38).
(d) His substitutionary work on the cross (1 Cor. 15:3; 2 Cor. 5:21).
(e) His bodily resurrection from the dead (Matthew 28:6; Luke 24:39; 1 Cor. 15:4).
(f) His exaltation to the right hand of God (Acts 1:9, 11; 2:33; Philippians 2:9-11; Hebrews 1-3).

4. The Fall of Man

Man was created good and upright; for God said, "Let us make man in our image, after our likeness." However, man by voluntary transgression fell and thereby incurred not only physical death but also spiritual death, which is separation from God (Genesis 1:26, 27; 2:17; 3:6; Romans 5:12-19).

5. The Salvation of Man

Man's only hope of redemption is through the shed blood of Jesus Christ the Son of God.

(a) Conditions to Salvation

Salvation is received through repentance toward God and faith toward the Lord Jesus Christ. By the washing of regeneration and renewing of the Holy Ghost, being justified by grace through faith, man becomes an heir of God according to the hope of eternal life (Luke 24:47; John 3:3; Romans 10:13-15; Ephesians 2:8; Titus 2:11; 3:5-7).

(b) The Evidences of Salvation

The inward evidence of salvation is the direct witness of the Spirit (Romans 8:16). The outward evidence to all men is a life of righteousness and true holiness (Eph. 4:24; Titus 2:12).

6. The Ordinances of the Church

(a) Baptism in Water

The ordinance of baptism by immersion is commanded in the Scriptures. All who repent and believe on Christ as Saviour and Lord are to be baptized. Thus they declare to the world that they have died with Christ and that they also have been raised with Him to walk in newness of life. (Matthew 28:19; Mark 16:16; Acts 10:47, 48; Romans 6:4).

(b) Holy Communion

The Lord's Supper, consisting of the elements—bread and the fruit of the vine—is the symbol expressing our sharing the divine nature of our Lord Jesus Christ (2 Peter 1:4); a memorial of His suffering and death (1 Cor. 11:26); and a prophecy of His second coming (1 Cor. 11:26); and is enjoined on all believer "till He come!"

7. The Baptism in the Holy Ghost

All believers are entitled to and should ardently expect and earnestly seek the promise of the Father, the baptism in the Holy Ghost and fire, according to the command of our Lord Jesus Christ. This was the normal experience of all in the early Christian Church. With it comes the enduement of power for life and service, the bestowment of the gifts and their uses in the work of the ministry (Luke 24:49; Acts 1:4, 8; 1 Cor. 12:1-31). This experience is distinct from and subsequent to the experience of the new birth (Acts 8:12-17; 10:44-46; 11:14-16; 15:7-9). With the baptism in the Holy Ghost come such experiences as an overflowing fullness of the Spirit (John 7:37-39; Acts 4:8), a deepened reverence for God (Acts 2:43; Heb. 12:28), an intensified consecration to God and dedication to His work (Acts 2:42), and a more active love for Christ, for His word, and for the lost (Mark 16:20).

8. The Evidence of the Baptism in the Holy Ghost

The baptism of believers in the Holy Ghost is witnessed by the initial physical sign of speaking with other tongues as the Spirit of God gives them utterance (Acts 2:4). The speaking in tongues in this instance is the same in essence as the gift of tongues (1 Cor. 12:4-10, 28), but different in purpose and use.

9. Sanctification

Sanctification is an act of separation from that which is evil, and of dedication unto God (Rom. 12:1, 2; 1 Thess. 5:23; Heb. 13:12). The Scriptures teach a life of "holiness without which no man shall see the Lord" (Heb. 12:14). By the power of the Holy Ghost we are able to obey the command: "Be ye holy, for I am holy." (1 Peter 1:15, 16)

Sanctification is realized in the believer by recognizing his identification with Christ in His death and resurrection, and by faith reckoning daily upon the fact of that union, and by offering every faculty continually to the dominion of the Holy Spirit. (Rom. 6:1-11, 13; 8:1, 2, 13; Gal. 2:20; Phil. 2:12, 13; 1 Peter 1:5)

10. The Church and Its Mission

The Church is the Body of Christ, the habitation of God through the Spirit, with divine appointments for the fulfillment of her great commission. Each believer, born of the Spirit, is an integral part of the General Assembly and Church of the Firstborn, which are written in heaven (Ephesians 1:22, 23; 2:22; Hebrews 12:23).

Since God's purpose concerning man is to seek and to save that which is lost, to be worshiped by man, and to build a body of believers in the image of His Son, the priority reason-for-being of the Assemblies of God as part of the Church is:

a. To be an agency of God for evangelizing the world (Acts 1:8; Matthew 28:19, 20; Mark 16:15, 16).
b. To be a corporate body in which man may worship God (1 Corinthians 12:13).
c. To be a channel of God's purpose to build a body of saints being perfected in the image of His Son (Ephesians 4:11-16; 1 Corinthians 12:28; 1 Corinthians 14:12).

The Assemblies of God exists expressly to give continuing emphasis to this reason-for-being in the New Testament apostolic pattern by teaching and encouraging believers to be baptized in the Holy Spirit. This experience:

a. Enables them to evangelize in the power of the Spirit with accompanying supernatural signs (Mark 16:15-20; Acts 4:29-31; Hebrews 2:3, 4).
b. Adds a necessary dimension to worshipful relationship with God (1 Corinthians 2:10-16; 1 Corinthians 12, 13, and 14).
c. Enables them to respond to the full working of the Holy Spirit in expression of fruit and gifts and ministries as in New Testament times for the edifying of the body of Christ (Galatians 5:22-26; 1 Corinthians 14:12; Ephesians 4:11, 12; 1 Corinthians 12:28; Colossians 1:29).

11. The Ministry

A divinely called and scripturally ordained ministry has been provided by our Lord for the threefold purpose of leading the Church in: (1) Evangelization of the world (Mark 16:15-20), (2) Worship of God (John 4:23, 24), (3) Building a body of saints being perfected in the image of His Son (Ephesians 4: 11-16).

12. Divine Healing

Divine healing is an integral part of the gospel. Deliverance from sickness is provided for in the atonement, and is the privilege of all belivers (Isaiah 53:4, 5; Matt. 8:16, 17; James 5:14-16).

13. The Blessed Hope

The resurrection of those who have fallen asleep in Christ and their translation together with those who are alive and remain unto the coming of the Lord is the imminent and blessed hope of the church (1 Thess. 4:16, 17; Romans 8:23; Titus 2:13; 1 Cor. 15:51, 52).

14. The Millennial Reign of Christ

The second coming of Christ includes the rapture of the saints, which is our blessed hope, followed by the visible return of Christ with His saints to reign on the earth for one thousand years (Zech. 14:5; Matt. 24:27, 30; Revelation 1:7; 19:11-14; 20:1-6). This millennial reign will bring the salvation of national Israel (Ezekiel 37:21, 22; Zephaniah 3:19, 20; Romans 11:26, 27) and the establishment of universal peace (Isaiah 11:6-9; Psalm 72:3-8; Micah 4:3, 4).

15. The Final Judgment

There will be a final judgment in which the wicked dead will be raised and judged according to their works. Whosoever is not found written in the Book of Life, together with the devil and his angels, the beast and the false prophet, will be consigned to everlasting punishment in the lake which burneth with fire and brimstone, which is the second death (Matt. 25:46; Mark 9:43-48; Revelation 19:20; 20:11-15; 21:8).

16. The New Heavens and the New Earth

"We, according to His promise, look for new heavens and a new earth wherein dwelleth righteousness" (2 Peter 3:13; Revelation 21;22).

APPENDIX B

DECLARATION AT ST. LOUIS

Recognizing the end times in which we live and the evident hand of God which has rested upon the Assemblies of God for these times, and having engaged together in prayerful study in this Council on Evangelism concerning God's purpose in the world today and our place in His purpose, we make the following declaration.

DECLARATION

Because the Assemblies of God came into being as the Holy Spirit was poured out in prophetic fulfillment at the turn of the century and a body of like-minded Pentecostal believers voluntarily joined together in worship, ministry, and service; and

Because the Assemblies of God has accepted the Bible as the inerrant Word of God and has declared it as the whole counsel of God, giving emphasis to the full gospel; and

Because the Assemblies of God has grown rapidly both at home and abroad and has continued to experience the blessing of God as it has sought to do His will and to be an instrument of divine purpose; and

Because the Assemblies of God determines to remain a body of believers responding fully to the divine working in these last days; therefore, be it

Declared, That the Assemblies of God considers it was brought into being and built by the working of the Holy Spirit as an instrument of divine purpose in these end times; and be it
Declared further, That the Assemblies of God recognizes God's purposes concerning man are:

1. To reveal Himself through Christ to seek and to save that which is lost,
2. To be worshiped in spirit and in truth,
3. To build a body of believers in the image of His Son; and be it

Declared further, That the Assemblies of God recognizes that its mission is:

1. To be an agency of God for evangelizing the world,
2. To be a corporate body in which man may worship God,
3. To be a channel of God's purpose to build a body of saints being perfected in the image of His Son; and be it

Declared further, That the Assemblies of God exists expressly to give continuing emphasis to this mission in the New Testament apostolic pattern by encouraging believers to be baptized in the Holy Spirit, which enables them:

1. To evangelize in the power of the Holy Spirit with accompanying supernatural signs,
2. To worship God in the fullness of the Spirit,
3. To respond to the full working of the Holy Spirit in expressing His fruit and gifts as in New Testament times, edifying the body of Christ and perfecting the saints for the work of the ministry.

RESPONSE

LEADERS: In response to this declaration of mission of the Assemblies of God, we affirm that God is not willing that any should perish but is revealing Himself through Jesus Christ and is seeking to save the lost, calling man to Himself in Christ.

CONGREGATION: *This we affirm!*

LEADERS: We affirm that God desires to build a body of believers in the image of His Son, separating them unto Himself.

CONGREGATION: *This we affirm!*

LEADERS: We give ourselves to be an agency of God for evangelizing the world through Jesus Christ.

CONGREGATION: *We give ourselves to Him for this mission.*

LEADERS: We give ourselves to be a spiritual body in which man may worship God in the beauty of holiness and may be separated unto Him.

CONGREGATION: *We give ourselves to Him for this mission.*

LEADERS: We give ourselves to build a body of saints being perfected in the image of His Son, conforming unto Him.

CONGREGATION: *We give ourselves to Him for this mission.*

LEADERS: We dedicate ourselves to Spirit-filled living and teaching, to encourage believers likewise to be baptized in the Holy Spirit, knowing this will enable us to evangelize in the power of the Spirit with signs following.

CONGREGATION: *We dedicate ourselves to this mission.*

LEADERS: We dedicate ourselves to be filled with the Spirit so we will worship God in the fullness of the Spirit and minister before Him in spirit and in truth.

CONGREGATION: *We dedicate ourselves to this mission.*

LEADERS: We dedicate ourselves to respond to the full working of the Holy Spirit, praying He will use us mightily even as He worked in the New Testament Church, granting expression of fruit and gifts and ministries for the edifying of the body of Christ.

CONGREGATION: *We dedicate ourselves to this mission.*

LEADERS: This purpose of God and this mission of the Assemblies of God we affirm this day, and to this mission we dedicate ourselves, praying always to be kept in the faith, to evangelize in the power of the Spirit, to worship in spirit and in truth, and to conform to the image of His Son—so help us God!

CONGREGATION: *To this purpose of God and to this mission of the Assemblies of God we give ourselves this day—so help us God!*

APPENDIX C

A STATEMENT OF SOCIAL CONCERN[1]

"THE ASSEMBLIES OF GOD recognizes with growing solicitude the grave crises existing in every segment of our contemporary society. In order to relate our church meaningfully to its social responsibilities to men as well as its spiritual obligations to God, we make the following affirmations:

"As members of the evangelical Christian community, we believe that the Church has a unique and indispensable contribution to make in the current efforts at improving human conditions. We oppose the social ills that unjustly keep men from sharing in the blessings of their communities; and we abhor the moral evils that destroy human dignity and prevent men from receiving the blessings of heaven.

"As sons of God as well as citizens on earth, we reaffirm the Biblical view that man is a sinner and inclined to evil by his nature; that crises in human affairs are produced by selfishness and pride resulting from separation from God; and, that the spirit of alienation, rebellion, and racism is a universal human weakness reflecting the native spirit of fallen humanity.

"Because of this Biblical view of the human race, we neither believe that alienations are healed by devised confrontations between those alienated, nor that revolution is the key to social progress. Community-betterment projects and legislative actions on social improvement may alleviate the symptoms of a fundamental human problem (and by all means they should be prominent in our society); but the human solutions to social problems are not enough. Man's greatest need is his need of God; and without God he can hope for no just and equitable society.

"It is here that the Church makes its most significant social contribution. This contribution is not of goods and services only, however urgent may be the need for economic justice. And this contribution is not all good will and recognition merely, however alienated and oppressed any people may be. A sin-sick world needs the salvation of God. The first and foremost obligation of the Church to society is to preach publicly in every community the Biblical gospel of the Lord Jesus Christ.

"We of the Assemblies of God intend as citizens to make our influence felt where concrete social action is justified in areas of domestic relations, education, law enforcement, employment, equal opportunity, and other worthwhile and beneficial matters. However,

---

[1]General Presbytery minutes, August 21, 1968, pp. 24-26.

we reaffirm our deep conviction that the greatest need of man is for personal salvation through Jesus Christ, and we give this spiritual need its due priority. It is only as men become right with God that they can truly become right with one another.

"As a community of Christians we labor to *win* men, not merely to move men. We are called to accomplish our objectives not by coercion, but by conversion. It is not in clashes and confrontations that we manifest God to the world, but it is in demonstrating the power of the Holy Spirit to change men's lives.

"In these matters the world does not write our agenda. Nor do the circumstances of our times dictate our mission. These are given to us by God. Our calling is to be faithful to Him.

"WE THEREFORE PLEDGE to humble ourselves before God, to pray, and to seek the power of the Holy Spirit to change the lives of men; and

"We further PLEDGE to give ourselves in the Biblical way to meet today's challenge by a renewed dedication to proclaim the fullness of the universal gospel of Jesus Christ both at home and abroad without respect to color, national origin, or social status!

"WE FURTHER PLEDGE to exert our influence as Christian citizens to justifiable social action in areas of domestic relations, education, law enforcement, employment, equal opportunity, and other beneficial matters."

Appendix D

OFFICERS OF THE GENERAL COUNCIL: 1914-1979

1. HOT SPRINGS, ARKANSAS—APRIL 2-12, 1914

Chairman: Eudorus N. Bell — Secretary: J. Roswell Flower

2. CHICAGO, ILLINOIS—NOVEMBER 15-29, 1914

Chairman: Arch P. Collins — Secretary: J. Roswell Flower
Asst. Chm.: Daniel C. O. Opperman — Asst. Secretary: Bennett F. Lawrence

3. ST. LOUIS, MISSOURI—OCTOBER 1-10, 1915

Chairman: John W. Welch — Secretary: J. Roswell Flower

4. ST. LOUIS, MISSOURI—OCTOBER 1-7, 1916

Chairman: John W. Welch — Secretary: Stanley H. Frodsham

5. ST. LOUIS, MISSOURI—SEPTEMBER 9-14, 1917

Chairman: John W. Welch — Secretary: Stanley H. Frodsham

6. SPRINGFIELD, MISSOURI—SEPTEMBER 4-11, 1918

Chairman: John W. Welch — Secretary: Stanley H. Frodsham

7. CHICAGO, ILLINOIS—SEPTEMBER 25-30, 1919

Chairman: John W. Welch — Secretary and Editor: Eudorus N. Bell
Foreign Missions Secy.: J. Roswell Flower

8. SPRINGFIELD, MISSOURI—SEPTEMBER 21-27, 1920

Chairman: Eudorus N. Bell — Secretary: John W. Welch
Foreign Missions Secy.: J. Roswell Flower
Editor: J. T. Boddy

9. ST. LOUIS, MISSOURI—SEPTEMBER 21-28, 1921

Chairman: Eudorus N. Bell — Secretary: John W. Welch
Foreign Missions Secy.: J. Roswell Flower
Editor: Stanley H. Frodsham

(E. N. Bell died in Springfield, Missouri, June 15, 1923. His office was not filled until the 1923 General Council.)

10. ST. LOUIS, MISSOURI—SEPTEMBER 13-18, 1923

Chairman: John W. Welch — Secretary: J. R. Evans
Asst. Chairman: David H. McDowell — Foreign Missions Secy.: William Faux
Foreign Missions Treas.: J. Roswell Flower
Editor: Stanley H. Frodsham

11. EUREKA SPRINGS, ARKANSAS—SEPTEMBER 17-24, 1925

Chairman: W. T. Gaston — Secretary: J. R. Evans
Asst. Chairman: David H. McDowell — For. Miss. Secy.-Treas.: William Faux
Editor: Stanley H. Frodsham

12. SPRINGFIELD, MISSOURI—SEPTEMBER 16-22, 1927

General Superintendent: W. T. Gaston — General Secretary: J. R. Evans
Asst. General Superintendent: David H. McDowell — Foreign Missions Secy.: Noel Perkin
Editor: Stanley H. Frodsham

13. WICHITA, KANSAS—SEPTEMBER 20-26, 1929

Gen. Supt.: Ernest S. Williams — General Secretary: J. R. Evans
Asst. General Superintendent: (vacant) — Foreign Missions Secy.: Noel Perkin
Editor: Stanley H. Frodsham

14. SAN FRANCISCO, CALIFORNIA—SEPTEMBER 8-13, 1931

Gen. Supt.: Ernest S. Williams — General Secretary: J. R. Evans
Asst. Gen. Supt.: J. Roswell Flower — Foreign Missions Secy.: Noel Perkin
Editor: Stanley H. Frodsham

15. PHILADELPHIA, PENNSYLVANIA—SEPTEMBER, 14-20, 1933

All officers reelected.

16. DALLAS, TEXAS—SEPTEMBER 12-19, 1935

Gen. Supt.: ERNEST S. WILLIAMS
Asst. Gen. Supt.: J. ROSWELL FLOWER
General Secretary: J. ROSWELL FLOWER
Foreign Missions Secy.: NOEL PERKIN
Editor: STANLEY H. FRODSHAM

17. MEMPHIS, TENNESSEE—SEPTEMBER 2-9, 1937

Gen. Supt.: ERNEST S. WILLIAMS
Asst. Gen. Supt.: FRED VOGLER
General Secretary: J. ROSWELL FLOWER
Foreign Missions Secy.: NOEL PERKIN
Editor: STANLEY H. FRODSHAM

18. SPRINGFIELD, MISSOURI—SEPTEMBER 2-12, 1939

All officers reelected.

19. MINNEAPOLIS, MINNESOTA—SEPTEMBER 5-11, 1941

All officers reelected.

20. SPRINGFIELD, MISSOURI—SEPTEMBER 1-9, 1943

Gen. Supt.: ERNEST S. WILLIAMS
Asst. Gen. Supt.: RALPH M. RIGGS
General Secretary: J. ROSWELL FLOWER
Foreign Missions Secy.: NOEL PERKIN
Editor: STANLEY H. FRODSHAM

21. SPRINGFIELD, MISSOURI—SEPTEMBER 13-18, 1945

Gen. Supt.: ERNEST S. WILLIAMS
Asst. Gen. Supts.: RALPH M. RIGGS, GAYLE F. LEWIS, FRED VOGLER, and WESLEY R. STEELBERG
General Secretary: J. ROSWELL FLOWER
Foreign Missions Secy.: NOEL PERKIN
Editor: STANLEY H. FRODSHAM

22. GRAND RAPIDS, MICHIGAN—SEPTEMBER 4-11, 1947

Gen. Supt.: ERNEST S. WILLIAMS
Asst. Gen. Supts.: RALPH M. RIGGS, GAYLE F. LEWIS, FRED VOGLER, and WESLEY R. STEELBERG
General Secretary: J. ROSWELL FLOWER
General Treasurer: WILFRED A. BROWN
Foreign Missions Secy.: NOEL PERKIN
Editor: STANLEY H. FRODSHAM

23. SEATTLE, WASHINGTON—SEPTEMBER 8-14, 1949

Gen. Supt.: WESLEY R. STEELBERG
Asst. Gen. Supts.: RALPH M. RIGGS, GAYLE F. LEWIS, FRED VOGLER, and BERT WEBB
General Secretary: J. ROSWELL FLOWER
General Treasurer: WILFRED A. BROWN
Foreign Missions Secy.: NOEL PERKIN
Editor: ROBERT C. CUNNINGHAM
(Cunningham has continued to serve as editor of *The Pentecostal Evangel*, an appointive position, to the present time).

24. ATLANTA, GEORGIA—AUGUST 16-23, 1951

(All officers were reelected. Wesley R. Steelberg died in Cardiff, Wales, July 8, 1952. Gayle F. Lewis was chosen to fill the unexpired term of General Superintendent by the General Presbytery on September 2, 1952. James O. Savell was selected as an Asst. General Superintendent to fill the vacancy created by Lewis's election.)

25. MILWAUKEE, WISCONSIN—AUGUST 26-SEPTEMBER 2, 1953

Gen. Superintendent: RALPH M. RIGGS
Asst. Gen. Supts.: GAYLE F. LEWIS, BERT WEBB, J. O. SAVELL, and T. F. ZIMMERMAN
General Secretary: J. ROSWELL FLOWER
General Treasurer: WILFRED A. BROWN
Foreign Missions Secy.: NOEL PERKIN

26. OKLAHOMA CITY, OKLAHOMA—SEPTEMBER 1-6, 1955

(All officers reelected. Wilfred A. Brown died on September 19, 1955, in Springfield, Missouri. Atwood Foster was appointed by the General Presbytery to fulfill the unexpired term.)

27. CLEVELAND, OHIO—AUGUST 28-SEPTEMBER 3, 1957

Gen. Superintendent: RALPH M. RIGGS
Asst. Gen. Supts.: GAYLE F. LEWIS, BERT WEBB, C. W. H. SCOTT, and T. F. ZIMMERMAN
General Secretary: J. ROSWELL FLOWER
General Treasurer: MARTIN B. NETZEL
Foreign Missions Secy.: NOEL PERKIN

28. SAN ANTONIO, TEXAS—AUGUST 26-SEPTEMBER 1, 1959

Gen. Supt.: THOMAS F. ZIMMERMAN
Asst. Gen. Supts.: GAYLE F. LEWIS, C. W. H. SCOTT, BERT WEBB, and HOWARD S. BUSH
General Secretary: BARTLETT PETERSON
General Treasurer: MARTIN B. NETZEL

(The director of Foreign Missions was given the title of Assistant General Superintendent, carrying the portfolio of Foreign Missions. J. Philip Hogan was elected to this position, filling the position vacated by Noel Perkin, who retired in 1959. Hogan has continued to fill that post to the present time.)

29. PORTLAND, OREGON—AUGUST 23-29, 1961

(All officers were reelected.)

30. MEMPHIS, TENNESSEE—AUGUST 21-26, 1963

(All officers reelected.)

31. DES MOINES, IOWA—AUGUST 25-30, 1965

Gen. Supt.: THOMAS F. ZIMMERMAN
Asst. Gen. Supts.: HOWARD S. BUSH, THEODORE E. GANNON, C. W. H. SCOTT, BERT WEBB, and J. PHILIP HOGAN
General Secretary: BARTLETT PETERSON
General Treasurer: MARTIN B. NETZEL

32. LONG BEACH, CALIFORNIA—AUGUST 24-29, 1967

(All officers reelected. In 1965, the office of General Superintendent was made a four-year term, so that office was not voted upon in 1967. Howard S. Bush died in Springfield, Missouri on March 26, 1969. His office was left vacant until the August, 1969 General Council.)

33. DALLAS, TEXAS—AUGUST 21-26, 1969

Gen. Supt.: THOMAS F. ZIMMERMAN
Asst. Gen. Supts.: G. RAYMOND CARLSON, T. E. GANNON, KERMIT RENEAU, C. W. H. SCOTT, and J. PHILIP HOGAN
General Secretary: BARTLETT PETERSON
General Treasurer: MARTIN B. NETZEL

34. KANSAS CITY, MISSOURI—AUGUST 19-24, 1971

Gen. Supt.: THOMAS F. ZIMMERMAN
Asst. Gen. Supt.: G. RAYMOND CARLSON
General Secretary: BARTLETT PETERSON
General Treasurer: MARTIN B. NETZEL

(Martin B. Netzel died in Springfield, Missouri on May 20, 1973. His office was left vacant until the August, 1973 General Council.)

35. MIAMI BEACH, FLORIDA—AUGUST 16-21, 1973

Gen. Supt.: THOMAS F. ZIMMERMAN
Asst. Gen. Supt.: G. RAYMOND CARLSON
General Secretary: BARTLETT PETERSON
General Treasurer: RAYMOND H. HUDSON

36. DENVER, COLORADO—AUGUST 14-19, 1975

Gen. Supt.: THOMAS F. ZIMMERMAN
Asst. Gen. Supt.: G. RAYMOND CARLSON
General Secretary: JOSEPH R. FLOWER
General Treasurer: RAYMOND H. HUDSON

37. OKLAHOMA, CITY, OKLAHOMA, AUGUST 18-23, 1977

(All officers reelected.)

38. BALTIMORE, MARYLAND—AUGUST 16-21, 1979

(All officers reelected.)

Appendix E

STATISTICAL DATA (1914-1969)

ORDAINED MINISTERS IN THE U.S.A. 1914 - 1969
GENERAL COUNCIL - ASSEMBLIES OF GOD

CHART NO. 1

Year	Ordained Ministers
1914	300
1925	1,155
1927	1,457
1929	1,641
1931	1,851
1933	2,086
1935	2,606
1937	3,086
1939	3,592
1941	4,159
1943	4,664
1945	5,016
1947	5,746
1949	6,225
1951	7,210
1953	7,641
1955	8,650
1957	8,878
1959	9,273
1961	9,428
1963	9,872
1965	10,237
1967	11,168
1969	11,459

Scale: 1,000 · 2,000 · 3,000 · 4,000 · 5,000 · 6,000 · 7,000 · 8,000 · 9,000 · 10,000 · 11,000

1982 Data: 15,744 Ordained Ministers in the U.S.A.

ASSEMBLIES OF GOD CHURCHES IN THE U.S.A. 1914 - 1969

CHART NO. 2

Year	Churches
1914	
1925	909
1927	1,353
1929	1,612
1931	2,030
1933	2,562
1935	3,149
1937	3,473
1939	3,496
1941	4,348
1943	5,106
1945	5,311
1947	5,548
1949	5,950
1951	5,854
1953	6,400
1955	7,320
1957	7,929
1959	8,094
1961	8,233
1963	8,302
1965	8,452
1967	8,506
1969	8,570

1,000
2,000
3,000
4,000
5,000
6,000
7,000
8,000
9,000

1982 Data: 10,173 Churches in the U.S.A.

CHURCH MEMBERSHIP IN THE U.S.A. 1914-1969
GENERAL COUNCIL - ASSEMBLIES OF GOD

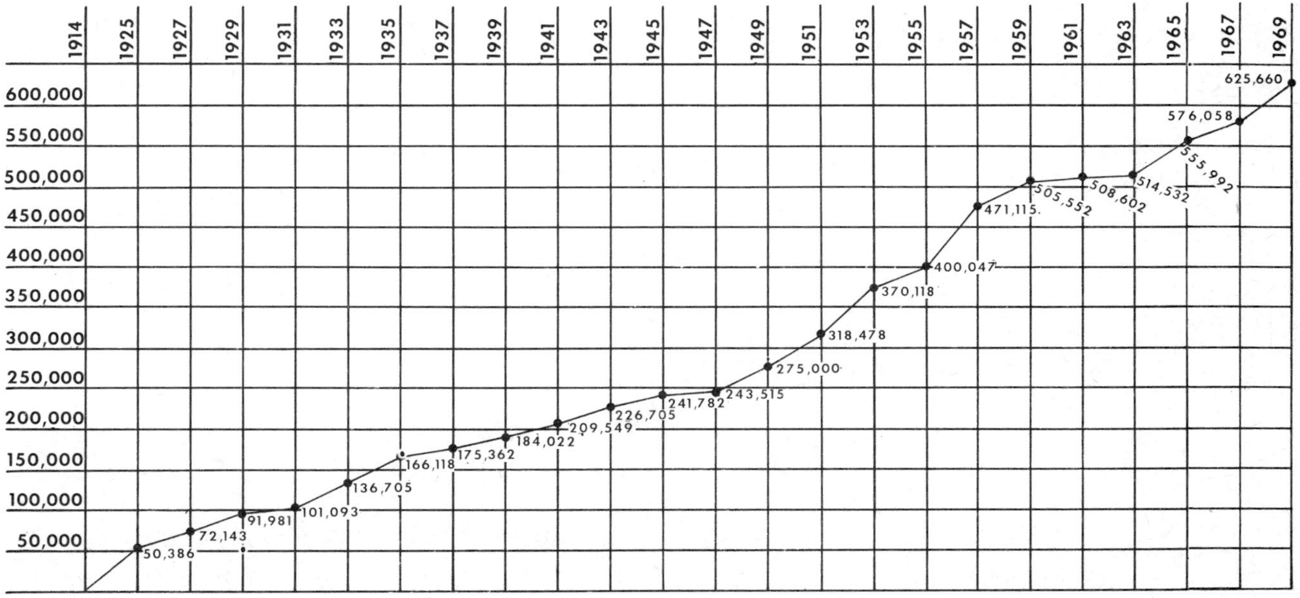

CHART NO. 3

1914
1925
1927
1929
1931
1933
1935
1937
1939
1941
1943
1945
1947
1949
1951
1953
1955
1957
1959
1961
1963
1965
1967
1969

600,000
550,000
500,000
450,000
400,000
350,000
300,000
250,000
200,000
150,000
100,000
50,000

50,386
72,143
91,981
101,093
136,705
166,118
175,362
184,022
209,549
226,705
241,782
243,515
275,000
318,478
370,118
400,047
471,115
505,552
508,602
514,532
555,992
576,058
625,660

1982 Data: 1,119,686 Members in the U.S.A.

ASSEMBLIES OF GOD **CHART NO. 4**

SUNDAY SCHOOL ENROLLMENT, 1951 - 1969

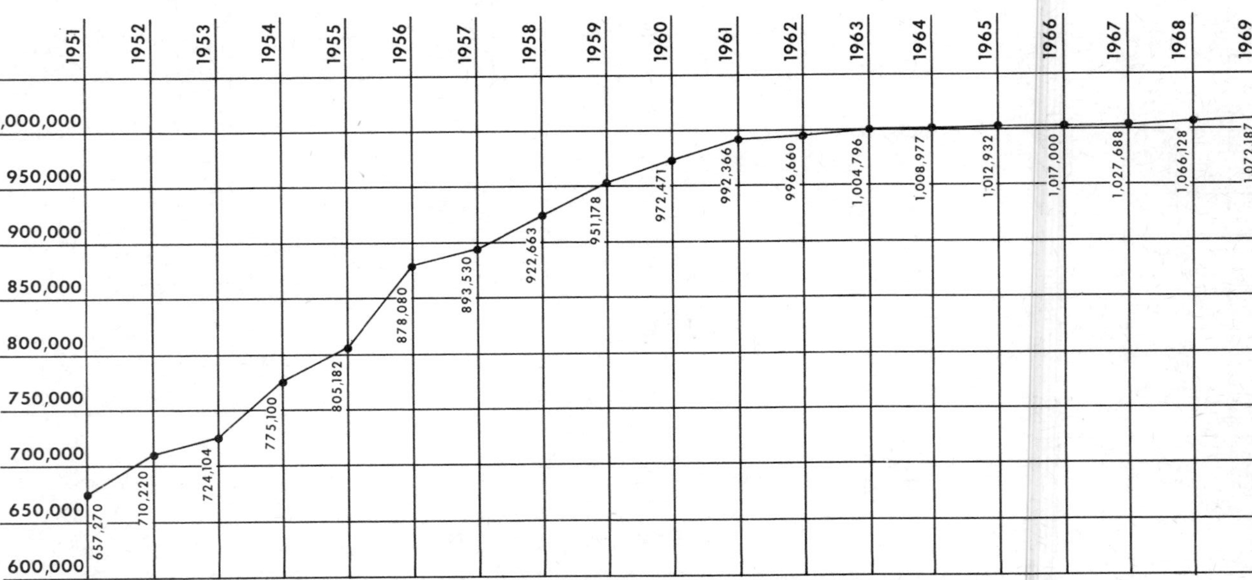

[1] Accurate figures for years prior to 1951 are not available.
Foreign Branch schools in the U.S.A. are included from 1956 on.

1982 Data: 1,421,924 Enrollment

NUMBER OF ASSEMBLIES OF GOD FOREIGN MISSIONARIES, 1914-1969

CHART NO. 5

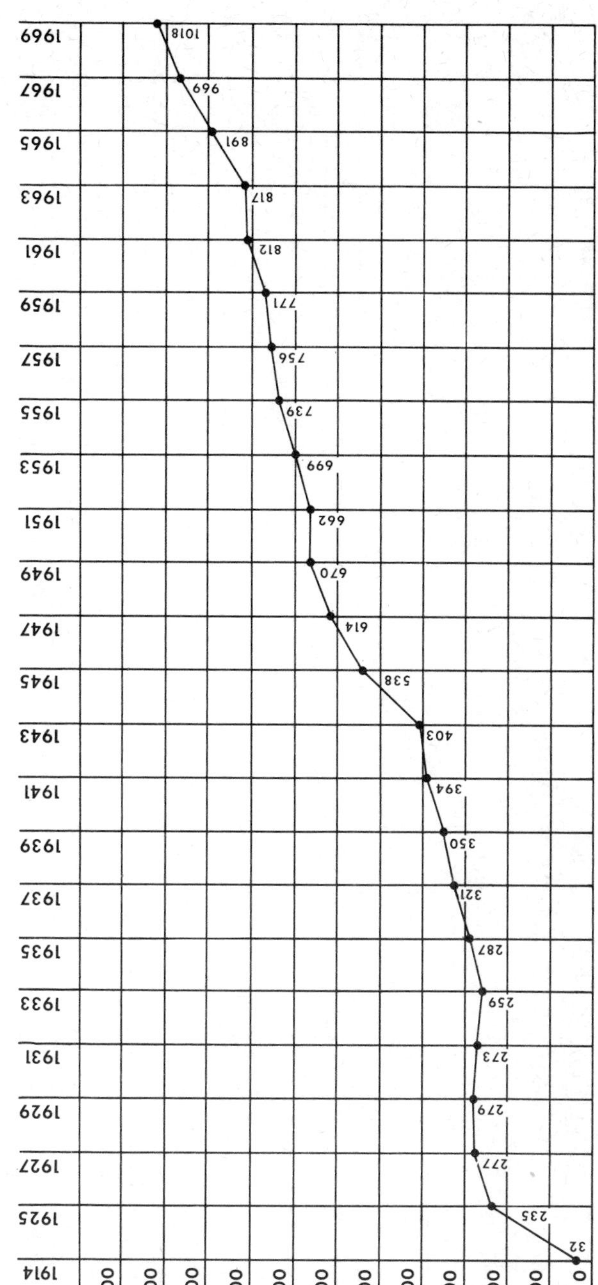

1982 Data: 1,220 Missionaries

CHART NO. 6

OVERSEAS CONSTITUENCY OF THE ASSEMBLIES OF GOD, 1951 - 1969

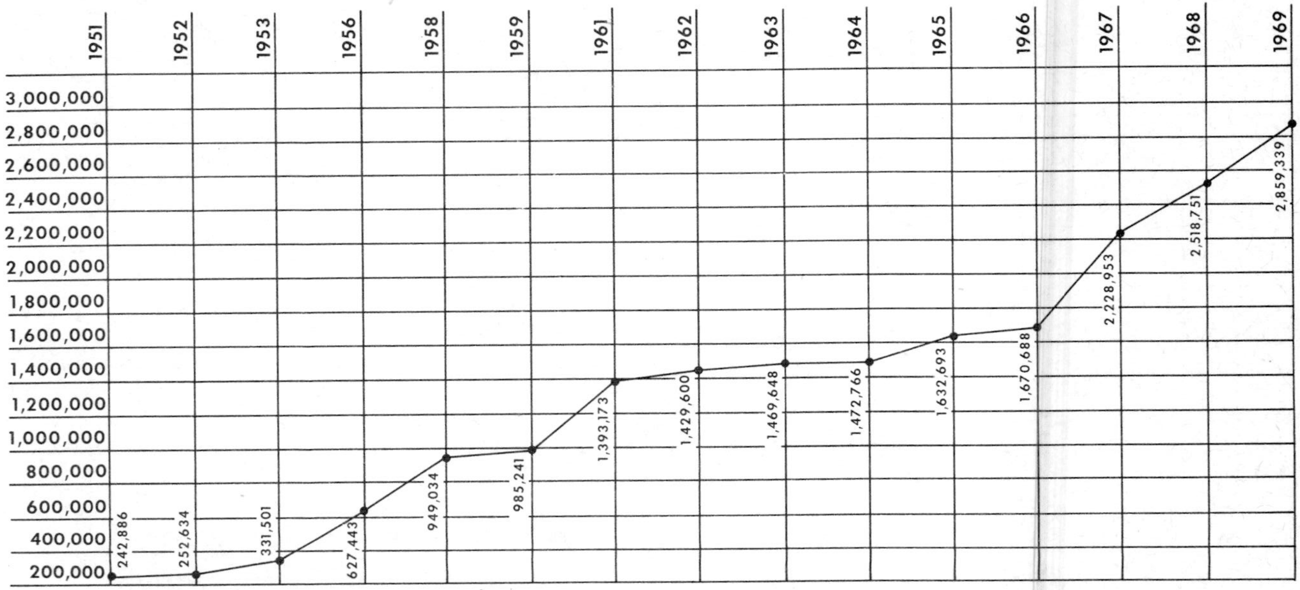

1982 Data: 10,250,571 Overseas Constituency

CHART NO. 7

FOREIGN MISSIONS GIVING OF THE ASSEMBLIES OF GOD IN THE U.S.A., 1916-1969

(IN DOLLARS)

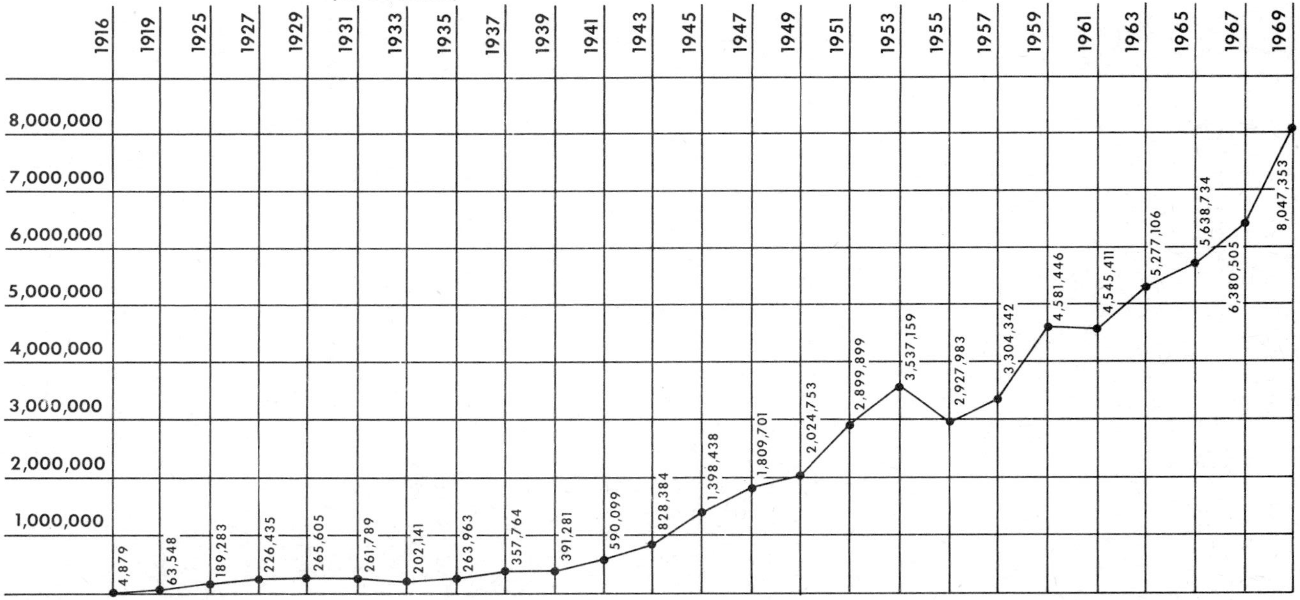

Year	Giving
1916	4,879
1919	63,548
1925	189,283
1927	226,435
1929	265,605
1931	261,789
1933	202,141
1935	263,963
1937	357,764
1939	391,281
1941	590,099
1943	828,384
1945	1,398,438
1947	1,809,701
1949	2,024,753
1951	2,899,899
1953	3,537,159
1955	2,927,983
1957	3,304,342
1959	4,581,446
1961	4,545,411
1963	5,277,106
1965	5,638,734
1967	6,380,505
1969	8,047,353

Axis: 1,000,000; 2,000,000; 3,000,000; 4,000,000; 5,000,000; 6,000,000; 7,000,000; 8,000,000

1982 Data: $48,453,712 Foreign Missions Giving

Bibliography

BOOKS

Arthur, W. *The Tongue of Fire.* London: Charles H. Kelly, 1856.

Atter, Gordon F. *The Third Force.* Peterborough, Ontario: The College Press, 1962.

Barabas, Steven. *So Great Salvation.* Westwood, New Jersey: Fleming H. Revell, n.d.

Barratt, T. B. *In the Days of the Latter Rain.* London: Elim Publishing Company, n.d.

______. *When the Fire Fell.* Norway: Alfons Hansen and Soner, 1927.

Bartelman, Frank. *How Pentecost Came to Los Angeles.* Los Angeles: Privately printed, 1928.

______. *What Really Happened at Azusa Street.* Northridge, California: Voice Publications, 1962.

Benson, Clarence. *A Popular History of Christian Education.* Chicago: Moody Press, 1943.

Bloch-Hoell, Nils. *The Pentecostal Movement.* Oslo: Universitetsforlaget, 1964.

Boer, Harry R. *Pentecost and Missions.* Grand Rapids: Eerdmans, 1961.

Boyd, Frank M. *Ages and Dispensations.* Springfield, Missouri: Gospel Publishing House, 1949.

______. *Introduction to Prophecy.* Springfield, Missouri: Gospel Publishing House, 1948.

Braden, Charles S. *These Also Believe.* New York: Macmillan, 1950.

Bresson, Bernard L. *Studies in Ecstasy.* New York: Vantage Press, 1966.

Brumback, Carl. *Suddenly . . . from Heaven.* Springfield, Missouri: Gospel Publishing House, 1961.

______. *What Meaneth This?* Springfield, Missouri: Gospel Publishing House, 1947.

Brunner, Emil. *The Misunderstanding of the Church.* Translated by Harold Knight. Philadelphia: Westminster Press, 1953.

Buntain, D. N. *The Holy Ghost and Fire.* Springfield, Missouri: Gospel Publishing House, 1956.

Cairns, Earle E. *Christianity in the United States.* Chicago: Moody Press, 1964.

Campbell, Joseph E. *The Pentecostal Holiness Church* 1898-1948. Franklin Springs, Georgia: Publishing House of the Pentecostal Holiness Church, 1951.

Carter, Howard. *The Gifts of the Holy Spirit.* London: Defoe Press, 1946.

Champion, Richard; Caldwell, E. S.; Leggett, Gary (eds.). *Our Mission in Today's World.* Springfield, Missouri: Gospel Publishing House, 1968.

Clark, Elmer T. *The Small Sects in America.* Rev. ed. New York: Abingdon Press, 1949.

Clark, Glenn. *The Holy Spirit.* St. Paul, Minnesota: Macalester Park, 1954.

Commager, Henry S. *The American Mind.* New Haven: Yale University Press, 1950.

Conn, Charles W. *Like A Mighty Army.* Cleveland, Tennessee: Church of God Publishing House, 1955.

Crayne, Richard. *Pentecostal Handbook.* Morristown, Tennessee: Privately printed, 1963.

Curran, Francis X. *Major Trends in American Church History.* New York: The American Press, 1946.

Cutten, George B. *Speaking with Tongues.* New Haven: Yale University Press, 1927.

Dalton, Robert Chandler. *Tongues Like as of Fire.* Springfield, Missouri: Gospel Publishing House, 1945.

Duffield, G. P. *Pentecostal Preaching.* New York: Vantage Press, 1957.

Du Plessis, David. *The Spirit Bade Me Go.* Rev. ed. Dallas, Texas: Privately printed, 1963.

Evans, W. I. *This River Must Flow.* Springfield, Missouri: Gospel Publishing House, 1954.

Ewart, Frank J. *The Phenomenon of Pentecost.* St. Louis: Pentecostal Publishing House, 1947.

Ferguson, Charles W. *The Confusion of Tongues.* Grand Rapids: Zondervan, 1940.

Fischer, Harold A. *Reviving Revivals.* Springfield, Missouri: Gospel Publishing House, 1950.

Flower, Alice R. *Grace for Grace.* Springfield, Missouri: Privately printed, n.d.

Frodsham, Stanley H. *Rivers of Living Water.* Springfield, Missouri: Gospel Publishing House, n.d.

———. *Smith Wigglesworth, Apostle of Faith.* Springfield, Missouri: Gospel Publishing House, 1951.

———. *This Pentecostal Revival.* Springfield, Missouri: Gospel Publishing House, 1941.

———. *With Signs Following.* Rev. ed. Springfield, Missouri: Gospel Publishing House, 1946.

Furniss, Norman F. *The Fundamentalist Controversy,* 1918-1931. Hamden, Connecticut: Archon Books, 1963.

Gee, Donald. *After Pentecost.* Springfield, Missouri: Gospel Publishing House, 1945.

———. *All With One Accord.* Springfield, Missouri: Gospel Publishing House, 1961.

———. *Concerning Spiritual Gifts.* Rev. ed. Springfield, Missouri: Gospel Publishing House, 1937.

———. *Pentecost.* Springfield, Missouri: Gospel Publishing House, 1932.

———. *Spiritual Gifts in the Work of the Ministry Today.* Springfield, Missouri: Gospel Publishing House, 1963.

——— (ed.). *The Fifth World Pentecostal Conference, Toronto, Canada,* 1958. Toronto: Testimony Press, 1958.

———. *The Glory of the Assemblies of God.* Luton, England: Redemption Tidings Bookroom, n.d.

———. *The Ministry-Gifts of Christ.* Springfield, Missouri: Gospel Publishing House, 1930.

———. *The Pentecostal Movement.* Enlarged ed. London: Elim Publishing Company, 1949.

———. *The Phenomena of Pentecost.* Springfield, Missouri: Gospel Publishing House, 1931.

———. *Upon All Flesh.* Rev. ed. Springfield, Missouri: Gospel Publishing House, 1947.

———. *Why Pentecost?* London: Victory Press, 1944

Geiger, Kenneth E. (compiler). *The Word and the Doctrine.* Kansas City: Beacon Hill Press, 1965.

Glover, Robert H. *The Progress of World-wide Missions.* Rev. ed. New York: Harper and Brothers, 1960.

Goldman, Eric F. *The Crucial Decade—and After: America,* 1945-1960. New York: Random House, 1960.

Gordon, A. J. *The Ministry of the Spirit.* Reprinted. Philadelphia: Judson Press, 1949.

Gordon, Ernest. *An Ecclesiastical Octopus.* Boston: Fellowship Press, 1948.

Goss, Ethel E. *The Winds of God.* New York: Comet Press, 1958.

Gruits, Patricia D. *Understanding God.* Detroit: The Evangel Press, 1962.

Harnack, Adolf. *What Is Christianity?* New York: G. P. Putnam's Sons, 1904.

Harper, Michael. *As at the Beginning.* London: Hodder and Stoughton, 1965.

Hastie, Eugene N. *History of the West Central District Council of the Assemblies of God.* Fort Dodge, Iowa: Walterick Printing Company, 1948.

Hayes, D. A. *The Gift of Tongues.* New York: The Methodist Book Concern: 1913.

______. *The Drift of Western Thought.* Grand Rapids: Eerdmans, 1951.

Henry, Carl F. H. *Frontiers in Modern Theology.* Chicago: Moody Press, 1966.

Henry, C. F. H. and Mooneyham, W. S. (eds.). *One Race, One Gospel, One Task.* 2 vols. Minneapolis: World Wide Publications, 1967.

Historical Account of the Apostolic Faith, A. Portland, Oregon: The Apostolic Faith Publishing House, 1965.

Hodges, Melvin L. *The Indigenous Church.* Springfield, Missouri: Gospel Publishing House, 1953.

Hoffer, Eric. *The True Believer.* New York: The New American Library of World Literature, 1951.

Horton, Harold. *The Gifts of the Spirit.* Luton, England: Redemption Tidings Bookroom, 1934.

Horton, Stanley. *Into All Truth.* Springfield, Missouri; Gospel Publishing House, 1955.

______. *The Promise of His Coming.* Springfield, Missouri: Gospel Publishing House, 1967.

Horton, Wade H. (ed.). *The Glossolalia Phenomenon.* Cleveland, Tennessee: Pathway Press, 1966.

Howard, Rick. *Chi Alpha Manual.* Springfield, Missouri: Gospel Publishing House, 1966.

Hurst, D. V. and Jones, T. J. *The Church Begins.* Springfield, Missouri: Gospel Publishing House, 1959.

Ironside, H. A. *Holiness: The False and the True.* New York: Loizeaux Brothers, n.d.

Johnson, Charles A. *The Frontier Camp Meeting.* Dallas: Southern Methodist University Press, 1955.

Kelsey, Morton T. *Tongue-Speaking.* Garden City, New York: Doubleday and Company, 1964.

Kendrick, Klaude. *The Promise Fulfilled.* Springfield, Missouri: Gospel Publishing House, 1961.

Kincheloe, Samuel C. *Research Memorandum on Religion in the Depression.* Bulletin 33. New York: Social Science Research Council, 1937.

King, Joseph H. *Yet Speaketh, Memoirs of the Late Bishop Joseph H. King.* Franklin Springs, Georgia: The Publishing House of the Pentecostal Holiness Church, 1949.

Knox, Ronald A. *Enthusiasm.* Oxford: Clarendon Press, 1951.

Kulbeck, Gloria C. *What God Hath Wrought.* Toronto: Pentecostal Assemblies of Canada, 1958.

Lawrence, B. F. *The Apostolic Faith Restored.* St. Louis, Missouri: Gospel Publishing House, 1916.

Lemons, Frank W. *Our Pentecostal Heritage.* Cleveland, Tennessee: Pathway Press, 1963.

Lindquist, Frank J. *The Truth About the Trinity and Baptism in Jesus Name Only.* Minneapolis: Northern Gospel Publishing House, n.d.

Lindsay, Gordon. *Bible Days Are Here Again.* Shreveport, Louisiana: Privately printed, 1949.

———. *The Gordon Lindsay Story.* Dallas: The Voice of Healing Publishing Company, n.d.

Lindsell, Harold. *The Church's Worldwide Mission.* Waco, Texas: Word Books, 1966.

Litzman, Warren. *The Rebirth of Pentecost.* Waxahachie, Texas: Litzman Pentecostal Campaigns, 1960.

Luce, Alice E. *Pictures of Pentecost.* Springfield, Missouri: Gospel Publishing House, 1950.

McCrossan, T. J. *Speaking With Other Tongues: Sign or Gift, Which?* Harrisburg, Pennsylvania: Christian Alliance Publishing Company, 1927.

MacDonald, William G. *Glossolalia in the New Testament.* Springfield, Missouri: Gospel Publishing House, 1964.

McGavran, Donald (ed.). *Church Growth and Christian Mission.* New York: Harper and Row, 1965.

Mackay, John A. *Ecumenics.* Englewood Cliffs, New Jersey: Prentice-Hall, 1964.

Mackie, Alexander. *The Gift of Tongues.* New York: George H. Doran Company, 1921.

McPherson, Aimee Semple. *The Foursquare Gospel.* Los Angeles: Echo Park Evangelistic Association, 1946.

———. *The Story of My Life.* Los Angeles: Echo Park Evangelistic Association, 1951.

Martin, Ira Jay. *Glossolalia in the Apostolic Church: A Survey Study of Tongue-Speech.* Berea, Kentucky: Berea College, 1960.

Mathison, Richard R. *Faiths, Cults, and Sects of America.* New York: Bobbs-Merrill, 1960.

Mavity, Nancy B. *Sister Aimee.* Garden City, N. Y.: Doubleday, Doran, and Co., 1931.

May, Henry F. *Protestant Churches and Industrial America.* New York: Harper and Brothers, 1949.

Mead, Sidney E. *The Lively Experiment.* New York: Harper and Row, 1963.

Miller, Elmer C. *Pentecost Examined by a Baptist Lawyer.* Springfield, Missouri: Gospel Publishing House, 1936.

Moberg, David O. *The Church as a Social Institution.* Englewood Cliffs, New Jersey: Prentice-Hall, 1962.

Montgomery, Carrie Judd. *Under His Wings, The Story of My Life.* Oakland, California: Office of Triumphs of Faith, 1936.

Murch, J. D. *Christian Education and the Local Church.* Cincinnati: Standard Publishing Company, 1943.

———. *Cooperation Without Compromise.* Grand Rapids: Eerdmans, 1956.

Myland, D. W. *The Latter Rain Covenant and Pentecostal Power.* 2nd ed. Chicago: The Evangel Publishing House, 1911.

Nash, Ronald H. *The New Evangelicalism.* Grand Rapids: Zondervan, 1963.

Nelson, P. C. *Bible Doctrines.* Springfield, Missouri: Gospel Publishing House, 1948.

Newbigin, Lesslie. *The Household of God.* London: SCM Press, 1957.

Nichol, John T. *Pentecostalism.* New York: Harper and Row, 1966.

Nickel, Thomas R. *Upon All Flesh.* Monterey Park, California: Great Commission International, 1965.

Nida, Eugene A. *Message and Mission.* New York: Harper and Brothers, 1960.

Niebuhr, H. Richard. *The Kingdom of God in America.* New York: Harper and Brothers, 1937.

———. *The Social Sources of Denominationalism.* New York: World Publishing Company, 1929.

Ockenga, Harold John. *Our Evangelical Faith.* Grand Rapids: Zondervan, 1946.

Olmstead, C. E. *History of Religion in the United States.* Englewood Cliffs, New Jersey: Prentice-Hall, 1960.

Orr, J. Edwin. *The Light of the Nations.* Grand Rapids: Eerdmans, 1965.

Pardington, George P. *The Crisis of the Deeper Life.* Harrisburg, Pennsylvania: Christian Publications, n.d.

Parham, Sarah E. *The Life of Charles F. Parham.* Joplin, Missouri: Tri-State Printing Company, 1930.

Parr, J. Nelson. *Divine Healing.* Springfield, Missouri: Gospel Publishing House, 1955.

Paton D. M. (ed.). *The Ministry of the Spirit: Selected Writings of Roland Allen.* London: World Dominion Press, 1960.

Paulk, Earl P. *Your Pentecostal Neighbor.* Cleveland, Tennessee: Pathway Press, 1958.

Pearlman, Myer. *Knowing the Doctrines of the Bible.* Springfield, Missouri: Gospel Publishing House, 1937.

Penn-Lewis, Jessie. *The Awakening in Wales.* New York: Fleming H. Revell, 1905.

Perkin, Noel and Garlock, John. *Our World Witness.* Springfield, Missouri: Gospel Publishing House, 1963.

Persons, Stow. *American Minds.* New York: Holt, Rinehart and Winston, 1958.

Pethrus, Lewi. *The Wind Bloweth Where It Listeth.* Translated by Harry Lindblom. Chicago: Philadelphia Book Concern, n.d.

Plymire, David V. *High Adventure in Tibet.* Springfield, Missouri: Gospel Publishing House, 1959.
Pope, Liston. *Millhands and Preachers.* New Haven: Yale University Press, 1942.
Price, Charles S. *Divine Intervention.* Pasadena, California: Charles S. Price Publishing Company, n.d.
———. *The Story of My Life.* 4th ed. Pasadena, California: Charles S. Price Publishing Company, 1947.
Ranaghan, Kevin and Dorothy. *Catholic Pentecostals.* New York: The Paulist Press, 1969.
Rice, John R. *Speaking with Tongues.* Murfreesboro, Tennessee: Sword of the Lord Publishers, 1965.
Riggs, Ralph M. *The Spirit Himself.* Springfield, Missouri: Gospel Publishing House, 1949.
———. *The Spirit-filled Pastor's Guide.* Springfield, Missouri: Gospel Publishing House, 1948.
———. *We Believe.* Springfield, Missouri: Gospel Publishing House, 1954.
Roberts, Oral. *My Story.* Tulsa, Oklahoma: Summit Book Company, 1961.
Rose, Delbert R. *A Theology of Christian Experience.* Wilmore, Kentucky: The Seminary Press, 1958.
Scharpff, Paulus. *History of Evangelism.* Translated by H. G. Henry. Grand Rapids: Eerdmans, 1966 (English ed.).
Schlesinger, A. M. *The Rise of the City,* 1878-1898. Vol. X. of *A History of American Life.* Edited by Dixon R. Fox and Arthur M. Schlesinger. 13 vols. New York: Macmillan Company, 1933.
Schneider, Herbert W. *Religion in Twentieth Century America.* Rev. ed. New York: Atheneum, 1964.
Shaw, P. E. *The Catholic Apostolic Church, Sometimes Called Irvingite.* Morningside Heights, New York: King's Crown Press, 1946.
Shelley, Bruce. *Evangelicalism in America.* Grand Rapids: Eerdmans, 1967.
Sherrill, John L. *They Speak with Other Tongues.* New York: McGraw-Hill, 1964.
Shoemaker, Samuel M. *With the Holy Spirit and Fire.* New York: Harper and Row, 1960.
Smith, H. Shelton, Handy, R. T., and Loetscher, L. A. *American Christianity.* 2 vols. New York: Charles Scribner's Sons, 1963.
Smith, Timothy L. *Called Unto Holiness.* Kansas City: Nazarene Publishing House, 1962.
———. *Revivalism and Social Reform in Mid-Nineteenth Century America.* New York: Abingdon Press, 1957.
Steiner, Leonhard. *Mit Folgenden Zeichen.* Basel: Verlag Mission fur das volle Evangelium, 1954.
Stiles, J. E. *The Gift of the Holy Spirit.* Glendale, California: The Church Press, n.d.

Stokes, Louie W. *The Great Revival in Buenos Aires.* Buenos Aires: Casilla de Correo, n.d.

Stolee, H. J. *Speaking in Tongues.* Minneapolis: Augsburg Publishing House, 1963.

Sumrall, Lester. *All for Jesus: the Life of Wesley R. Steelberg.* Springfield, Missouri: Gospel Publishing House, 1955.

———. *Lillian Trasher, Nile Mother,* Springfield, Missouri: Gospel Publishing House, 1951.

———. *Through Blood and Fire in Latin America.* Grand Rapids: Zondervan, 1944.

Sweet, W. W. *Revivalism in America.* New York: Abingdon Press, 1944.

———. *The Story of Religion in America.* Rev. ed. New York: Harper and Brothers, 1950.

Torrey, R. A. *The Holy Spirit.* New York: Fleming H. Revell, 1927.

Tozer, A. W. *How to Be Filled with the Holy Spirit.* Harrisburg, Pennsylvania: Christian Publications, n.d.

———. *Wingspread: Albert B. Simpson, A Study in Spiritual Altitude.* Harrisburg, Pennsylvania: Christian Publications, 1943.

Troeltsch, Ernst. *The Social Teaching of the Christian Churches.* 2 vols. Translated by Olive Wyon. London: George Allen and Unwin, 1931.

Tucker, Angeline. *He Is in Heaven.* New York: McGraw-Hill Book Company, 1965.

Unger, Merrill F. *The Baptizing Work of the Holy Spirit.* Wheaton, Illinois: Van Kampen Press, 1953.

Wach, Joachim. *Sociology of Religion.* Chicago: University of Chicago Press, 1944.

Warfield, Benjamin B. *Perfectionism.* Grand Rapids: Baker, 1958.

White, Alma. *Demons and Tongues.* Zarephath, New Jersey: Pillar of Fire Publishers, 1919.

Whitehead, Alfred N. *The Aims of Education.* New York: Macmillan, 1959.

Wierwille, Victor P. *Receiving the Holy Spirit Today.* 4th ed. rev. New Knoxville, Ohio: The Way, Incorporated, 1962.

Wilkerson, David. *The Cross and the Switchblade.* New York: Random House and the Gospel Publishing House, 1963.

———. *Twleve Angels from Hell.* Westwood, New Jersey: Fleming H. Revell, 1965.

Williams, Ernest S. *Systematic Theology.* 3 vols. Springfield, Missouri: Gospel Publishing House, 1953.

Wilson, Elizabeth. *Making Many Rich.* Springfield, Missouri: Gospel Publishing House, 1955.

Winehouse, Irwin. *The Assemblies of God, A Popular Survey.* New York: Vantage Press, 1959.

Witmer, Safara A. *Education with Dimension.* Manhasset, New York: Channel Press, 1962.

———. *Report: Preparing Bible College Students for Ministries in Christian Education*. Fort Wayne, Indiana: Accrediting Association of Bible Colleges, 1962.

Womack, David. *Wellsprings of the Pentecostal Movement.* Springfield, Missouri: Gospel Publishing House, 1968.

WMC Leader, The. Springfield, Missouri: Gospel Publishing House, 1967.

Wood, William W. *Culture and Personality Aspects of the Pentecostal Holiness Religion.* The Hague: Mouton, 1965.

Woodworth-Etter, Mrs. M. B. *Acts of the Holy Ghost.* Dallas, Texas: John F. Worley Printing Company, n.d.

Wotherspoon, H. J. *What Happened at Pentecost?* Edinburgh: T. and T. Clark, 1937.

Wright, J. Elwin. *Death in the Pot.* Boston: Fellowship Press, 1944.

Yinger, J. Milton. *Sociology Looks at Religion.* New York: Macmillan, 1963.

PERIODICALS

Advance. Vols. I-III. October, 1965–December, 1969.

Assemblies of God Educator. Vols. I-XII. May-June, 1956–November-December, 1969.

Campus Ambassador. Vols. V-XX. October, 1952–April, 1967.

Chicago Daily Tribune. December 20, 1960.

Christ's Ambassadors Herald. Vols. XVIII–XL. January, 1945–December, 1967.

Full Gospel Business Men's Voice. Vols. I-XV. February, 1953–December, 1967.

General Council, Assemblies of God Minister. Issued irregularly, generally four times a year, since June 20, 1940. Known popularly as the "Quarterly Letter." June, 1940–July, 1967.

Global Conquest. Vols. I-IX. August, 1959–November-December, 1967. Now known as *Good News Crusades.*

Los Angeles Times. March 17, 1963.

Missionary Challenge, The. Vols. IV-XIX. January-March, 1944–March, 1959.

Paraclete. Vols. I-II, No. 1. Fall, 1967–Winter, 1968.

Pentecostal Evangel, The. Nos. 1182-2799. January 2, 1937–December 31, 1967.

Pulpit. Vols. I-VII. August, 1958–December, 1965.

Slant. Vols. I-XI, No. 1. January, 1958–January, 1968.

Sunday School Counselor, The. Vols. I-XXV. August, 1941–December, 1966.

Team. Vols. I-XIV. October-December, 1954–December, 1967.

Trinity. Vols. I-IV, No. 2. Trinitytide, 1961–Christmastide, 1965.

Voice of Healing, The. Vols. IV-XIX. April, 1951–March, 1967.

Word and Witness. Vol. IX, No. 12 (December 20, 1913), and Vol. X, No. 4 (April 20, 1914).

ARTICLES

Ahlstrom, Sydney E. "Theology and the Present-Day Revival," *The Annals of the American Academy of Political and Social Science,* CCCXXXII (November, 1960), 20-36.

Aikman, Duncan. "The Holy Rollers," *American Mercury,* XV (October, 1928), 180-91.

Bois, Jules. "The New Religions of America, I. The Holy Rollers, the American Dervishes," *Forum,* LXXIII (February, 1925), 145-55.

"But What About Tommy Hicks?" Christian Century, LXXI (July 7, 1954), 814-15.

Edman, V. Raymond. "Spiritual Discernment: Are Tongues Divine or Devilish?" *The United Brethren,* LXXXII (January 3, 1968), 4, 5, 18.

Frodsham, S. H. "Disfellowshiped!" *The Pentecostal Evangel,* August 18, 1928, 7.

Gee, Donald. "Why is 'Pentecost' Opposed?" *The Pentecostal Evangel,* May 18, 1929, 2-3.

Gilkey, Langdon. "Social and Intellectual Sources of Contemporary Protestant Theology in America," *Daedalus,* XCVI (Winter, 1967), 69-98.

Hanson, James H. et al. "A Symposium on Speaking in Tongues," *Dialog,* II (Spring, 1963), 152-59.

Hollenweger, Walter J. "The Pentecostal Movement and the World Council of Churches," *The Ecumenical Review,* XVIII (July, 1966), 310-20.

———. "A Vision of the Church of the Future," *Laity,* No. 20 (November, 1965), 5-11.

Kendrick, Klaude. "The Pentecostal Movement," *Christian Century,* LXXX (May 8, 1963), 608-10.

MacDonald, William G. "Glossolalia in the New Testament," *Bulletin of the Evangelical Theological Society,* XVII (Spring, 1964), 59-67.

McDonnell, Kilian. "The Ecumenical Significance of the Pentecostal Movement," *Worship,* XL (December, 1966), 608-29.

McIntire, Carl. Editorial, *Christian Beacon,* VII (December 17, 1942), 1.

———. Editorial, *Christian Beacon,* IX (April 20, 1944), 1.

———. Editorial, *Christian Beacon,* IX (April 27, 1944), 1.

McLoughlin, William G. "Is There a Third Force in Christendom?" *Daedalus,* XCVI (Winter, 1967), 43-68.

Marty, Martin E. "Sects and Cults," *The Annals of the American Academy of Political and Social Science,* CCCXXXII (November, 1960), 125-34.

———. "The Spirit's Holy Errand: The Search for a Spiritual Style in Secular America," *Daedalus,* XCVI (Winter, 1967), 99-115.

May, Carlyle. "A Survey of Glossolalia and Related Phenomena in Non-Christian Religions," *American Anthropologist,* LVIII (February, 1956), 75-96.

Muelder, W. G. "From Sect to Church," *Christendom,* X (October-December, 1945), 450-62.

O'Connor, Edward. "A Catholic Pentecostal Movement," *Ave Maria,* CV (June 3, 1967), 6.

Nouwen, Henri. "A Critical Analysis," *Ave Maria,* CV (June 3, 1967), 11.

Phillips, McCandlish. "And There Appeared to Them Tongues of Fire," *Saturday Evening Post,* CCXXXVII (May 16, 1964), 30-40.

Smith, Timothy L. "Historic Waves of Religious Interest in America," *The Annals of the American Academy of Political and Social Science,* CCCXXXII (November, 1960), 9-19.

Trinterud, L. J. "The Task of the American Church Historian," *Church History,* XXV (March, 1956), 3-15.

Van Dusen, H. P. "Caribbean Holiday," *Christian Century,* LXXII (August 17, 1955), 946-48.

_______. "The Third Force in Christendom," *Life,* XLIV (June 9, 1958), 113-24.

Van Elderen, Bastian. "Glossolalia in the New Testament," *Bulletin of the Evangelical Theological Society,* XVII (Spring, 1964), 53-58.

Walker, Alan. "Where Pentecostalism is Mushrooming," *Christian Century,* LXXXV (January 17, 1968), 81-82.

"Where We Stand on the Revived Tongues Movement," *Alliance Witness,* XCVIII (May 1, 1963), 5, 6, 19.

Wilson, Bryan R. "An Analysis of Sect Development," *American Sociological Review,* XXIV (February, 1959), 3-15.

Zimmerman, Thomas F. "Plea for the Pentecostalists," *Christianity Today,* VII (January 4, 1963), 11-12.

MINUTES AND REPORTS

Accrediting Association of Bible Colleges. "Annual Report," *AABC Newsletter,* XII (Winter, 1968), 2-3.

American Lutheran Church. "Progress Report, Committee on Spiritual Gifts," 1962.

Board of Education. Official minutes, September 7, 1956–August 24, 1967. The name of this body had been Committee on Education until August 26, 1959.

Department of Education. "Annual Report," October 31, 1967, and October 31, 1969.

Evangelical Theological Society. "Minutes of the Fifteenth Annual Meeting," *Evangelical Theological Society Bulletin,* VII (Winter, 1964), 28-29.

General Council of the Assemblies of God. Minutes, 1914-1969.

_______. Reports and Financial Statements, 1945-1969.

_______. Executive Presbytery Minutes, March 22, May 31, and November 30, 1967.

———. General Presbytery Minutes, 1933-1969.

Men's Fellowship Advisory Committee. Minutes, May 23, 1958.

National Association of Evangelicals. Board of Administration Minutes, April 29, 1946 and October 1-2, 1946.

———. Board of Directors Minutes, April 15, 1944.

———. Committee on Education Minutes, November 20, 1942, and December 6-7, 1943.

———. .Executive Committee Minutes, June 17-18, 1943, December 13, 1944, November 13, 1945, and June 11, 1946.

National Sunday School Association. Board of Directors Minutes, October 5, 1946.

———. Executive Committee Minutes, April 30-May 1, 1945.

Pentecostal Fellowship of North America. Board of Administration Minutes, October 28, 1957.

———. Business Session Minutes, November 1, 1962.

Publications Committee. Official minutes, January 12, 1948.

"Report of the Special Commission on Glossolalia to the Right Reverend Gerald Francis Burrill, Bishop of Chicago," December 12, 1960.

"Status Report of Action Proposed at Men's Fellowship Seminar," August 30, 1958.

"Youth Action Study Committee Minutes," July 31, 1958.

PAMPHLETS AND BROCHURES

"Alaska Evangelism," Springfield, Missouri: Home Missions Department, 1967.

"American Indian Bible Institute," Springfield, Missouri: Home Missions Department, 1967.

"Branch Out!" Springfield, Missouri: Home Missions Dept., 1967.

"Constitution and By-laws of the Pentecostal Fellowship of North America," n.d.

"Constitution of the National Association of Evangelicals," n.d.

"Do All Speak with Tongues?" by F. F. Bosworth. Dayton, Ohio: John J. Scruby, n.d.

"Evangelical Press Association Membership Directory," 1969.

"Evangelical Theological Society, The," n.d.

"In the Last Days," Springfield, Missouri: Public Relations Office, 1962.

"'Like a River," Springfield, Missouri: Gospel Publishing House, Fiftieth Anniversary Souvenir Brochure, 1964.

"National Religious Broadcasters, Inc.," n.d.

"Our Campus Is the World," Springfield, Missouri: Foreign Missions Department, International Correspondence Institute, 1968.

"Pentecostal Fellowship of North America," n.d.

"Reaching Our American Indian," Springfield, Missouri: Home Missions Department, 1967.

"Who We Are and What We Believe," Springfield, Missouri: Gospel Publishing House, n.d.

"Working Together," Springfield, Missouri: Gospel Publishing House, 1960. General Council Headquarters policy manual.

THESES AND UNPUBLISHED DOCUMENTS

"Assemblies of God Series of the Graded Sunday School Lessons, The," 1946. Mimeographed.

"Building, The," n.d. Mimeographed. History of the Gospel Publishing House.

Carmen, Calvin. "The Posture of Contemporary Pentecostalism in View of the Fundamentalist-Neo-Evangelical Debate." Unpublished M.A. thesis, Central Bible College, 1964.

Carroll, Grace. "The Evolution of Centralized Accounting," n.d. Mimeographed.

Collins, Millard E. "Establishing and Financing of Higher Educational Institutions in the Church Body of the Assemblies of God in the U.S.A." Austin, Texas, 1959. Typewritten.

Corvin, Raymond O. "Religious and Educational Backgrounds in the Founding of Oral Roberts University." Unpublished Ph. D. dissertation, The University of Oklahoma, 1967.

Fischer, Harold A. "Progress of the Various Modern Pentecostal Movements Toward World Fellowship." Unpublished M.A. thesis, Texas Christian University, 1950.

Flower, J. Roswell. "History of the Assemblies of God," 1949. Mimeographed.

Fulton, Everett P. "An Investigation of the Changing Theological Concepts of the Ministers of Open Bible Standard Churches." Unpublished M.A. thesis, Drake University, 1964.

Gross, George. "A Study of Norms of Conduct in the Assemblies of God." Unpublished M.A. thesis, Central Bible College, 1961.

Guynes, Eleanor R. "Development of the Educational Program of the Assemblies of God from the School Year 1948-49 up to the Present Time." Unpublished M.A. thesis, Southern Methodist University, 1966.

Harris, Ralph W. "Development of Graded Material," n.d. Mimeographed.

______. "Graded Course for Adults and Young People," 1960. Mimeographed.

______. "History of Christian Education Objectives," 1963. Dittoed.

______. "The Development of Church School Curricula of the Assemblies of God During the Period 1954-1966." Unpublished M.A. thesis, Central Bible College, Springfield, Missouri, 1969.

Harrison, Irvine J. "A History of the Assemblies of God." Unpublished Th. D. dissertation, Berkeley Baptist Divinity School, 1954.

Henstock, Thomas F. "A History and Interpretation of the Curriculum of Central Bible Institute." Unpublished M.A. thesis, Central Bible College, 1963

"Historic Highlights of CA Development," n.d. Dittoed.

Hollenweger, Walter J. "Handbuch der Pfingstbewegung." Unpublished D. Theol. dissertation, Theological Faculty of the University of Zurich, 1965. Xeroxed.

Hoover, Mario G. "Origin and Structural Development of the Assemblies of God." Unpublished M.A. thesis, Southwest Missouri State College, Springfield, Missouri, 1968.

Howard, Ivan. "A Review of the Assemblies of God," 1952. Typewritten.

Jackson, Rex. "The Literature Program of the Assemblies of God." Unpublished M.S. thesis, Kansas State University, Manhattan, Kansas, 1963.

Johns, Donald F. "A Philosophy of Religious Education for the Assemblies of God." Unpublished Ph.D. dissertation, New York University, 1962.

Keene, Gertrude B. "Distinctive Social Values of the Pentecostal Churches: A Sociological Field Study." Unpublished M.A. thesis, University of Southern California, 1938.

Littell, Franklin H. "The Historical Free Church Tradition Defined," n.d. Mimeographed.

Masserano, Frank C. "A Study of Worship Forms in the Assemblies of God Denomination." Unpublished Th.M. thesis, Princeton Seminary 1966.

Moore, E. L. "Handbook of Pentecostal Denominations in the United States." Unpublished M.A. thesis, Pasadena College, 1954.

Oliver, John B., Jr. "Some Newer Religious Groups in the United States: Twelve Case Studies." Unpublished Ph.D. dissertation, Yale University, 1946.

Paul, George H. "The Religious Frontier in Oklahoma: Dan T. Muse and the Pentecostal Holiness Church." Unpublished Ph.D. dissertation, The University of Oklahoma, 1965.

Rasnake, John S. "An Investigation of the Policy of the Assemblies of God on Glossolalia and Its Effects on Education in Their Colleges." Unpublished M.A. thesis, East Tennessee State University, 1965.

Riggs, Ralph M. "The Men's Fellowship of the Assemblies of God," 1952. Dittoed.

Rose, Delbert. "The Theology of Joseph H. Smith." Ph.D. dissertation, The University of Iowa, 1952.

Scott, C. W. H. "What Is the Latter Rain?" Sermon notes, February 14, 1949. Typewritten.

Strahan, Richard D. "A Study to Introduce Curriculum Approaches and Student Personnel Services for Evangel College." Unpublished Ed.D. dissertation, The University of Houston, 1955.

Synan, Harold Vinson. "The Pentecostal Movement in the United States." Unpublished Ph.D. dissertation, The University of Georgia, Athens, Georgia, 1967.

Taylor, Rachel Jean. "The 'Return to Religion' in America After the Second World War: A Study of Religion in American Culture, 1945-1955." Unpublished Ph.D. dissertation, The University of Minnesota, 1961.

"The E. S. Williams Story." Unpublished mimeographed manuscript, n.d.

Vitello, J. L. "A History and Evaluation of the Attitudes of the Assemblies of God Toward Post-Secondary Education." Unpublished M.A. thesis, Central Bible College, 1962.

Vivier, L. M. "Glossolalia." Unpublished M.D. thesis, University of Witwatersrand, Johannesburg, Union of South Africa, 1960. Xeroxed.

LETTERS

Armeding, Hudson, President of Wheaton College, Wheaton, Illinois.

Armstrong, B. L, Executive Secretary, National Religious Broadcasters.

Beall, James L., Pastor, Bethesda Missionary Temple, Detroit, Michigan.

Bethany, Edgar, Executive Presbyter.

Bosworth, Mrs. F. F., The widow of Rev. Bosworth, strategic figure in the "Initial Evidence" controversy.

Burnett, C. C., President, Bethany Bible College; Secretary, National Association of Evangelicals.

Clark, E. M., Executive Presbyter.

Colombo, Joseph, Chairman, Home Missions Church Building Committee.

Conner, Carl G., Pastor, First Assembly of God, Winston-Salem, North Carolina.

Davidson, N. D., Executive Presbyter.

Dobbins, R. D., Pastor, Evangel Temple, Akron, Ohio.

Gaston, W. T., District Superintendent, Northern California-Nevada District Council. Letter dated March 29, 1956 addressed to Ralph M. Riggs, General Superintendent of the Assemblies of God.

Graves, Arthur, President, South-Eastern Bible College.

Hardcastle, G. W., Executive Presbyter.

Hollenweger, Walter J., Associate Secretary, World Council of Churches, Division of Studies, Department on Studies in Mission and Evangelism, Geneva.

Littell, Franklin H., President, Iowa Wesleyan College.

Litzman, Warren, Evangelist.

Lowenberg, Paul, Executive Presbyter.

Menzies, Mrs. W. E. (Sophie B.), The mother of the author of this volume.

Mjorud, Herbert, Evangelist, American Lutheran Church.

Moberg, David O., Bethel Seminary.

Mostert, John, Executive Secretary, AABC.

Rose, Delbert R., Professor of Biblical Theology, Asbury Theological Seminary.

Sawyers, Lindell, Division of Lay Education, United Presbyterian Church.

Shingler, A. Lewis, Layman, Church of the Nazarene.

Smith, Eugene, American Secretary, World Council of Churches.

Stanger, Frank B., President, Asbury Theological Seminary.

Strickland, Charles H., President, Nazarene Bible College.

Trueblood, Elton, Professor at Large, Earlham College.

Unger, Merrill F., Professor of Bible, Dallas Theological Seminary.

Van Dusen, Henry P., President Emeritus, Union Theological Seminary.

Watson, Philip S., Professor of Systematic Theology, Garrett Theological Seminary.

Wead, Roy, Executive Presbyter.

INTERVIEWS

Assemblies of God

Adams, Joe, District Secretary-Treasurer, North Texas District Council.

Ahlf, Ann, Editor, *Slant*.

Ashcroft, J. Robert, President, Evangel College.

Barnes, Johnnie, National Commander, Royal Rangers.

Bates, A. C., Retired Assemblies of God minister.

Beem, C. T., Office Manager, "Revivaltime."

Bonds, Glen, National Secretary, Men's Fellowship Department.

Boyd, Frank M., Retired professor and author.

Bresson, Bernard, Professor of History, Evangel College.

Bush, Howard S, Former Assistant General Superintendent.

Carlson, G. Raymond, Assistant General Superintendent.

Colbaugh, Wildon F., Editor, *TEAM;* Coordinator, Action Crusades.

Correll, Norman, National Secretary, Christ's Ambassadors Department.

Cowart, H. S., Pastor, Dallas, Texas

Cox, Russell, National Secretary, Christ's Ambassadors Department.

Crouch, Philip., President, Central Bible College.

Cunningham, Robert C., Editor, *The Pentecostal Evangel.*

Denton, Charles W., Coordinator, Spiritual Life–Evangelism Commission.

Drake, David, Registrar, Central Bible College.

Dunham, Evelyn, Budget Accountant.

Eastlake, William, Manager, Marketing Services Division.

Emery, Paul J., President, Northeast Bible Institute.

Flower, J. Roswell, Former General Secretary.

Gannon, T. E., Assistant General Superintendent.

Garlock, John, Academic Dean, Continental Bible College, Brussels, Belgium.

Grable, Marcus, Former National Secretary of the Sunday School Department.

Grant, U. S., Pastor, First Assembly of God, Kansas City, Kansas.

Guynes, Delmar, Academic Vice-president, Southwestern Assemblies of God College.

Hamill, James, Pastor, First Assembly of God, Memphis, Tennessee.

Harrell, J. Otis, Retired Manager, Gospel Publishing House.

Harris, Ralph, Editor, Church School Literature.

Hodges, Melvin, Field Secretary, Latin America.

Hogan, J. Philip, Assistant General Superintendent; Executive Director, Foreign Missions Department.

Horton, Stanley, Chairman, Bible Department, Central Bible College.

Howard, Rick, National College Youth Representative.

Hurst, D. V., President, Northwest College of the Assemblies of God.

Jansen, Harris, Editor, *Sunday School Counselor.*

Johns, Donald F., Dean, Central Bible College.

Johnston, David, Manager, Merchandising Division, Gospel Publishing House.

Johnston, E. Daniel, Sales Manager, Merchandising Division, Gospel Publishing House.

Jones, Gwen, Editor, *Advance.*

Kamerer, Mrs. J. Z., Retired Director, Personnel Office.

Kendrick, Klaude, Professor of History, Texas Wesleyan College, Fort Worth, Texas.

Kirschke, William E., National Secretary of Sunday School Department.

Kraiss, Wayne, Vice-President, Evangel College.

Krogstad, E. Elsworth, Retired Pastor, Central Assembly of God, Springfield, Missouri.

Lewis, Gayle F., Retired General Superintendent.

Lindsay, Zella, General Council Headquarters Librarian.

McGlasson, Robert, Secretary, Foreign Missions Department.

MacKinney, Verne, Speed-the-Light Coordinator.

McLellan, Cyril, Director, "Revivaltime" Choir.

McPherson, Warren F., Secretary, Public Relations Office.

Markstrom, Paul, National Prison Representative.

Menzie, J. D., Retired minister, Bloomington, Minnesota.

Menzies, Homer, Former Manager, Gospel Publishing House.

Michael, Stanley, National Secretary, Department of Benevolences.

Morris, Dorothy, Associate Editor, Church School Literature.

Myers, Harry, Pastor, Tulsa, Oklahoma.

Nelli, Andrew, Vice-President, General Milk Corporation.

Netzel, M. B., General Treasurer.

Noah, H. C., Pastor, Oak Cliff Assembly of God, Dallas, Texas.

Ohler, Sam, Administrative Assistant, Department of Finance.

Perkin, Noel, Retired Secretary, Foreign Missions Department.

Peterson, Bartlett, General Secretary.

Reneau, Kermit, Assistant General Superintendent.

Riggs, Ralph M., Former General Superintendent
Ringness, Curtis W., National Secretary of the Home Missions
Sandidge, Jerry, National College Youth Representative.
Schumitsch, Charlotte, Director, Missionettes; Editor, *Missionettes Memos.*
Shultz, Leland, National Secretary of the Radio Department.
Scott, Charles W. H., Assistant General Superintendent.
Smuland, Mildred, National Secretary of the Women's Missionary Council Department.
Snyder, Melvin, Technician, Audio-Visual Division, Public Relations Office.
Steinberg, Hardy, National Secretary of the Department of Education.
Tregenza, Mary. Editor, *CA Herald.*
Tucker, Angeline, Director, Young Missionettes.
Ward, C. M., Speaker, "Revivaltime."
Watters, Lillian, Evangelist.
Watters, Robert, Evangelist.
Way, Robert, Servicemen's Division Representative, CA Department.
Webb, Bert, Former Assistant General Superintendent.
Wilkerson, David, Evangelist, Teen Challenge.
Williams, Ernest S, Retired General Superintendent.
Williams, Ward, Chairman, Department of Religion, Evangel College.
Wilson, Aaron A, Retired minister, Springfield, Missouri.
Womack, David, Foreign Missions Home Secretary.
Zimmerman, Thomas F., General Superintendent.

Non-Assemblies of God

Arrington, French, Professor of Bible, Lee College, Cleveland, Tennessee.
Broughton, William, Ministerial staff, Christ Church (Episcopal), Winnetka, Illinois.
Calvanico, Anthony, Business Administrator, Full Gospel Business Men's Fellowship, International.
Carter, Herbert, General Superintendent, Pentecostal Free Will Baptist Church, Dunn, North Carolina; Secretary, Pentecostal Fellowship of North America.
Climenhaga, Arthur, Past-Executive Director, National Association of Evangelicals.
Conn, Charles W., General Overseer, Church of God, Cleveland, Tennessee.
Du Plessis, David, Pentecostal ambassador-at-large.
Frodsham, Stanley H., Former editor, *The Pentecostal Evangel.*
Gause, R. H., Dean, Bible Department, Lee College, Cleveland, Tennessee.
Goddard, Burton. Retired dean of the Gordon Divinity School, Beverly Farms, Massachusetts; Librarian, Gordon Divinity School.
Handy, Robert, Professor of American Church History, Union Theological Seminary, New York City.

Henry, Carl F. H., Editor, *Christianity Today.*

Lindsay, Gordon, Editor, *Christ for the Nations;* Secretary, Full Gospel Fellowship of Churches and Ministers, International.

McGavran, Donald, Director, School of World Missions and Institute of Church Growth, Fuller Seminary, Pasadena, California.

McPherson, Rolf, President, International Church of the Foursquare Gospel.

Manschreck, Clyde, Professor of History of Christianity, Chicago Theological Seminary, Chicago, Illinois.

Mitchell, R. Bryant, Director of World Missions, Open Bible Standard Churches; Chairman, Pentecostal Fellowship of North America; Past-General Chairman, Open Bible Standard Churches.

Moreau, Jules, Professor of Ecclesiastical History, Seabury-Western Theological Seminary, Evanston, Illinois.

Nichol, John T., Professor of History, Bentley College, Boston, Massachusetts.

Pelikan, Jaroslav, Professor of Church History, Yale Divinity School, New Haven, Connecticut.

Satre, Lowell J., Professor of New Testament, Luther Theological Seminary, St. Paul, Minnesota.

Smith, Eugene, American Secretary, World Council of Churches.

Sonmore, Clayton, Vice-President, Full Gospel Business Men's Fellowship, International.

Synan, A. J. Bishop, Pentecostal Holiness Church, Franklin Springs, Georgia.

Taylor, Clyde, Executive Director, National Association of Evangelicals.

Walker, Robert, Editor, *Christian Life.*

Winkler, Richard E, Rector, Trinity Episcopal Church, Wheaton, Illinois.

Index

Notes

Notes

Notes

Notes

Notes

Notes

Notes

Notes

Notes

Notes

Notes